Samuel Rawson Gardiner

The Fall of the Monarchy of Charles I, 1637-1649

Samuel Rawson Gardiner

The Fall of the Monarchy of Charles I, 1637-1649

ISBN/EAN: 9783743406834

Manufactured in Europe, USA, Canada, Australia, Japa

Cover: Foto ©ninafisch / pixelio.de

Manufactured and distributed by brebook publishing software (www.brebook.com)

Samuel Rawson Gardiner

The Fall of the Monarchy of Charles I, 1637-1649

THE

FALL OF THE MONARCHY

OF

CHARLES I.

1637–1649

BY

SAMUEL RAWSON GARDINER, LL.D.
HONORARY STUDENT OF CHRIST CHURCH
PROFESSOR OF MODERN HISTORY AT KING'S COLLEGE, LONDON; CORRESPONDING
MEMBER OF THE MASSACHUSETTS HISTORICAL SOCIETY, AND OF
THE ROYAL BOHEMIAN SOCIETY OF SCIENCES

VOL. I.

1637—1640

LONDON
LONGMANS, GREEN, AND CO.
1882

All rights reserved

PREFACE
TO
VOLUMES I. AND II.

IN the two volumes which are now given to the public, and more especially in the second, I have reached a part of my work to which all that I have hitherto done has been leading up, and of which all that I can hope to accomplish in the future can be but the development. If I have judged rightly the first fourteen months of the Long Parliament, I am likely to judge rightly the future course of the parties which then came into collision. If I have erred seriously here, I am not likely to find anything worth saying hereafter.

What the difficulties of the task have been can only be fully known to those who have attempted to face a similar problem. It is not merely that the subject-matter is one which, even at the present day, strangely evokes the divergent sympathies and passions of Englishmen, and that it has been already attempted by writers of no mean reputation, some of whom have succeeded in convincing their readers that there is nothing more to be said about the matter; but that even the richest materials fail to yield all that the historian requires. Again and again, however, the frontier of knowledge may be advanced, the enquirer is confronted by darkness into which he cannot safely penetrate.

Yet in spite of all risks I have ventured to tell again a familiar tale. It has not, I hope, been for nothing that many years ago, as a young and unknown writer, I deliberately refrained from selecting a subject more attractive in its own nature than the reign of James I. could possibly be. It seemed to me then, as it seems to me now, that it was the duty of a serious inquirer to search into the original causes of great events rather than, for the sake of catching at an audience, to rush unprepared upon the great events themselves. My reward has been that, whether the present work is well or ill done, it is at all events far better done than it could have been if I had commenced with the tale of the Puritan Revolution itself. Whether that tale will ever be told in its completeness by me, neither I nor any one can tell. To me personally, as a descendant of Cromwell and Ireton, it would be a special satisfaction to call up them and their contemporaries before me, and to learn the true secret of their success and failure. To the historian no more interesting period can be found than one in which men of virtue and ability strove with one another in seeking the solution of the highest problems at a time when the old chain of precedent had been violently snapped, and when all things seemed possible to the active intelligence.

, Whatever the future may have in reserve, this present work has constantly reminded me by how deep a gulf we are separated from the time when I commenced my labours, now some twenty-two years ago. Macaulay and Forster were then in possession of the field. The worship of the Puritans was in the ascendant, and to suggest that it was possible to make out a reasonable case for Bacon and Strafford was regarded as eccentric. All this is changed now. Few are to be found to say a good word for Puritanism, and the mistakes of the Long Parliament are unveiled with an unsparing hand. A dislike of agitation and disturbance has in some quarters taken the place of a dislike of arbitrary power, whilst reverence for culture has often left little room for reverence for liberty.

If I have striven, with what success I know not, to take a broader view of the deeds of the great men who made this England in which we live, and to realise and measure the greatness of Pym, as I have formerly attempted to realise and measure the greatness of Strafford, it must not be forgotten that this has been in great measure rendered possible by the amount of new material which has come into my hands, and which till very lately was entirely inaccessible. The invaluable diary of Sir Symonds d'Ewes, and the State Papers in the Public Record Office, have indeed been studied by previous inquirers, though I have found amongst them gleanings not wholly despicable. The Clarendon MSS., the Carte and Tanner MSS. in the Bodleian Library have also been helpful. But even if these mines had been more thoroughly worked than they have been, little or nothing would have been found in them to fill up the great deficiency which every previous historian of the period must have felt. The suspicions entertained of Charles I. by the Parliamentary leaders forms the most prominent feature of the history of the Long Parliament. The whole narrative will be coloured by the conviction of the writer that these suspicions were either well or ill founded. Yet hitherto there has been no possibility of penetrating, except by casual glimpses, behind the veil of Charles's privacy. What evidence has been forthcoming was too scattered and incoherent to convince those who were not half convinced already. Though even now much remains dark, considerable light has been thrown upon the secrets of Charles's policy by the copies, now in the Record Office, of the correspondence of Rossetti, the Papal Agent at the Court of Henrietta Maria, with Cardinal Barberini. The originals are preserved in the Barberini Palace, where the agents of the Record Office were permitted, by the courtesy of the librarian, Don Sante Picralisi, to make the copies of them which have stood me in such good stead. I do not know any literary service for which I have had reason to be more profoundly grateful than that which was performed by these gentlemen by directions from the authorities at the Record Office, and of which I and my readers have been the first to reap the benefit.

Scarcely less is the gratitude which I feel to Mr. Rawdon Brown, through whose kindness a great part of the Venetian despatches relating to this period were copied and sent to the Record Office. Those thus forwarded by him are referred to in these volumes as 'Venetian Transcripts.' The few with which I became acquainted through my own exertions are quoted as 'Venetian MSS.'

Of less importance only than these authorities are the French despatches in the National Library at Paris or in the Archives of the Ministry of Foreign Affairs, the Dutch despatches and the letters of Salvetti, the agent of the Grand Duke of Tuscany, copies of which are to be found in the British Museum. References to other MSS. in that collection will be found in their proper place. The recently acquired Nicholas Papers have already been of considerable service, and will probably be even more useful at a later period. It will be understood that where the name of a printed tract is followed by the letter E. and a number, the reference is to the press-mark of the Thomason tracts in the Museum. A number without the preceding letter is a reference to the press-mark of other tracts in the same library.

Outside the walls of our two national repositories, I have, with considerable advantage, had access, through the kind permission of the Library Committee at Guildhall, to the records of the Common Council of the City of London. Something too has been gained from the Register House and the Advocates' Library at Edinburgh. In the latter is to be found a full account of the proceedings of the Scottish Commissioners in London during the first months of 1641, which seems to have escaped the notice of Scottish antiquarians. Of a very different character are the Verney MSS. preserved at Claydon. After the close of 1639, when Mr. Bruce's selection, published by the Camden Society, ends, the correspondence of the Verney family deals less directly with public affairs, and there are therefore fewer extracts quoted from them in the latter part of these volumes than in the former. But it would be a great mistake to measure the historical value of this correspondence by the number of references to it in these pages. After reading such a mass of letters from men and women of very different characters and in various positions in society, the mind of an historian becomes saturated with the thoughts and ideas of the time, in a way which is most helpful to him, though he may not be making even a mental reference to the writers of the letters themselves, or to the subjects which interest them. Any regret that I have been unable to bring before my readers many of the topics of this most interesting correspondence, is qualified by the knowledge that Lady Verney is engaged upon a sketch of the lives of the early members of the family, drawn from those papers which she has herself so admirably arranged, and with the contents of which she is so familiarly acquainted. No words of mine could adequately express my feeling of the kindness with which I have been received at Claydon by her and by Sir Harry Verney, and of the liberality with which they regard their possession of these inestimable treasures as a trust committed to them for the benefit of all who know how to make use of them.

In one quarter only have I found any difficulty in procuring access to MSS. of importance. I regret that Lord Fitzwilliam has not considered it to be consistent with his duty to allow me to see the Strafford correspondence preserved at Wentworth Woodhouse.

It would not be becoming to enter into a criticism of modern writers, as the points at issue could only be made intelligible at far greater length than I have here at my disposal; but as it has been necessary in the interests of truth to speak clearly on the extreme carelessness of some of Mr. Forster's work, I should not like to be considered to be without sense of the high services rendered by him to students of this period of history, especially in quickening an intelligent interest in the events of the seventeenth century. Nor will it, I trust, be presumptuous in me to record my admiration of the thoroughness and accuracy of the work of Mr. Sanford and Professor Masson. I have thought it due to their high reputation to point out in every case the few inaccuracies in matters of fact which I have detected, excepting where the fault lay in their not having before them evidence which has been at my disposal. I have little doubt that if my work were subjected to as careful revision it would yield a far greater crop of errors.

Unfortunately in the second, and part of the first, volume, I have no longer the benefit of Mr. Hamilton's calendar of the Domestic State Papers. Happily for me he had achieved the greater part of his work before I outstripped him in my lighter labours. After the opening of the Long Parliament the State Papers decrease in volume and interest.

The map at the beginning of the second volume

is founded on the lists published by Mr. Sanford in his 'Studies on the Great Rebellion.' The red lines denote not merely those who joined the King at the commencement of the Civil War, but also those who subsequently took his side. I have, however, allowed Sir Ralph Verney's name to remain with a blue line, as Mr. Sanford was certainly wrong in speaking of him as having at any time gone over to the King. He simply went into exile because he refused to take the Solemn League and Covenant.

I cannot conclude without especially thanking Mr. Reginald Palgrave, who kindly consented to look over these volumes in proof, and whose great knowledge of the documents relating to the history of the time enabled him to supply me with most valuable corrections and suggestions.

CONTENTS

OF

THE FIRST VOLUME.

CHAPTER I.

THE RELIGIOUS OPPOSITION.

		PAGE
1637	Ecclesiastical difficulties	1
	Prynne, Bastwick, and Burton	3
	Their trial in the Star Chamber	6
	Laud's defence of himself	7
	Execution of the sentence on Prynne, Bastwick, and Burton	9
	The Press muzzled	13
	Laud and the Catholics	14
	Con as the Papal Agent at Court	15
	The Queen's support of the Catholics	16
	The Catholic converts	17
	Laud urges strong measures against proselytism	19
	Struggle between Laud and the Queen	20
	The Queen's triumph	22
1638	The Earl of Newcastle appointed Governor of the Prince	24
	English Puritanism—Milton's *Lycidas*	25
	John Hutchinson	27
1637	John Lilburn	30
	His sentence in the Star Chamber	31
	George Wither	32
1628	Bishop Williams prosecuted in the Star Chamber	33
1635	His second prosecution	34
	The Holy Table, Name, and thing	36
1637	Sentence on Williams	37
	The Latitudinarians—Falkland	38
	Chillingworth	42
	The religion of Protestants	46
	John Hales of Eton	49
1638	His interview with Laud	52
	Influence of Latitudinarianism not immediate	53

CHAPTER II.

THE CONSTITUTIONAL OPPOSITION.

		PAGE
1637	Ship-money provided for an actual want	55
	The expedition to Sallee	56
	Constitutional objection to ship-money	57
	Hampden's case in the Exchequer Chamber	58
1638	The decision of the Judges	65
	Extravagant language of Finch	67
	Arrears of ship-money collected	69
	The Forest Courts	70
	Corporate monopolies	71
	Brickmakers	72
	Coal-shippers and soap-makers	73
	Salt works	74
	Starch-makers—maltsters and brewers	75
	Vintners	76
	City petition against the growth of London	78
	Demolition of houses	79
	The Londonderry forfeiture	80
	The new Corporation	81
	Hackney coaches—the letter-post	82
	Drainage of Hatfield Chase	83
	Drainage of the Great Level	85
	Riots in the Fens	88
	Intervention of the King	90
	Charles's position in the country	91
	The City of London a type of the local organisations	93
	Hopelessness of the King's aim	95

CHAPTER III.

THE RIOTS IN EDINBURGH, AND THE SCOTTISH COVENANT.

1633	Feeling of the Scottish nobility towards the Bishops	97
	The Scottish Church	98
1635	Notes of an English traveller in Scotland	100
1634	Charles resolves to introduce a new Prayer-Book	101
	The Church Courts	102
1635	Preparation of Canons and a Prayer-Book	103
1636	Issue of the Canons	104
	The Prayer-Book submitted to a few Bishops	105
	It is disliked as English	106
1637	It is sent to Scotland	107
	Temper of the nobility	108

		PAGE
	The tumult at St. Giles'.	109
	Traquair's management	111
	The King's annoyance	112
	Henderson's petition	113
	Charles unable to draw back	114
	The Council does not support him	115
	The second riot at Edinburgh	116
	Persistence of Charles	117
	The third riot at Edinburgh	118
	Commissioners chosen by the leaders of the Opposition	120
	Organised resistance	121
1638	Traquair's visit to London	122
	Charles justifies the Prayer-Book	123
	Rothes appeals to the gentry of Scotland	124
	The Tables	125
	The National Covenant	126
	Scene in the Grey Friars' Church	130
	Traquair's account to the King	131
	An Assembly and a Parliament demanded	132
	General circulation of the Covenant	133
	Ill-treatment of those who refuse to sign it	134
	Practical unity of the nation	136
	Charles resolves to negotiate in order to gain time	137
	Hamilton appointed Commissioner	138
	He arrives in Scotland	140
	His account of the situation	141
	His reception at Edinburgh	143
	Charles prepares for war	144
	Hamilton offers to induce the King to consent to summon an Assembly and a Parliament	145
	The Divine Right of Assemblies	146
	Hamilton's intrigue with the Covenanters	147
	He returns to England	148

CHAPTER IV.

THE ASSEMBLY OF GLASGOW.

1638	The English Council informed on Scottish affairs	149
1637	Wentworth's progress in the West of Ireland	150
	His views on the conduct of Prynne and Hampden	152
1638	His opinion of the Scottish Covenanters	153
	Suggests a policy to be pursued in Scotland	154
	Early life of Montrose	156
	Montrose as a Covenanter	158
	The Aberdeen doctors	159

	PAGE
Huntly and Argyle	160
Montrose at Aberdeen	161
Hamilton's second mission to Scotland	162
He attempts to divide the Covenanters	163
His return to England and third mission to Scotland	164
The King's Covenant	165
An Assembly and a Parliament summoned	165
Resistance to the King's Covenant	166
Election of the Assembly	167
Charles resolves to resist	168
The Bishops cited before the Assembly	170
Meeting of the Assembly at Glasgow	171
It declares itself duly constituted	173
Question whether the Bishops are subject to censure by the Assembly	174
Hamilton dissolves the Assembly	175
Argyle's position in Scotland	175
The Assembly continues sitting and abolishes Episcopacy	177

1639	Hamilton's report on his mission	179
1638	The Congress at Hamburg	180
	Unsuccessful expedition of the Elector Palatine	181
	Secret negotiations at Brussels	182
	Mary de Medicis proposes to visit England	184
	Her arrival in London	186
	Bernhard of Weimar's successes on the Upper Rhine	187
1639	Relation of the Scottish troubles to Continental politics	188
	Charles drifting into war	189
	Preparations for levying an army	190
	Want of national support	191
	Charles asks that Spanish troops may be sent to England	193
	The Scottish army	194
	Alexander Leslie	195
	The Scottish manifesto	196
	Williams before the Star Chamber	197
	Publication of the *Large Declaration*	198

CHAPTER V.

THE MARCH TO THE BORDERS AND THE PACIFICATION OF BERWICK.

1639	The Covenanters take the castles of Edinburgh, Dumbarton, and Dalkeith	200
	Morton's success in the North	201
	Huntly carried to Edinburgh	204
	The King at York	205
	His financial difficulties	207

THE FIRST VOLUME. xvii

	PAGE
Wentworth's review of the situation	208
The King appeals to the Scottish tenants	209
State of the King's army	210
Disaffection of the English nobles	211
The military oath	212
Feeling of the English army	213
Hamilton in the Firth of Forth	214
His despondency	215
Failure of the King's appeal to the tenants	216
Hamilton proposes to negotiate	217
Quality of Charles's army	219
Hamilton's conference with the Covenanters	220
The Trot of Turriff	222
Montrose returns to the North	223
The King at Berwick	224
Arundel at Dunse	225
The King prepares to take the aggressive	226
His financial position	227
Attempts to obtain money	228
The Scots at Kelso	229
Holland's march to Kelso	230
Condition of Charles's army	231
The Scots on Dunse Law	233
They offer to negotiate	235
Hamilton arrives at the Camp	236
Opening of negotiations	237
The King fails to obtain money from the City	239
Signature of the Treaty of Berwick	241
Storming of the Bridge of Dee	242
Project of sending a Scottish army to Germany	243
Obstacles in the way of carrying out the Treaty	244

CHAPTER VI.

THE ASSEMBLY AND PARLIAMENT OF EDINBURGH.

1639	Charles summons the Bishops to the Assembly	246
	Riot at Edinburgh	247
	The Covenanting leaders invited to Berwick	248
	Traquair's instructions as High Commissioner	249
	Charles returns to Whitehall	250
	Secret protestation of the Scottish Bishops	251
	The Assembly at Edinburgh confirms the abolition of Episcopacy	252
	Parliament meets and proposes Constitutional changes	253
	Charles looks for support to Montrose	254

		PAGE
	He refuses to rescind the Acts in favour of Episcopacy	255
	Argyle's policy	256
	Legislative changes proposed	257
	Charles determines to resist, and orders the adjournment of the Parliament	258
	The war in Germany	259
	Charles turns to a Spanish alliance	260
	Dispute with the Dutch about the right of search	261
	A Spanish fleet sails for the Channel	262
	Is defeated by the Dutch in the Straits of Dover	263
	Takes refuge in the Downs	264
	Charles's secret negotiation with Spain	265
	Bellievre's diplomacy	266
	The negotiation for Bernhard's army	267
	Oquendo and Tromp in the Downs	268
	The sea-fight in the Downs	272
	Imprisonment of the Elector Palatine	274
	Wentworth's case against Crosby and Mountnorris	275
	Case of Lord Chancellor Loftus	276
	Wentworth arrives in England and becomes the King's principal adviser	278
	The Scottish Commissioners in London	279
	Prorogation of the Scottish Parliament	280
	Wentworth advises the King to summon a Parliament in England	281
	His advice accepted	282
	The Privy Councillors' Loan	283
	Suspicions that Parliament is to be intimidated	284
	The political and ecclesiastical opposition	285
	Spread of the sects	288
	Trendall's case	289
1640	Wentworth created Earl of Strafford—Preparations for war	291
	Finch Lord Keeper	292
	Lady Carlisle	293
	Vane replaces Coke as Secretary	294

CHAPTER VII.

THE SHORT PARLIAMENT.

1640	Release of Valentine and Strode—The Queen and the Catholics	295
	Charles's foreign relations	297
	Proposed application of the Scots to France	300

THE FIRST VOLUME.

	PAGE
A letter of the Scots to Lewis XIII. falls into Charles's hands	301
Scottish Commissioners in England	302
Strafford sets out for Ireland	303
The Irish Parliament	304
The English Elections	306
Opening of the Short Parliament	307
The letter to the French King produced	308
Grimston's speech	309
Feeling against Laud in the House of Lords	310
Pym's speech	311
Pym accepted as leader	317
The three estates of the realm	318
The Houses summoned to Whitehall	319
Strafford advises an appeal to the Lords	320
The Lords support the King	321
The Commons complain of the breach of privilege	322
The Lords maintain their position	323
The King demands an immediate grant	324
Debate in the Commons	325
Twelve subsidies demanded	326
Ship-money and the military charges challenged	327
Vane's intervention	328
Proposed petition against war with Scotland	329
The Council votes for a dissolution	330
Dissolution of the Short Parliament	331
Strafford's view of the situation	332
Discussion in the Committee of Eight	333
Strafford argues for an aggressive war	334
Proposes to make use of the Irish army	336
English feeling on the subject	340
Unpopularity of Strafford	341

CHAPTER VIII.

PASSIVE RESISTANCE.

1640		
	Imprisonment of members of Parliament	344
	Efforts made to obtain money	345
	Spanish Ambassadors arrive to negotiate an alliance	346
	Strafford asks for a loan from Spain	347
	Riots at Lambeth	348
	The Queen's intrigue with Rome	350
	Concessions made	351
	Proposed negotiation with Scotland	352
	Financial difficulties	353

		PAGE
	Strafford's conversation with Bristol	354
	Strafford's illness	355
	The war with Scotland persisted in	357
	The last case of judicial torture	358
	Convocation continues sitting	359
	It grants six subsidies and passes new Canons	360
	Doctrine of the Canons on the Divine Right of Kings	362
	Laud on taxation	363
	The Etcetera Oath	364
	The convention of Estates at Edinburgh	366
	Resistance to the King's order for the prorogation of the Scottish Parliament	367
	His deposition canvassed	368
	Session of Parliament	369
	Condition of the English army	371
	Failure of the attempt to collect ship-money in the City	372
	The Second Session of the Irish Parliament	374
	Opposition to the Government in it	375
	Financial difficulties in England	376
	Dissatisfaction of the soldiers	377
	Distrust of Catholic officers	379
	Murder of Lieutenant Mohun	380
	Cases of Chambers and Pargeter	381
	Proposed issue of Commissions of Array	382
	Execution of a mutineer by martial law	383
	Newcastle left unfortified	384
	Astley's report on the army	385
	Monro and Argyle in the Highlands	386
	Argyle's raid	387
	Burning of the House of Airlie	388
	Resistance at an end in Scotland	389

CHAPTER IX.

THE SCOTTISH INVASION.

1640	Loudoun's mission	390
	Fresh schemes for raising money	391
	Proposal to seize the bullion in the Tower and to debase the coinage	392
	Mutinies in the army	394
	The City refuses to lend money	396
	Fresh efforts to obtain a loan from Spain	397
	Proposal to bring in Danish soldiers	398
	Attacks on the Communion rails	399

THE FIRST VOLUME.   xxi

	PAGE
The Yorkshire petition	399
The City again refuses to lend	400
Communications between the English leaders and the Scots	401
Savile's forgery	402
The bond of Cambernauld	404
Vacillation at Court	406
Strafford and the Irish army	407
The Spanish loan again	408
State of the forces in the North	409
Scottish manifestoes	410
The King resolves to go to York	411
The Scots cross the Tweed	413
Money raised upon pepper	414
Preparations for resistance	415
Strafford appeals to the Yorkshire gentry	416
Conway and Astley at Newcastle	417
The Rout at Newburn	419
Newcastle occupied by the Scots	420
The Scots advance to the Tees	421
Conference of the leaders of the Opposition	422
The Peers demand a Parliament	423
A Great Council proposed	424
The Great Council summoned	426
Strafford's view of the situation	430
Public feeling in London	431
The King is reluctant to call a Parliament	432
Fall of the strong places in Scotland	433
Opening of the Great Council	434
The Peers give their security for a loan	435
Negotiations begin at Ripon	436
Savile confesses his forgery	437
Disturbances in London	438
The progress of the negotiation	439
Strafford proposes to drive the Scots from Ulster	440
The treaty of Ripon	441
The City loan	442
Last meeting of the Great Council	443
The King's expectation of a happy Parliament	444

MAPS.

The Borders from Berwick to Kelso	224
The Tyne from Newcastle to Newburn	417

Errata.

Page 88, line 14, *for* "Wisbech" *read* "Wisbeach."
„ 192, „ 7, *for* "And the" *read* "The."
„ 225, „ 17, *for* "his proclamation" *read* "the proclamation which he had issued in April."
„ 225, note 2, *for* "171" *read* "177."
„ 228, line 5, *for* "Mastership in Chancery" *read* "Mastership of the Rolls."
„ 249, „ 17, *for* "Dumfermline" *read* "Dunfermline."
„ 284, „ 18, *for* "Councillor's" *read* "Councillors'."
„ 286, „ 5 from bottom, *for* "Officials'" *read* Official's."
„ 307, „ 18, *after* "Parliament" *insert* "Loudoun was soon removed to stricter confinement in the Tower."
„ 307, footnote 2, *for* "Avenal" *read* "Avenel."
„ 319, line 19, *for* "fresh" *read* "Irish."
„ 344, „ 19, *for* "Earle" *read* "Erle."
„ 399, „ 2 of note, *for* "Ulfield" *read* "Ulfeld."
„ 399, „ 8 of note, *for* "Fredericia" *read* "Fridericia."

THE
FALL OF THE MONARCHY OF CHARLES I.

CHAPTER I.

THE RELIGIOUS OPPOSITION.

IN the summer of 1637 more than eight years had passed away since a Parliament had met at Westminster. During those years, in spite of threats of war which Charles had neither the nerve nor the means to carry out, peace had been maintained, and with the maintenance of peace the material prosperity of the country had been largely on the increase. But the higher aspirations of the nation remained unsatisfied. England had been without a government, in the best sense of the word, as truly as she had been without a Parliament. That pacification of hostile ecclesiastical parties which Charles had undertaken to bring about was further off than when the doors closed upon the Commons after the last stormy meeting in 1629. The attempt to restore harmony to the Church by silencing Puritan doctrine, and by the revival of obsolete ceremonies, had only served to embitter still more that spirit of opposition which was bitter enough already. The enforced observance of rites enjoined by external authority had not as yet produced a temper of acquiescence. Yet it was in the firm belief that in

CHAP. I.
1637.
The result of eight years of Charles's rule.

Ecclesiastical difficulties.

CHAP. I.
1637.

Wren's view of the point at issue.

this way alone could the spiritual welfare of the nation be promoted, that men like Laud and Wren were labouring against the stream which threatened to sweep them away. "The Fountain of holiness," wrote Wren, who as Bishop of Norwich found himself in charge of one of the most Puritan districts in England, "is the Holy Spirit, God blessed for ever. God the Holy Ghost breathes not but in his Holy Catholic Church. The Holy Church subsists not without the Communion of Saints—no communion with them without union among ourselves—that union impossible unless we preserve a uniformity for doctrine and a uniformity for discipline." [1]

Unity to be reached through uniformity.

What Laud and Wren were unable to perceive was that their attempt to reach unity through uniformity was a sign of weakness. They seized upon the bodies of men because they were unable to reach their hearts. Yet, as far as could be judged by the avowed ecclesiastical literature of the day, they were everywhere triumphant. White and Dow, Heylyn and Shelford, poured forth quarto after quarto in defence

Ecclesiastical literature.

[1] Wren to ——— (?), May 27. *Tanner MSS.* lxviii. fol. 92. The following passage from the same letter shows how Wren was prepared to carry out his principles in detail:—"Here I must be bold to say plainly the breach of that unity and uniformity in the Church hath principally been caused . . . . by lectures and lecturers. . . . Now, therefore, for the advancing the holy discipline of the Church, and for preserving uniformity therein, I am resolved to let no man preach in any place where he is not also charged with the cure; thereby to put a straiter tie upon him to observe and justify the rites and ceremonies which the Church enjoineth; and I shall be very careful, if any man be found opposite or negligent in the one, without any more ado to render him unfit and unworthy of the other. For the preserving of unity of doctrine I dare promise myself nothing where the preacher shall be forced to suit his business to the fancy of his auditors, and to say nothing but what pleases them, at leastwise nothing that may displease them; and this needs he must do if his means have not some competency in it, and if a competency, then so much the worse if no certainty, but wholly depending on the will and pleasure of the hearers."

of the festive character of the Lord's Day, or of the new position assigned to the Communion table. No writer who thought it sinful to shoot at the butts on Sunday or to kneel at the reception of the Communion was permitted to make himself heard. As might have been expected, indignation found a way. There were presses in Holland which would print anything sent to them; presses too in London itself which did their work in secret. The risk to which the authors of unlicensed books were exposed imparted acrimony to their style. Many a pamphlet, sharp and stinging, passed rapidly and secretly from hand to hand. Laud found himself the object of fierce and angry vituperation. No misstatement was too gross, no charge too insulting, to be believed against a man who refused to his adversaries all chance of speaking in their own defence.

CHAP. I.
1637.

The unlicensed press.

Laud knew no other course than to persist in the path which he had hitherto followed. The terrors of the Star Chamber and the High Commission must be evoked against the misleaders of opinion. Three pamphleteers—William Prynne, Henry Burton, and John Bastwick—were selected for punishment.

Laud resolves to suppress it.

Prynne's style of writing had not grown less bitter since his exposure in the pillory in 1634. Under the title of *A Divine Tragedy lately acted* he clandestinely printed a collection of examples of God's judgments upon Sabbath-breakers. He told of the sudden deaths of young men who had on that day amused themselves by ringing a peal of bells, and of young women who had enjoyed a dance on the same day. He went on to argue that this wickedness was but the natural fruit of the King's *Declaration of Sports*, and of other books which had been published by authority. He attributed a fresh outbreak of the

1636. Prynne's *Divine Tragedy*.

plague to the special sin of Sabbath-breaking. In another pamphlet, called *News from Ipswich*, he directed a violent attack upon Bishop Wren, after which he proceeded to charge the Bishops as a body with suppressing preaching in order to pave the way for the introduction of Popery. He called upon 'pious King Charles' to do justice on the whole episcopal order by which he had been robbed of the love of God and of his people, and which aimed at plucking the crown from his head, that they might 'set it on their own ambitious pates.'

Burton was as outspoken as Prynne. On November 5, 1636, he preached two sermons which he afterwards published under the title of *For God and the King*. In these he attacked the tables turned into altars, the crucifixes set up, and the bowing towards the East, with a fierce relentlessness which was certain to tell on the popular mind. The inference which would be widely drawn was that these innovations being the work of the Bishops, the sooner their office was abolished the better it would be for the nation.

The inference at which Burton arrived was the starting-point of Bastwick. Born in Essex, and brought up, like so many Essex men, in the straitest principles of Puritanism, he had, after a short sojourn at Emmanuel College, the stronghold of Puritanism at Cambridge, left England to serve as a soldier, probably in the Dutch army.[1] He afterwards studied medicine at Padua, and returned home in 1623 to practise his profession at Colchester.

Ten years later he published his *Flagellum Pontificis* in Holland. It was an argument in favour of Presbyterianism. He was, in consequence, brought

---

[1] This is nowhere stated; but his constant use of the word "groll" as a term of reproach indicates familiarity with the Dutch language.

before the High Commission and sentenced to a fine of 1,000*l.*, to exclusion from the practice of medicine, and to an imprisonment which was to last till he saw fit to retract his opinions.¹

The *Flagellum Pontificis* was a staid production, unlikely to inflame the minds even of those who were able to read the Latin in which it was couched. Bastwick's next book was the *Apologeticus*, more fiery in its tone, but still shrouding its vehemence in Latin from the popular eye.² At last he flung off all restraint and struck fiercely at his persecutors. *The Litany of John Bastwick* kept no quarter with the Bishops. "From plague, pestilence, and famine," he prayed, "from bishops, priests, and deacons, good Lord, deliver us!" The Prelates, he said, were the enemies of God and the King. They were the tail of the Beast. They had opened 'the very schools to ungodliness and unrighteousness, impiety and all manner of licentiousness.' The Church was 'as full of ceremonies as a dog is full of fleas.' "To speak the truth, such a multitude of trumperies and grollish³ ceremonies are brought in by the Prelates as all the substance of religion is thrust out." Churchwardens were ordered to inform 'about capping, ducking, standing, and kneeling,' as well as to accuse persons wandering from their own parishes in search of more palatable doctrine than was to be found at home, and persons who met in private for mutual edification and prayer. In Bastwick's eyes the Ecclesiastical Courts were altogether abominable. "I shall ever be of this opinion," he wrote, "that there is never a one of the Prelates' Courts but the wickedness of that alone and

---

¹ Sentence, Feb. 12, 1635. *S. P. Dom.* cclxi. 178.
² Its first title is πράξεις τῶν ἐπισκόπων.
³ Dutch, 'grollig,' foolish.

CHAP. I.
1637.

their vassals in it is able to bring a continual and perpetual plague upon the King's three dominions." All manner of wickedness was there vendible, so that if men would but open their purses 'remission of sins and absolution, with a free immunity from all dangers,' would be 'with facility granted them.' "Take notice," he wrote in conclusion, "so far am I from flying or fearing, as I resolve to make war against the Beast, and every limb of Antichrist, all the days of my life. . . . If I die in that battle, so much the sooner I shall be sent in a chariot of triumph to heaven; and when I come there, I will, with those that are under the altar, cry, 'How long, Lord, holy and true, dost Thou not judge and avenge our blood upon them that dwell upon the earth?'"

June 14. The Star Chamber trials.

On June 14 the three assailants of the Bishops appeared before the Star Chamber to answer to a charge of libel. Even men who were attached to the existing system of government long remembered with bitterness the scene which followed. When Prynne took his place at the bar, Finch called upon the usher of the Court to hold back the locks with which he had done his best to cover the scars left by the execution of his former sentence. "I had thought," said the Chief Justice with a sneer, "Mr. Prynne had no ears, but methinks he hath ears." The executioner had dealt mercifully with him three years before, and there was still a possibility of carrying out the sentence which Finch had made up his mind to inflict. The three cases were practically undefended. Burton's answer had been signed by his counsel, but was rejected by the Court as irrelevant. The answers of the other two were so violent that no lawyer could be induced to sign them. The three accused persons said what they could, but in the place in which they stood nothing that they could say was likely to avail them. "There are some honourable Lords in this Court," said Bastwick, his old military instincts stirring strongly within him, "that have been forced out as combatants in a single duel.[1] It is between the Prelates and us at this time as between two that have been appointed the field; the one, being a coward, goes to the magistrate, and by virtue of his authority disarms the other of his weapons, and gives him a bulrush, and then challanges him to fight. If this be not base cowardice, I know not what belongs to a soldier. This is the case between the Prelates and us; they take away our weapons— our answers—by virtue of your authority, by which we should defend ourselves; and yet they bid us fight. My Lord, doth not this savour of a base, cowardly spirit? I know, my Lord, there is a decree gone forth—for my sentence was passed long ago— to cut off our ears."

The sentence was indeed a foregone conclusion. At Cottington's motion the three accused men were condemned to lose their ears, to be fined 5,000*l.* apiece, and to be imprisoned for the remainder of their lives in the castles of Carnarvon, Launceston, and Lancaster, where, it was fondly hoped, no breath of Puritan sympathy would reach them more. Finch savagely added a wish that Prynne, as a seditious libeller, should be branded on the cheeks with the letters S L, and Finch's suggestion was unanimously adopted.[2]

The speech which Laud delivered in Court was long and argumentative.[3] The main charge against

[1] The reference was to the Earl of Dorset, whose duel, when he was Sir E. Sackvile, with Lord Bruce is well known.
[2] A brief relation. *Harl. Misc.* iv. 12.
[3] Laud to Wentworth, June 28. *Works*, vii. 355.

him was that the ceremonies which he had enforced were innovations on established usage. His answer was in effect that they were not innovations on the established law. On many points of detail he had far the better of the argument. The removal of the Communion table to the east end he treated as a mere matter of convenience, for the sake of decency and order; and he quoted triumphantly an expression of the Calvinistic Bishop Davenant, " 'Tis ignorance to think that the standing of the holy table there relishes of Popery." His own practice of bowing he defended. "For my own part," he said, "I take myself bound to worship with body as well as soul whenever I come where God is worshipped; and were this kingdom such as would allow no holy table standing in its proper place—and such places some there are—yet I would worship God when I came into His house." He flatly denied that he had compelled anyone to follow his example. "Yet," he said, "the Government is so moderate that no man is constrained, no man questioned, only religiously called upon—'Come, let us worship.'" True perhaps in the letter, this defence was not true in spirit. Even if those cathedrals and chapels, where the statutes inculcated the practice of bowing upon entrance, had been left out of sight, there was an almost irresistible influence exercised in favour of the general observance of the custom.

To the question of the King's jurisdiction in ecclesiastical matters Laud answered with equal firmness. One of the charges brought against the Archbishop was that he was undermining the Royal authority by laying claim to a Divine right for his own order. On this point the speech was most emphatic. "Though our office," Laud said, "be from

God and Christ immediately, yet may we not exercise that power, either of order or jurisdiction, but as God hath appointed us; that is not in his Majesty's or any Christian king's kingdoms, but by and under the power of the King given us so to do." So pleased was Charles with the language of the Archbishop that he ordered the immediate publication of his speech. He also referred to the Judges the question whether the Bishops had infringed on his prerogative by issuing processes in their own names, and the Judges unanimously decided that they had not.[1]

Whatever the Judges might say they could not meet the rising feeling that the power of the Crown was being placed at the disposal of a single ecclesiastical party. Large numbers of Englishmen leapt to the conclusion that the object of that party was the restoration of the Papal authority. The three years which had just gone by—the years of the metropolitical visitation—had effected a great change in the temper of the nation. In 1634, as far as any evidence has reached us, Prynne had suffered uncheered by any sign of sympathy. There was no lack of sympathy now. As he stepped forth, with Burton and Bastwick by his side, on his way to the place where the sentence of the Star Chamber was to be carried out, he found the path strewed with herbs and flowers. Bastwick was the first to mount the scaffold. He was quickly followed by his wife. She kissed him on his ears and mouth. The crowd set up an admiring shout. "Farewell, my dearest," said her husband as she turned to descend, "be of good comfort; I am nothing dismayed."

For two hours the three stood pilloried, conversing freely with the bystanders. "The first occa-

CHAP. I.
1637.
June.

July 1.

June 30. Execution of the sentence of the Star Chamber.

[1] *Rymer*, xx. 143, 156.

sion of my trouble," said Bastwick, "was by the Prelates, for writing a book against the Pope, and the Pope of Canterbury said I wrote against him, and therefore questioned me; but if the presses were as open to us as formerly they have been, we should scatter his kingdom about his ears." Prynne characteristically employed his time in explaining that his sentence was not warranted by precedent. The real cause of his coming there, he said, was his refusal to acknowledge that the Prelates held their office by Divine right. He was ready to argue the question against all comers, and, if he did not make his point good, to be 'hanged at the Hall Gate.' Once more the people shouted applaudingly. Burton followed, thanking God that He had enabled him thus to suffer. Even the rough men whose duty it was to superintend the execution were melted to pity, and sought to alleviate his suffering by placing a stone to ease the weight of the pillory on his neck. His wife sent him a message that 'she was more cheerful of' that 'day than of her wedding-day.' "Sir," called out a woman in the crowd, "every Christian is not worthy of the honour which the Lord hath cast on you this day." "Alas!" replied Burton, "who is worthy of the least mercy? But it is His gracious favour and free gift to account us worthy in the behalf of Christ to suffer anything for His sake."[1]

At last the time arrived for sharper suffering. "After two hours," wrote a collector of news, "the hangman began to cut off the ears of Mr. Burton, and at the cutting of each ear there was such a roaring as if every one of them had at the same instant lost an ear." Bastwick, making use of his surgical knowledge, instructed the executioner how 'to cut off his

[1] *Harl. Misc.* iv. 19.

ears quickly and very close, that he might come there no more.' "The hangman," wrote one who recorded the scene, "burnt Prynne in both the cheeks, and, as I hear, because he burnt one cheek with a letter the wrong way, he burnt that again; presently a surgeon clapped on a plaster to take out the fire. The hangman hewed off Prynne's ears very scurvily, which put him to much pain; and after he stood long in the pillory before his head could be got out, but that was a chance."[1] Amongst the crowd not all were on Prynne's side. "The humours of the people were various; some wept, some laughed, and some were very reserved." A story got about which, whether it were true or false, was certain to be eagerly credited, that 'a Popish fellow told some of those which wept that, if so be they would turn Catholics, they need fear none of this punishment.' On his way back to prison Prynne composed a Latin distich, in which he interpreted the S L which he now bore indelibly on his cheeks as *Stigmata Laudis*, the Scars of Laud.[2]

Well might Laud come to the conclusion that his purposes were hindered rather than furthered by such an exhibition. "What say you," he wrote to Wentworth, "that Prynne and his fellows should be suffered to talk what they pleased while they stood in the pillory?"[3] Even here his policy of the enforcement of silence had broken down. The very executioners had turned against him.

The manifestation of popular feeling round the scaffold was repeated when the prisoners were led out of London to their far-distant dungeons. Of Bast-

[1] Not 'a shame,' as printed by Mr. Bruce.
[2] Rossingham's Newsletter, July 6. *Documents relating to Prynne,* Camd. Soc., 86.
[3] Laud to Wentworth, Aug. 28. *Straf. Letters,* ii. 99.

wick's journey, indeed, no account has reached us. Prynne, as he passed along the Northern Road, was greeted with the loudest declarations of sympathy, which were at the same time declarations of hostility to Laud. At Barnet friendly hands prepared for him a dinner. At St. Albans six or seven of the townsmen joined him at supper with hospitable greeting. At Coventry he was visited by one of the aldermen. At Chester he became an object of interest to the townsmen. When Burton left London by the Western Road, crowds joined in shouting 'God bless you!' as he passed with his gaolers.[1]

The conditions under which the three were imprisoned were hard enough. The use of pen and ink was strictly prohibited. No book was allowed to enter the cells of the prisoners except 'the Bible, the Book of Common Prayer, and such other canonical books as were consonant to the religion professed in the Church of England.' Anxious as the Privy Council was for the orthodoxy of the prisoners, it was still more anxious that no voice of theirs should again be heard to lead astray the silly sheep who were unable to distinguish between the false shepherds and the true. Launceston and Carnarvon and Lancaster were far enough removed from the centres of population, but the keepers reported that they were unable to make adequate provision for the isolation of their charges from the outer world. Fresh orders were therefore issued to transfer the prisoners to still more inaccessible strongholds, where their persuasive tongues might find no echo. Bastwick was to be immured in a fort in the Scilly Isles. Burton was to be confined in Cornet Castle in Guernsey, Prynne in

[1] Examinations of Maynard and Ingram, Sept. 22. *S. P. Dom.* ccclxviii. 14.

Mont Orgueil in Jersey. The object of the Council was not that they should be separated from the world, but that the world should be separated from them. Burton and Bastwick were married men; and strict orders were given that their wives should not be allowed to land in the islands in which the prisoners were detained, lest they should 'be evil instruments to scatter abroad their dangerous opinions and designs.'[1]

The three men, victims to Laud's terror rather than to his hatred, were thus doomed, to all appearance, to a life-long seclusion from mankind. Other voices took up their tale. Libels picked up in the streets charged the Archbishop with being the captain of the army of the Devil in his war against the saints. A copy of the Star Chamber decree was nailed to a board. Its corners were cut off as the ears of Laud's victims had been cut off at Westminster. A broad ink-mark was drawn round his own name. An inscription declared that "The man that puts the saints of God into a pillory of wood stands here in a pillory of ink."[2]

Laud could but press on to the end in the path on which he had entered. The silence requisite for the success of his scheme must be enforced still more strictly. There must be no weak concession, no idle folding of the hands whilst the enemy was on the alert. The policy of 'Thorough' must take its course. As far as statute law was concerned, the English press was as free in the reign of Charles as it is in the reign of Victoria. It was muzzled by a decree of the Star Chamber, issued at the time when the throne of Elizabeth was assailed by bitter and

[1] *Documents relating to Prynne*, Camd. Soc. 62-69.
[2] Laud to Wentworth, Aug. ? *Works*, vii. 364.

CHAP. I.

1637. Aug.

Star Chamber decree on the press.

Clandestine publications.

Laud and the Catholics.

unscrupulous attacks. That decree was now reinforced by another still more sharp. The number of printers authorised to carry on their trade in London was to be reduced to twenty. Even books formerly licensed were not to be republished without a fresh examination. Any man not of the number of the privileged twenty who ventured to print a book was 'to be set in the pillory and whipped through the City of London.'[1]

The appetite for unlicensed literature was too strong to be thus baulked. Clandestine presses continued to pour forth pamphlets to be read by admiring and increasing crowds. Laud's attempt to silence his accusers only added fresh zest to the banquet of libel and invective. The decorous tones which issued from the licensed press to bewail the folly and ignorance of the times convinced none who were not convinced already.

Under no circumstances was this system of repression likely to take permanent root in England. To have given it even a temporary chance of success it must have been applied fairly on the right hand as well as on the left. The Catholic must suffer as well as the Puritan.

So much Laud clearly saw. He knew full well that the charge brought against him of complicity with the Church of Rome was entirely false; and as he could not prove his Protestantism by tenderness to the Puritans, the only way open to him to convince the world that he was not a secret emissary of the Pope was to persecute the members of the Papal Church. For some time, therefore, he had been pleading earnestly with the Council to take steps to

[1] *Rushw.* ii. 450. App. 306. Lambe's List of Printers, July. *S. P. Dom.* ccclxiv. 111.

limit the freedom of action recently enjoyed by the Catholics.

One invincible stumbling-block stood in Laud's way. For no persistent course of policy was Charles's support to be relied on. With no imaginative insight into the condition of the world around him, he did not share in Laud's prognostications of evil. Puritanism was not to him a wolf held by the ears, but simply a troublesome and factious spirit which needed to be kept down by sharp discipline, but which was not likely to be really formidable. His fear of danger from the Catholics was even less than his fear of danger from the Puritans. To him they were merely well-disposed, gentlemanly persons with improper notions about some religious doctrines, and more especially with some theoretical objections to the Royal supremacy, which were not very likely to influence their practice. It never entered his head that familiarity with such pleasant companions was the most dangerous course which he could possibly pursue.

The King's friendly intercourse with Panzani had been continued with Con, the Scotchman who succeeded him as Papal Agent at the Queen's Court. Con dropped the subject of the reunion of the Churches, which had now served its purpose; and if the negotiation for a modification of the oath of allegiance was still occasionally heard of, it was more for the sake of appearance than from any expectation that it would be really possible to come to an understanding with the King on this subject. Charles was quite satisfied to find in Con a well-informed and respectful man, ready to discuss politics or theology without acrimony by the hour, and to flatter him with assurances of the loyalty of his Catholic subjects,

CHAP. I.
1637.
April.
Con at Court.

without forgetting to point to the sad contrast exhibited by the stiff-necked and contemptuous Puritan.

There were quarters in which ordinary Puritanism met with but little sympathy where offence was given by this unwise familiarity. At the festival of the Knights of the Garter the brilliant assembly was kept waiting for the commencement of the service in the Royal Chapel till the King had finished exhibiting his pictures to the representative of the Pope. On another occasion, when the Court was assembled to witness the leave-taking of the French Ambassador, Seneterre, the Privy Councillors occupied their accustomed positions at the King's right hand, Laud, in virtue of his Archbishopric, standing next to the throne. The Queen was on Charles's left, and next to her was Con. "Now," said a lady of the Court to the Scottish priest, "there is only a step between the Archbishop and you. Shake hands and agree together." "Our Lord," answered Con significantly, "stands with his arms open to receive all men into the bosom of the Holy Church."[1]

July.

The Queen and the Catholics.

Panzani had striven in vain to win Charles to more than well-bred friendliness. Con turned his attention to the Queen. It had never hitherto been possible to rouse her to more than spasmodic efforts even on behalf of the Catholics. Averse to sustained exertion, and intervening only from some personal interest or momentary pique, she had contented herself with the consciousness that the persecution under which the Catholics suffered had been gradually relaxed. Con wished to make her an active agent in the propagation of the faith, and he was seconded by Walter Montague, who had been recently allowed to return to England, though he was received more

[1] Con to Barberini, $\frac{\text{Apr. 21}}{\text{May 1}}$, July $\frac{7}{17}$. *Add. MSS.* 15,390, fol. 246, 346.

warmly at Somerset House than at Whitehall. Between them they succeeded in securing the support of the Queen for that work of individual proselytism which was to supersede Panzani's fantastic scheme for the absorption of the Church of England. It is true that in the actual work of gaining converts Henrietta Maria took but little part; but she showed a warm interest in the process, and she prided herself in protecting the converts made by others. It was her part to win from her fond husband, by arguments, by prayers, if need be by tears, their release from the consequences of a too open violation of the harsh laws which still held their place on the Statute Book, and which were supported by a widely diffused public opinion. At one time she was closeted every morning with Con in eager consultation over the best means of swaying Charles's mind in favour of the Catholics.

<small>CHAP. I.
1637.</small>

The protection of the Queen was invaluable to Con. For active energy he looked elsewhere. The soul of the proselytising movement was Mrs. Porter, the wife of that Endymion Porter who had been employed in so many secret missions by James and Charles. By her mother she was a niece of Buckingham, and she had inherited the quick decision and the prompt impetuosity of the splendid favourite. One day she heard that her father, Lord Boteler, was seriously ill. At once she drove down to his country seat, hurried the old man into her coach, and carried him up to London. She then brought the priests around him, and was able, before he died, to boast of him as a convert. Her triumph was the greater because her Protestant sister, Lady Newport, had also driven off to secure the sick man, and had arrived at his house too late.

<small>Mrs. Porter's converts.</small>

<small>March. Lord Boteler.</small>

¹ Con to Barberini, March 30/Apr. 9. *Add. MSS.* 15,390, fol. 213.

The next object of Mrs. Porter's attack was the Marchioness of Hamilton, another of Buckingham's nieces. Her bright beauty had not long since been the theme of admiring tongues, which had celebrated her gentleness of heart as equal to the attractions of her person. She was now fading away under that wasting disease which carried her off a few months later. In this condition she was peculiarly susceptible to religious impressions, and she was plied with controversial books till she was almost ready to surrender. Her father, Lord Denbigh, 'a Puritan ass,' as Con contemptuously called him, summoned the Bishop of Carlisle to his assistance. The old argument that there was no safety in the next world for those who died outside the pale of the Roman Church was plentifully used. The Bishop replied that if the lady remained a Protestant he would be ready to pledge his soul for her salvation.[1] "It will profit you little, my sister," sneered Mrs. Porter, " that this old man's soul should keep company with yours in the Devil's house." Lady Hamilton's conversion, however, was never openly avowed, either because, as Mrs. Porter fancied, she shrank from giving pain to her relations, or because, as is more probable, the influences of her old faith were still living in her heart, and made themselves heard as soon as she was removed from the overpowering presence of her impetuous cousin.[2]

Other converts, ladies for the most part, followed in no inconsiderable numbers. At last the world was startled by the news that even Lady Newport had announced herself a Catholic. In an unguarded moment she had undertaken the part of a champion

---

[1] 'Che metterà la sua anima per quella di lei.'
[2] Con to Barberini, Oct. $\frac{13}{23}$. *Add. MSS.* 15,390, fol. 453.

of Protestantism, for which neither her temperament nor her knowledge fitted her. Once engaged in argument with the priests, she was beaten from point to point till she laid down her arms. Her husband, the eldest son of the adulterous union between the Earl of Devonshire and Lady Rich, and thus the half-brother of Warwick and Holland, was high in Charles's favour. As Master of the Ordnance he held an important post in the service of the State. A Protestant by position and from a sense of honour rather than from a closely reasoned conviction, he felt his wife's change of religion as a slur upon his own good name. Hurrying to Lambeth, he adjured Laud to punish the instruments of his misfortune. Together with Con he named Walter Montague and Sir Toby Matthew, though it would seem that the two latter had had no part in the affair. Laud was eager enough to do as Newport wished. On the next Council day he spoke his mind freely on the unusual favours accorded to the Catholics, and begged the King to forbid Montague's access to Court, and to allow proceedings to be taken against him in the High Commission. He knew well that he would himself be held accountable for these defections from the English Church. This time it seemed as if he would have his way. Charles expressed his displeasure at what had occurred, and declared his intention of providing a remedy. But Laud had counted without the Queen. Con had urged her to stand up stoutly for her religion. When once Henrietta Maria was really interested in a cause, difficulty and danger only produced on her an exhilarating effect. The language held by Laud in the Council was reported to her almost immediately. In the evening, when the King visited her in her apartments, she spoke her mind freely to him of the insolence of the Archbishop. Charles could not make up his mind to fly in his wife's face. "I doubt not," wrote Laud to Wentworth, after recounting what had taken place, "but I have enemies enough to make use of this. But, howsoever, I must bear it, and get out of the briars as I can. Indeed, my Lord, I have a very hard task, and God, I beseech Him, make me good corn, for I am between two great factions, very like corn between two mill-stones."[1]

Laud's appeal to the King.

In his distress Laud appealed to the King. Charles recommended him to seek out the Queen. "You will find my wife reasonable," he said. He did not see that his wife had made herself the centre of the opposition of which Laud complained. The Archbishop replied by proposing in full Council that her chapel at Somerset House, as well as the chapels of the Ambassadors, should be closed against the entrance of English subjects. His proposal received warm support, and orders were given for the preparation of a proclamation against the Catholics.

The Queen's displeasure.

Con was warned of what had happened by his friends in the Council, and the Queen was warned by Con. Henrietta Maria took up the quarrel so warmly that Con besought her to moderate her excitement. She felt that in defending the liberty of her chapel she was warding off insult from herself.

Nov. Threatened proclamation kept back by Con and the Queen.

Charles tried to effect a compromise with his wife. He would leave Somerset House alone; but he insisted that something must be done with the chapels of the Ambassadors. Oñate, the Spanish Ambassador, who since his arrival in England had been

---

[1] Con to Barberini, Oct. $\frac{20}{30}$. *Add. MSS.* 15,390, fol. 461. Laud's Diary, Oct. 22. Laud to Wentworth, Nov. 1. *Works*, iii. 229, vii. 378. Garrard to Wentworth, Nov. 9. *Straf. Letters*, ii. 128.

making himself as disagreeable as he possibly could, had lately given offence by announcing that he would build a larger chapel than the Queen herself could boast of. A proclamation therefore there must be. But Charles did his best to explain it away. "This sort of thing," he assured Con, "is done every year. No one would say a word against it if you would let my wife alone." Con had no intention of letting her alone. Her new position of protectress of her Church in England flattered her vanity. Her chapel was thronged with worshippers. The Holy Sacrament was on the altar till noon, to satisfy the devotion of the multitude of communicants. On festivals nine masses were celebrated in the course of the morning. The Queen strove hard to induce the King to refrain from issuing any proclamation at all. It was a struggle for influence between her and Laud, and she threw herself into it with all the energy of which she was capable. To his astonishment, Con found himself growing in favour even with men who were known as Puritans, as soon as he measured his strength with the man whom they most abhorred. He at least, they said, professed his belief openly, which was more than could be said of Laud.[1]

All through the month of November the struggle lasted. It was not till December that Con learnt that orders had been secretly given for the issue of the proclamation. He again begged Charles to withdraw it, and Charles answered that it was merely directed against the scandal given by indiscreet Catholics. "With your good leave," he said, "I wish to show that I am of the religion which I profess. . . . Everyone ought to know that the quiet which the Catholics enjoy is derived from my clemency. It is necessary

[1] Con to Barberini, Nov. $\frac{8}{15}, \frac{19}{20}$. *Add. MSS.* 15,390, fol. 469, 476.

to remind them that they live in England, not in Rome." Con tried to irritate him against Laud. He replied that he was following the advice of the whole Council, not that of Laud alone. The proclamation, he added, would be moderate enough. In fact, as Con afterwards learnt, Charles had promised his wife to omit anything to which she might take exception. So complete was the Queen's triumph that she even consented to admit Laud to her presence, and to extend to him some qualified tokens of her favour.[1]

Dec. 20. Issue of the proclamation.

Thus manipulated, the proclamation was at last issued on December 20. In its final shape it could hardly give offence to anyone. Even Con described it as 'so mild as to seem rather a paternal admonition to the Catholics than a menace.' The Puritans, he added, were of the same opinion. In fact, it contained nothing more than a threat that those who persisted in withdrawing his Majesty's subjects from the Church of England would do so 'under pain of the several punishments' provided by the law, and that all who gave scandal by the celebration of masses would be punished according to their offence. No definition was given of the amount of notoriety which was to constitute scandal.[2]

Dec. 25. The mass at the Queen's chapel.

Gentle as the admonition was, Henrietta Maria could not resist the temptation to treat it with contempt. On Christmas Day, by her special orders, Lady Newport and the other recent converts were marshalled to receive the Communion in a body at Somerset House. As soon as the Queen returned to her apartments she called Con to her side. "You have now seen," she said to him triumphantly, "what has come of the proclamation."[3]

---

[1] Con to Barberini, Dec. $\frac{8}{18}$. *Ibid.* fol. 498. Laud's Diary, Dec. 12. *Works*, iii. 230. [2] Proclamation, Dec. 20. *Rymer*, xx. 180.
[3] Con to Barberini, $\frac{Dec. 29}{Jan. 8}$. *Add. MSS.* 15,391, fol. 1.

The Queen's open defiance of the proclamation gave the tone to every priest in England. Never were masses more publicly celebrated in the Ambassadors' chapels, or with less concealment in the houses of the Catholic laity. "Before you came," said Lady Arundel to Con, "I would not for a million have entertained a priest at my table, and now you see how common a thing it is." The proclamation, in fact, had been merely wrung from Charles by Laud's insistence, supported by the special annoyance caused by the bravado of the Spanish Ambassador. He was too sure of his own position, too blind to the real dangers by which it was surrounded, to sympathise with Laud's perception of the risk which he would incur by holding the balance uneven between the Puritans and the Catholics. "The Archbishop," he said to Con, "is a very honest man, but he wants to have everything his own way."[1]

There is no reason to regret that Laud did not in this case have his way. The danger from Rome was less serious than it seemed. The bait held out by the Papal clergy appealed to the lower and more selfish side of human nature. Fantastic speculators like Sir Kenelm Digby, witty intriguers like Walter Montague, brought no real strength to the cause which they espoused; whilst the gay Court ladies, whose life had hitherto been passed in a round of amusement,

---

[1] Con to Barberini, June $\frac{7}{17}$, July $\frac{13}{23}$, 1638. *Ibid.* fol. 164, 204. Laud's bewilderment at the charge brought against him of being secretly a Roman Catholic is well expressed by some words which he made use of nearly two years previously. "Because," he said, "he strove to maintain the old orders of the Church, the common people, who were enemies to all order and government, proclaimed him a Papist; but (if he had been one) he had had reason enough—besides his ill-usage he had when he had no friend at Court but the King—to have left the Church and have gone beyond seas." Charles Lewis to Elizabeth, May 31, 1636. *Forster MSS.*, in the South Kensington Museum.

were personally the better by submitting to a sterner discipline than any which they had hitherto known. The arguments by which they had been moved appealed to motives too low to exercise any attractive force over the real leaders of the age, or to be otherwise than repulsive to the sense of honour which was the common property of English gentlemen.

The Earl of Newcastle.

Such a man, for instance, as William Cavendish, Earl of Newcastle, was entirely beyond the reach of Con. In the summer of 1638 he was selected by Charles to be the governor of his eldest son. "He was a fine gentleman," wrote Clarendon, who knew him well; "active and full of courage, and most accomplished in those qualities of horsemanship, dancing, and fencing which accompany a good breeding, in which his delight was. Besides that, he was amorous in poetry and music, to which he indulged the greatest part of his time. . . . He loved monarchy, as it was the foundation of his own greatness; and the Church, as it was constituted for the splendour and security of the Crown; and religion, as it cherished and maintained that order and obedience that was necessary to both, without any other passion for the particular opinions which were grown up in it and distinguished it into parties, than as he detested whatsoever was like to disturb the public peace."[1] Con's report of Newcastle tallies almost exactly with that of the English historian. "In matters of religion," he wrote, "the Earl is too indifferent. He hates the Puritans, he laughs at the Protestants, and has little confidence in the Catholics. In speaking with him, therefore, I have been obliged to touch upon first principles, and to bring him to the axiom that in things doubtful the safer part is to be

[1] Clarendon, viii. 82.

chosen."[1] It was to no purpose that the temptation was held out to such a man as this. The careless, worldly temper of a Newcastle gave as little hold to Con as the higher virtue of nobler men.

{CHAP. I. 1638.}

Enough was, however, done to alarm English Protestants. The charge, indeed, which a later age has to bring against Charles is not that he abstained from persecuting the Catholics, but that he failed to give fair play to the diverse elements of which the English Church was compounded. Catholic books passed from hand to hand. Puritanism was an object of derision to all who took their tone from Whitehall, and of stern repression in the Ecclesiastical Courts. Men who had no sympathy with Calvinistic dogmatism were attracted by that stern morality which rebuked the solemn trifling which was the atmosphere of Charles's Court.

{English feeling about the Catholic conversions.}

To such a feeling as this Milton at last gave expression in that high satire which bursts forth, as if from some suddenly raised volcano, out of the smooth and graceful lamentations of the *Lycidas*. Nothing in Milton's past life gave warning of the intensity of his scorn. Nothing in the subject which he had chosen invited him to check the flow of his private grief that he might bewail the public sorrows of his time. Yet from these public sorrows he could not avert his gaze. As it had been with Dante, the poet of medieval Catholicism, so was it with the man who was training himself to be one day the poet of English Puritanism. The living interest in the joys and sorrows of the great world around him, even the mere official acquaintance with the dry details of public business, by which rulers attempt, if they rise at all to the height of their duty, to increase those

{Milton's Lycidas.}

---

[1] Con to Barberini, Sept. $\frac{7}{17}$. *Add. MSS.* 15,391, fol. 235.

joys and to alleviate those sorrows, were to strengthen the Englishman as they strengthened the great Italian to seek for consolation in a serener and purer atmosphere than that in which the best and wisest of statesmen must be content to work. Milton had not as yet had any close insight into the difficulties of government. He saw the evil; he could not descry the hindrances to good. Before the eye of his imagination rose the Apostle Peter, mournfully addressing the dead Lycidas, lost too early to earthly service. The indignant poet cannot choose but to tell how 'the pilot of the Galilean lake'

> Shook his mitred locks, and stern bespake,
> " How well would I have spared for thee, young man,
> Enow of such as for their bellies' sake
> Creep and intrude, and climb into the fold!
> Of other care they little reckoning make,
> Than how to scramble at the shearers' feast
> And shove away the worthy bidden guest.
> Blind mouths! that scarce themselves know how to hold
> A sheep-hook, or have learnt aught else the least
> That to the faithful herdsman's art belongs,
> What recks it them? What need they? They are sped,
> And when they list their lean and flashy songs
> Grate on their scrannel pipes of wretched straw.
> The hungry sheep look up and are not fed,
> But swoln with wind, and the rank mist they draw,
> Rot inwardly, and foul contagion spread,
> Besides what the grim wolf with privy paw
> Daily devours apace and nothing said."

Character of Milton's Indignation.

Milton's indignation was not as the indignation of Prynne or Bastwick. He did not approach the Church question from the ceremonial side. He did not as yet care to ask whether the Church ought to be Episcopalian or Presbyterian. There is still a touch of the poet of *Il Penseroso* and of the *Elegy on Bishop Andrewes* in the 'mitred locks' of Peter. He is kindled to wrath by the moral results of Laud's discipline—results which he doubtless exaggerated, but which were certainly not entirely imaginary. He saw that, whether Laud were consciously tending towards the Roman Church or not, his superabundant care for the externals of religion was eating the heart out of English Protestantism. It invited the allegiance of men to whom nothing was easier than to assume a posture or to clothe themselves in a vestment. It repelled the allegiance of men who saw in that posture or that vestment a token of the subordination to external forms of the spiritual life itself.

Milton did more than denounce the system which he hated so thoroughly. He predicted its speedy overthrow. He announced that

> That two-handed engine at the door
> Stands ready to smite once and smite no more.[1]

The prophecy was doubtless intentionally left in vague and mysterious outline, but its general intention was unmistakable.

Milton's voice expressed the deepest feelings of the nation. Slowly and reluctantly the generation of serious Englishmen now advancing towards middle age was coming to the conclusion that the overthrow of the Laudian system was the one thing necessary for

---

[1] It is impossible to be dogmatical on the precise meaning of the words, but the interpretation of its referring to the two Houses of Parliament cannot be right. Not only was an impeaching Parliament out of the range of probability in 1637, but the engine was to be held by two hands, not to be two engines held by one. The idea of the axe laid to the root of the tree seems most natural. Professor Masson says (*Milton's Works*, iii. 455) that the engine here 'is at the door of an edifice, not at the root of a tree.' Milton, however, may have meant to mingle the idea of smiting the system with the idea of smiting the persons who supported it. He may not have wished to be too definite, and the expression 'blind mouths' shows that we must not look for rigid consistency. Perhaps, too, he was thinking in an indistinct way of the iron flail with which Talus stormed the castle of the Lady Munera, and wished to intensify the crushing nature of the blow by turning the one-handed weapon of Spenser into a two-handed engine.

the restoration of a healthy spiritual life. The feeling was all the stronger because all moral earnestness was repelled by the loose follies of the Court. The growth of this feeling may be traced in the career of John Hutchinson, whose character has been portrayed by his widow, under the mellowing light of wifely affection. He was educated at Peter House, the college of Cosin and Crashaw, the college which, more than any other, attempted to exorcise the spirit of Puritanism. Yet he was able to boast that, after five years, he came away untainted with the principles or practices of the followers of Laud. On the other hand, he did not come away with any confirmed dislike of the Church in which those principles and practices had taken root. He was 'not yet enlightened to discern the spring of them in the rites and usages of the English Church.' His was the Puritanism of the polished and practical country gentleman, versed from his youth up in the conduct of business, and accustomed to conduct it with a strict but not ungraceful morality, which left room for the ornaments and enjoyments of life. At college 'he kept not company with any of the vain young persons, but with the graver men and those by whose conversation he might gain improvement. . . . For his exercise he practised tennis, and played admirably well at it; for his diversion he chose music, and got a very good hand, which afterwards he improved to a very good mastery on the viol.' He danced and vaulted with grace and agility, studied eagerly, learning being regarded by him 'as a handmaid to devotion and as a great improver of natural reason.' His choice of the decorations of life was made under a sense of serious self-restraint. "In those things that were of mere pleasure he loved not to aim at that he could not attain; he would rather wear clothes absolutely plain than pretend to gallantry, and would rather choose to have none than mean jewels or pictures and such other things as were not of absolute necessity . . . His whole life was the rule of temperance in meat, drink, apparel, pleasure, and all those things that may be lawfully enjoyed, and herein his temperance was more excellent than in others, in whom it is not so much a virtue, but proceeds from want of appetite or gust of pleasure; in him it was a true, wise, and religious government of the desire and delight he took in the things that he enjoyed. He had a certain activity of spirit which could never endure idleness either in himself or others, and that made him eager for the time he indulged it, as well in pleasure as in business; indeed, though in youth he exercised innocent sports a little while, yet afterwards his business was his pleasure. But how intent soever he were in anything, how much soever it delighted him, he could freely and easily cast it away when God called him to something else. He had as much modesty as could consist with a true virtuous assurance, and hated an impudent person. Neither in youth nor in riper age could the most fair or enticing women ever draw him into unnecessary familiarity or vain converse or dalliance with them, yet he despised nothing of the female sex but their follies and vanities; wise and virtuous women he loved, and delighted in all pure, holy, and unblamable conversation with them, but so as never to excite scandal or temptation. Scurrilous discourse even among men he abhorred; and though he sometimes took pleasure in wit and mirth, yet that which was mixed with impurity he never would endure. The heat of his youth a little inclined him to the passion of anger, and the goodness of his nature to those of love and grief; but reason was never dethroned by them, but continued governor and moderator of his soul."

Such was the character—for Hutchinson was but a type of a large section of society—of the noblest class of English Puritans, of men who possessed their souls in patience, uttering no cry of scorn or anger. It was the steady and persistent refusal of these men to countenance the Court and its ways which made the opposition of such as Prynne and Bastwick really formidable, and which gave weight to the forlorn hopes which from time to time dashed themselves, apparently in vain, against the defences of the Government.

Of such forlorn hopes there were enough and to spare. In the winter of 1637 it was the turn of John Lilburn, a youth of twenty, who had just returned from Holland. A certain Chillington, accused of circulating Puritan books printed beyond the sea, saved himself by charging Lilburn with having them printed at Rotterdam. Lilburn was arrested and interrogated, but he absolutely denied that he had had anything to do with Chillington's books. When asked questions on more general matters he refused to answer. No one, he said, had a right to make him criminate either himself or others. He was brought before the Star Chamber, and ordered to take the usual oath that he would answer truly to all questions that might be put to him. This he steadily refused to do. He came of a sturdy and self-willed race. His father was a Yorkshire gentleman, who was the last man in England to compel the unwilling judges to allow him to commit a lawsuit to the chances of trial by battle.[1] Of this opinionativeness he had inherited

---

[1] The King, however, refused to allow the combat to proceed. The case in 1818 did not proceed so far, as the demand was withdrawn.

his full share. In the course of a stirring life he was never in accord with any Government, and never missed an opportunity of making known to the world the grievances which he entertained against every Government. The claim which he now made went far beyond the doctrine ultimately accepted by English Courts that no man may be compelled to criminate himself. He refused to swear to answer truly to any questions of which he did not at the time of his oath know the import—a claim which, if admitted, would make it impossible to cross-examine any witness whatever. Like all the Courts, the Star Chamber was peculiarly sensitive to any attack upon its rules, and especially upon the system under which it had been for so many years in the habit of procuring evidence from unwilling witnesses. Lilburn was accordingly sentenced to be whipped from the Fleet to Palace Yard, and then to be placed in the pillory. All along the Strand the lash descended on his back. Smarting with pain, he was placed in the pillory. In spite of his agony he exhorted the bystanders to resist the tyranny of the Bishops, and scattered amongst them a few copies of Bastwick's pamphlets which he had in his pockets. The Court of Star Chamber was in session hard by, and an angry order to gag him was issued at once. Another order directed the Warden of the Fleet to place him in irons on his return, and to keep him in solitary confinement 'where the basest and meanest sort of prisoners are used to be put,' to prohibit his friends from visiting him or supplying him with money. But for the persistent contrivance of his admirers Lilburn would have been starved to death. The Warden held that it was no part of his duty to supply the prisoners with food. Those who had no money were accustomed to beg their food from the charitable who passed the door; but Lilburn was debarred even from that wretched resource. The other prisoners, half-starved and ragged as they were, entered into a conspiracy in his favour. They shared their crusts and broken victuals with him, in spite of blows and kicks from the turnkeys. Sometimes this precarious aid failed, and on one occasion the unfortunate man passed ten whole days without tasting food. Yet, broken in health as he could not fail to be, his indomitable spirit held up, and he survived to unfold the horrors of his prison house to sympathising ears.[1]

It is the nature of a government like that of Laud to be too readily terrified to take advantage of the real strength of its position. Englishmen had not so changed since the days of Elizabeth as to be anxious to deliver themselves over to be manipulated by a Prynne or a Bastwick, or even by a Milton or a Hutchinson. There were many thousands who still regarded with reverent admiration the old Prayer Book, which they had learned to love as children. There were probably many more thousands who had no wish to see cakes and ale banished from life. The most popular verse-writer of the day was George Wither, and Wither was neither a Laudian nor a Puritan. Endowed with considerable poetic gifts, he had unfortunately mistaken his vocation in life. He had given up writing good songs in order to write bad satire. He derided alike new practices and abstruse doctrines. His view of government was the simple one that kings ought not to be tyrannical and that parliaments ought not to be exacting. People were to be content with the rule in Church and State under which they were born, provided that it made

[1] *State Trials*, iii. 1315.

no very violent demands upon their conscience, and provided that they could attain under it to a placid and decorous virtue. Of this virtue, as far as can be judged by Wither's own example, the chief constituent was to be found in a self-complacent recognition of the extreme sinfulness of others and an equally self complacent assurance that this sinfulness of others was certain to bring Divine vengence down upon the world.[1]

Men of this temper—and there can be little doubt that the middle classes of the towns were very much of this temper—would have formed the best security that a government could have wished against Puritan violence. Laud's proceedings irritated them in every possible way, till they forgot that Puritanism could be irritating at all.

The only man who was fitted by his mental qualities for the task of mediation in the dark days which were approaching was unhappily disqualified for the work by his own moral defects as well as by the King's dislike. Bishop Williams had been for many years an object of a Star Chamber prosecution, on the ground that he had betrayed some secrets entrusted to him as a Privy Councillor. The charge seems to have been a frivolous one, and it was probably only brought in order to frighten Williams into the surrender of the Deanery of Westminster, which he still held, together with his bishopric. In 1633 the affair took an unexpected turn. A certain Kilvert, to whom the case against the Bishop had been entrusted, and who was himself a man of low moral character, discovered that one of Williams's

---

[1] See especially *Britain's Remembrancer*, published in 1628. The idea of the subject of predestination being one for the devils in hell to discuss appears here long before *Paradise Lost* was written.

witnesses, named Pregion, was the father of an illegitimate child, and he fancied that by attacking Pregion on this score he might succeed in discrediting his evidence in the Bishop's favour.

<small>1634. Williams obtains false evidence.</small>

Williams threw himself into the cause of his witness with characteristic ardour. It is possible that at first he may have regarded Kilvert's story as an impudent fabrication, but he can hardly have retained that opinion long; and there can be little doubt that he demeaned himself to the subornation of false evidence in order to support the character of a man who was enlisted on his side in his own quarrel with the Court.[1]

<small>1635. Fresh prosecution of Williams.</small>

A fresh prosecution of Williams on the charge of subornation of perjury was now commenced in the Star Chamber. Williams saw his danger, and asked Laud to be his mediator with the King.[2] He could hardly have expected Laud to throw much warmth into his mediation, and he turned with greater hope to Portland, and after Portland's death to Cottington. Cottington was importunate and Charles was weak.

<small>Nov. He has hopes of a pardon.</small>

Before the end of 1635 the King had promised to pardon the Bishop. The only question related to the rate at which the pardon was to be purchased. "Thus much," wrote Laud in despair, "can money and friends do against honour in movable Courts." [3]

<small>Dec. Charles's hesitation.</small>

Suddenly Williams found the bark of his fortunes drifting out again to sea. Fresh evidence of his

---

[1] Notes of proceedings, May 27, June 16, 23, 1637. *S. P. Dom.* ccclvii. 104; ccclxi. 99; ccclxii. 34. Hacket's narrative is too inaccurate to be accepted as a firm foundation. I have drawn my own conclusions from the evidence produced at the trial. Mr. Bruce appears, from his preface to the Calendar for 1637, to have come to much the same conclusion as I have.

[2] Laud to Williams, Jan. 10, 1635. *Works*, vi. 402.

[3] Laud to Wentworth, Jan. 12, Oct. 4, Nov. 30. *Ibid.* vi. 138. 171, 202.

misdemeanours reached the King's ears,¹ and Charles withdrew his promise of a pardon. A few months later the King was again hesitating. Sir John Monson, who had been maligned by Williams, and by whom the new accusations had been brought, was informed that Williams had been boasting that he was now reconciled to the King, and that those who appeared against him had better be careful of attacking a man who would soon be in full enjoyment of the Royal favour. Monson asked Charles if there was any foundation for this assertion. "The King," he afterwards informed Laud, "answered he would be free with me, and thereupon said it was true that he was in some treaty with the Bishop, who had enlarged his offers, and was now willing to yield his deanery, give 8,000*l.*, and leave me to my course in law for my repair, but that he had not given him any assurance of his acceptance of these terms, nor would if my information were truth." Williams only looked upon his present rebuff as a mischance originating from his neglect to offer a bribe sufficiently high. He soon gained over Lennox as well as Cottington to his side, and, unless Monson was misinformed, he assured the courtiers who were pleading his cause that whatever the sum might be which he was required to pay to the King, they should have as much again to divide amongst themselves. Monson took care that this should reach the King's ears, and told Charles that he would make a better bargain by allowing the law to take its course, and by taking all the money that could be got from Williams for himself. In the end this reasoning prevailed.² The whole negotiation

CHAP. I.

1636. Aug.

¹ Lambe to Laud, Dec. 3, 10; Monson to Laud, Dec. 11; Monson's petition. *Lambeth MSS.* mxxx. Nos. 39, 40, 41, 42.

² Letters and Papers of Sir J. Monson, Aug. 1636. *Lambeth MSS. Ibid.* Nos. 47, 48.

CHAP. I.
1636.

Nov.
The Holy Table, Name and Thing.

1637.
June 16.
The case in the Star Chamber.

did no credit to Charles. The lower side of Wentworth's 'Thorough' was perfectly intelligible to him. The higher side he was unable to comprehend.

Stung by his failure to bribe his way to impunity, Williams threw himself once more into ecclesiastical controversy. A book recently published by Laud's chaplain, Heylyn, *A Coal from the Altar*, had contained an attack upon Williams's well-known views about the position of the Communion table. To this he replied anonymously in *The Holy Table, Name and Thing*.[1] The authorship of the book was an open secret. It was one long argument in favour of that compromise which Williams had recommended from the beginning as the only legal arrangement; the compromise by which the table, usually standing at the east end of the church, was to be brought down to some place in the church or chancel at the time of the administration of the Communion. As might be expected, Williams preserved the courtesies of debate far better than Prynne or Bastwick. His work was, perhaps, all the more galling for that. Heylyn deemed it worthy of a serious reply, and Laud referred to it bitterly in the speech which he delivered at the censure of Prynne; but neither Laud nor Heylyn made any serious effort to refute its main position.

By this book Williams, who had sought to escape by the aid of the Catholics and semi-Catholics of the Court,[2] threw himself once more on the side of the Puritans and semi-Puritans. For the present his change of front was likely to avail him little. On

---

[1] Heylyn's book was licensed May 5; Williams's licensed for his own diocese Nov. 30.

[2] Panzani had hitherto regarded Williams as a friend of the Catholics.

June 16, 1637, the next Court day after sentence had been pronounced on Prynne, Bastwick, and Burton, his case was called on in the Star Chamber. The evidence for the prosecution was too strong to be resisted. When the day of sentence arrived, Williams's old patron, Cottington, led the way by suggesting a fine of 10,000*l.* to the King and one of 1,000 marks to Sir John Monson. The Bishop was also to be referred to the High Commission for ecclesiastical censure, to be suspended from the exercise of his functions, to be deprived of the profits of all his benefices, and to be imprisoned during the King's pleasure. This proposal was unanimously adopted, and the High Commission confirmed the decree of the Star Chamber so far as it related to matters within its special jurisdiction.[1]

Williams was sent to the Tower. The administration of his diocese was confided to his most bitter adversaries. By the King's command Laud offered him the terms on which alone he could recover his freedom. He must either pay his fine or give good security for its payment. He must surrender his bishopric, receiving in return another either in Wales or Ireland, and must give up all his other benefices. He must further acknowledge that he had committed the crime imputed to him, and that he had erred in writing *The Holy Table, Name and Thing*.[2] Many weary months passed over the prisoner's head before he was ready to accept these hard conditions even in part.

---

[1] *Rushw.* ii. 416. Commissioners for causes ecclesiastical to Williams, July 18. Sentence of suspension, July 24. *S. P. Dom.* cclxiv. 12, 43. See also Rossingham's Newsletters in *Documents relating to Prynne* (Camd. Soc.)

[2] The paper containing these terms is in Laud's hand, and endorsed, "The King commanded me to set them down." Aug. 30. *Lambeth MSS.* mxxx. fol. 68*b*.

1637.
The Latitudinarians.

In Williams the spirit of compromise, which was the characteristic mark of his genius, was marred by his moral defects. No such complaint could be made of a group of men who were working in the same direction, and who, if they failed to mould their own age after their image, have long been looked up to by later generations as the pioneers of thought. These men were Lucius Cary, Viscount Falkland; William Chillingworth, and John Hales.

1622.
Lord Falkland.

Lucius Cary was the son of the Lord Deputy who had preceded Wentworth in Ireland. When he was but twelve years old he was taken by his father to Dublin, and was there educated at Trinity College.[1] As soon as he had completed his academical course he prepared for a soldier's life, and, young as he was, was entrusted by his father's ill-judged weakness with the command of a company. As soon as the Lord Deputy was recalled, the Lords Justices, glad to make a cheap exhibition of virtue at the expense of the son of a man with whom they had been at variance, deprived the lad of his military rank, and appointed

1629.
Challenges Sir F. Willoughby.

Sir Francis Willoughby, an abler and more experienced soldier,[2] in his place. Young Cary, being unable to reach the Lords Justices, sent a challenge to Willoughby, and was consequently committed to prison and threatened with a prosecution in the Star Chamber. Charles, however, set him free after a short confinement of ten days,[3] allowing him the arrears of his pay and adding a special acknowledgment that he had lost his command through no fault of his own.[4]

[1] On his mysterious connection with St. John's, Cambridge, see Tulloch's *Rational Theology*, i. 183.
[2] He did good service afterwards in defending Dublin Castle in 1641.
[3] Lady Theresa Lewis, *Lives of the Friends of Clarendon*, i. 189.
[4] I found this in some formal document in the Record Office, I think

The young man was doubtless gratified by the compliment. He stood in no need of the money. His mother, a violent and overbearing woman, the daughter of Chief Baron Tanfield, had lately declared herself a Catholic—a step which so annoyed her father that he passed her over in his will and left his estates directly to his grandson. As soon, therefore, as he came of age young Cary found himself master of Great Tew, in Oxfordshire. Scarcely was he settled there when he gave offence to his father by entering upon a marriage of affection with a portionless lady. With the warm impulsiveness which was the principal charm of his character and at the same time the source of his greatest errors, he offered to resign the whole estate into his father's hands if only he might have a father's love. The offer was made in vain. The first Lord Falkland died in 1633, unreconciled to his son. The young man who now inherited the Scottish title of Falkland was as yet but little known to the world at large. For some years he devoted himself to his books and his friends. Falkland's house was the meeting-place for wits and poets as well as for scholars and divines. Carew and Suckling, Walter Montague and Sir Kenelm Digby were counted amongst his friends, whilst Sheldon and Morley knew how to lead the conversation to severer topics. Falkland himself played the part of host to perfection. All who had any serious purpose on hand had generous welcome at Great Tew. University men from Oxford 'found their lodgings there as ready as in the colleges; nor did the lord of the house know of their coming or going, nor who were in his house, till he came to dinner or supper, where

in the enrolment of the Privy Seal granting the arrears; but I have lost the reference.

all still met; otherwise there was no trouble, ceremony, or restraint to forbid men to come to the house or to make them weary of staying there; so that many came thither to study in a better air, finding all the books they could desire in his library, and all the persons together whose society they could wish, and not find it in any other society.'[1]

Falkland's mind was as hospitable as his house. He was in the highest sense of the words a seeker after truth, and he was unable to conceive that anything could be true which was not pure and of good report. His virtues were accompanied by their attendant defects. He was more keen to detect faultiness than to provide a remedy. He missed being a great man by a little, but that little was enough. He was too large-minded to take a mere party mould, and he was not sufficiently large-minded to stand above party altogether. He swayed from side to side as the special evils of each struck him more vividly. It was characteristic of him that of all poets he rated Ben Jonson most highly, and that in the catalogue of poetic gifts which he attributed to his favourite—

> Wit, judgment, learning, art, or industry,

the highest of all, the supreme gift of imagination, was wanting. It is equally missing in Falkland's own versification, and in this his versification was but the expression of his life. He was too clear-sighted to make a great party-leader, like Wentworth or Pym. He could not work out the results of a special political principle, and push it to its extreme consequences regardless of other principles which might commend themselves to other minds. His gentle, loving heart

---

[1] Clarendon, *Life*, i. 41. There is a curious echo of this description in the account of Allworthy's hospitality in *Tom Jones*.

longed to compose the differences of the world, and to bid the weapons fall from hands which were prepared for bitter war. But the comprehensiveness of his heart was not supported by comprehensiveness of brain. The desire for reconciliation vented itself in impulsive anger against those who at any given time stood forth as obstacles to reconciliation; it did not lead up to the reconciling thought which would have satisfied the reasonable desires of both parties. When he chose a side he did not know half its faults. When he deserted it he did not know half its merits.

Falkland had not yet thrown himself into opposition. In 1637 he went out of his way to praise the King, complimenting him on the sovereignty of the seas in a way which was not very consistent with any strong feeling on the subject of ship money, though the fact that he was a defaulter in respect of at least one of his estates may be allowed to stand for something on the opposite side.[1] Ben Jonson had just been carried to the grave full of years and honours. He, wrote Falkland, would have told in befitting verse

> How mighty Charles, amidst that weighty care
> In which three kingdoms as their blessing share
> (Whom as it tends with ever watchful eyes,
> That neither power may force nor art surprise,
> So, bounded by no shore, grasps all the main,
> And far as Neptune claims extends his reign),
> Found still some time to hear and to admire
> The happy sounds of his harmonious lyre.[2]

It was on a question of religion that Falkland was first drawn into the controversies of the world around him. His mother, having changed her own religion,

---

[1] Arrears for Hertfordshire, 1637. *S. P. Dom.*, ccclxxvi. 106.
[2] *Falkland's Poems*, ed. Grosart.

was anxious to make proselytes of all upon whom her influence could be brought to bear. Assailed by the usual argument that there was no infallibility but in the Roman Church, and no salvation without infallibility, Falkland was driven to examine the grounds of his faith. Under no circumstances is it conceivable that a mind so rational and so candid could have accepted these propositions. But though Falkland's tendencies of thought were his own, there was something in the very gentleness of his nature which led him at every important crisis in his life to seek out the support of a mind stronger and more self-reliant than his own. In different phases of his political career he rested alternately on Hampden and on Hyde. In his earlier days he rested on Chillingworth in their common effort to free religious belief from bondage to human authority.[1]

The two men so nearly akin in their aims differed widely from one another in their mental characteristics. In Falkland the reasoning powers were subordinate to the moral perceptions. In Chillingworth they exercised almost undivided sway. He was above all things a thinker. His singularly clear intellect met with but little resistance from those sympathies and antipathies which with most men count for so much. When once he had made up his mind that any given course was dictated by reason, nothing except conviction by argument that he had been mistaken would deter him from acting on his belief.

Chillingworth's early life was passed in circumstances which boded for him a prosperous career. Born at Oxford in 1602, he had Laud for his god-

[1] I am aware that the reverse has been asserted, but the relation of the two minds seems too clear to admit of any other view than this.

father. He received a good education, and in 1628 he became a Fellow of Trinity. Suddenly his friends learnt to their consternation that he had betaken himself to Douai as a convert to the Papal Church. The Jesuit Fisher had laid before him the argument that an infallible guide in matters of faith was necessary for salvation, and that such a guide was only to be found in the Roman Church. Chillingworth was at a loss for a reply, and, as usual, he followed the superior argument. A very brief residence at Douai convinced him that he had not searched the question to the bottom. Books of Jesuit theology were in the habit of applying the test of probability to moral action, and it is by no means unlikely that from them Chillingworth drew the unintended inference that, if it was enough to act upon the mere probability that the action was right, it might be enough to believe on the mere probability that the belief was true. If he accepted this as the best theory which he could form, it was evident that he had no further need of an infallible guide.

In making up his mind to return to the English Church Chillingworth had been helped by letters from Laud. The positions assumed by the two men were in the main identical. In his conference with Fisher, Laud had declared that it was unnecessary to require assent to more than the fundamental articles of the Christian faith.[1] But it was not likely that any argument would fare in Laud's hands exactly as it would fare in Chillingworth's. Laud would be sure

[1] Such a sentence as the following, for instance, has a very Chillingworthian ring: "The Church of England never declared that every one of her articles are fundamental in the faith; for it is one thing to say, No one of them is superstitious or erroneous, and quite another to say, Every one of them is fundamental, and that in every part of it, to all men's belief." Laud's *Works*, ii. 60.

to add something about the consent of antiquity and the practical advantages of submission to authority. Chillingworth would leave it in its own naked simplicity.

Chillingworth had not been long in England before he began to prepare himself for that great controversial work by which he hoped to guide others along the path in which his own feet had stumbled.

In 1630 a Jesuit who passed by the name of Edward Knott had published a book under the name of *Charity Mistaken*, in which he argued that, except under exceptional circumstances, there was no salvation for Protestants. In 1633 Dr. Potter had answered the book, and the Jesuit then replied to him in support of his former reasoning. It was here that Chillingworth intervened in the controversy. For three years he was laying the foundations of the book in which the great weapon of the Catholic armoury was to be put to the proof.

The attraction of the library at Great Tew drew Chillingworth to Falkland. Intercourse quickly ripened into intimacy, and tradition tells how much of the arguments of the scholar was owing to the suggestions of the peer. Those who have read with attention the writings of the two men will probably come to the conclusion that the peer owed more to the scholar than he gave. Falkland's reply to the letter in which Walter Montague announced his conversion goes over much the same ground as that which was subsequently occupied by Chillingworth. But the arguments are urged without that sharp incisiveness which marks the work of the stronger reasoner.

It is by no means unlikely that Chillingworth had braced himself to his labours at Laud's instigation, though no evidence to that effect is in existence. At all events, before the book was published Laud had ample reason to look upon it with interest. In a short pamphlet Knott sought to discredit by anticipation the reply which he expected. He charged the author with Socinianism, and flouted him on his pretension to appear as the advocate of a religion which no longer dared to deck itself in its own colours. "Protestantism," he wrote, "waxeth weary of itself. The professors of it, they especially of greatest worth, learning, and authority, love temper and moderation, and are at this time more unresolved where to fasten than at the infancy of their Church." Their doctrine, he added, was undergoing a change: they now denied that the Pope was antichrist; they had begun to pray for the dead, to use pictures, to adopt in many points the teaching of Rome. The articles were 'impatient, nay, ambitious, of some sense wherein they might seem Catholic.' Calvinism was 'accounted heresy and little less than treason.' The 'once fearful names of priests and altars' were widely used, and men were bidden to expound Scripture according to the sense of the Fathers—a practice which would evidently land them at the feet of the Pope, 'seeing that by the confession of Protestants the Fathers were on the side of the Catholic Church.'[1]

No wonder such words as these were gleefully quoted by the Puritans. It was exactly what they had been reiterating for years. No wonder, too, Laud and Charles were deeply annoyed by so unexpected an attack. Charles weakly allowed Windebank to apply to Con, asking him to express his displeasure to the audacious Jesuit.[2] As might have been ex-

Charles tries to get Knott banished.

---

[1] In addition to Chillingworth's quotation, De Maiseaux gives an account of Knott's work, of which he had seen a copy.

[2] Con to Barberini, $\frac{Nov. 24}{Dec. 4}$. *Add. MSS.* 15,389, fol. 384.

pected, Con expressed his inability to do anything of the sort; and Laud, with greater wisdom, turned his attention to hastening the appearance of Chillingworth's reply.[1] Towards the end of 1637, in the very heat of the excitement engendered by Lady Newport's conversion, *The Religion of Protestants* was issued to the world.

In his main argument that 'nothing is necessary to be believed but what is plainly revealed'[2] Chillingworth did little more than put in a clearer and more logical form, with all its excrescences stripped away, the contention of Laud in the conference with Fisher. That which marks the pre-eminence of the younger writer is his clear sense of the subordination of intellectual conviction to moral effort. If men, he says, 'suffer themselves neither to be betrayed into their errors, nor kept in them by any sin of their will; if they do their best endeavour to free themselves from all errors, and yet fail of it through human frailty, so well am I persuaded of the goodness of God, that if in me alone should meet a confluence of all such errors of all the Protestants of the world that were thus qualified, I should not be so much afraid of them all as I should be to ask pardon for them.'[3]

In these words, not in the counter-dogmatism of the Puritan zealot, lay the true answer to the claim to infallibility which was so ostentatiously flaunted before the world by the Roman missionaries. It was the old doctrine of Sir Thomas More and the men of the new learning coming to the surface once more, under happier auspices. It breathed the very spirit of mutual regard for zeal and earnestness in the midst of intellectual differences. It became men, Chilling-

---

[1] Chillingworth's reasons, Sept. 19. *S. P. Dom.* ccclxvii. 116.
[2] *Works*, i. 230.   [3] *Ibid.* i. 81.

worth held, to be very careful how they set up the creatures of their own imaginations as if they were the veriest certainties of Divine revelation. "This presumptuous imposing of the senses of men upon the general words of God," he writes, "and laying them upon men's consciences together, under the equal penalty of death and damnation; this vain conceit that we can speak of the things of God better than in the words of God; this deifying our own interpretations and tyrannous enforcing them upon others; this restraining of the Word of God from that latitude and generality, and the understandings of men from that liberty wherein Christ and the Apostles left them—is and hath been the only fountain of all the schisms of the Church, and that which makes them immortal; the common incendiary of Christendom, and that which tears into pieces, not the coat, but the bowels and members of Christ. . . . Take away these walls of separation, and all will quickly be one. Take away this persecuting, burning, cursing, damning of men for not subscribing to the words of men as the words of God; require of Christians only to believe Christ, and to call no man master, but Him only; let those leave claiming infallibility that have no title to it, and let them that in their words disclaim it disclaim it also in their actions." "Christians," he says again, "must be taught to set a higher value upon those high points of faith and obedience wherein they agree than upon those matters of less moment wherein they differ, and understand that agreement in those ought to be more effectual to join them in one communion than their difference in other things of less moment to divide them. When I say in one communion, I mean in a common profession of those articles wherein all consent, a joint worship of God, after such a way as all esteem lawful, and a mutual performance of all those works of charity which Christians owe one to another."[1]

Defects of Chillingworth's system.

It is not given to any one man, even if he be a Chillingworth, to make out with complete fulness the remedies needed for the evils of his age. Dogmatism, too, has its functions to perform in the work of the world. The vain belief in the possession of all truth is higher and more ennobling than the disbelief that truth exists at all; and it is impossible to deny that to the mass of Chillingworth's contemporaries the suspension of judgment, which was to him the ultimate goal of a keen and earnest search after truth, would seem to be the very negation of the existence of truth itself. Even calmer judgments might well doubt whether Chillingworth's notion of a 'joint worship of God after such a way as all esteem lawful' was feasible, or whether, even if it proved feasible, it was at all desirable. Chillingworth's mind was too purely intellectual to enable him to understand how any given ritual could either raise admiration or provoke hostility. He cared much whether a proposition were true or not. He had but a languid interest in forms of prayer. In his reply to Knott's last pamphlet he took up the defence of the recent charges. "What," he said, "if out of fear that too much simplicity and nakedness in the public service of God may beget in the ordinary sort of men a dull and stupid irreverence, and out of hope that the outward state and glory of it, being well-disposed and wisely moderated, may engender, quicken, increase, and nourish the inward reverence, respect, and devotion, which is due unto God's sovereign majesty and power; what if, out of a persuasion and desire that Papists

[1] *Works*, ii. 37.

may be won over to us the sooner by the removing of this scandal out of their way, and out of a holy jealousy that the weaker sort of Protestants might be the easier seduced to them by the magnificence and pomp of their Church service, in case it were not removed—I say, what if, out of these considerations, the governors of our Church, more of late than formerly, have set themselves to adorn and beautify the places where God's honour dwells, and to make them as heaven-like as they can with earthly ornaments?"[1] There is something contemptuous in such a defence as this. Above all, there is no acknowledgment by Chillingworth of the fact that moral influence may spread abroad from men who are very wrong-headed and very positive. The toleration which cheerfully grants free liberty to those who differ irreconcilably from us is the complement of the tolerance which seeks out by preference the points in which others agree with us rather than those in which they differ. The latter was Chillingworth's contribution to the peace of the Church and nation; for the former we must look elsewhere. Yet, before we plunge into the strife out of which the better thought was to be evolved, we may well linger a moment to contemplate the life of one whose nature was more complete, and whose personality was more altogether lovely, than that of the great controversialist. Rather than to Chillingworth, rather than to Falkland, the discerning eye is attracted to one who was in his own estimation less than either, but of whom those who knew him best loved to speak as the ever-memorable John Hales.

The genial recluse, with his prodigious memory and his keen, rapier-like thrust of argument, was the

[1] *Works*, i. 23.

most loving and tender-hearted of men. In his Eton fellowship he found himself at home under the provostship of the large-minded Sir Henry Wotton. His views of life and religion were in the main identical with those of Chillingworth, but he approached the subject from the other side. In Chillingworth the logical faculty was supreme. In Hales it was at the service of a singularly gentle and affectionate heart. Hence he began where Chillingworth left off. He did not argue himself into the belief that the intention to go wrong, and not the failure itself, was culpable. He rather made it the starting-point of his reasoning. "He would often say that he would renounce the religion of the Church of England to-morrow if it obliged him to believe that any other Christian should be damned, and that nobody would conclude another man to be damned that did not wish him so."[1] "Every Christian," he wrote, "may err that will; for if we might not err wilfully, then there would be no heresy, heresy being nothing else but wilful error. For if we account mistakes befalling us through human frailties to be heresies, then it will follow that every man since the Apostles' times was an heretic."[2] Hence he could take but little interest in Chillingworth's search after fundamental truths. That men should err was, in his eyes, a necessity of their nature. The venerable names of the Fathers of the ancient Church, the imposing solemnity of ecclesiastical councils, conferred no exemption from the universal law. "If truth and goodness," he wrote, "go by universality and multitude, what mean then the prophets and holy men of God everywhere in the Scripture so frequently,

---

[1] Clarendon, *Life*, i. 54.
[2] On the Sacrament of the Lord's Supper. *Works*, i. 63.

so bitterly to complain of the small number of good men careful of God and truth? Neither is the complaint proper to Scripture; it is the common complaint of all that have left any records of antiquity behind them. Could wishing do any good, I could wish well to this kind of proof; but it shall never go so well with mankind that the most shall be the best. The best that I can say of argument and reason drawn from universality in multitude is this: such reason may perchance serve to excuse an error, but it can never serve to warrant a truth."

Yet, for all this, the investigation of truth was the highest work of man. The words of the Apostle, "Be not deceived," were spoken not only to the wise and learned, but 'to everyone, of whatever sex, of whatever rank or degree and place soever, from him that studies in his library to him that sweats at the plough-tail.' But the command is not obeyed by those who content themselves with storing their memories with opinions learned by rote. He that would not be deceived must not only know 'what it is that is commanded,' must not therefore take his duties on trust from a Church claiming to be infallible, or from a venerated preacher, but must also know 'wherefore—that is, upon what authority, upon what reason.'[1] At last the new thought which was to form the modern world had reached its full and clear expression.

Like Chillingworth, Hales too had his dream of Utopian harmony of worship. "Were liturgies and public forms of service so framed," he argued, "as that they admitted not of particular and private fancies, but contained only such things as in which all Christians do agree, schisms in opinion were

The search for truth.

Public worship.

---
[1] Sermon on private judgment in religion. *Works*, iii. 141.

utterly vanished. For consider of all the liturgies that are or ever have been, and remove from them whatsoever is scandalous to any party, and leave nothing but what all agree on, and the event shall be that the public service and honour of God shall no ways suffer; whereas to load our public forms with the private fancies upon which we differ is the most sovereign way to perpetuate schism unto the world's end. Prayer, confession, thanksgiving, reading of Scripture, exposition of Scripture, administration of sacraments in the plainest and simplest manner, were matter enough to furnish out a sufficient liturgy, though nothing else of private opinion, or of church pomp, of garments, of prescribed gestures, of imagery, of music, of matter concerning the dead, of many superfluities which creep into churches under the name of order and decency, did interpose itself."[1]

Hales sent for by Laud.

The tract on schism in which these words occur was circulated in manuscript in the spring of 1638. No wonder that when a copy fell into Laud's hands he sent for the author to Lambeth. And yet he could not but know that Hales, if not his ally, was at least the assailant of his enemies. A few years before, perhaps, he would have dealt harshly with him. He could not find it in his heart now to visit very severely a man whose thrusts were directed against Puritan and Papist alike. The two men walked up and down the garden in friendly, if sometimes in warm, argument. Laud breathed a word of caution. The time, said the Archbishop, was 'very apt to set new doctrines on foot, of which the wits of the age were too susceptible.'[2] 'There could not

---

[1] Tract concerning schism. *Works*, i. 114.
[2] This is Clarendon's account. *Life*, i. 55.

be too much care taken to preserve the peace and unity of the Church.' As Hales came away he met Heylyn, and fooled him to the top of his bent,[1] assuring him that the Archbishop had proved far superior in controversy, ferreting him 'from one hole to another till there was none left to afford him any further shelter; that he was now resolved to be orthodox, and to declare himself a true son of the Church of England both for doctrine and discipline.'[2] Hales, no doubt, was laughing in his sleeve at the pompous chaplain. Yet it must be remembered that it is not from men of Hales's stamp that vigorous self-assertion is to be expected. In writing to Laud he did not, it is true, retract any of his positive opinions, but he certainly explained away some of his utterances. Laud was satisfied with his explanation, and in the following year he procured for him a canonry at Windsor.

In the days of conflict Falkland and Chillingworth and Hales would be found on Charles's side. In the long run the spirit which inspired them would be found a far more powerful dissolvent of Laud's system than the Puritanism which he dreaded. Its time was not yet come. Two theories of the religious life were in presence of one another, and those theories were entwined with a whole mass of habits which could not readily be shaken off. The strife was approaching, and it was not till the combatants had measured their strength with one another that they would be ready to listen to the words of peace. Even when that time came the solution would not be altogether such as Hales would have approved. The

[1] This is Principal Tulloch's explanation, and is, I have no doubt, the right one.
[2] Heylyn, *Cyprianus Anglicus*, 340.

religious conscience would demand a more definite creed, and a more definite ceremonial, than that for which he had asked. By the side of the idea of comprehension would arise the idea of toleration. The one would soften down asperities, and teach the assured dogmatist to put on something of that humility in which the controversialist of all periods is so grievously deficient. The other would prepare room for the unchecked development of that individuality which is the foundation of all true vigour in Churches and in nations.

CHAPTER II.

THE CONSTITUTIONAL OPPOSITION.

The ecclesiastical grievances were only felt by a part of the community. Financial burdens were felt by everyone who had property. In the summer of 1637 the outcry against ship money had become general.

No unprejudiced person can deny that the existence of a powerful fleet was indispensable to the safety of the State, or that the amount of money demanded by Charles for the equipment of that fleet was no more than the case required. The charge which has frequently been brought against him of spending the money thus levied on objects unconnected with its ostensible purpose is without a shadow of foundation; and it is perfectly certain that, though the grant of tonnage and poundage had originally been made in order to provide the Crown with the means of guarding the seas, the expenses of government had so far increased that if tonnage and poundage were to be applied to that purpose on the scale that had now become necessary, the Exchequer would soon be in a condition of bankruptcy.

Even the most just and necessary taxation, however, is sometimes received with murmurs. If such murmurs are not to lead to actual resistance, it is incumbent on those who impose the tax to explain to the tax-payer the necessity under which they are placed, and if possible to find some way of obtaining his consent. It was the very thing that Charles had not dared to do. He well knew that to summon a Parliament would be to endanger the success of his ecclesiastical policy, and he had no mind to run the risk.

Services of the fleet.

The fleet obtained by the levy of ship money had done nothing sufficiently striking to make men forget the faults of its origin. The maintenance of trade with Dunkirk in the face of threats of a Dutch or French attack upon that nest of privateers interested only a few traders in London or Dover, and the exploits of the King's ships amongst the Dutch fishermen[1] in the summer of 1637 would, if the truth had been known, have awakened scorn rather than admiration. If a less inglorious success was achieved in the same summer by a squadron of six vessels

The expedition to Sallee.

under Captain Rainsborough at Sallee, it was due to other causes than the skill of the commander or the efficiency of the armament. Rainsborough was sent to deliver from slavery the European captives of the Barbary pirates, but his efforts to overcome their stronghold by attack or blockade were entirely ineffectual. Luckily, however, a civil war broke out amongst the Moors, and the King of Morocco purchased the neutrality of the English fleet by the surrender of 271 prisoners.[2]

Ship money attacked as illegal.

Yet it was not because ship money was badly spent that the impost was assailed in England. Voices were raised on every side declaring it to be utterly illegal. Ship money, it was loudly declared, was

---

[1] *Personal Government of Charles I.*, ii. 336.

[2] Brissenden to Nicholas, Sept. 21. Rainsborough's journal. *S. P. Dom.* ccclxviii. 6, ccclxix. 72 ; Carteret to Coke, Sept. 21. List of prisoners released. *S. P. Morocco.* Garrard's statement (*Straf. Letters*, ii. 118) that Rainsborough 'put the new town of Sallee into the King of Morocco's hands' is exaggerated.

undeniably a tax, and the ancient customs of the realm, recently embodied in the Petition of Right, had announced with no doubtful voice that no tax could be levied without consent of Parliament. Even this objection was not the full measure of the evil. If Charles could take this money without consent of Parliament, he need not, unless some unforeseen emergency arose, ever summon a Parliament again. The true question at issue was whether Parliament formed an integral part of the Constitution or not.

The constitutional objection.

A charge has sometimes been brought against the Englishmen of that day that they concerned themselves overmuch with legality and precedent. Undoubtedly they loved to dwell upon the antiquity of the rights which they claimed. Antiquarians like Selden or Twysden expressed the tendencies of their age as truly as thinkers like Voltaire and Rousseau expressed the tendencies of theirs. But the legality which they cherished was the legality of a nation which had hitherto preserved unbroken the traditions of self-government. Spoken or unspoken, beneath all the technicalities of the lawyers, beneath all the records of the antiquaries, there remained an undertone of reliance upon the nation itself. Parliaments had been established to gather into a focus the national resolve. Kings had been established to give prompt efficacy to the resolve which had been formed. It was a new thing that a king should treat the policy and religion of the nation as if they concerned himself alone. But the men who opposed it because it was new opposed it still more because it was degrading.

Attachment of the nation to legality.

Charles fancied that the question of the legality of ship money had been settled for ever in his favour

The question of ship money to be argued.

CHAP. II.
1637.

Difficulties in the way.

Nov. 6.
St. John's argument.

by the declaration of the Judges.[1] Lord Saye and John Hampden thought otherwise. They resolved that, whatever the result might be, the argument against ship money should be heard in open Court, and Charles was too confident of the justice of his cause to offer any opposition.

For some unknown reason—perhaps because his case was more simple than that of Saye—Hampden's refusal was selected to test the opinion of the Judges. The counsel employed by him were St. John and Holborne, lawyers connected with the Earl of Bedford. They would have to argue with the full knowledge that the Court was against them, and they would have therefore to put forward just that side of the argument which would not call down the violent censure of the Judges. It would be far easier to show that Charles was politically in the wrong than to show that he was legally in the wrong; but they were bound by their position to urge legal objections, only indirectly touching upon the political objections, if they touched on them at all. They knew that the Judges had acknowledged the King to be the sole judge of danger from abroad, and they therefore did not venture to question a maxim adopted on such authority.

St. John accordingly began by making a great concession. He abandoned any attempt to draw a distinction between the levy of ship money in the inland counties and its levy in the maritime counties. He acknowledged, too, that the King was the sole judge of the existence of danger. The law, he said, had given the King power, 'by writ under the Great Seal of England, to command the inhabitants of each county to provide shipping for the defence of the

[1] *Pers. Gov. of Charles I.*, ii. 322.

kingdom, so that he might by law compel the doing thereof.' The only question was in what manner he was to exercise this power. St. John answered his own question by arguing that as the King could not set fines nor deliver judgment except through the Judges, so he could not raise money beyond his ordinary revenue except by Parliament. He showed that there were special reasons for this restriction. A representative assembly was likely to be a jealous guardian of the property of its constituents. The King was under no such bonds. If he could lay what charge he pleased on his subjects ' it would come to pass that, if the subject hath anything at all, he is not beholden to the law for it, but it is left entirely in the mercy and goodness of the King.'

The remainder of St. John's argument may profitably be stripped of its technicalities. It is a good thing, he said in effect, that there should be some one to keep an eye on the possibility of danger. It is also a good thing that property should be guarded against unnecessary claims. It was, therefore, well that the King, when he had discovered the danger, should, under ordinary circumstances, be compelled to apply to Parliament for the taxation needed to meet it. It might be, indeed, that the danger developed so rapidly that time for an application to Parliament was wanting. In that case the rights of property would be simply in abeyance. If a French or a Spanish army landed unexpectedly in Kent or Devonshire, no one would blame the Government because it seized horses from a gentleman's stable to drag artillery, or ordered its troops to charge across a farmer's cornfields. It was a matter of notoriety, however, that in the present case no such danger had occurred. Writs had been issued in August for the purpose of

CHAP. II.
1637.
Nov. 6.

equipping a fleet which was not needed till March. What possible reason could be alleged why Parliament had not been summoned in the course of those seven months, to grant a subsidy in the regular way?

A reason no doubt there was, to which St. John did not venture even to allude, but which his hearers were not likely to forget. A Parliament, once summoned, would have been certain to discuss other matters than ship money, and it would most probably demand an entire reversal of the civil and ecclesiastical policy of the reign.

St. John had supported his arguments by the usual store of antiquarian learning. He had been able to show that the Kings of England had frequently paid for services done in defence of the realm, even when they had been forced to borrow money to enable them to do so. Surely, he urged, no king would have done this if he had been aware that he might legally impose the burden on his subjects.

When St. John sat down he found himself famous. The crowded audience drank in every word that he said, listening as men would listen who believed their property and their rights to be at stake.

Nov. 11.
Lyttelton's argument.

As Solicitor General, Lyttelton undertook to reply. It would have been strange if he had failed to find cases in which English kings had occasionally taken money irregularly. The struggle between Crown and Parliament had been a conflict of strength as well as a conflict of principle, and an advocate of the Government might easily go astray by quoting acts of aggression as if they had embodied the very spirit of the law. When Lyttelton ascended from precedent to principle, the weakness of his case must have been manifest even to those who knew little of constitutional law. He acknowledged that the King had no right to impose ship money, excepting in time of danger, and he made the most of the argument that the rights of property were not weakened by taking so much of it as was needed for its defence. All laws must give way to the law of necessity, and in times of necessity it was impossible to appeal to Parliament. Forty days must elapse after the issue of the writs before Parliament could meet, and then would follow long debates and conferences between the Houses. Before an agreement could be arrived at the kingdom would be lost.

Lyttelton's argument would have been an excellent one if it had had the slightest relation to the actual circumstances of the case. Even supposing that the seven months which passed between the issue of the writ and the assemblage of the fleet had been insufficient to enable Parliament to come to a decision on that year's supply, no such excuse could be pleaded on behalf of an exaction which was now being renewed for a fourth annual period. Evidently the danger was considered at Court to be a permanent one, and to a permanent danger Lyttelton's reasoning had no application whatever.

Holborne in a few words blew down the house of cards which had been erected by the Solicitor General. The writ, he said, did not mention the existence of imminent danger. Then, rising to the occasion, he argued, amidst interruptions from the Bench, 'that by the fundamental laws of England the King cannot, out of Parliament, charge the subject—no, not for the common good unless in special cases.' Not only could not the King do it 'for the guard of the sea against pirates, but he could not even do it for the ordinary defence of the kingdom unavoidably in

Dec. 2. Holborne's argument.

danger to be lost.' Then, going further than St. John had ventured to go, he refused to acknowledge that the King was the proper judge of danger, unless when that danger was so closely impending that it was impossible to consult Parliament at all.

The great constitutional issue was raised more distinctly by Holborne than by St. John. For him Parliament, not the King, was the main organ of the sovereignty of the nation over itself. Bankes, the Attorney General, refused to meet him on that ground. The Court, he argued, had no right to inquire under what circumstances the King could exercise his judgment. It was enough to know that it had been exercised. His power of forming the necessary decision was 'innate in the person of an absolute king and in the persons of the Kings of England; so inherent in the king that it is not any ways derived from the people, but reserved to the king when positive laws first began.'

In the course of his three days' argument Bankes had many precedents to show, in which the obligation of the subject to defend the realm in person, by land or sea, was often confused with the special obligation of dwellers on the coast to provide ships for its defence. Nor did he omit to quote a few cases in which in older times the inhabitants of inland counties had been compelled to find money for the provision of ships. But he was totally unable to show anything like a general contribution enforced from year to year. In the end he repeated his declaration that the King was an absolute monarch and the sole judge of danger. To 'distrust that he will command too great a power or aid, it is a presumption against the presumption of the law.'

"My Lords," he said in conclusion, "if there

were no law to compel unto this duty, yet nature and the inviolate law of preservation ought to move us. These vapours which are exhaled from us will again descend upon us in our safety and in the honour of our nation; and therefore let us obey the King's command by his writ, and not dispute. He is the first mover among these orbs of ours, and he is the circle of this circumference, and he is the centre of us all, wherein we all as the loins should meet. He is the soul of this body, whose proper act is to command."

Importance of Bankes's argument.

Bankes thus supplied whatever defects there might be in Holborne's argument. When he sat down it must have been abundantly clear to all men that if his view was accepted as the true one, the old Parliamentary constitution of England was at an end. If that were the case, as they had already learned from St. John, no man could hold his property except on sufferance. Those who cared less for pelf, and more for the old constitutional inheritance of their race, learned from the glib utterance of a lawyer's tongue that the system under which they fondly believed that long generations of their ancestors had lived and died had never had any real existence. The assemblies of early times before the Conquest, the Great Councils of Norman kings, the Parliaments of the Plantagenets were, it would seem, merely ornamental appendages to the substantial edifice of the monarchy. No doubt the King still professed his intention of ruling according to the law. No doubt the Great Charter, the confirmation of the Charters, and the recent Petition of Right would still be quoted and wrangled over in Westminster Hall, but their living force would be gone. The representative monarchy of Henry VIII. and Elizabeth would cease to be, as completely as the Parliamentary monarchy of the

CHAP. II.
1637.
Dec. 18.

House of Lancaster would cease to be. In its stead was to be raised the authority of a king ruling in accordance with his own inscrutable counsels, whilst the English people was to wait patiently for the decision of its master. His was the wisdom which foresees everything and arranges everything, which no contingency could take by surprise and no calamity find without resource. Theirs was the ignorance of a herd of cattle contentedly grazing in the fat pastures prepared for them till their owner thought good to send them forth to the slaughter-house of war.

Conditions under which the claim to absolute power was made.

It is certain that, whether Charles were or were not possessed of the profound wisdom needed to make good the claim advanced in his name, no time could be conceived more unfitted for its general acceptance. So far as the King's advocate demanded that complicated affairs should be entrusted to the decision of the few rather than of the many, they merely asked what was in accordance with the necessities of human nature, though they left out of sight the fact that it is equally in accordance with those necessities that the decision of the few should be openly or tacitly submitted to the approval of the many. At the moment, however, the very success of Charles's fleet made the mystery in which he veiled his resolutions more unintelligible. When a great crisis arrives in the national fortunes, when an invasion by a foreign Power is impending and the means of resistance are scanty, it is far more important that the plans for meeting the danger should proceed from one brain, and that the forces of resistance should be concentrated in one hand, than that there should be a public Parliamentary discussion on the proper tactics to be pursued. Nothing of the kind was impending now. When Richelieu determined to keep his new fleet out of the English Channel, he struck a decisive stroke, though he knew it not, on behalf of the Parliamentary liberties of England. If a combined French and Dutch fleet had attacked Dunkirk, and had threatened English commerce on the English coasts, all the patriotism in England would have been loud in demanding that the powers of Government should be increased, though it is quite possible that it might also have demanded that a thoughtful and able Government should be substituted for one which had proved itself shiftless and inefficient. As it was, there was no reason whatever that special powers should be conceded where no special reasons existed for their exercise.

CHAP. II.
1637.
Dec. 18.

The decision of the Judges remained to be heard. As only two were to deliver their opinion on the same day, and in consequence of the claims of other business, a considerable delay would intervene between the utterances of each speaker; some months must elapse before the judgment of the whole bench could be known.

1638.
The opinion of the Judges.

It was not likely that the Judges would break away from their declaration of the preceding winter. On some of them no doubt the dependent position to which they had been reduced by Charles may have not been without its influence. But it must not be forgotten that the question itself was rather one for political than for judicial settlement. Hampden and his supporters were only careful to establish a negative. They saw clearly that the right assumed by the King was fatal to the Parliamentary constitution of England. The Judges might well ask what was the alternative proposed. Was a House of Commons, as yet unguided by any Cabinet and undisciplined by

VOL. I.   F

CHAP. II.
1638.

any party ties, to be expected to meet with wise forethought all the exigencies of foreign affairs? What was really wanted, if there was not to be a political revolution, was that the King should not only exercise his discretion, but should really be discreet, should only use extraordinary powers in extraordinary circumstances, and should withhold his confidence from the nation no further than it might be in the interest of the nation that secresy should be maintained for a time. Unfortunately, such a consummation was beyond the power of any judicial decision to effect.

Judgment of Weston;

Something of this difficulty seems to have been felt by Baron Weston, who delivered judgment first. He believed that the King had decided rightly in fitting out the fleet. If, indeed, it had been done by Parliament, it had been done by the happiest means. But he could not lay down the law that it must always be done by Parliament. If the enemy had come ' before the Parliament had met, or before they had granted any aid, should the safety of the kingdom depend upon such contingencies?'

of Crawley and Berkeley;

This reluctance to acknowledge the existence of a general prohibitory law was the strongest ground on which the King's supporters could rely. It was not likely that all of Weston's brethren would be content to give so half-hearted a support to the Crown. Crawley, who followed, declared that it was a royal prerogative ' to impose taxes without common consent of Parliament.' Berkeley went further still. He fixed upon Holborne's argument that, by the fundamental policy of the realm, sovereigns who wished to exact money at their pleasure ought to be restrained by Parliament. "The law," he said, "knows no such king-yoking policy. The law is of itself an old and trusty servant of the King's; it is his instrument and means which he useth to govern his people by. I never read nor heard that *Lex* was *Rex*, but it is common and most true that *Rex* is *Lex*, for he is *Lex loquens*, a living, a speaking, an acting law."

Vernon and Trevor followed on the same side. It was not till five of the Judges had declared for the King that one was found to take part with the defendant. Sir George Croke is said to have hesitated what he should say, but to have been encouraged by his wife to speak his mind without fear of consequences. The tale has no sufficient evidence to support it, and he was hardly the man to need such an exhortation. However this may have been, he spoke distinctly and emphatically. It was utterly contrary to law, he said, to set any charge whatever upon the subject except in Parliament. Even under this condition the King could not possibly find any difficulty in providing for the defence of the realm. He had power to press into his service every single man and every single ship in England. 'The imagination of man,' he said, 'could not invent a danger, but course might be taken till Parliament be had.' No example of such a writ as that before the Court could be produced from the whole course of English history.

Of the remaining Judges Hutton followed decisively in Croke's steps. Denham, who was ill, gave a brief judgment in Hampden's favour, and Brampston and Davenport placed themselves, for technical reasons, on the same side. Jones and Finch pronounced for the King. Charles could count as his own but seven voices out of twelve, giving him the smallest of all possible majorities.

Of all the arguments delivered on the side of the Crown none created so profound an impression as

of Vernon, Trevor, and Croke.

Seven Judges for the Crown.

Finch's constitutional views.

that of Finch. It had at least the merit of plain speaking, and the spontaneity of its tone is such as to raise a suspicion that the Chief Justice of the Common Pleas, overbearing and brutal as he could be upon this occasion, was not the mere time-server that he is generally reckoned. Finch held, as all reasonable politicians now hold, that in every State some man or body of men must exist above all human control, which may be wisely subjected to checks and hindrances, but which must be able in case of supreme necessity to brush aside those checks and hindrances without appeal. This power, which is now attributed to the constituencies, was by Finch attributed to the King. The law, he said, having given to the King the duty of defending the country, had of necessity given him the right of laying the charge which would enable him to fulfil the duty imposed upon him. "Acts of Parliament," he boldly added, "to take away his Royal power in the defence of his kingdom are void. . . . They are void Acts of Parliament to bind the King not to command the subjects, their persons and goods, and I say their money too, for no Acts of Parliament make any difference."[1]

This was at least plain speaking. After this, what was the use of going back to those ancient laws which were fondly regarded as the bulwarks of English liberty? Precedent and statute had been quoted in vain. There was, it seemed, a transcendent authority in the King which neither law nor Parliament could fetter. No wonder men took alarm at so portentous a doctrine, and that those who claimed sovereignty for the law and those who claimed sovereignty for Parliaments were equally roused to indignation. "Undoubtedly," wrote Clarendon long

[1] *State Trials*, iii. 825.

afterwards, "my Lord Finch's speech made ship money much more abhorred and formidable than all the commandments by the Council table and all the distresses taken by the sheriffs of England."[1] It did more than that. It taught men to know, beyond all possibility of mistake, that the reign of Parliament and the reign of law were indissolubly connected, and that the fond idea of an unparliamentary government acting under legal restraint must be cast aside for ever.

The speeches of the popular lawyers, and the judgments of the popular Judges, were circulated from hand to hand. A settled conviction took possession of Englishmen that, if the majority of the Judges was against them, the weight of argument was on their side. Never had the authority of Charles sunk so low as after the victory which he counted himself to have won.

Charles acted as if doubt were no longer possible. The voice of the Judges, when it spoke in his own favour, was to him as the voice of the law itself. Sharp orders were at once issued for the immediate collection of the arrears. Sheriffs were to bring in the money on pain of a summons before the Council. Constables refusing to assess, magistrates of towns refusing to collect, and men of standing refusing to pay were to be treated in the same manner. This pressure was not exerted entirely in vain. Even the sturdy Richard Chambers, who had refused to pay ship money as he had refused to pay Tonnage and Poundage before, was liberated from prison upon payment of the 10*l*. charged upon him, though he consoled himself by bringing an action against the Lord Mayor, who had assessed it, upon the ground of some

[1] *Clarendon,* i. 71.

technical informality.¹ At the end of July 78,000*l.* were still in arrear. By the end of October 30,000*l.* of this sum had been paid in, though even this left the arrears twice as large as those remaining at the end of October 1637.² If this, however, could be recovered there was no reason to despair of the Exchequer. Never since the accession of the Stuart dynasty had the finances been in so flourishing a condition as in the spring of 1638. The Great Customs, which had for some years been farmed for 150,000*l.*, were let afresh for 165,000*l.*³ The new burdens laid since Portland's death were beginning to tell, and with ordinary prudence the King would be certain to secure himself from a deficit.

Other grievances besides ship money.

The great case of ship money was peculiarly adapted to bring into a focus all the political dissatisfaction which existed in England. The incidence of the tax was felt by all but the very poorest, and the question at issue, with its wide and far-reaching consequences, was capable of being summed up in a few terse words which would fix themselves in the dullest understanding. As was, however, to be expected, the grievance of ship money did not stand alone. Other complaints were heard of mischiefs inflicted for the most part on special classes or special localities, which were each of them separately of less importance than that caused by the ship money, but which, taken together, were sufficient to cause a considerable amount of irritation.

The Forest Courts.

First of these was the complaint of the action of

---

¹ Rossingham's Newsletter, June 16, 1640. *S. P. Dom.* ccclvii. 36.

² *Council Register*, June 30, July 15. Russell's account, Oct. 27, 1637, July 28, Oct. 27, 1638. *S. P. Dom.* ccclxx. 57, cccxlv. 93, 95, cccc. 114, 115.

³ Indenture, March 17, 1638. *Patent Rolls*, 13 Charles I., Part 41, No. 1.

the Forest Courts, the unwonted activity of which had been in operation ever since 1634. In the course of three years Holland, as Chief Justice in Eyre, had held his justice seat in the Forest of Dean, in Waltham Forest, and in the New Forest.[1] In 1637 the turn of the Forest of Rockingham arrived. The fines set by Holland were enormous. The Earl of Salisbury was called on to pay 20,000*l.*, the Earl of Westmoreland 19,000*l.*, Sir Christopher Hatton 12,000*l.* The bounds of the forest had been reckoned as measuring six miles in circumference. They were now to measure sixty.[2] As usually happened, the fines actually levied were far less than those originally set. In November Commissioners were named to compound with all persons guilty of offences against forest law.[3] After the Commission had been in action two years and a half, only 23,000*l.* had been brought by it into the Exchequer from all the forests in England.[4] The sum paid was indeed small enough when compared with the original demand, but it was large enough to cause considerable discontent in the minds of those who believed themselves to be buying off, on compulsion, a purely imaginary claim.

No public object was aimed at by Charles in these exactions. In the institution of new corporations with exclusive rights of manufacture, or of sale, he, or those who acted in his name, were doubtless guided to a large extent by considerations of public benefit. The Monopoly Act of 1624 had been the result partly of the jealousy aroused amongst traders, who

---

[1] *Personal Government of Charles I.*, ii. 73, 76, 172, 182.
[2] Garrard to Wentworth, Oct. 9. *Straf. Letters*, ii. 114.
[3] Commission, Nov. 4. *Patent Rolls*, 13 Charles I., Part 14, Dors. 6.
[4] Breviates of the receipt.

saw the profits of trade going into the hands of courtiers, and partly of the pressure felt in consequence of the violation of economic laws by those who could give no account of the true cause of the mischief. Not only had that Act left untouched the general power of the Crown to institute corporations with the right of monopoly, but it had not been accompanied, as the Free-Trade measures of our own time were accompanied, by any intellectual enlargement of the traditional sphere of thought upon the subject. The Privy Council of Charles, therefore, not only believed itself to be empowered by law to establish new corporations with the sole right of trade, but they shared the feelings of a generation which regulated trade in every possible way. Justices of the peace had long counted it to be a part of their business to settle the rate of wages and to keep down the price of food. Inhabitants of towns petitioning for the erection of a municipal corporation were in the habit of ascribing all the vice and misery of over-populated districts to the 'want of governance' which allowed each man to come and go, to manufacture or not to manufacture, as he pleased.[1] It is impossible for any candid person to read the numerous entries on the subject of trade which crowd the Register of the Privy Council without coming to the conclusion that they were the work of men desirous, perhaps, here and there to obtain a little fragmentary relief for the impoverished Exchequer, but who were desirous to have honest work done at low prices, and conspicuously failed in the attempt.

In 1636, for instance, a Corporation of Brick-

[1] Several petitions state this in the *Petition Books* at Crowcombe Court.

makers was established for the benefit of the builders of London. These men were to make good bricks at the rate of six shillings the thousand. At the end of three years it was discovered that they made very bad bricks indeed, and that, though they sold them at the stipulated price, they kept the carriage of them in their own hands and charged exorbitantly for it.[1]

Still more difficult was the task of bringing the London coal supply to an ideal standard. The owners of the coal ships were formed into a corporation, and bound themselves to pay one shilling to the King on every chaldron imported from Newcastle. They also bound themselves never to charge more than seventeen shillings the chaldron in summer and nineteen shillings in winter. Yet, strict as were the rules laid down, the coal-shippers gave endless trouble to the Government. Again and again there was a scarcity in the London market, and prices rose in defiance of the Privy Council. Sometimes blame was attributed to a combination amongst the shippers to delay their vessels on the way from the North, in order to create an unusual demand, under the pressure of which they might run up prices in defiance of their agreement; sometimes to improper regulations imposed in the London market; sometimes to the greed of the retailers. But, in spite of the reasoning and the activity of the Council, it was only at rare intervals that coals were not above the regulation price in London.[2]

The Corporation of Soap-makers, which had caused such excitement in 1635,[3] underwent a com-

---

[1] *Patent Rolls*, 13 Charles I., Part 7, No. 5. *Council Register*, Apr. 24, 1639.
[2] The *State Papers* and the *Council Register* are full of this business.
[3] *Personal Gov. of Charles I.*, ii. 165.

plete change in 1637. With Juxon as Treasurer Laud at last had his way. The company formed of Portland's friends disappeared. The old independent soap-makers were erected into a corporation, buying out their predecessors with 43,000*l*., and agreeing to pay to the King 8*l*. on every ton of soap manufactured by them. The very men who had raised the outcry against the search for illicit soap now made exactly the same use of their monopoly as that of which they had themselves complained. They constantly applied to the Council to assist them in the suppression of unauthorised manufacture, and the Council seldom failed to comply with their request.[1]

The original object of the incorporation of the Soap Company had been the encouragement of domestic industry. With the same object a company was formed at Shields for the production of salt. All port towns from Berwick to Southampton were ordered to provide themselves with this salt alone in place of that which came from the shores of the Bay of Biscay, and which was at that time regarded as the best salt in the world. The company was to pay to the King ten shillings on every wey sold. for home consumption, and three shillings and fourpence on every wey of that coarser sort which was used by fishermen.[2] Complaints were soon heard. The owners of the Yarmouth fishing boats declared that they could not obtain salt in sufficient quantity, and that what they did receive was not as good as the old bay salt had been.[3] The King had a plan of his own

[1] Agreement, July 3, 1637. *Patent Rolls*, 13 Charles I., Part 39, No. 10. There are also frequent entries relating to the subject in the *Council Register*.

[2] Indenture, Nov. 4, 1635. *Patent Rolls*, 11 Charles I., Part 26, No. 4.

[3] Bailiffs of Great Yarmouth to the Council, Nov. 13, 1636. *S. P. Dom.* cccxxxv. 51.

to meet the difficulty. A certain Nicholas Murford had invented a new method of making salt, and had obtained leave to establish his works in the neighbourhood of Yarmouth, with special permission to sell his salt in spite of the monopoly of the Shields manufacturers. An influential company was formed to carry out Murford's project. The King interested himself so deeply in the affair that he granted lands to the new company, which turned out to be the property of others, and was consequently compelled to retract his gift.[1]

The King's claim to levy impositions on soap and salt may have received a sort of justification as a mere demand for an equivalent for the loss of his customs caused by the prohibition of importation. Other interferences with domestic trade reposed simply on the ground that it was the King's business to see that his subjects were provided with articles of good quality, though even in these cases he did not disdain to make a profit for himself. The Company of Starchmakers was to take care that good wheaten flour was not wasted in their unprofitable manufacture. In order that grain might not be misused in brewing beer unnecessarily strong, all persons except a certain number of licensed maltsters and brewers were prohibited from making malt and brewing beer. This last prohibition caused such an outcry that even Charles gave way before it and threw open the trade once more.[2]

---

[1] Grant to Murford and Hanworth, May 25, 1636. *Patent Rolls*, 12 Charles I., Part 7, No. 6. The King to Wentworth and others, Jan. 18. Wentworth's petition, Feb. 22, 1637. Murford to Sherwood, 1637? *S. P. Dom.* cccxliv. 35, cccxlvii. 80, ccclxxvii. 84.

[2] Proclamation, July 9, 1637, June 18, 1638. *Rymer*, xx. 157, 234. Appointment of Brewers for Essex, Feb. 28, 1638. *Patent Rolls*, 13 Charles I., Part 18, No. 6.

For these encroachments some reason, however unsatisfactory, could, in every case, be alleged. For Charles's interference with the wine trade no reason whatever could be produced. As early as in 1632 a demand was made upon the sellers of wine in London for a premium of 4*l*. per tun. Upon their refusal, it was discovered that the Vintners were in the habit of dressing meat for sale to their customers, a mode of obtaining money which was not authorised by their charter. A decree of the Star Chamber put a stop to the practice. At the Council Board the Vintners were urged to be wise in time. "It is folly in travellers," said Dorset, "to deny their purses to robbers upon the way, and to draw harm upon themselves thereby, when they have no sufficient force either to defend their purses or their own persons." A proposal was then made that if the Vintners would lend the King 6,000*l*. the prohibition should be relaxed for some months, and that then they should be secured from further molestation. They paid the money, but the promised security was not forthcoming. They complained to the Council, but met with no redress. "Will you not be satisfied," said Arundel, "with the word of a king?" Upon this they imagined that they would be allowed to dress meat, as they had hitherto done. They were at once called in question. The Attorney General offered to overlook the offence for the future if they would pay the King a penny on every quart of wine sold. On their refusal they were again prosecuted in the Star Chamber for dressing meat. When the cause was ready for sentence, Alderman Abell, the Master of the Vintners' Company, came to a bargain with the King through the interposition of the Marquis of Hamilton. To Hamilton had been granted the fines which were recoverable in the Star Chamber from the offenders in the matter of dressing meat. He now explained to the Vintners that he had no wish to ruin so many honest men, and that it would be far better for them to comply with the King's wish. His arguments were warmly supported by Abell, and by Kilvert, the wretch who had been the main agent in the ruin of Williams, and who was now currying favour at Court by providing for the increase of the revenue at the expense first of the Vintners and ultimately of the consumers of wine. Before this pressure the unfortunate Company gave way. They agreed to all that was asked. They were to be permitted to dress meat and sell beer. They were to be allowed to charge an additional penny on every quart of wine sold, and they were to grant to the King a payment of 20*l.* on every tun, or, as was subsequently settled, a rent of 30,000*l.* a year.[1] All the vintners in England were compelled by the Council to conform to the arrangements made with the London Company. Hamilton obtained 4,000*l.* a year from the rent, and 1,500*l.* a year more were assigned to two members of his family. No doubt Kilvert had his profit too.[2]

[1] *Rushw.* iii. 277. *Council Register*, March 2, 1635. Garrard to Wentworth, Jan. 8, 1636. *Straf. Letters*, i. 507. Indenture, Sept. 7, 1638, *Patent Rolls*, 14 Charles I., Part 18, No. 2. This is no doubt the indenture assigned by Rushworth to 1634. See also *The Vintners' Answer to some Scandalous Pamphlets*, 1642. (E. 140.) "Those of the better sort which did give their counsel," says the writer of this pamphlet (p. 7), "did it not with any true liking to the project, but merely to avoid ruin in the Star Chamber. For the shipwreck of the soap-boilers and others was then fresh in view; and that Court had then gotten them the same repute as a Timariot's horse has in Turkey, where they say no grass ever grows after the impression of his fatal hoof." The early form of this saying, which is still current, with a slight change, is curious.

[2] Kilvert's remonstrance, *Harl. MSS.* 1,219, fol. 3. Grants to Hamilton and others, *Patent Rolls*, 14 Charles I., Part 9, Nos. 25, 31, 32.

The great body of consumers of wine suffered in order that the King and the courtiers might increase their profits. It is not always by the most hurtful actions that the greatest discredit is gained. In our eyes nothing could be so injurious as any attempt to limit the size of London by prohibiting the erection of new houses. England was growing in prosperity and wealth, and the effects of prosperity were felt in the increase of the population of the capital. In the early part of the reign houses began to spring up for the accommodation of the new comers, and a new and fashionable quarter arose in the neighbourhood of Drury Lane. To provide the requirements necessary for the maintenance of health would have taken some trouble and some thought. It was easier to say that no houses should be built than to regulate the mode in which they were to be erected. At first, indeed, the anxiety to restrain the increase of buildings gave way before the desire to fill the Exchequer, and fines were readily accepted in the place of the demolition of houses. When at last a serious effort was made to check the supposed evil, the initiative did not proceed from the King. A petition from the Lord Mayor and aldermen drew the attention of the Council to the growing mischief. They alleged that swarms of beggars were attracted by the new houses. Prices had risen in consequence of the increasing demand for the necessaries of life. Many of the houses were built over water-pipes, and cut off the supply of water. The danger of infection was increased. Soil was carried down to the river, which threatened to impede navigation.[1]

[1] *Council Register*, Oct. 29, 1632. How strongly the corporation felt on this subject is shown by the presentation of a petition to the House of Commons on June 14, 1642, praying that a Bill might be passed against new buildings. *Common Council Journal Book*, xi. 33.

Doubtless something more than pure enthusiasm for the public good was at work in the minds of the petitioners. The population within the City looked on the population outside the City as its rival in trade.

After a year's consideration the Council responded to the City petition. One valuable suggestion they made, but it was made only to be dropped. They advised that the streets and alleys which had grown up to the north of the Strand should be brought under municipal government by being divided between the cities of London and Westminster. For the rest, they simply adopted the recommendations of the City. In order to ascertain the extent of their legal powers a test case was brought into the Star Chamber, when Attorney General Noy argued that though there was no statute to authorise the demolition of the new buildings, they might be proceeded against as nuisances under the Common Law. Coventry and the two Chief Justices accepted this doctrine, and orders were given to commence the demolitions.[1] As long as Charles retained authority permission to build was seldom granted, though in a few exceptional cases the prohibition was relaxed on payment of a fine.

The natural result was the overcrowding of existing houses. To provide a remedy householders were ordered to forbear from taking lodgers. It was not easy to enforce the order. A return made in 1637, when the ravages of the plague had frightened the authorities, who were ignorantly doing their best to promote the dissemination of disease, shows how little their edicts were observed. In one house were found eleven married couples and fifteen single persons. In

[1] *Council Register*, Oct. 23, 1633. *Add. MSS.* 11,764, fol. 2.

another the householder had taken in eighteen lodgers; and even the Company of Freemasons had cut up their common hall into tenements.¹ The wisest were as far to seek as the most ignorant. In a report on the causes of the plague made by the College of Physicians, the chief blame is thrown not on restriction, but on the increase of building, 'by which multitudes of people are drawn hither to inhabit, by which means both the air is much offended and provision is made more scarce.' It is true that this statement is followed by a list of nuisances to be abated. The sewers and ditches were not properly cleansed. Ponds which should have been filled up were left to collect refuse. The streets were not swept as they should be. Lay stalls were allowed to remain close to the habitations of man. Those who died of the plague were buried within the City, and some of the graveyards were so full that partially decomposed bodies were taken up to make room for fresh interments. Corn, meat, and fish unfit for consumption were sold to the poor. The physicians recommended the erection of a Health Office to provide a remedy, a recommendation which no one attempted to carry into effect.²

For good or for evil it was dangerous to interfere with the great City commonwealth. The settlement of the affairs of Londonderry,³ though more favourable to the City than had been at one time expected, was long cherished as a deadly grievance. The Irish lands, settled at the cost of so much labour and capital, were forfeited to the Crown. The greater part of the fine imposed was indeed remitted, but 12,000*l.*

---

¹ Returns, May 1637. *S. P. Dom.* ccclix.
² The College of Physicians to the Council, Aug. (?) 1637. *S. P. Dom.* ccclxvi. 78.   ³ Pers, *Government of Charles I.*, ii. 152.

were exacted for the use of the Queen,[1] who happened to be in want of that sum. Another subject of irritation was an arrangement for increasing the tithes due to the City clergy. On the face of the matter, Laud, who pushed it on in the Council, had justice on his side. The tithes by which the clergy were supported had sunk to a mere pittance through under-valuation of the property on which they were charged, and Laud insisted on a more accurate valuation. The citizens regarded his demand from a very different point of view. If they were illiberal in the payment of tithe, they had been very liberal in irregular payments to preachers and lecturers. They liked, however, to select the recipients of their bounty—as Laud would have put it, to bring the clergy into subservience to themselves, or, as they would have put it, to take care that their ministers were not infected by the new ceremonialism.

Collisions between the Council and the City were indeed of constant occurrence. In 1636 the failure of the proposal to extend the municipal governments of London and Westminster over the districts covered with recent buildings was followed by the establishment of a new corporation for those districts, which, by establishing the usual trade regulations, should prohibit the intrusion of persons who had not served their regular apprenticeship. The citizens of London regarded the new arrangement with a jealous eye, and a proposal that apprentices who had served their time under the new corporation should be admitted to trade in the City found no favour in their sight.[2]

---

[1] There is a Privy Seal to this effect.
[2] Charter, June 2, 1636. *Patent Rolls*, 12 Charles I., Part 20, No. 7. Proclamation, Nov. 22, 1637. *Rymer*, xx. 173. *Council Register*, May 6, 1638.

VOL. I.　　　　　G

1634.
Hackney coaches.

The spirit of monopoly was everywhere vigorous. In 1634, when an enterprising stable-keeper for the first time sent hackney coaches to stand for hire in the streets, many persons held up their hands in horror at the innovation. It was seriously proposed that no coach should be hired for less than a three miles journey, and that unmarried gentlemen should be forbidden to ride in them except when accompanied by their parents.[1] The London watermen made objections of a different kind. They were quite ready to see any number of coaches driving northwards towards Islington and Hoxton, but they held it to be intolerable presumption in them to compete with the wherries on the river by driving from the City to Westminster. For a time these objections prevailed.

1636.

In 1636 a proclamation was issued forbidding the hiring of hackney coaches for a shorter journey than one of three miles. Too extensive a use of coaches, it was said, would block up the streets, break up the pavements, and raise the price of hay.[2] It was not long before it was discovered that the coaches which had been so severely condemned were not without their use. Like the vintners, the coachmen applied to Hamilton to license fifty hackney coachmen for London and Westminster, and as many as he thought right for other places in England. Hamilton did not grant these licenses for nothing,[3] but he provided London with vehicles which were to be hired by all who wished to employ them.

1637.

1635.
The letter-post.

Another salutary innovation was the establishment of a post-office for the transmission of letters.

[1] Paper of suggestions, May 5, 1634. *S. P. Dom.*, cclxvii. 36.
[2] Watermen's Petition, June, 1634. *S. P. Dom.*, cclxix. 52; Proclamation, June 19, 1636. *Rymer*, xix. 721.
[3] A bundle of these licenses are preserved amongst the Verney Papers at Claydon.

Hitherto, any one who wished to communicate with his friends, and who was not sufficiently wealthy to send his letters by a private messenger, was obliged to entrust them to a carrier, who conveyed them over the miry roads at the rate of sixteen or eighteen miles a day. Under this system, the few persons who had communications with Scotland or Ireland were well content if they received an answer within two months. In 1635 the Government adopted a proposal for establishing a regular post on the principal roads. Six days were allowed for going to Edinburgh and back. The other main routes were from London to Plymouth, and from London to Holyhead, but cross posts were established to serve the principal towns lying off the road. The charge for a single letter was twopence for a distance of eighty miles.[1] By an arrangement with the King of France and the Cardinal Infant, the system was extended beyond the Channel, and merchants were able to send a single letter to Antwerp for eightpence, and to Paris for ninepence.[2]

Like all the Stuart Kings, Charles took an interest in those improvements which were likely to increase the material prosperity of the country. In his father's reign there had been many projects for reclaiming inundated lands, but it was not till after Charles's accession that anything serious was attempted. In 1626 a commencement was made with Hatfield Chase, where 70,000 acres were flooded by the rivers which converge to form the Humber. A Dutchman, Cornelius Vermuyden, skilled in the art of raising embankments and cutting canals, was brought over from

---

[1] Proposition, June. *S. P. Dom.*, ccxci. 114, Proclamation, July 31, 1635. *Rymer*, xix. 649.

[2] Commission, April 5, 1637. *Patent Rolls*, 13 Charles I. Part 41, Dors. No. 3.

Holland. Dutch capitalists were induced to provide money for the venture, and the strong arms of Dutch labourers, not without some admixture of Flemish refugees and French Huguenots, were ready to wield the pickaxe and the spade. The operation was certain to be unpopular amongst the surrounding peasantry. Voices were raised in complaint that water was being forced over fields which had once been dry; and the grievances of landowners were echoed by the grievances of large numbers without avowed occupation, who had gathered round the waste grounds, and who made a livelihood by catching fish and snaring ducks, as well as by various other contrivances, for the cessation of which the undertakers of the works would hardly be able to find an exact pecuniary compensation. Jealousy of foreigners fanned the flame of hatred. The embankments were broken through and the workmen were attacked. The foreigners took up arms in self defence, and an Englishman was killed in the struggle. The sheriff of the county restored order, and Vermuyden, made wise by experience, offered to employ native labourers at high wages, and to compensate those whom he had unintentionally damaged. In 1629 Vermuyden was knighted, and received a grant of the lands which he had recovered on payment of a yearly rent, and a fine of 16,000*l*.[1]

The old difficulties were not yet at an end. The Government found it a hard task to keep the peace. The enthusiastic and quick-tempered Dutch engineer was apt to regard the English peasants in the light of ignorant and selfish obstructives. The peasants looked

---

[1] Hunter, *Hist. of the Deanery of Doncaster*, i. 160. Ansbie to Buckingham, Aug. 21. Vernatti to St. Gilles, Oct. 1628. *S. P. Dom.* cxiii. 38; cxix. 73.

upon every accidental injury as a premeditated wrong. At last, the whole dispute was committed to the mediation of Wentworth and Hutton, the best men for the purpose to be found in England. After full inquiry, they drew up an award, which was subsequently confirmed by the Court of Exchequer, by which the rights of the tenants and the commoners were fully protected. Vermuyden, in dudgeon, parted with his interest. The immigrants whom he had employed, about two hundred families of foreign origin, remained on the soil which they had rescued. Grass grew, and corn waved, where a few years before Henry, Prince of Wales, had captured from boats a whole herd of deer swimming in the waters. The neighbours still remonstrated that they were occasionally deluged by artificial floods; but when once the drainage was fully completed, the inundations ceased.[1] From another kind of hardship the foreigners found no escape. They had been permitted to erect a chapel in which they might worship God in their native tongues, and they interpreted that permission as conveying a license to use the forms of their native land. Archbishop Neile was horrified to find that these Dutchmen and Frenchmen had established a Presbyterian congregation on English soil, that they baptized infants without a font, and received the Communion without kneeling at the rail. Neile at once intervened. The strangers were compelled to dismiss their minister, to pull down their chapel, and to attend the parish churches of the neighbourhood.[2]

The draining of Hatfield Chase was not the only

CHAP. II.

1630.

1636. The foreigners compelled to conform to the English Church.

1629. The Great Level.

---

[1] *Hunter,* i. 162.
[2] Neile to Laud, June 23, Sept. 8, 1636; Neile's report. *S. P. Dom.* cccxxvii. 47, cccxxxi. 71, cccxlv. 85, i. 5.

work of the kind accomplished in England during these years. Many thousands of acres were reclaimed in Lincolnshire. But of all the fens the largest was that known as the Great Level, which spread round the Isle of Ely over some 36,000 acres, which was covered by the overflow of the Ouse, the Nen, and the Welland. What was in winter a vast expanse of water was in summer a dreary swamp. On the damp islets an ague-stricken population gathered a coarse hay and cut the willows to supply the basket-makers of England. Wild ducks and wild geese were to be captured by hundreds, and pike and other freshwater fish were to be had in plenty. Men who passed half of their lives in boats, and who, when they left their boats, strapped on the long stilts which enabled them to stride from one piece of dry ground to another, were terrified when they heard of a coming change. Their scared feelings were well expressed by words placed in their mouths by a rhymester of the day.

> Behold the great design, which they do now determine,
> Will make our bodies pine, a prey to crows and vermin;
> For they do mean all fens to drain and waters overmaster,
> All will be dry, and we must die, 'cause Essex calves want pasture.[1]

The first serious attempt to deal with the Great Level was made in 1629 by the Commissioners of Sewers, a body composed of the neighbouring gentry acting under the authority of the Crown. They entered into a contract with Vermuyden to drain the level. But the proposal to introduce foreigners was as unpalatable in Lincolnshire and Cambridgeshire as it had been in Yorkshire, and the Commissioners were forced by the public opinion of the district to rescind the contract. They urged the Earl of Bedford

[1] Dugdale's *Hist. of Embanking*, 391.

to place himself at the head of the work. On his consent, it was arranged that 95,000 acres of the drained land should be allotted to him. Of this share, however, he was to set apart 12,000 for the King, and the profits of 40,000 were to serve as a security for keeping up the works after their completion. The amount of land which he was actually to enjoy would therefore be reduced to 43,000 acres. He divided the undertaking into twenty shares, and in 1634 the shareholders were incorporated by Royal Charter. The work proceeded rapidly, and in October 1637 the Commissioners of Sewers decided that it had been completed, and adjudged the stipulated reward to the Earl and his associates.[1]

The associates, however, were not satisfied. They complained that Bedford had pursued his own interests at their expense, and they threatened him with a prosecution in the Star Chamber unless he treated them more fairly.[2] Vermuyden too, who had been employed by Bedford, was equally discontented. Bedford, it was alleged, had claimed his reward before he had fully carried out his contract. In summer the reclaimed land was tolerably dry. In winter, the streams swelled as before, and the waters poured over the level plain. Bedford, it would seem, had done all that was in his power to do. He had spent 100,000*l.* on the undertaking. Yet, unless more were done, his labours would have been almost in vain.[3]

On April 12, 1638, a new body of Commissioners,

---

[1] Cole, *Collection of Laws*, xxiii.

[2] Complaints of the shareholders, Oct. 1637. *Harl. MSS.* 5011, fol. 37.

[3] This is distinctly stated by Vermuyden, *A Discourse touching the Draining*, &c. Compare Dugdale, 411, and the Act of 1649, which shows that the drained land was even then under water in winter. The accounts

appointed for the purpose, opened a session at Huntingdon. Whilst they were still sitting, they received from the King a letter in which, with his accustomed indiscretion, he announced that he had formed a decided opinion that the works were incomplete, and then added that he was prepared to take them into his own hands.[1] The Commissioners took a personal survey of the works, and obtained verdicts from seven different juries. Upon this evidence they declared the drainage to be unfinished.[2] Whether they were acting under pressure or not, they were, necessarily, after the reception of the King's letter, liable to the imputation of doing so. At their next meeting at Wisbech in May, they imposed a taxation varying from 10s. to 40s. an acre, to support the expense of carrying out the original plan.

The money was to paid at their next meeting at Huntingdon in July.[3] Before the appointed day arrived, other voices made themselves heard. Imperfect as it was, Bedford's work had created sore discontent amongst many of the inhabitants of the district.[4] Landowners complained that they were worse off than they had been before his intervention. The whole tribe of fishermen and willow-cutters

---

usually given, as for instance in Cole's *Collection of Laws*, ignore this ground of the King's interference. Wells reprints Cole's objurgations, though he interlaces them with remarks of his own, conceived in a different spirit, giving, however, no intimation which are Cole's sentences and which are his own.

[1] We have only the abstract of this letter in *Cole* xxviii. He misdates it as written in 1639.

[2] Inrolments of the laws of sewers, Part I. *R. O.*

[3] *Dugdale*, 411.

[4] A pamphlet, the *Anti-Projector*, written after 1649, asserts that Bedford's grant was illegal; and that, whereas by the Act of 43 Eliz. cap. 11, a lord of the manor was bound to obtain the consent of the majority of owners and commoners before commencing drainage works, he had falsely stated that this had been obtained.

proclaimed themselves grievously wronged. Their commons, as they called the swamp, had been taken from them, and at the best they would have to betake themselves to an uncongenial life of hard agricultural labour. From the moment that the Commissioners declared against the Earl, a vague hope spread that the King might be on their side. In May, Bedford's workmen were interrupted by a disorderly mob.[1] On June 4 the magistrates of the Isle of Ely were informed that there had been an assemblage of forty or fifty men, at which it had been resolved to collect at least six hundred on the following day, on the pretext of a football match, to destroy the drainage works. Two of the ringleaders were arrested. The next day was rainy, and only two hundred persons appeared to begin the work of destruction. There were more arrests, and the mob was dispersed. One of the prisoners gave expression to the thought which was doubtless present to the minds of all. He would not leave his commons, he said, till he saw the King's hand and seal. He would obey God and the King, and no one else, for they all were but subjects. "What," he asked, "if one might be inspired to do the poor good, and help them to their commons again?"[2]

[1] Windebank to Peachy, May 16. *S. P. Dom.* cccxc. 89.
[2] Justices of the Peace to the Council, June 9. *S. P. Dom.* cccxcii. 45. It is difficult to say what Cromwell had to do with the matter. Sir Philip Warwick's statement that he threw himself into opposition to the King has led every one astray. Probably Warwick, when he wrote his Memoirs, could not conceive Cromwell as acting except in opposition to the King. Mr. Forster in his *Life of Cromwell* has a highly imaginative narrative of Cromwell's proceedings which has no support in any known evidence. If Cromwell had really bearded the Court, his name would have appeared on the Council Register as a prisoner. Mr. Sanford (*Studies of the Great Rebellion*, 252) is far more moderate; but even he suggests that Cromwell appeared on behalf of the commoners, 'turning that amount of popular opinion against the King's undertaking, which

1638.
July 18.
Decision of the Commissioners.

When the Commissioners met on July 18, it was to declare their determination to enforce the taxation which they had ordered, and to announce that the inhabitants were to continue in possession of their lands and commons till the drainage was completed. Nor were Bedford and his partners to have any reasonable cause for dissatisfaction. By the original arrangement, after providing 12,000 for the King and 40,000 to form a provision for the maintenance of the works, they would have had 43,000 to divide amongst themselves. They were now offered 40,000 without the obligation of finishing the works at all. If, as is said, the annual value of the reclaimed land was 30s. an acre, they would obtain a yearly income of 60,000*l*. by a capital expenditure of 100,000*l*. They had certainly no reason to complain.

The King is to undertake the work.

The King himself was to undertake the work, receiving 57,000 acres in return. Little was, however, done by him. Troubles were coming thickly

had been created to resist his illegal proceedings; so that the Commissioners, afraid of meeting the whole of the parties, made an order to permit the landholders to take the profits of the lands, and to the generality granted commons of pasture over the whole of the acreage. . . . Both these concessions, without doubt, were owing to the skilful opposition of Oliver.' The simple answer to this hypothesis is, that the Commissioners met on July 18, and that Charles had on July 10 announced his intention of making these concessions (Bankes to Windebank, July 21. *S. P. Dom.* cccxcv. 77), when he can have had no fear of Oliver before his eyes. Nevertheless, it is highly probable that Cromwell did take the part of these poor men. If he did so, he must have been on the King's side against Bedford, and not, as is always asserted, on Bedford's side against the King. This would be the more creditable to him, as political motives would have drawn him to Bedford, and his cousin St. John was Bedford's counsel and one of the adventurers. There is nothing whatever to connect the nickname 'Lord of the Fens' with these proceedings. It simply occurs as one of the many names for the leading Parliamentarians in the *Mercurius Aulicus* of Nov. 6, 1643. Sir H. Vane appears as 'an old New England man,' Rudyerd as 'a grave senator,' &c. &c. All that can be meant is, that Cromwell lived in the fens.

upon Charles, and he had neither money nor time to bestow upon the fens. Possibly he might not have succeeded even under more favourable circumstances. He selected Vermuyden as his engineer, and even then voices were raised to argue that Vermuyden's ideas were unpractical. Modern engineers have decided that the objections then brought were of great weight.[1]

The story of the first attempt to effect the drainage of the great fens is worthy of notice by the historian as well as by the engineer. It brings out into clear relief both the merits and the defects of Charles's character. It is evident that he was anxious to carry out a work of real importance, both when he entrusted it to Bedford and when he took it into his own hands. It is evident, too, that he desired both that the rich should be benefited and that the poor should not be wronged. Yet he gained no credit for his good intentions. He took his decision in private before any inquiry had been held, and he stultified his Commissioners by announcing to them his decision just as they were starting to make the inquiry upon which it was ostensibly to be based. When all this parade of investigation ended in the assignment of a large number of acres to himself, it was easy to leap to the conclusion that the sole object of the whole proceeding was to fill the Exchequer at the expense of a popular nobleman, whose advocates before the Commissioners were St. John and Holborne, the very men who had recently been retained by Hampden.

From whatever side Charles's conduct is approached, the result is the same. He failed because morally, intellectually, and politically he was isolated

---

[1] Burrell, *Exceptions against Vermuyden's Discourse.* "One of the principal labours of modern engineers has been to rectify the errors of Vermuyden and his followers." Smiles' *Lives of the Engineers*, i. 56.

in the midst of his generation. He had no wish to erect a despotism, to do injustice, or to heap up wealth at the expense of his subjects If he had confidence in his own judgment, his confidence was not entirely without justification. He was a shrewd critic of other men's mistakes, and usually succeeded in hitting the weak point of an opponent's argument, though it often happened that, taken as a whole, the argument of his opponents was far stronger than his own. Especially on theological questions, he was able to hold his own against trained disputants. On all matters relating to art, he was an acknowledged master. His collection of pictures was the finest and most complete in Europe. He had that technical knowledge which enabled him instinctively to distinguish between the work of one painter and another He was never happier than when he was conversing with musicians, painters, sculptors, and architects. He treated Rubens and Vandyke as his personal friends. But the brain which could test an argument or a picture could never test a man. Nothing could ever convince him of the unworthiness of those with whom he had been in the long habit of familiar intercourse. Nothing could ever persuade him of the worthiness of those who were conscientiously opposed to his government. There was no gradation either in his enmity or his friendship. An Eliot or a Pym was to him just the same virulent slanderer as a Leighton or a Bastwick. A Wentworth and a Holland were held in equal favour, and some who were ready to sacrifice their lives in his cause were constantly finding obstacles thrown in their path through the King's soft-hearted readiness to gratify the prayers of some needy courtier.

In his unwarranted self-reliance Charles enormously under-estimated the difficulties of government, and especially of a government such as his. He would have nothing to say to 'thorough,' because he did not understand that thoroughness was absolutely essential. He would not get rid of slothful or incompetent officials, would not set aside private interests for great public ends, would not give himself the trouble to master the details of the business on which he was engaged. He thought that he had done everything in ridding himself of Parliaments, though in reality he had done but little. He did not see that Parliaments had roots in the local organisations of the country, and that, as long as these organisations remained intact, they would be ready to blossom into Parliaments again at the first favourable opportunity. Sheriffs and Justices of the Peace, no doubt, were appointed by the King. In his name they administered justice or executed the directions of the Council. But they were not, as the Intendants of the old French Monarchy or the Prefects of the Empire, entirely dependent upon the master in whose name they acted. They were country gentlemen with the same habits of thought, the same feelings of independence, as their neighbours around them. If they collected ship money, they collected it unwillingly, and there were few indeed amongst them who did not sympathise with the gallant resistance of Hampden.

In the towns the local organisation was far more independent of the government than it was in the counties. Such a city as that of London, for instance, contained a potential force which it would be hard to beat down. It was no mere assemblage of individual units, content to store up wealth, or to secure their daily bread. It had an organisation of

CHAP. II.
1638.
estimates his difficulties.

The local organisation of the country untouched.

The City of London.

its own, reaching from the highest to the lowest. Its Lord Mayor, its Aldermen, its Common Council, and Common Hall constituted a municipal republic. Its great merchant societies were busily engaged in pushing back the limits of English commerce in the most distant lands. At home the great City Companies maintained the traditions of trade and manufacture, and looked with a jealous eye on all attempts made by those outside their pale to participate in their profits. If the richer merchants were sometimes tempted into subserviency by the timidity of wealth and by the allurements of such gains as were attainable by a farmer of the Customs, or a shareholder in one of the new monopolies, the mass of the citizens had nothing directly to hope or fear from the Crown; whilst the habit of participating in the election of those by whom the affairs of the City were directed, and in the actual decision of more important questions, inspired them with that mutual reliance which is the ripest fruit of community of action. Nor was that action confined to speech and counsel. The defence of the City was not confided to an army paid and commanded by the central authority of the State, but to the trained bands composed of its own citizens. The protection of life and property was not entrusted to a salaried police. The citizens themselves kept watch and ward. When trouble was abroad, when apprentices were likely to be riotous, or when some unwonted pageant attracted denser crowds than usual into the streets, the householder was still required, as in days of remote antiquity, to be answerable for the conduct of every member of his household, and to pay the penalty for the wrong-doing of his children and servants.[1]

[1] The *Journal Book of the Court of Common Council* is full of information on these points.

Such a people—and if other town corporations were far behind the capital in wealth and population, they were not far behind in self-reliance—was not likely to endure for ever to be entirely excluded from all participation in the direction of the national policy, especially as the freeholders and gentry of the counties were very much like-minded with the inhabitants of the towns.

"The blessing of Judah and Issachar," wrote Bacon, "will never meet, that the same people or nation should be both the lion's whelp and the ass between burdens . . Although the same tribute and tax laid by consent or by imposing be all one to the purse, yet it works diversely upon the courage." From the wisdom which had dictated these words Charles had gone very far astray.

Yet it is no matter of surprise that the inevitable resistance was so long delayed. In the midst of material prosperity there was no sharp sting of distress to goad the masses to defiance of authority. Men of property and education had, in the intermission of Parliaments, no common centre round which they could rally. Those who were united in political opposition to the Crown were divided by their religious sympathies. The feeling of irritation against Laud's meddlesome interference with habitual usage was indeed almost universal; but Puritanism was, after all, the creed only of a minority. Many of those who detested the High Commission most bitterly would be no partners in any violent or revolutionary change.

If the nation, however, was not ready to overthrow its government by force, it was not prepared to make any effort to sustain it. How long this state of things would have endured, if no impulse had come from without, it is impossible to say. The

CHAP. II.
1638.
Charles's task a hopeless one.

The Revolution delayed.

The nation needed an impulse from without.

impulse came from a quarter from which Englishmen had long ceased to expect either good or evil. In 1636, Scotland, with its scanty population and its hardy poverty, was as seldom mentioned in London as the Republic of Genoa or the Electorate of Brandenburg. In 1638 it was in the mouths of all men. Charles had inflicted on the Scottish nation a blow which it deeply resented, and its resentment had already led to avowed resistance.

CHAPTER III.

THE RIOTS IN EDINBURGH AND THE SCOTTISH COVENANT.

SCOTSMAN as he was by birth, Charles knew even less of his Northern than of his Southern kingdom. Since his early childhood he had only paid one brief visit to Scotland. That visit had witnessed an outburst of dissatisfaction amongst the nobility with that Episcopal Government which they had eagerly assisted James to impose on a Presbyterian Church.

The nobles had discovered that in placing a yoke on the necks of the clergy they had raised up rivals to themselves. Everywhere in Scotland the Bishops were thrusting them aside. The Archbishop of St. Andrews was Lord Chancellor of Scotland. Other Bishops were members of the Privy Council. Whenever Parliament met, the Bishops had in their hands the selection of the Lords of the Articles, and experience had shown that resistance to the decisions of the Lords of the Articles was not likely to be successful. In the country districts the Bishops claimed that respect and submission which the earl or the lord believed to be due to himself alone. Although Charles had given to the holders of Church property an indefeasible title to the estates which their fathers had usurped, and had actually purchased lands with English money to serve as an endowment for the revived Bishoprics, it was hard for him to allay the suspicion that he intended sooner or later to reconfiscate to the use of the Church that which had been confiscated from the Church by an earlier generation of landowners. The greater part of the nobility, therefore, hated the Bishops thoroughly, and those few who did not hate them were not inclined to move a finger in their behalf. Of all the Scottish lords not one was more loyal than Lord Napier, the son of the inventor of logarithms. But he was as intolerant as Rothes or Loudoun of the political eminence into which the Bishops had been thrust. "That Bishops have a competence," he wrote, " is agreeable to the law of God and man ; but to invest them into great estates and principal officers of the State is neither convenient for the Church, for the King, nor for the State."[1]

If Charles could have been content to leave the Scottish Church as he found it at the time of his visit, it is hardly likely that the nobles would ever have gathered courage to resist him. It is true that their power over their tenants was far greater than that possessed by English landowners, but it was less than that which had been possessed by their fathers. The middle classes had been growing in importance and cohesion, and even the peasants looked for guidance to their minister rather than to their lord. Till very recently the bulk of the clergy was tolerably contented. Here and there was to be found a man who had remained faithful to the extreme Presbyterianism of a former generation, and a large number felt the Articles of Perth to be a serious grievance. But their material comfort had been greatly increased by Charles and his father, at the expense of the neighbouring landowners. The Bishops interfered but little with their parochial ministrations. Above all, they were free to preach the whole Calvinistic creed, and to fulminate anathemas against Popery and

[1] Napier, *Memorials of Montrose*, i. 70.

Arminianism to their hearts' content. No Royal Declaration bound them, as it bound the Southern clergy, to abstain from enlarging on controverted topics. No canons or rubrics existed which could be quoted as sanctioning an obsolete ceremonial.

<small>CHAP. III.
1633</small>

The direction of the Articles of Perth to kneel at the reception of the Communion roused, it is true, no little opposition. It sometimes happened that when a minister asked the congregation to kneel, they flocked out of the church, leaving him alone at the table.[1] But in general, either by the connivance of the Bishops or by the submission of the congregations, there was less trouble caused by this injunction than might have been expected. Here and there, under the shelter of episcopal authority, there were even to be found islands of a faith and practice which contrasted strangely with the level waters around. The colleges of Aberdeen were notorious for their adherence to a more tolerant creed than that of the rest of the clergy. At the King's Chapel at Holyrood, at one of the colleges at St. Andrews, and at some of the cathedrals, the English Prayer Book was used without giving offence.[2] If matters had been allowed to take their course, it is not impossible that the Church of Scotland would have been the first to give an example of that comprehensive tolerance which was the ideal of Chillingworth and Hales.

<small>Kneeling at the Communion.</small>

<small>Varieties of doctrine and ceremony.</small>

Of no such elasticity in doctrine and practice was Charles likely to approve. When Laud accompanied the King to Scotland, he was struck by the mean aspect of many of the Scottish churches. Some of them were plain square buildings, looking, as he said, very like pigeon-houses. The galleries inside re-

<small>Charles determines to coerce the Scottish Church.</small>

---

[1] This happened at Ayr. *Brereton's Travels*, Chetham Society, 121.
[2] *Large Declaration*, 20.

minded him of seats in a theatre.¹ On one occasion, when he found an old Gothic building thus maltreated, and was told that the change had been made at the Reformation, he answered sharply that it was not a reformation, but a Deformation.²

This carelessness about external propriety was no doubt to be attributed in great part to the prevalence of Calvinism. Yet it cannot be altogether dissociated from that carelessness about the external decencies of life which was simply the result of poverty. The England of the seventeenth century was assuredly far behind the England of our own times in sanitary precautions. An English traveller who visited Edinburgh in 1635, spoke with amazement of the filth which was allowed to accumulate even in the best houses. "This city," he wrote, "is placed in a dainty, healthful, pure air, and doubtless were a most healthful place to live in, were not the inhabitants most sluttish, nasty, and slothful people. I could never pass through the hall, but I was constrained to hold my nose; their chambers, vessels, linen, and meat nothing neat, but very slovenly." Linen which had been washed was in much the same state as dirty linen would be in England. 'To come into their kitchen, and to see them dress their meat, and to behold their sink' was 'a sufficient supper, and' would 'take off the edge of the stomach.' The writer is the more to be credited, because in higher matters he is extremely laudatory. "The greatest part of the Scots," he declares, "are very honest and zealously religious. I observed few given to drink or swearing; but if any oath, the most ordinary oath was 'Upon my

---

¹ *Works*, iii. 365.

² This fling at the ugliness of the Scottish churches is usually quoted by writers who ought to know better, as if it implied that the Scotch had been better off under the Pope.

soul.' The most of my hosts I met withal, and others with whom I conversed, I found very sound and orthodox, and zealously religious. In their demands they do not so much exceed as with us in England, but insist upon and adhere unto their first demand for any commodity."[1]

For all this hard-headed zeal and honesty, Charles had no admiration. His eye did not penetrate beneath the external crust of Scottish life. To him, as to Laud, a Reformation which had produced churches so ill-built, and a ritual so unadorned, was no better than a Deformation. The long extemporary prayers of the ministers annoyed him, as they have annoyed many an Englishman since.[2] For all this he had a fitting remedy. "We," he wrote to the Scottish Bishops soon after his return to England, "tendering the good and peace of that Church by having good and decent order and discipline observed therein, whereby religion and God's worship may increase, and considering that there is nothing more defective in that Church than the want of a Book of Common Prayer and uniform service to be kept in all the churches thereof, and the want of canons for the uniformity of the same, we are hereby pleased to authorise you as the representative body of that Church, and do herewith will and require you to condescend upon a form of Church service to be used therein, and to set down canons for the uniformity of the discipline thereof."[3]

[1] *Brereton's Travels*, 102, 106, 110.   [2] *Large Declaration*, 15.
[3] The King to the Bishops, May 13. Sprott's *Scottish Liturgies*, Introd. xlviii. Compare Keble's feeling when he visited Scotland. "The kirks, and the manner in which they defile and insult the sacred places, e.g. Jedburgh Abbey, are even more horrid than I had expected. I would not be in one of them at service time on any consideration. They proclaim aloud, every inch of them, 'Down with the altar.'" Coleridge, *Memoir of Keble*, 350.

1634.
The Bishops and the Church Courts.

Officially, no doubt, the Bishops might be held to be 'the representative body of that Church.' Of the religious heart and soul of Scotland they were in no sense the representatives. Even in relation to the organisation of the Church, their position was very different from that of their English brethren. An English Bishop had the Church Courts at his disposal. The churchwardens, as English Puritans bitterly complained, were bound by oath to present offenders against Church law before authorities entirely independent of the parishioners. In Scotland, the Episcopal jurisdiction had taken no such deep root. In the general management of ecclesiastical affairs the Bishops had taken the place of the assembly, but the local management of parochial affairs was still in the hands of elected officers. Deacons were chosen by the parishioners to take charge of the provision for the poor, and elders to take cognisance of moral faults committed by members of the congregation. The deacons and elders held weekly meetings with the ministers to consult on the affairs of the parish. Acts of immorality were punished, as in England, by exposure on the stool of repentance in the face of the congregation. Persons loitering in the streets or tippling and gaming during service time were sent to prison.[1]

Political education of the middle class.

In this way the Scottish middle class received its political education. Men learned to act together in the Church Courts, where they were not overshadowed, as they were in their single House of Parliament, by great lords and ministers of State. It was not an education which would encourage variety of character. The established principles of morality and religion were taken for granted in every discus-

[1] *Brereton's Travels*, 106.

sion. But if the system bred no leaders of thought, it bound man to man in an indissoluble bond.

Such courts necessarily placed themselves in opposition to the Bishops, who were every year becoming more distinctly the instruments of Laud. As the Bishops of the stamp of Patrick Forbes died, they were succeeded by men after Laud's own heart, such as Wedderburn and Sydserf. Yet, even these men would hardly have entered on a hopeless struggle with the popular feeling, but for the urgency of Laud. Laud, indeed, was far too strong an advocate of ecclesiastical propriety, to attempt to interfere as Archbishop of Canterbury with the Scottish Church. But if the King asked his advice as a private person, he saw no reason why he should decline to give it. Nor did he see any reason why he should not convey the King's directions to the Northern prelates, if Charles asked him to do so. As the King's secretary, he conveyed instructions to the Bishops, remonstrated with proceedings which shocked his sense of order, and held out prospects of advancement to the zealous. Scotchmen naturally took offence. They did not trouble themselves to distinguish between the secretary and the Archbishop. They simply said that the Pope of Canterbury was as bad as the Pope of Rome.

In the meanwhile, preparations for applying a remedy to the evils which were supposed to afflict the Church of Scotland were strenuously urged on in London. A draft of the new canons was submitted by the King to Laud and Juxon, and a draft of the new Prayer Book to Laud and Wren. The alterations proposed were forwarded to Scotland for the approval of the Scottish Bishops; but the brain which had conceived them was that of the restless Archbishop of Canterbury.

Marginalia:
CHAP. III.
1634. Growing opposition to Episcopacy.
Laud and the Scottish Bishops.
1635. The Canons and the Prayer Book.

CHAP. III.

1636.
Issue of the Canons.

The Canons authorised in 1635 were issued in the following year. In them is to be discerned an attempt to bridge over the gap between the Bishops and the Parochial Courts. There were to be diocesan and national synods; and such synods, if fairly constituted and fairly treated, might have gone far to keep the existing constitution of the Church in working order. But the mode in which these canons were issued was in itself an unmistakable intimation that Charles had no intention of seriously consulting either the clergy or the laity. They came forth to the world on the Royal authority alone. Even High Churchmen in the next generation shook their heads at the slight shown to the Church. Two or three of the Bishops had been privately consulted on the matter, and that was all.[1]

The canons thus sent into the world contained some good advice. Ministers were directed to abstain from long and tedious sermons, and to inculcate the duty of righteousness of life as well as that of doctrinal orthodoxy. Other commands there were, which no one who had the slightest respect for the feelings of Scotsmen would have thought of inserting. The Communion Table was to be placed 'at the upper end of the chancel or church.' Though 'sacramental confession and absolution' had in some places been abused, all who felt their consciences burdened were to be encouraged 'to confess their offences to the bishop or presbyter.' In every department of ministerial work the minister was to be strictly subordinated to the Bishop, and above the Bishops stood the King, whose authority was to be exercised in all ecclesiastical causes in the same way as that which 'the godly kings had among the Jews, and the Chris-

[1] Burton, *Hist. of Scotland*, vi. 397.

tian emperors in the Primitive Church.' The Prayer Book, as yet unpublished, was already placed under the guardianship of the law of the Church. To assert that it contained 'anything repugnant to the Scriptures,' or that it was 'corrupt, superstitious, or unlawful,' was to incur excommunication.[1]

CHAP. III.
———
1636.

Like the Canons, the Prayer Book was submitted to no ecclesiastical body whatever.[2] Of the few Bishops who had been consulted, not one had any knowledge of the temper of the nation; and one of them, Wedderburn, Bishop of Dumblane, had spent many years of his life in England. He strongly advocated the omission, from the sentences spoken at the Administration of the Communion, of the clauses which owed their origin to the second Prayer Book of Edward VI. These clauses, he said, seemed 'to relish somewhat of the Zwinglian tenet that the Sacrament is a bare sign, taken in remembrance of Christ's passion.' This argument, as a mere matter of reasoning, may have been good enough. The clauses from the first Prayer Book of Edward VI. which he proposed to retain lent themselves easily to the Calvinistic doctrine of a real, though spiritual presence. What was wanting to Wedderburn was the imaginative eye which could see beyond the shelves of his episcopal library to the manses of the country clergy, and the ability to discover that any unnecessary change was certain to arouse suspicion.[3] Nothing can be more unfair than to argue

The Prayer Book disliked as Popish.

---

[1] Canons. *Laud's Works*, v. 583.

[2] For the earlier history of this Prayer Book, see *Pers. Government of Charles I.*, i. 354.

[3] *Laud's Works*, iii. 357. Wedderburn, however, was not the first to originate the proposal. It is acted upon in the MS. corrections, probably made in 1628, to a Prayer Book now in the British Museum. *Egerton MSS.*, 2417.

that the authors of this unlucky liturgy had any intention of approximating to the Roman ritual; but they could hardly have given greater offence if they had introduced the missal at once. If the old forms of prayer contained in Knox's *Book of Common Order* were to be abolished, it was only natural that a bewildered people, who had not even been consulted on the subject, should ask themselves what was the hidden object with which the change had been made.

<small>The Prayer Book disliked as English.</small>

Other alterations, slight in themselves, pointed in the same direction as the omission of the strongly Protestant clauses in the Administration of the Communion. Another defect was almost equally fatal. Whether the book were Popish or not, there could be no doubt that it was English. It had been touched and re-touched by English hands. The knowledge that this had been the case was enough to make it odious in Scotland. If the gift offered by Laud had been one of priceless value, it would have been dashed scornfully aside.

<small>The moderates.</small>

In such a cause as this, the clergy and their congregations were certain to be of one mind. Here and there, no doubt, there were a few men who, like Robert Baillie, of Kilwinning, had done their best to fit themselves into the scheme of Church government which existed around them, but who kept themselves as much as possible aloof from Bishops on the one side, and from fanatics on the other. It was precisely men of this class that Charles was doing everything in his power to alienate. Yet there is every reason to believe that neither Charles nor Laud had any conception that the new Prayer Book would meet with any serious opposition. It has sometimes been asked whether Charles was urged on by love of despotism or love of religion. It does not need much knowledge of his character to see that neither of these formed the motive power. What he was doing he did from a love of order, combined with sheer ignorance of mankind. He could see nothing in the book but the decent comeliness of its arrangements and the well-chosen suitability of its expressions.[1]

To the very last, Laud thought more of polishing the language of the Prayer Book than of securing for it a favourable reception. It was printed and reprinted, till it seemed to have reached typographical perfection. In October 1636, Charles wrote to the Privy Council informing them that, 'having taken the counsel of his clergy,' he thought fit that the book should 'be used in God's public worship.' In December a proclamation ordered every parish to adopt it, and to procure two copies of it before the following Easter.[2]

Easter came, and still the book was not ready. Rumours were rife that it had been seen in England, and that it differed from the English Prayer Book 'in addition of sundry more Popish rites.' Others whispered that it was merely the Mass in disguise. As time went on, the impending danger grew more terrible in its vagueness. Yet it is worthy of notice that there was as yet no thought of resistance. The utmost to which extreme Puritans ventured to aspire was permission to form themselves into a non-conformist body, worshipping apart with the connivance of the Government.[3]

At last, in the spring of 1637, the long-dreaded

[1] One of the parts of the book which gave offence was the direction for the position of the minister at the consecration. See Burton, *Hist. of Scotland*, vi. 424. The book at Lambeth, which has Laud's annotations, differs from the Scottish book in directly ordering the eastward position. Possibly, though the handwriting is Laud's, the suggestion may have been Wren's.

[2] The King to the Council, Oct. 18. *Balfour*, ii. 224. *The Preface to the Prayer Book.*

[3] *Baillie*, i. 4.

volume reached Scotland. In May every minister received orders to buy two copies on pain of outlawry. The Bishops, though they had never consulted their synods on the preparation of the book, now called them together to urge them to obedience. Openly no word of resistance was heard. It was hard for a single minister to expose himself to certain ruin. But in private men spoke their minds more freely. The Book, they said, was more Popish than the English one. It had no authority either from Assembly or Parliament. The Scottish Puritan feeling and the Scottish national feeling were rising higher every day.

It was hardly likely that the temper thus aroused would be suffered to die away for lack of leadership. With one or two brilliant exceptions, the Scottish nobles of that day were not remarkable for ability. But they had the habit of authority which had long been lost by the English Peers, and they would ill brook the continuance of a system which placed the Bishops above their heads. It is easy to speak of the zeal of men like Rothes and Loudoun as sheer hypocrisy. It is far more likely that they felt strongly in a direction in which it was their interest to feel strongly. Men of advanced age could indeed remember that the yoke of Presbytery had once been as heavy as the yoke of Episcopacy. Men even of middle age knew nothing of Presbyterianism except by report. They saw the Bishops outvying them in the Royal favour, and reducing them to comparative insignificance even on their own estates. Whatever religious feeling was in them had been nurtured through the old Calvinistic doctrine, and jealousy for the national honour of Scotland burnt in them as strongly as in their tenants and dependents.

It is impossible to say with certainty what truth

there may be in the story that a meeting in which some of the malcontent nobles took part with the leading clergy and a few of 'the devouter sex,' was held in Edinburgh for the purpose of organising resistance.[1] Attachment to tried religious forms is always stronger in women than in men, and it may well be that some of the Edinburgh ladies stirred up the indignation of the fishwives and serving-women of the city. But no mistake would be greater than to imagine that they created the spirit which they directed. The insult to the Scottish nation and the Scottish Church was one to kindle resentment in the humble and the exalted alike.

CHAP. III.
1637. June. Alleged meeting at Edinburgh.

July 23 was at last fixed as the day on which the patience of the citizens of Edinburgh was to be put to the test, in the hope that the submission of the capital would furnish an example to the rest of the country. The confidence felt by the Bishops received a rude shock. At St. Giles', recently erected into the Cathedral Church of the new diocese of Edinburgh, a large number of maid-servants were gathered, keeping seats for their mistresses, who were in the habit of remaining at home till prayers were over and the preacher was ready to ascend the pulpit. The Dean opened the book and began to read. Shouts of disapprobation from the women drowned his voice. "The Mass," cried one, "is entered amongst us." "Baal is in the Church," called out another. Opprobrious epithets were applied to the Dean. Lindsay, the Bishop of Edinburgh, ascended the pulpit above the reading desk, and attempted to still the tumult. He begged the noisy zealots to desist from their profanation of holy ground. The words conveyed an

July 23. The reading of the Book.

The tumult at St. Giles'.

[1] The story comes from Guthry's *Memoirs*, 23. It was written down after the Restoration, and is certainly inaccurate in its details.

CHAP. III.
1637.
July 23.

idea which was utterly abhorrent to the Puritan mind, and the clamour waxed louder under the ill-judged exhortation. A stool aimed at the Bishop all but grazed the head of the Dean. At this final insult Archbishop Spottiswoode called on the magistrates to clear the church of the rioters. The noisy champions of Protestantism were with much difficulty thrust into the streets, and the doors were barred in their faces. They did not cease to knock loudly from without, and to fling stones at the windows. Amidst the crash of broken glass, the service proceeded to the end. One woman, who had remained behind unnoticed, stopped her ears with her fingers to save herself from the pollution of the idolatrous worship, whilst she read her bible to herself. Suddenly she was roused by a loud Amen from a young man behind her. "False thief!" she cried, dashing her bible in his face, "is there no other part of the kirk to sing Mass in, but thou must sing it in my lug?" When the doors were at last thrown open, and the scanty congregation attempted to withdraw, the crowd outside dashed fiercely at the Bishop. But for the intervention of the Earl of Wemyss, he would hardly have escaped alive.

The afternoon service.

Such Privy Councillors as could be hastily convened gave immediate orders to the magistrates to protect the afternoon service. Guards were marched to the church, and a select few were alone permitted to enter. Special directions were given that no woman should be allowed to pass the doors. The Earl of Roxburgh drove the Bishop home in his coach amidst a shower of stones. His footmen were obliged to draw their swords to keep off the mob.[1]

[1] Setting aside later narratives, we have two contemporary accounts to rest on, one from the King's *Large Declaration*, the other, written in a

The next day the Council met. It can hardly be doubted that its lay members sympathised heartily with any kind of resistance to the Bishops. Sir Thomas Hope, the Lord Advocate, is said to have been one of those who instigated the disturbance. Lord Lorne, the heir of the Catholic Earl of Argyle, a man of scheming brain, and consummate prudence, is not likely to have gone so far. But he shared in the prevalent feeling, and had recently come to high words with the Bishop of Galloway on the subject of the imposition of fine and imprisonment on one of his followers by the High Commission.[1] For the present, however, the guidance of affairs rested in the hands of the Lord Treasurer, the Earl of Traquair. In after times Traquair was accused of playing a double game. It is more probable that he sympathised with neither party. A cool and wary man of business, immersed in the details of government, he fell a victim to his attempt to play the moderator in the impending collision of fanaticisms. He had opposed the Bishops when they attempted to force their own ideas on an unwilling Church, especially as he had reason to believe that one of their number, Bishop Maxwell, was intriguing to supplant him as Treasurer of Scotland. But by instinct and position he disliked the domination of a mob, and especially of a mob with clerical backers. Such a man was capable of conveying words of common sense to Charles's ear, though it was most improbable that they would ever penetrate to his mind.

marginalia: CHAP. III. — 1637. July 24. The Privy Council. Sir T. Hope. Lorne. Traquair.

---

violent Puritan spirit, printed in the Appendix to Rothes' *Proceedings*. On the whole they agree very well together. Both agree that only one stool was thrown. The tradition which names Jeanie Geddes as the heroine of the day has long been abandoned. See Burton's *Hist. of Scotland*, vi. 443. Gordon's account is a mere copy of the Declaration with a few additions.   [1] *Baillie*, i. 16.

CHAP. III.
1637.
July 24.
Action of the authorities.

The Council, in appearance at least, took instant measures to carry out the King's wishes. Six or seven of the rioters were arrested. The Edinburgh ministers were assured that they might read the prayers without danger, and the magistrates were ordered to protect them in so doing. As far as words could go, the Council had done its duty. Words, however, would not suffice. Some of the ministers had no wish to read the book, and those who were willing to read the book did not wish to risk being torn in pieces by the mob. They declared that they had no confidence in the power of the magistrates to preserve order, and it is not unlikely that most of the councillors were of the same opinion. At Spottiswoode's motion, both the old and the new forms of prayer were suspended in Edinburgh till the King's pleasure could be known. The sermons were to be delivered as usual.[1]

Dissatisfaction of the King.

The King was not likely to be satisfied with such timidity. Of the difficulties of his representatives in Scotland he understood nothing. He ordered strict measures of repression to be taken. He forgot to inquire whether the Government had force enough at its disposal to enable it to carry out his orders. As soon as the magistrates attempted to do as they were bidden, they found that the rioters had all Edinburgh at their backs. The Privy Council gave to the magistrates but a lukewarm support. Its lay members threw the blame on the Bishops. The Bishops threw it back on the laymen. Laud, writing by the King's orders, distributed it equally between both. He scouted the idea of abandoning the Prayer Book because a band of secret conspirators had hounded on an unruly mob against it. It was un-

Aug. 7.
Laud's view of the case.

[1] *Baillie*, i. 18, 447. Gordon, *Hist. of Scots Affairs*, i. 12.

worthy of the Bishops, he said, to disclaim the book as their own. It was their work, and it was for them to support it. "Will they now," he added, "cast down the milk they have given because a few milk-maids have scolded at them? I hope they will be better advised."[1]

1637. Aug. 7.

It was easy to write thus in the safe privacy of Lambeth. It was hard to obey the command at Edinburgh. The magistrates stated plainly that no one would read the service on any conditions. They had offered a large sum of money to any one who would do so, but none had been found sufficiently hardy to accept the offer.[2]

Aug. 19. Failure to enforce the King's orders.

The viragoes of St. Giles' were backed by the population of Edinburgh. If Edinburgh were backed by Scotland, Charles would have work enough before him. A threat of outlawing the ministers who had refused to purchase their two copies of the Prayer Book, put the feeling of the country clergy to the test. Petitions drawn up in due legal form began to drop in upon the Council. The only one which has reached us was drawn up by Alexander Henderson, Minister of Leuchars. Its wording carried the controversy out of the region of passion into the region of argument. Henderson descended into the strife as a champion worthy of a great cause. He had not leapt forward impatiently to testify his displeasure at the proceedings of the Bishops. He had not been hasty to judge the practice of kneeling at the Communion as altogether evil. The time had now come when it behoved every honourable man who believed, as he believed, in the old Scottish creed, to lift up his voice on behalf of his Church and nation. Hen-

Aug. 23. Henderson's petition.

---

[1] Laud to Traquair, Aug. 7. *Works,* vi. 493.
[2] The Magistrates to Laud, Aug. 19. *Large Declaration,* 28.

CHAP. III.
1637.
Aug. 23.

derson would not be the more likely to hang back in the end, because his protest was studiously moderate now. He did not say, as so many others were saying, that the new Prayer Book was actually Popish, but he professed his readiness to argue that it contained matters 'far from the form and worship and reformation' of the 'Kirk,' and 'drawing near in material points to the Church of Rome.' It was not in this reasoning, however, that the main stress of his argument lay. The old form of worship, he said, had been recognised by Assembly and Parliament. The new form of worship had been recognised by neither. Further, the Church of Scotland was free and independent. Its own pastors knew best what was suitable to their people, who 'would be found unwilling to the change when they should be assayed.'[1]

Meaning of Henderson's protest.

In these sober words, Henderson raised a standard of resistance for the Scottish people. He did not plead the cause of Presbyterianism against Episcopacy. He simply announced that the religion of a people was under its own guardianship.

Charles cannot draw back.

Charles was in a great strait. Humiliating as it would have been, a frank acknowledgment of his mistake would doubtless have been his wisest course. But the shock which his authority would receive would not be limited to Scottish ground. What was true in Scotland was also true in England, and the artificial edifice of the Laudian Church would feel the blow struck at the house of cards which had been built up beyond the Tweed. Nor was it easy to persuade Charles that the riot in Edinburgh had been a genuine result of popular indignation. He saw in it only the concealed hands of the angry nobles, grasping at Church lands, and at the dignities worthily accorded to men who were better than themselves.

[1] Supplication. *Baillie*, i. 449.

Yet how was Charles to procure obedience in Scotland? Military force he had none, and the Scottish Council was likely to yield him but a half-hearted support, even if it yielded him any support at all. Only in five or six places was the Prayer Book read. When Henderson appeared before the Council, he was accompanied by a crowd of gentry. Letters which poured in from distant parts left no doubt that the feeling in his favour was not confined to the neighbourhood of the capital. Even if the Council had been willing to take severe measures, it would have been helpless to overcome resistance. Henderson was told that he had been ordered to buy the books, not to read them. "We found ourselves," wrote the Council to Charles, "far by our expectations surprised with the clamours and fears of your Majesty's subjects from almost all the parts and corners of the kingdom, and that even of those who otherways had heretofore lived in obedience and conformity to your Majesty's laws, both in ecclesiastical and civil business, and thus we find it so to increase that we conceive it to be a matter of high consequence in respect of the general murmur and grudge in all sorts of people for urging of the practice of the Service Book, as the like hath not been heard in this kingdom." They could therefore only leave it to his Majesty, 'in the deepness of his Royal judgment, to provide a remedy.'[1]

Charles had no remedy to provide. He sent back a scolding answer, in which he found fault with everyone except himself, and ordered the immediate enforcement of the use of the Prayer Book. No

---

[1] Act of Council, Aug. 25. The Scottish Council to the King, *Baillie*, i. 449, 451. Traquair to Hamilton, Aug. 27. Burnet, *Lives of the Dukes of Hamilton*, ii. 18.

CHAP. III.
1637.

Sept. 18.
The new Provost of Edinburgh.

General resistance.

Sept. 20.

Sept. 25.
Second riot in Edinburgh.

magistrates were to be allowed to hold office in any borough who would not give their support to the new service.¹ In Edinburgh a few partisans of Charles's ecclesiastical system were still to be found amongst the official class. Sir John Hay, the Clerk Register, was thrust as Provost upon the unwilling townsmen. Nowhere else was such an arrangement possible. "If it were urged," wrote Baillie, "we could have in all our towns no magistrates at all, or very contemptible ones."² Those ministers who in any place tried to read the book were roughly handled, especially by the women. When the Council met to take the King's last letter into consideration, it was evident that nothing could be done to carry out his orders. Petitions poured in from every quarter. Twenty noblemen, with a crowd of gentlemen and ministers in their train, appeared to enforce by their presence the language of the petitions.³ The Council could but assure Charles that they had done their best, sending him, at the same time, the petitions, sixty-eight in number, for his perusal.⁴

Before long there was worse news to be told. The new Provost had attempted to hinder the town from sending in a petition against the Prayer Book. An angry mob burst into the Tolbooth, where the Town Council was in session. "The Book," they shouted, "we will never have." They forced the magistrates to promise that the petition should be sent. This second entry of the mob upon the scene shocked some even of those who had no love for the Bishops. "What shall be the event," wrote Baillie,

¹ The King to the Council, Sept. 12. *Baillie*, i. 452.
² *Ibid.* i. 25.   ³ *Rothes*, 7. *Baillie*, i. 33.
⁴ The Council to the King, Sept. 20. *Baillie*, i. 453.

"God knows. There was in our land never such an appearance of a stir. The whole people thinks Popery at the doors. . . . No man may speak anything in public for the King's part, except he would have himself marked for a sacrifice to be killed one day. I think our people possessed with a bloody devil, far above anything that ever I could have imagined, though the Mass in Latin had been presented. The ministers who have the command of their mind do disavow their unchristian humour, but are no ways so zealous against the devil of their fury as they are against the seducing spirit of the Bishops."[1]

CHAP. III.
1637.
Sept. 25.

If such was the language of a Scottish minister, what must have been Charles's indignation? The courtiers at Whitehall might persuade themselves that but for Laud's interference he would have given way.[2] It is far more likely that, whether Laud had been there or not, he would have persisted in the course which he believed to be the course of duty. "I mean to be obeyed," were the words which rose to his lips when he was interrogated as to his intentions.[3]

Persistence of Charles.

Even Charles, however, could see that he could not expect to be obeyed at once. He must postpone, he wrote, his answer on the main subject of the petitions. For the present, therefore, the Council were to do nothing in the matter of religion. But they must try to punish the ringleaders of the late disturbances, and they must order all strangers to leave Edinburgh on pain of outlawry.[4] Another

Oct. 9.
His directions to the Council.

The Council and the Court of Session to be removed.

---
[1] *Baillie*, i. 23.
[2] Correr's Despatches, Sept. $\frac{15}{28}$, $\frac{Sept. 27}{Oct. 7}$. *Venetian MSS.*
[3] Con to Barberini, Oct. $\frac{13}{23}$; *Add. MSS.*, 15,390, fol. 453.
[4] The King to the Council, Oct. 9; *Balfour*, ii. 23.

letter directed the removal of the Council and the Court of Session—first to Linlithgow, and afterwards to Dundee.[1]

If Charles had had no more than a riot to deal with, it would have been well that the offending city should learn that the lucrative presence of the organs of government and justice could only be secured by submission to the law. Because he had more than a riot to deal with, his blow recoiled on himself. He had chosen to fling a defiance in the face of the Scottish nation, and he must take the consequences.

When these letters arrived in Edinburgh the petitioners had returned to their homes, not expecting so speedy an answer. But they had left behind the shrewdest of lawyers, Archibald Johnston of Warriston, and Johnston at once gave the alarm. On October 17 they were back again, black-gowned ministers and gay noblemen, waiting for what might befal. In the evening the substance of the King's orders was proclaimed from that Market Cross,[2] where, according to legend, a ghostly visitant had taken his stand to summon Charles's ancestor from the field of Flodden to the judgment-seat of God. The simple officer who read the formal words of the proclamation was as truly the messenger of ill to Charles. He was pointing to the track which led to the battle-field, the prison, and the scaffold.

The next morning all Edinburgh was astir. The city had not, like London, an independent commercial life of its own. To lose the Council and the Court of Session was to dwindle to the insignificance of a provincial town. The inhabitants, whose very means

---

[1] This letter has not been preserved, but is referred to in a subsequent proclamation.
[2] Proclamations, Oct. 17; *Large Declaration*, 33.

of livelihood was at stake, raved against the Bishops as the cause of the mischief. Bishop Sydserf, of Galloway, who was reported to wear a crucifix beneath his dress, was driven by an angry crowd to take refuge in the Council House. Another crowd surrounded the magistrates, and insisted on their joining in a protest. The magistrates, glad to escape with their lives, did all that was required. The mob still thronged the streets, shouting, "God defend all those who will defend God's cause, and God confound the Service Book and all the maintainers of it." Traquair came out to quell the tumult. Hustled and thrown down, he struggled back with loss of hat and cloak, as well as of his white rod of office. Sydserf was still a prisoner in the Council House. The Provost declared that he was unable to help him. No one else ventured to move a finger in his behalf. One course, dishonourable as it was, remained to be tried. The noblemen and gentry who had been ordered the day before to leave Edinburgh were sitting in consultation on the best way of opposing the King's orders. To them the King's Council sent, begging them to use their influence with the enraged multitude. What the King's representatives were powerless to effect, his opponents did with the greatest ease. The Lord Provost of Edinburgh and the whole body of the Privy Council, including the fugitive Bishop, only reached their homes under the protection of the men who were treated as rebels by their master.[1]

Forty-one years earlier, Charles's father had quelled a Presbyterian riot by the removal of the

Contrast between Charles and his father.

---

[1] *Rothes,* 19. *Large Declaration,* 35. Gordon again simply borrows from the Declaration. It is quite a mistake to treat him, as Mr. Burton does, as an original authority for these events.

CHAP. III.
1637.
Oct. 18.

Council and the Court of Session from Edinburgh. He had been able to do so because he had the nobility and the country at large on his side. The men who guarded his Councillors through the streets were no longer, as their fathers had been, on the side of the King against the Capital.

The General Supplication.

The reply of the petitioners was a General Supplication, in which the Bishops were pointed at as the authors of the calamities of the Church. Charles was asked to allow them to be put on their trial, and, as they were now parties in the case, to prohibit them from sitting in the Council as judges of matters relating to the present dispute.[1]

The petitioners assume the offensive.

The petitioners had thus changed their defence into an attack. Not we, they said in effect, but the Bishops are the breakers of the law. The demand that the Bishops should not be judges in their own case was the same as that which, four months before, had been received with derision when it proceeded from the lips of Bastwick in the English Star Chamber. In the heat of discussion before the Council, Bishop Sydserf and Hay threw out a suggestion which had unexpected consequences. Why should not the mass of the petitioners return home, leaving behind a few of their number to speak in their name? The petitioners took them at their word. They chose a body of Commissioners from amongst themselves. From that moment, if the nation rallied round the new Commissioners, it would have a government, and that government would not be the King's. There were no more riots in Edinburgh.[2]

They choose Commissioners.

Oct. 19.
Traquair's proposal.

To a man of practical instincts, like Traquair, the outlook was indeed pitiable. "I am in all things,"

[1] *Large Declaration*, 42.   [2] *Rothes*, 17. *Baillie*, 35, 38.

he wrote, "left alone, and, God is my witness, never so perplexed what to do. Shall I give way to this people's fury which, without force and the strong hand, cannot be opposed?" It was hard for him to believe that a compromise was no longer possible. Why, he asked Rothes, could they not agree to accept the English.Prayer Book as it stood? Rothes would not hear of it, and the resolution of Rothes was the resolution of his countrymen.[1]

<small>CHAP. III.
1637.
Oct. 19.</small>

On November 15, the petitioners returned to Edinburgh. Their Commissioners, hastily chosen, were to give way to a more permanent body, composed of six or more noblemen, two gentlemen from each shire, one townsman from each borough, and one minister from each Presbytery. Traquair, seeing that authority was slipping out of his hands, remonstrated warmly; but Sir Thomas Hope, the Presbyterian Lord Advocate, gave an opinion that the petitioners were acting within their rights, and further opposition was impossible.[2]

<small>Nov. 15. Organisation of the Commissioners.</small>

In the persons of the Commissioners, Scotland waited, not impatiently, for an answer. If Charles could frankly abandon the Service Book, as Elizabeth had once abandoned the monopolies, he might, perhaps, have saved some fragments of authority for the Bishops. He could not even make up his mind to announce his intentions plainly. On December 7, a proclamation issued at Linlithgow, where the Council, in obedience to the King, was now sitting, declared that, on account of the riots at Edinburgh, the answer to the supplication would be delayed. All that Charles had to say was, that he abhorred Popery, and would consent to nothing which did not

<small>Scotland waits for an answer.</small>

<small>Dec. 7. The proclamation at Linlithgow.</small>

---

[1] Traquair to Hamilton, Oct. 19; *Hardw. St. P.* ii. 95. *Rothes*, 22.
[2] *Ibid.* 23.

CHAP. III.

1637.
Dec. 7.

tend to the advancement of the true religion as it was 'presently professed' in Scotland. "Nothing," the proclamation ended by saying, "is or was intended to be done therein against the laudable laws of this His Majesty's native kingdom."[1]

Dec. 21.
The Supplication and Declinator.

Scotsmen had made up their minds with almost complete unanimity that those laudable laws had been broken. In vain Traquair begged that the King should be propitiated. The deputation from the City of Edinburgh might wait on him at Whitehall, ' offering him their charter and the keys of their gates,' as a mere matter of course.[2] The Com-

Dec. 8.

missioners would not hear of the suggestion.[3] It must be settled once for all, whether it was in accordance with the law of Scotland that a king could change the forms of worship without the sanction of any legislative assembly whatever.

Dec. 21.
Protest against the Bishops remaining in the Council.

At last, on December 21, a copy of the General Supplication which had been drawn up in October, was formally handed in by the Commissioners to the Privy Council, accompanied by a formal demand that the case between themselves and the Bishops might be judicially determined, and that the Bishops might in the meanwhile be removed from the Council.

1638.
Feb.
Traquair in London.

Before long, Charles sent for Traquair, to hear from his own mouth his opinion on the state of affairs in Scotland. It would have been well if he had more seriously attended to that cool and dispassionate adviser. The Lord Treasurer assured him that the Scottish people had no wish to cast off his authority, but they would not look on idly whilst their religion was assailed. Above all, they were proud of their

---

[1] Proclamation, Dec. 7; *Large Declaration*, 46.
[2] *Rothes*, 43.
[3] Bill and Declinator, Dec. 21; *Ibid.* 50.

ancient independence, and they would not take orders from the Archbishop of Canterbury.¹ His Majesty must plainly understand, that if he wished the new Prayer Book to be read in Scotland, he must support it with an army of 40,000 men.

To withdraw the Service Book and to assert his civil authority, was the substance of this advice. Charles listened, but was not convinced. Traquair was sent back with orders to issue a proclamation which was virtually a declaration of war.²

That proclamation was read on February 19, in the streets of Stirling, where the Council, after leaving Linlithgow, had been allowed to take up its quarters, rather than in the more distant Dundee. Charles truly asserted that he, and not the Bishops, was responsible for the issue of the Prayer Book. "As much," he said, "as we, out of our princely care of maintenance of the true religion already professed, and for beating down of all superstition, having ordained a Book of Common Prayer to be compiled for the general use and edification of our subjects within our ancient kingdom of Scotland, the same was accordingly done, in the performing whereof we took great care and pains so as nothing passed therein but what was seen and approved by us, before the same was either divulged or printed, assuring all our loving subjects that not only our intention is, but even the very book will be a ready means to maintain

---

¹ Zonca's Despatches, Jan. $\frac{19}{29}$, Feb. $\frac{2}{12}$, $\frac{Feb. 24}{March 5}$. *Ven. Transcripts.*

² "Your Lordship can best witness how unwilling I was that our master should have directed such a proclamation; and I had too just grounds to foretell the danger and inconveniences which are now like to ensue thereupon." Traquair to Hamilton, March 5; *Hardw. St. P.* ii. 101. Mr. Burton must have overlooked this passage when he wrote that the proclamation was 'too nearly in the tone of the advice which Traquair had given.' *Hist. of Scotland,* vi. 477.

the true religion already professed, and beat out all superstition, of which we in our time do not doubt but in a fair course to satisfy our good subjects." His Royal authority, he proceeded to say, was much impaired by the petitions and declarations which had been sent to him. All who had taken part in them were liable to 'high censure, both in their persons and their fortunes, as having convened themselves without his permission. He was, however, ready to pass over their fault, provided that they returned home at once, and abstained from all further meetings. If they disobeyed, he should hold them liable to the penalties of treason.'[1]

Charles could not see why, if the Prayer Book had satisfied himself, it should not satisfy others. The objection that it had no legal authority he treated with contemptuous disregard. All the more tenaciously did the Scottish leaders cling to legal forms. As soon as the herald had finished his task, Johnston stepped forward to protest against it in their name. They treated the proclamation as the work of the Council alone, and announced that from that body they would accept no orders as long as the Bishops retained their places in it. They demanded to have recourse to their 'sacred sovereign, to present their grievances and in a legal way to prosecute the same before the ordinary competent judges, civil or ecclesiastical.'[2]

If this appeal to the law was to have any weight with Charles, it must be supported by an appeal to the nation. Rothes, who had been placed by his energy and decision at the head of the movement, despatched a circular letter to the gentlemen who

[1] Proclamation, Feb. 19; *Large Declaration*, 48.
[2] Protestation, Feb. 19; *Ibid.* 50.

had not hitherto supported the cause, urging them to lose no time in giving in their adhesion. The next step was to complete the work of organisation. The Commissioners appointed in November had been found too large a body to act as a central authority. From time to time a select Committee had been appointed to communicate with the Council, and that Committee had been naturally selected from the different classes of which the nation was composed. Four separate Committees were now appointed; one formed of all noblemen who might choose to attend, the other three of four gentlemen, four ministers and four borough representatives respectively. These Committees might meet either separately or as one body. Sometimes to them, and sometimes to the larger body of the Commissioners, the name of The Tables was given, in the popular language of the day.[1]

These Committees might form an unauthorised government, and the Commissioners an unauthorised parliament. But unless more were done, they would speak in their own name alone. Even Rothes's circular had been directed only to the upper classes.

CHAP. III.

1638. Feb. 19. The Tables set up.

Feb. 23. An appeal to the nation necessary.

[1] The question of the exact meaning of The Tables is not easy to answer. Row (*Hist. of the Kirk*, 486) speaks of the Commissioners by this name. Gordon, who is followed by Mr. Burton, confuses the Commissioners with the Committees. The *Large Declaration* puts the appointment of The Tables at this date, limiting the number of the noblemen to four. I follow Rothes, in whose *Relation* the gradual development of The Tables can be traced. The Commissioners were chosen on Nov. 15 (p. 23). On Nov. 16 thirteen were solicited to wait on the Council (p. 26). On the 18th six of the gentry and some representatives of the boroughs remained in Edinburgh (p. 32). In December six or seven noblemen met with four out of each of the other classes to hold communication with the Council (p. 34). On Dec. 19 we hear of only twelve performing this office (p. 38). On Feb. 22 we are told, 'there was one Committee chosen of four barons, four boroughs, and four ministers, to join with the noblemen,' the number not being specified (p. 69). This seems to have been the ultimate form taken. At one important meeting on June 9 (p. 146) there were six noblemen present.

CHAP. III.
1638.
Feb. 23.

It was necessary to touch the multitude. The thousands to whom it was a matter of indifference whether the Church were ruled by Bishops or by Presbyters, had been deeply wounded by the threatened interference with their worship. The plan by which this inarticulate dissatisfaction was converted into a definite force was suggested by Archibald Johnston.

Proposal to renew the covenant of 1580.

In the days in which life and property had found no security from the law, the nobility and gentry of Scotland had been in the habit of entering into 'bands' or obligations for mutual protection. In 1581, when the country was threatened by a confederacy of Catholic noblemen at home, supported by a promise of assistance from Spain, James had called on all loyal subjects to enter into such a 'band' or covenant. Those who had signed this covenant pledged themselves to renounce the Papal doctrines, to submit to the discipline of the Scottish Church, and to 'defend the same according to their vocation and power.' Johnston and Henderson were now entrusted with the composition of additions to this covenant appropriate to the actual circumstances, in order that the whole might be sent round to be subscribed by all who wished to throw in their lot with the resistance of the upper classes. As soon as Johnston and Henderson had completed their work it was revised by Rothes, Loudoun, and Balmerino, and on the 27th it was laid before the two or three hundred ministers who happened to be in Edinburgh at the time.[1]

Feb. 27.

The additions to the covenant.

The additions proposed consisted in the first place of a long string of citations of Acts of Parliament passed in the days of Presbyterian ascendency. To touch the heart of the people, something more than this was needed. "We," so ran the words which

[1] *Rothes*, 69.

were soon to be sent forth to every cottage in the land, "Noblemen, Barons, Gentlemen, Burgesses, Ministers, and Commons undersubscribing, considering divers times before, and especially at this time, the danger of the true reformed religion, of the King's honour, and of the public peace of the Kingdom, by the manifold innovations and evils generally contained and particularly mentioned in our late supplications, complaints, and protestations, do hereby profess, and before God, His angels, and the world, solemnly declare that with our whole hearts we agree and resolve all the days of our life constantly to adhere unto and to defend the foresaid true religion, and—forbearing the practice of all novations already introduced in the matters of the worship of God, or approbation of the corruptions of the public government of the kirk or civil places and powers of kirkmen, till they be tried and allowed in the Assemblies and in Parliaments—to labour by all means lawful to recover the purity and liberty of the Gospel, as it was established and professed before the foresaid novations. And because, after due examination, we plainly perceive, and undoubtedly believe, that the innovations and evils contained in our supplications, complaints, and protestations, have no warrant in the Word of God, are contrary to the articles of the foresaid confessions, to the intention and meaning of the blessed reformers of religion in this land, to the above-written Acts of Parliament, and do sensibly tend to the re-establishing of the Popish religion and tyranny, and to the subversion and ruin of the true reformed religion and of our liberties, laws, and estates; we also declare that the foresaid confessions are to be interpreted and ought to be understood of the foresaid novations and evils, no less

CHAP. III.
1638.
Feb. 27.

CHAP. III.
1638.
Feb. 27.

than if every one of them had been expressed in the foresaid confessions, and that we are obliged to detest and abhor them amongst other particular heads of papistry abjured therein; and therefore from the knowledge and conscience of our duty to God, to our King and country, without any worldly respect or inducement, so far as human infirmity will suffer, wishing a further measure of the grace of God for this effect, we promise and swear, by the great name of the Lord our God, to continue in the profession and obedience of the foresaid religion, that we shall defend the same and resist all these contrary errors and corruptions, according to our vocation, and to the uttermost of that power that God hath put in our hands all the days of our life; and in like manner with the same heart, we declare before God and men that we have no intention nor desire to attempt anything that may turn to the dishonour of God, or to the diminution of the King's greatness and authority; but on the contrary, we promise and swear that we shall, to the uttermost of our power with our means and lives, stand to the defence of our dread Sovereign, the King's Majesty, his person and authority, in the defence of the foresaid true religion, liberties, and laws of the kingdom; as also to the mutual defence and assistance, every one of us of another in the same cause of maintaining the true religion and his Majesty's authority, with our best counsel, our bodies, means, and whole power, against all sorts of persons whatsoever; so that whatsoever shall be done to the least of us for that cause shall be taken as done to us all in general and to every one of us in particular; and that we shall neither directly nor indirectly suffer ourselves to be divided or withdrawn by whatsoever suggestion, combination, allurement, or terror from this blessed and loyal conjunction, nor shall cast in any let or impediment that may stay or hinder any such resolution, as by common consent be found to conduce for so good ends; but, on the contrary, shall by all lawful means labour to further and promote the same, and if any such dangerous and divisive motion be made to us by word or writ, we and every one of us shall either suppress it, or if need be shall incontinent make the same known, that it may be timeously obviated; neither do we fear the foul aspersions of rebellion, combination, or what else our adversaries from their craft and malice would put upon us, seeing what we do is so well warranted and ariseth from an unfeigned desire to maintain the true worship of God, the majesty of our King, and the peace of the kingdom for the common happiness of ourselves and the posterity; and because we cannot look for a blessing from God upon our proceedings, except with our profession and subscription we join such a life and conversation as beseemeth Christians who have renewed their covenant with God, we therefore faithfully promise for ourselves, our followers, and all others under us, both in public, in our particular families and personal carriage, to endeavour to keep ourselves within the bounds of Christian liberty, and to be good examples to others of all godliness, soberness, and righteousness, and of every duty we owe to God and man; and that this our union and conjunction may be observed without violation, we call the living God, the searcher of our hearts, to witness, who knoweth this to be our sincere desire and unfeigned resolution, as we shall answer to Jesus Christ in the great day and under the pain of God's everlasting wrath, and of infamy and of loss of all honour and respect in this world; most humbly

CHAP. III.

1638. Feb. 27.

130   THE SCOTTISH COVENANT.

CHAP. III.
1638.
Feb. 27.

beseeching the Lord to strengthen us by His Holy Spirit for this end, and to bless our desires and proceedings with a happy success, that religion and righteousness may flourish in the land, to the glory of God, the honour of our King, and peace and comfort of us all." [1]

The Covenant signed by the nobility and gentry;

The Covenant thus worded was cheerfully accepted by the ministers to whom it was proposed.[2] On the 28th it was carried to the Grey Friars' Church, to which all the gentlemen present in Edinburgh had been summoned. Henderson and Dickson, a minister even more enthusiastic than himself, were prepared to give satisfaction to all who expressed doubt. Few came forward to criticise, and those few were easily persuaded. At four o'clock in the grey winter evening, the noblemen, the Earl of Sutherland leading the way, began to sign. Then came the gentlemen, one

March 1, by the clergy;

after the other, till nearly eight. The next day the ministers were called on to testify their approval, and nearly three hundred signatures were obtained before night. The Commissioners of the boroughs signed at the same time.[3]

March 2, and by the people.

On the third day the people of Edinburgh were called on to attest their devotion to the cause which was represented by the Covenant. Tradition long loved to tell how the honoured parchment, carried back to the Grey Friars, was laid out on a tombstone in the churchyard, whilst weeping multitudes pressed round in numbers too great to be contained in any building. There are moments when the stern Scottish nature breaks out into an enthusiasm less passionate, but more enduring, than the frenzy of a Southern race. As each man and woman stepped forward in turn, with the right hand raised to heaven

[1] *Large Declaration*, 57.   [2] *Rothes*, 71.   [3] *Ibid.* 79.

before the pen was grasped, every one there present knew that there would be no flinching amongst that band of brothers till their religion was safe from intrusive violence.¹

CHAP.
1638.
March 2.

Modern narrators may well turn their attention to the picturesqueness of the scene, to the dark rocks of the Castle crag over against the churchyard, and to the earnest faces around. The men of the seventeenth century had no thought to spare for the earth beneath or for the sky above. What they saw was their country's faith trodden under foot, what they felt was the joy of those who had been long led astray, and had now returned to the Shepherd and Bishop of their souls.

No one in Scotland had so much reason as Traquair to regret the King's ill-advised persistency. "Many things have been complained on," he wrote on the first day of signature; "but the Service Book, which they conceive by this proclamation, and the King's taking the same upon himself, to be in effect of new ratified, is that which troubles them most; and truly, in my judgment, it shall be as easy to establish the missal in this kingdom as the Service Book, as it is conceived. The not urging the present practice thereof does no way satisfy them, because they conceive that what is done in the delaying thereof is but only to prepare things the better for the urging of the same at a more convenient time; and, believe me, as yet I see not a probability of power within this kingdom to force them; and whoever has informed the King's Majesty otherwise, either of the Book itself or of the disposition of the subjects to obey his

Feb. 28.
Traquair's letter.

---

¹ The general signature is not described in contemporary accounts. The 28th and 1st were too fully occupied, and I have therefore assigned it to the 2nd, though there is no direct evidence about the date.

K 2

Majesty's commandments, it is high time every man be put to make good his own part."¹

Such views were not confined to Traquair. Spottiswoode, speaking on behalf of the Bishops, avowed to the Council that peace was hopeless unless the Service Book were openly withdrawn. The Council itself was of the same opinion, and they despatched one of their number to the King to implore him to listen to the grievances of his subjects, and to suspend all those orders which had given rise to the late disturbances."²

It is hardly likely that even the promptest acceptance of this advice would now have appeased the Scottish nation. The Covenant had appealed to Assembly and Parliament as the legal basis of the national religion, and no mere withdrawal of the obnoxious orders would now suffice. An Assembly and Parliament must meet to pronounce those orders to have been utterly and scandalously illegal.

Even the lesser demand of the Council met with apparently insuperable resistance in Charles's mind. He knew well that it was not the fortune of Scotland only which was involved in his decision. Englishmen about him, he believed, in all probability with truth, were already in correspondence with the Northern malcontents, and were hoping that the example which had been set at Edinburgh might one day be followed in London. His Scottish servants were not lacking in sympathy with their countrymen. One poor example was made. Archie Armstrong, the King's fool, railed at Laud in his cups as a monk, a rogue, and a traitor. Laud was unwise enough to complain to the King. The unlucky jester was called before

¹ Traquair to Hamilton, Feb. 28; *Hardw. St. P.*, ii. 99.
² Extracts from the Register of the Privy Council. *Baillie*, i. 458.

the Council, sentenced to have his coat pulled over his ears, to be discharged from the King's service, and to be sent before the Star Chamber for further punishment. The Star Chamber would probably have ordered him to be soundly flogged, but Laud at last interfered, and Archie escaped the lash.[1]

CHAP. III.
1638. March 17.

Others besides Archie bore ill will to Laud as the adviser of the King's refusal to content the Scots. The English Privy Councillors protested that they were not responsible for conduct on which their advice had not been asked. Charles was only annoyed at their evident belief that he had been acting under Laud's dictation. In an angry voice he assured the Council that he had never taken the advice of any Englishman in the affairs of Scotland.[2]

The English Councillors throw the blame on Laud.

It needs no proof to show that Charles's policy of procrastination was indeed his own. Week after week passed away, with no resolution taken. The Covenanters were not so remiss. By the end of April well-nigh the whole of Scotland had rallied to their cause. In every town, in every village, in every secluded nook, the most influential landowners, the most eloquent preachers were ready to pour their arguments into willing ears. No doubt, as in every such movement, much is to be laid to the account of the excellence of the organisation provided by its leaders. Much of the reasoning used would hardly bear the test of a critical examination. Charles's Service Book certainly did not deserve all the hard things that were said of it. None the less was the resistance of Scotland the result of a determination to be true to the motto of the Scottish Thistle. Scotland

The King's procrastination.

April. Circulation of the Covenant.

[1] *Council Register*, March 11, 17. Garrard to Wentworth, March 20. *Straf. Letters*, ii. 152. *Rushw.* ii. 47.
[2] Zonca's Despatches, March 23 30 / Apr. 2 9. *Ven. Transcripts*.

has never at any time distinguished itself as the originator of new ideas in religion or government; but it has ever shown itself to be possessed of the most indispensable quality of a hardy and vigorous people, the determination to be itself, and not what external force might choose to make it. The Scottish nation had done well to pay a heavy price in the thirteenth century for its political independence. It did well in the seventeenth century to pay a heavy price for its ecclesiastical independence. For the sake of that, it renounced the wide sympathies of the cultured intellect, and hardened its heart like a flint against all forms of spiritual religion which did not accord with the fixed dogmatic teaching which it had borrowed from Geneva. Calvinism had but scant regard for the liberty of the individual conscience. Its preachers felt themselves called upon to set forth the unalterable law, and the law which they preached came back to them in the voice of their congregations. In the many there was no sense of any restriction placed upon themselves. To the few it became an insupportable tyranny—a tyranny which would be more than ordinarily felt in the hours of danger through which the nation was then passing. To reject the Covenant was not merely to differ in belief from the multitude; it was to be a traitor to the country, to be ready to help on the foreign invasion which would soon be gathering in the South. Those who still held out were met with dark looks and threatening gestures. "The greater that the number of subscribents grew," we hear from one who remembered that time well, "the more imperious they were in exacting subscriptions from others who refused to subscribe, so that by degrees they proceeded to contumelies and reproaches, and some were threatened and beaten who durst refuse, especially in the greatest cities—as likewise in other smaller towns—namely, at Edinburgh, St. Andrews, Glasgow, Lanark, and many other places. Gentlemen and noblemen carried copies of it about in their portmantles and pockets, requiring subscription thereunto, and using their utmost endeavours with their friends in private for to subscribe. It was subscribed publicly in churches, ministers exhorting their people thereunto. It was also subscribed and sworn privately. All had power to take the oath, and were licensed and welcome to come in, and any that pleased had power and license for to carry the Covenant about with him, and give the oath to such as were willing to subscribe and swear. And such was the zeal of many subscribents that, for a while, many subscribed with tears on their cheeks, and it is constantly reported that some did draw their own blood, and used it in place of ink to underscribe their names. Such ministers as spoke most for it were heard so passionately and with such frequency, that churches would not contain their hearers in cities. . . . Nor were they scrupulous to give the Covenant to such as startled, at any point thereof, with such protestations as in some measure were destructive to the sense thereof; so that they got subscriptions enough thereunto; and it came to that height in the end, that such as refused to subscribe were accounted by the rest who subscribed no better than Papists."[1]

If honour be due to the nation which refused to shift its religion at the word of command, honour is also due to those who, from whatever conscientious motive, refused to sign their names to a lie for the sake of peace. Such men went about the streets of Edinburgh in fear of their lives. David Michell, one

[1] *Gordon*, 45.

of the recusant ministers, was dogged by gentlemen with drawn swords. The cry of "If we had the Popish villain" was thrown at him as he passed.[1] Yet it is worthy of notice that these threats led to nothing worse. No bloodshed, except in avowed war, stained the cause of the Covenant.

Practically the nation was united. A few great landowners stood aloof from the movement. A few amongst the clergy took alarm. Scholars like Drummond of Hawthornden dreaded the rising flood of popular passion which threatened to overwhelm their quiet studies. Some there were who signed in defiance of their conviction, and many more who signed in ignorance of the meaning of their promises. But on the whole the nation swayed forward under the influence of strong excitement, as the cornfield sways before the breeze.

To the King the Scottish Covenant was much more than an assertion of Puritanism. By its appeal from himself to Parliament and Assembly, it was in his eyes something very like a declaration of Republicanism. Yet, resolved as he was to resist such pretensions to the uttermost, he knew not where to turn for the force which he needed. Though he had little idea how deep the dissatisfaction in England was, he knew enough to be aware that there were many of his subjects who would not fight very enthusiastically in this cause. Army he had none, in the sense of a disciplined body of men, ready to act independently of the state of popular opinion, and his fleet would not be of much avail unless it could be used in support of an army.

It was at least possible to do something to improve the organisation of the navy. The Navy Commission

[1] Nichell to the Bishop of Raphoe, March 19, *Baillie*, i. 263.

which had been appointed on Buckingham's death was still in office, and Charles had perhaps intended that it should remain in office till his second son, James, whom he had created Duke of York, and who was not yet five years old, should become capable of performing the duties of a Lord Admiral. In view of the approaching conflict, it was necessary that some other arrangement should be made. Northumberland, who had commanded the fleet on its last year's cruise, was therefore created Lord Admiral during the King's pleasure. At the same time an instrument conveying the office to the young Prince was executed, and consigned to the safe recesses of the Council chest, to be drawn forth whenever the King wished it to be put in force.[1]

 Northumberland fell ill shortly after his appointment, and was therefore unable to command the fleet in person. Even if it had been otherwise, no scheme of warlike preparation had been framed in which the fleet could possibly have taken part. Charles fell back on diplomacy. It was necessary for him 'to gain time' till he might be able to intervene with effect. Yet it would be to misunderstand his character and position, to suppose, as has been so often supposed, that he had made up his mind to deceive the Scots by offering concessions which he never intended to make. He knew that he must abandon the position which he had taken up in the previous summer. He would modify the Court of High Commission, and would give assurance not to press the Canons and the Service Book, except in 'such a fair and legal way as' should satisfy his subjects; that he intended no 'innovation in religion or laws.' So far he was pre-

---

[1] Northumberland's appointment, April 13; *Patent Rolls*, 13 Charles I., Part 38. *Council Register*, April 18.

CHAP. III.
1638.
May.

pared to go. But he was strongly of opinion that the Scots would not be content with this. He believed that their leaders at least were bent upon throwing off his lawful authority. The Covenant must therefore be surrendered as a standard of rebellion.[1] Spottiswoode sensibly told him that this demand would make all negotiation impossible. He answered curtly, that till the Covenant were abandoned he had no more power than a Doge of Venice.[2] The request he plainly believed to be a righteous one. It was the fault of the Scots if they did not see it in the same light. The mere demand would give him time to push on his preparations. If that were to his advantage, the blame would lie with those who rejected such reasonable terms.

Hamilton to go as Commissioner.

As the bearer of this overture, Charles selected the Marquis of Hamilton, whom he had for many years consulted on every subject relating to Scotland. Of all men living he had the greatest share of the King's confidence, and was probably the most unfit to be trusted with the difficult task now assigned to him.

His character.

The charge which was often brought against him by contemporaries of wishing to seat himself upon his master's Scottish throne, as the next heir after the Stuart line, is doubtless without foundation.[3] Everything that we know of him lends itself to the supposition that he felt a warm personal affection for Charles. But even a warm personal affection may easily be clouded over by other passions. When the chivalrous Montrose assured the lady of his heart that he could not love her so much unless he loved honour more, he laid down a principle which holds good in other relations of life than those which exist

[1] Burnet, *Lives of the Hamiltons*, 43.   [2] *Ibid.* 46.
[3] *Pers. Gov. of Charles I.*, i. 222.

between man and woman. Attachment arising out of personal admiration, or out of the amenities of personal intercourse, is liable to interruption or decay. Attachment arising out of community of sentiment and community of sacrifice for a common object is subject to no such danger. The enduring loyalty of Wentworth saw in Charles not merely a gracious sovereign, but the symbol of a great political principle. The loyalty of Hamilton saw in Charles a blindly devoted master, who had been the founder of a great part of his personal fortune. He wished to support and maintain the King's authority, but he wished still more to foster his own wealth and state under the shadow of that authority. He would serve the King, but he could not serve him with a perfect heart. To the King he owed the high position which set him apart from other Scottish subjects, and which exposed him to the jealousy of his brother nobles. But the permanent supports of his family, the broad estates, the attached hearts of followers and dependents, were to be found in the rich valley through which the Clyde poured its stream, under skies as yet undimmed by the smoke of a mighty industry. Every feeling of his heart, every demand of his interest urged him to be the pacificator of the strife But he might easily be led to seek the accomplishment of his object by means which might possibly do credit to his impartiality, but which were by no means befitting an ambassador trusted by one of the parties in the quarrel.

To the religious aspect of the strife Hamilton was profoundly indifferent. If only the Scots would keep quiet, it mattered nothing to him whether they read their prayers out of the new book or not. It was the indifference of contempt, not the indifference of

CHAP. III.
1638. May.

His indifference to the religious side of the dispute.

wisdom. He was just the man to advocate a compromise, just the man too not to see on what terms a compromise was possible. He would shift his ground from day to day because, if he did not take his stand on the principles of either of the contending parties, he had no principles of his own to secure him against the attraction or repulsion of every accident that occurred.

His despondent temper.

It is not unlikely that this want of settled principle expressed itself, unconsciously to himself, in that gloomy despondency for which he was notorious. He never undertook any work without rapidly coming to the conclusion that success was only attainable by an entire change of plan. He was frequently engaged in war and in diplomacy. Whenever he was engaged in war he became absolutely certain that negotiation would give him everything that he wanted. Whenever he was engaged in diplomacy he was sure that war, and war only, would accomplish the ends which he had been sent to obtain by negotiation.

Hamilton despairs of success.

Already, before he could set out from England, he felt the difficulties of his task. "I have no hope in the world of doing good," he said to Con, "without coming to blows. Our countrymen are possessed by the devil. The judgment of God is to be seen in the business; for though the King is ready to pardon them, and to do all that they want, they continue to make new demands, and have now published orders that none of the Covenanters shall meet the King's Commissioners."[1]

June 4. His arrival in Scotland.

It was too true. Hamilton was made to understand that he was to treat with the Covenanting leaders, and must not pass them over to address their followers. Dalkeith was appointed as the place of

[1] Con to Barberini, June $\frac{1}{11}$, *Add. MSS.*, 15,391, fol. 164.

meeting. Before he reached it, an affair occurred which inflicted on him a fresh indignity. A vessel laden with warlike stores for the King's garrison in the Castle of Edinburgh arrived at Leith. The Covenanters would not allow it to land its cargo. At last Traquair carried off the gunpowder on board and stowed it away in Dalkeith House. The Covenanting leaders at once refused to go near so dangerous a spot, and set guards round the Castle to hinder the introduction of the powder.[1]

1638. June 4. The powder ship at Leith.

On June 7 Hamilton was able to give an account of the state of affairs. He had an interview with Rothes, and had told him that if the terms which he brought were rejected, the King would come in person to Scotland with 40,000 men at his back. Rothes did not appear to be terrified. All that Scotland wanted, he said, was that their religion might be so securely established that no man might alter it hereafter at his pleasure.[2]

June 5. Hamilton's interview with Rothes.

Before leaving England, Hamilton had received from Charles two alternative forms of a declaration which he was expected to publish. In the one the demand for the surrender of the Covenant was plainly worded. In the other it was shrouded in vague exhortations to obedience. Hamilton now assured the King that it was only in the latter form that it would be possible to read the declaration at all.[3] The Covenanters would be content with nothing short of an abolition of the obnoxious forms, including the Articles of Perth, by an Assembly and Parliament, together with a limitation placed upon the authority of the Bishops. The King must therefore be prepared

June 7. Hamilton's account of the situation.

---

[1] *Rothes*, 112, 129.   [2] *Ibid.*, 135.
[3] I suppose this is what he means by dividing the Declaration. At all events, this is what he resolved on two days later.

to invade Scotland with a royal army. He was certain to gain a victory, but he must remember that it would be gained over his 'own poor people,' and he might perhaps prefer 'to wink at their madness.' As long as that madness lasted, they would 'sooner lose their lives, than leave the Covenant, or part from their demands—impertinent and damnable as they were.' If the Covenanters could not force him to give way, they would call a Parliament themselves. "Be confident," he added, "they, by God's grace, shall neither be able to do the one nor the other in haste, for what I cannot do by strength I do by cunning."[1]

Hamilton was, perhaps, using his cunning to frighten Charles into those further concessions which now appeared to him to offer the only chance of peace. Charles, however, did not take the hint. He replied that he was hastening his preparations. "In the meantime," he continued, "your care must be how to dissolve the multitude, and—if it be possible—to possess yourselves of my castles of Edinburgh and Stirling, which I do not expect. And to this end I give you leave to flatter them with what hopes you please, so you engage not me against my grounds—and in particular that you consent neither to the calling of Parliament nor General Assembly, until the Covenant be disavowed and given up; your chief end being now to win time that they may not commit public follies until I be ready to suppress them."[2] In the main point, in short, there was to be no concession, but on matters of lesser importance Hamilton was to spin out the negotiation as long as he could.

---

[1] Hamilton to the King, June 7. *Hamilton Papers*, 3.
[2] The King to Hamilton, June 11. *Burnet*, 55. The letter is a reply to the one of the 7th, not to the one of the 4th, mentioned in the beginning of it.

Before this letter was written, Hamilton had entered Edinburgh. The whole population of the town, swollen by numbers who had flocked in from the country, appeared to receive him. He reported that at least sixty thousand lined the roads. Five hundred ministers in their black gowns were there. Eluding their purpose of greeting him with a public speech, he made his way to Holyrood to hear what they had to say in private. So pleased was he with his reception, that he requested the King to put off any warlike effort till he had seen what he was able to accomplish in Edinburgh. The Covenanters, it was true, were not to be induced to surrender the Covenant at once, but it would be possible to obtain other concessions which fell short of that.[1]

In less than a week Hamilton discovered that even these modified hopes had been far too sanguine. On the 15th he wrote that even the Councillors of State declared the Covenant to be justified by law, 'which,' he added, 'is a tenet so dangerous to monarchy, as I cannot yet see how they will stand together.' All that was to be done was to stave off the inevitable rebellion till the King was ready to crush it. He had not dared to publish the Declaration even in its curtailed form. Nothing short of the immediate meeting of an Assembly and Parliament would satisfy the Covenanters. On any terms short of this it was useless to continue the negotiation. Of the chance of a successful resistance he was equally hopeless. He had sent Huntly and a few other loyal noblemen to their homes to form the nucleus of opposition. Lord Antrim, who as a MacDonell had claims to lands in the Western Highlands, might bring an Irish force to the King's aid. But the immediate

[1] Hamilton to the King, June 9. *Hamilton Papers,* 7.

prospect was most gloomy. Edinburgh Castle would soon be lost. There was not much comfort to be given. "When your power comes," wrote Hamilton, "I hope in God, He will give you victory; but, believe me, it will be a difficult work and bloody."[1]

The next day Hamilton suggested a fresh way out of the difficulty. Might not the Covenanters add an explanation to the Covenant, declaring that they had no wish to infringe on the authority of the King?[2] Charles, however, shrunk from acknowledging a defeat so plainly. No explanation would conceal the fact that he had given way because he could not cope with the forces arrayed against him. He therefore replied that he was making ready for war. In six weeks he should have a train of artillery consisting of forty pieces of ordnance. Berwick and Carlisle would soon be secured against attack. He had sent to Holland for arms to equip 14,000 foot, and 2,000 horse. The Lord Treasurer had assured him that he would have no difficulty in providing 200,000*l*. He was about to despatch the fleet to the Firth of Forth, and 6,000 soldiers should be sent with it, if Hamilton could make sure that they would be able to land at Leith.[3]

A few days later Charles was still resolute. "I will only say," he wrote, "that so long as this Covenant is in force—whether it be with or without explanation—I have no more power in Scotland than as a Duke of Venice, which I will rather die than suffer; yet I commend the giving ear to the explanation, or anything else to win time, which now I see is one of your chiefest cares." He added that he should

---

[1] Hamilton to the King, June 15. *Hamilton Papers*, 9.
[2] *Burnet*, 58.
[3] The King to Hamilton, June 20. *Burnet*, 59.

not be sorry if the Covenanters even proceeded to call a Parliament and Assembly without authority from him. By so doing they would only put themselves more completely in the wrong.¹

<small>CHAP. III.
1638.</small>

Hamilton had already discovered that it was not so easy to win time as Charles imagined. He threatened to break off the negotiation, to return to England, and to advise the King to take another course. At last he obtained an engagement from the Covenanters that they would disperse to their homes, and would take no forward step for three weeks, during his absence, on the understanding that he would do his best to induce the King to summon an Assembly and a Parliament.

<small>June 24. Hamilton talks of returning to England.</small>

In announcing this arrangement to Charles, Hamilton made the most of the delay that he had gained. It was possible, he said, that having once dispersed, the Covenanters would return in a better frame of mind. They would certainly not surrender the Covenant, but they would perhaps 'not so adhere to it' as now they did. He had also something to say about the impending war. He could not secure the landing of the proposed force of 6,000 men, but a lesser number might be brought in the fleet to make incursions in Fife and the Lothians. Dumbarton was already in safe hands, and he was in treaty with the Earl of Mar for the surrender of Edinburgh Castle. Yet he could not deny that the Covenanters were also active, and were importing arms freely from the Continent.²

In reply, Charles gave the required permission to return. The Commissioner was to promise nothing which would afterwards have to be refused. He

<small>June 29. Hamilton has leave to return.</small>

¹ The King to Hamilton, June 25; *Burnet*, 60.
² Hamilton to the King, June 24. *Hamilton Papers*, 14.

VOL. I.   L

might, however, recall the law courts to Edinburgh, and give some vague hopes of a future Assembly and Parliament. On the other hand, the Declaration in its amended form must be published before he left Edinburgh.[1]

Hamilton had already set out for England when this letter reached him. He at once turned back, and on July 4 the King's Declaration was read at the Market Cross at Edinburgh. Covenanting Scotland was informed that the Canons and Service Book would only be pressed in a fair and legal way.

Once more, as soon as the herald had fulfilled his task, a Protestation was read in reply. The Covenanters again appealed to Assembly and Parliament as the only lawful judges of their cause. Nor did they fail to make it known that the Assembly which they contemplated was a very different one from those gatherings which had ratified the will of James with enforced subserviency. Bishops were to have no place there excepting as culprits to give an account of their misdeeds. Of this Assembly they began to speak in terms to which a servant of King Charles could hardly dare to listen. It was openly said that the right to hold Assemblies came direct from God, and that no earthly Prince might venture to interrupt them.[2]

The long controversy was slowly disentangling itself. The claim of Charles to cast the religion of his subjects in the mould which seemed fairest in his eyes was met by the stern denial of his right to meddle with religion at all.

This outburst of Scottish feeling penetrated to the Council Chamber itself. Before nightfall many of the

[1] The King to Hamilton, June 29; *Burnet*, 61.
[2] Protestation, *Large Declaration*, 98.

Privy Councillors, who in the morning had given an official approval to the Declaration, signified their determination to withdraw their signatures. Unless this were permitted, they would sign the Covenant at once. To save himself from this indignity, Hamilton tore up, in their presence, the paper on which their approval had been recorded.[1]

CHAP. III.
1638. July 4.
July 5.

Whilst the Lord Commissioner was still arguing with the Council, a deputation from the Covenanters arrived to remonstrate against the language of the Declaration. Hamilton replied with firmness. The Council, he said, 'knew what they did, and would answer it.'[2] When the members of the deputation took leave, he followed them out of the room. "I spoke to you," he is reported to have said as soon as he was in private with them, "before those Lords of the Council as the King's Commissioner; now, there being none present but yourselves, I speak to you as a kindly Scotsman. If you go on with courage and resolution, you will carry what you please; but if you faint and give ground in the least, you are undone. A word is enough to wise men."[3]

Deputation from the Covenanters.

They are encouraged by Hamilton.

"What I cannot do by strength," he had explained to Charles, "I do by cunning." Hamilton's cunning was as ineffectual as his strength. It is not necessary

---

[1] Hamilton to the King, July 4; *Hamilton Papers*, 21. *Burnet*, 64.
[2] *Rothes*, 175.
[3] These words are given by Guthry (*Memoirs*, 40). He says that he heard the story on the same day from a person who had been told it by Cant, who was himself one of the deputation, and heard it again, 'in the very same terms,' that evening from Montrose, who was another of the deputation. It does not follow that the very words are accurately set down by Guthry when he came to write his Memoirs. The belief that he was playing a double game was too common in Scotland not to have had some foundation. The English author of the curious narrative printed in the Appendix to the *Hamilton Papers* (263), says that 'he gave them advice as his countrymen to keep to their own principles, lest the English nation . . . . should encroach upon them.'

to suppose that he wished to ruin his master. He probably wanted simply to be on good terms with all parties, and thought, as was undoubtedly the case, that it would be better for Charles as well as for Scotland, that he should accept the terms which appeared to be inevitable. With this object in view, it was to him a matter of indifference whether Charles frightened the Scots into surrender, or the Scots frightened Charles into concessions. As the first alternative appeared to be more than ever improbable, he now took his journey southward, with the hope that Charles would give way more readily than his subjects. He was prepared to urge him to give his consent to the meeting of Assembly and Parliament, to allow them to give a legal condemnation to the recent ecclesiastical innovations, and even to place the Bishops for the future under the control of the General Assembly. It might well be doubted whether Charles would be prepared to yield so much. There could be no doubt whatever that the Scots would not be content with less.

CHAPTER IV.

THE ASSEMBLY OF GLASGOW.

On July 1, a few days before Hamilton set out for England, Charles for the first time broached the subject of the Scottish troubles in the English Privy Council. The necessity of placing Berwick and Carlisle in a state of defence, made it impossible to treat the matter any longer as one in which England was wholly unconcerned. The King spoke of his wish to have brought about a religious uniformity between the two kingdoms. He explained that he had now found it necessary to entrust Arundel with the work of strengthening the Border fortresses, but that he had no intention of dealing hardly with the wild heads in Scotland, if they went no farther than they had done as yet. Beyond this vague statement he did not go. No opinion was asked from the Privy Councillors, and none was given. Charles was doubtless not unconscious of the difficulty of gathering an adequate military force. That weary look, which, transferred to the canvas of Vandyke, gained for Charles so many passionate admirers, was now stealing over his countenance. For the first time in his life he left the tennis-court unvisited, and, except on rare occasions, he avoided the excitement of the chase. He announced that, this year, his progress would be but a short one, and that he would return to Oatlands before the middle of August at the latest.[1]

[1] Garrard to Wentworth, July 3. *Straf. Letters*, ii. 179. Zonca's Despatch, July $\frac{8}{13}$, *Ven. Transcripts*.

If the Council as a body was not consulted, a special Committee was formed from amongst its members, to discuss the practicability of an armed interference in Scotland. The Committee was soon hopelessly divided in opinion. The Catholics and semi-Catholics, Arundel, Cottington, and Windebank, were for instant war. Vane, Coke, and Northumberland hesitated in the face of its enormous difficulties. The promise of 200,000*l.* made by Juxon a few weeks before had melted away. Only 200*l.* were at the moment in the Exchequer. The utmost that could be raised by borrowing was 110,000*l.*, a sum which would go but a little way towards the maintenance of an army. What was of more consequence was, that the recent decision in the ship-money case had revealed the discontent of the English people, and it was freely acknowledged that they were more likely to support the Scots than to draw their swords for the King.[1]

In these desperate circumstances, it was natural that the thoughts of those who cared for the maintenance of the King's authority should cross St. George's Channel. There at least was a man who had shown that it was possible to educe order out of chaos. Might not the force which had curbed Ireland be employed to restore discipline in Scotland?

Never had Wentworth been so hopeful of the success of his great experiment as in the summer of 1637. In August, just as the Scottish resistance was growing serious, he set out for the West. In a letter to Conway he described, with much amusement, the triumphal arches erected in his honour, and the long speeches of welcome inflicted on him by the magistrates of the towns through which he passed. He

[1] Northumberland to Wentworth, July 23. *Straf. Letters*, ii. 185.

was well satisfied with the more serious business of his journey. "Hither are we come," he wrote from Limerick, "through a country, upon my faith, if as well husbanded, built, and peopled as are you in England, would show itself not much inferior to the very best you have there. The business we came about is most happily effected, and His Majesty now entitled to the two goodly counties of Ormond and Clare, and, which beauties and seasons the work exceedingly, with all possible contentment and satisfaction of the people. In all my whole life did I never see, or could possibly have believed to have found men with so much alacrity divesting themselves of all property in their estates, and, with great quietness and singleness of mind, waiting what His Majesty may in his gracious good pleasure and time determine and measure out for them. I protest I that am, to my truth, of a gentle heart, find myself extremely taken with the manner of their proceeding. They have all along, to the uttermost of their skill and breeding, given me very great expressions of their esteem and affection, so as I begin almost to be persuaded that they here could be content to have me the minister of His Majesty's favour towards them as soon as any other."[1]

Such a letter shows Wentworth at his best. It is probable that the days of this summer progress were the last of unalloyed happiness that he ever enjoyed. He could hardly doubt what was the cause of this unexpected loyalty. At Galway, two years before, he had acted in defiance of the great tribal lord the Earl of Clanrickard. At Limerick he was acting with the warm support of the Earl of Ormond.

Whether it would have been possible by patience

[1] Wentworth to Conway, Aug. 21, 1637. *S. P. Ireland*, Bundle 286.

to bring the other lords to follow Ormond's example, it is impossible now to say. Patience was no part of Wentworth's character. In any case, the impulse to improvement must have come from the Crown, and the improvement to which he looked was rather to be found in the benefits derived by the poor from orderly government, than in the increased activity of the rich. "It is most rare," he wrote about this time, "that the lower sort of the Irish subject hath not in any age lived so preserved from the pressures and oppressions of the great ones as now they do; for which, I assure you, they bless God and the King, and begin to discern and taste the great and manifold benefits they gather under the shadow, and from the immediate dependence upon the Crown, in comparision of the scant and narrow coverings they formerly borrowed from their petty yet imperious lords."[1]

Such work was not likely to conduce to the formation of a correct judgment on English and Scottish affairs. "Mr. Prynne's case," he wrote in October, " is not the first wherein I have resented the humour of the time to cry up and magnify such as the honour and justice of the King and State have marked out and adjudged mutinous to the Government, and offensive to the belief and reverence the people ought to have in the wisdom and integrity of the magistrate. Nor am I now to say it anew . . . . that a Prince that loseth the force and example of his punishments, loseth withal the greatest part of his dominion, and yet still, methinks, we are not got through the disease—nay, I fear, do not sufficiently apprehend the malignity of it. In the mean time a liberty thus assumed, thus abused, is very insufferable ;

[1] Wentworth to Coke, Aug. 15. *Straf. Letters*, ii. 88.

but how to help it I know not, till I see the good as resolute in their good as we daily observe the bad to be in their evil ways, which God of His grace infuse into us; for such are the feeble and faint motions of human frailty, that I do not expect it thence."[1]

To Wentworth, Hampden's case appeared no better than that of Prynne. "Mr. Hampden," he complained to Laud, "is a great Brother, and the very genius of that nation of people leads them always to oppose civilly as ecclesiastically all that ever authority ordains for them; but, in good faith, were they right served, they should be whipped home into their right wits, and much beholden they should be to any that would thoroughly take pains with them in that kind." "In truth," he wrote some months later, "I still wish . . . Mr. Hampden and others to his likeness were well whipped into their right senses; if that the rod be so used that it smarts not, I am the more sorry."[2]

Whatever may have been the exact form of punishment which Wentworth designed for Hampden, there can be no doubt that he was ready to expend all his energy on the Scottish Covenanters. One plan, indeed, which had been suggested in London, that the Earl of Antrim, who had married Buckingham's widow, should be allowed to raise a force to attack the West of Scotland, found no favour in his eyes. He told the King that he thought but meanly of Antrim's 'parts, of his power, or of his affections.' It would not be safe to trust him with arms. If he did not misuse them himself, the Scottish colonists were strong enough to seize upon them for their own ends. The Irish Government could not spare a man of its small

---

[1] Wentworth to Laud, Oct. 18. *Straf. Letters*, ii. 119.
[2] Wentworth to Laud, Nov. 27, Apr. 10. *Straf. Letters*, ii. 136, 156.

army for service in Scotland. Three or four thousand foot, however, might be levied for the purpose. If this were done, the greater number ought to be of English birth. If Irishmen received a military training in Scotland, they might be dangerous after their return.

When Wentworth wrote this letter, he had in his hand a copy of the last Protestation of the Scots. It left no doubt on his mind that they were aiming at a change in the basis of government. One of his chaplains had recently visited Edinburgh. An attempt, Wentworth said, had been made to force him 'to sign and swear something which' he thought they called 'their Covenant with God.' If it be such, he sneeringly added, 'it will learn them obedience to their King very shortly.'[1]

As yet Wentworth's advice on the policy to be pursued towards the Scots had not been asked. He therefore unbosomed himself in a private letter to Northumberland. If the insolency of the Scots, he said, were not 'thoroughly corrected,' it was impossible to foresee all the evil consequences that would follow. It was true that the preparations in England were not sufficiently advanced to justify an immediate declaration of war. But there should be no further concessions to the Scots. 'To their bold and unmannerly demand' for a Parliament, 'mixed with a threat that otherwise they' would 'betake themselves to other counsel,' His Majesty should reply that 'it was not the custom of the best and mildest of kings to be threatened into parliaments, or to be circumscribed with days and hours by their subjects.' Their present conduct, he should say, was 'more than ever he expected from them' which profess the religion

[1] Wentworth to the King, July 28. *Straf. Letters*, ii. 187.

which decries all such tumultuous proceedings of people against their sovereign.' He should ask what they would have thought 'if the Papists of England or Ireland' had done the like, and should inform them that he would give them leisure 'to consider the modesty, the reverence, wherewith they were to approach God's anointed, and their King, and so to frame their petitions and supplications as that they might be granted without diminution to his height and Royal estate.'

To prepare for the worst, Berwick and Carlisle must be garrisoned, and the troops there, as well as the trained bands of the northern counties, must be diligently exercised during the winter, so as to have a disciplined army ready at the commencement of the summer, without any previous expense to the exchequer. It the Scots continued refractory their ports could then be blockaded, and their shipping seized. Under this stress, their new unity would speedily be dissolved. Partisans of the King would spring up on every side. No unnecessary cruelty must delay the work of submission. Seditious ministers must be merely imprisoned. There must be no death on the scaffold, however richly it might be deserved. Scotland would soon prostrate itself at the feet of the King.

Then—for Wentworth never failed to form a clear conception of his ultimate aim—would come a new day of government for Scotland. It was to be ruled as Ireland was ruled, by a Council of its own, acting in strict subordination to the English Privy Council. The religious difficulty was to be settled on much the same principle. No extemporary prayers, no Book of Common Order was to be tolerated. Neither was any new-fangled Liturgy to be forced upon the people. But they must be content to accept the time-honoured Prayer Book of the English Church, the Protestantism of which was beyond dispute.

If Wentworth, as he undoubtedly did, underestimated the strength which a struggle for national existence would give to Scotland, he overestimated still more the devotion of the English people to their King. He imagined that his countrymen were still animated by that fiery loyalty which was peculiarly his own. "Your Lordship," he wrote in conclusion, "may say:—How shall money be found to carry us through the least part of this? In good faith, every man will give it, I hope, from his children, upon such an extremity as this, when no less verily than all we have comes thus to the stake. In a word, we are, God be praised, rich and able, and in this case, it may be justly said, *Salus populi suprema lex*, and the King must not want our substance for the preservation of the whole."[1]

Such was Wentworth's confession of faith. He believed in his heart of hearts that to fight for the King in this cause was to fight 'for the preservation of the whole.'

It may well be that in Scotland no middle course between a complete conquest and an absolute relinquishment of power was in any way possible. After all that had passed, it was hopeless to expect that Charles's authority would ever again strike root in the heart of the Scottish nation. One man indeed there was who, in after years, was to believe it possible, and who was destined to dash himself to pieces, in the Royal cause, against the rocky strength of Covenanting Scotland. That man was still a fiery youth, throwing himself heart and soul into the cause

[1] Wentworth to Northumberland, July 30. *Straf. Letters*, ii. 189.

of the Covenant. James Graham, Earl of Montrose, was born in 1612, and succeeded to his father's title as a mere lad in 1626. Educated at St. Andrews, he was easily supreme in those bodily exercises in which youths of gentle birth sought distinction. He bore away the prize for archery; he was noted for his firm seat on horseback, and for the skill with which he managed his arms. Married at the early age of seventeen, after four years of wedded happiness, he sought pleasure and instruction in a prolonged tour on the Continent. When he returned in 1636 he passed through England, and asked Hamilton for an introduction to the King. Hamilton, if report speaks truly, was jealous of the young man, and played off on him one of his master-pieces of deception. Telling him that the King could not endure a Scotchman, he prepared him for an unfavourable reception. He then warned the King that Montrose was likely to be dangerous in Scotland. The traveller was therefore received with coolness, and returned home highly discontented. The man with whom he was most closely connected, his brother-in-law, the excellent Lord Napier, and his kinsman, the Earl of Airth, were at the same time loyal to their Sovereign and hostile to Hamilton, whom they regarded with disfavour, as withdrawing the management of Scottish affairs from Edinburgh to Whitehall, and against whom they were embittered by one of those family feuds which were still potent in Scotland.[1]

CHAP. IV.
1638.

1626.
1629.
1633.
1636.
Is tricked by Hamilton.

[1] The story of Hamilton's treatment of Montrose comes from Heylyn (*Life of Laud*, 350). It is there connected with a story about another Graham, Earl of Menteith, who had a kind of claim to the throne of Scotland on the ground of the questionable legitimacy of Robert III., through whom the Crown had descended. The King, through a legal process, had deprived him of his titles, though he subsequently granted him the Earldom of Airth by a fresh creation. The whole of his story will be found in Masson's *Drummond of Hawthornden*, 185.

*1637.
Montrose's character.*

Before 1637 came to an end, Montrose was in the thick of the opposition. When once he had chosen his side, he was sure to bear himself as a Paladin of old romance. If he made any cause his own, it was not with the reasoned calculation of a statesman, but with the fond enthusiasm of a lover. When he afterwards transferred his affections from the Covenant to the King, it was as Romeo transferred his affections from Rosaline to Juliet. He fought for neither King nor Covenant, but for that ideal of his own which he followed as Covenanter or Royalist. He went ever straight to the mark, impatient to shake off the schemes of worldly-wise politicians and the plots of interested intriguers. Nature had marked him for a life of meteoric splendour, to confound and astonish a world, and to leave behind him an inspiration and a name which would outlast the ruin of his hopes.

*1638.
Montrose as a Covenanter.*

In 1637 Montrose could be nothing but a patriotic Scotsman, and as a patriotic Scotsman he threw himself without an afterthought into the whirl of political strife. He detested and distrusted Hamilton, as he afterwards detested and distrusted Argyle. He had been one of those who had listened to Hamilton's appeal to the 'kindly Scots,' and the incident had made a deep impression on his mind. When a de-

Heylyn says that Hamilton told the King that Montrose was 'of such esteem amongst the Scots, by reason of an old descent from the Royal family, that he might take part in supporting his kinsman's claim.' It must be remembered that though Hamilton did not put in any claim to the throne against Charles, he was in the line of succession, and was therefore personally interested in the putting down any claim by Menteith. Mr. Napier has pointed out that Heylyn probably derived his information from Lord Napier. It is difficult to say what amount of credit is due to the narrative printed in the Appendix to the *Hamilton Papers*, but the rivalry between Montrose and Hamilton, there alleged to have existed, falls in very well with Heylyn's story.

cision was to be taken or a protestation read, he was certain to be foremost.[1] The Covenanting leaders knew how to make good use of his fervid energy. Scarcely had Hamilton turned his back on Edinburgh, when they launched Montrose against Aberdeen.

CHAP. IV.
1638. July.

A great national uprising makes scant account of corporate privilege or individual liberty. He who stands sneeringly, or even hesitatingly apart from it, is soon regarded as a possible traitor, if not as an actual traitor, who waits for an opportunity to strike. Ministers who had refused to sign the Covenant had been silenced, ill-treated, and driven from their homes. Only in one place in Scotland did they gather thickly enough to hold their own. The Aberdeen doctors, indeed, were no enthusiastic supporters of Charles's ill-fated Prayer Book. They felt no attraction to Laud and his Beauty of Holiness. They were faithful disciples of the school which had been founded by Patrick Forbes. The danger which they foresaw was that which is inseparable from every popular excitement, and especially from every popular religious excitement. They feared for their quiet studies, for their right to draw unmolested their own conclusions from the data before them. They were Royalists; not as Laud and Wren were Royalists, but after the fashion of Chillingworth and Hales. Under the name of authority they upheld the noble banner of intellectual freedom. Under Charles they had such liberty

The Aberdeen doctors.

---

[1] Gordon's story (i. 33) may be true, though it looks as if it were dressed up after the event, and was certainly written after 1650. "It is reported that at one of these protestations at Edinburgh Cross, Montrose standing up upon a puncheon that stood on the scaffold, the Earl of Rothes in jest said unto him, 'James,' says he, 'you will not be at rest till you be lifted up there above the rest in three fathom of rope.' . . . . This was afterwards accomplished in earnest in that same place. Some say that the same supports of the scaffold were made use of at Montrose's execution."

CHAP.
IV.
───
1638.
July.
Danger from Aberdeen.

as they needed; under the Covenant they were not likely to have any liberty at all.

So matters looked at Aberdeen. It was impossible that they should be so regarded in Edinburgh. The liberty of the Aberdeen doctors might easily become the slavery of Scotland. If the Northern City were occupied by the King's forces, it would become to Covenanting Scotland what La Vendée afterwards became to Republican France. The risk was the greater because Aberdeen had other forces behind it than those which were supplied by the logic of its colleges. It lay close to the territory occupied by the powerful Gordon kindred, at the head of which was the Marquis of Huntly. Huntly in the north-east, like Argyle in the south-west, was more than an eminent Scottish nobleman. These two were as kings within their own borders. Each of them had authority outside the mountains. Each of them was a Celtic chieftain as well as a Peer of the realm. Far away from Argyle's castle at Inverary, far away from Huntly's castle at the Bog in Strathbogie, the frontiers of rival authority met.

Huntly and Argyle.

Huntly's royalism.

Of the two, Huntly's power was less Celtic than that of Argyle, and was therefore more exposed to attack from the southern populations. An invading army might easily keep clear of the mountains by clinging to that strip of lowland country which stretches along the shores of the Moray Firth. Huntly's family had risen to power by the defence of this more civilised district against lawless attacks from the dwellers in the hills. It was a district scarcely less isolated from Southern influences, and Huntly's immediate predecessors had retained the faith of the ancient Church. They had therefore looked with jealousy upon any government seated at

Edinburgh, and in proportion as the King had become estranged from the sentiments prevailing in the south of Scotland, he would be regarded as the natural ally of his subjects in the North. Huntly's own position was such as to place him at the head of a struggle for local independence. The victory of the national party would reduce his power to that of an ordinary nobleman. To a messenger sent to urge him to throw in his lot with his countrymen, he replied that 'his family had risen and stood by the kings of Scotland, and for his part, if the event proved the ruin of this king, he was resolved to lay his life, honours, and estate under the rubbish of the King's ruins.'[1]

CHAP. IV.
1638. July.

On July 20, Montrose entered Aberdeen. According to the custom of the place, a cup of wine was offered to him as an honoured guest. He refused to drink it till the Covenant had been signed. He brought with him three preachers—Henderson, Dickson, and Cant. All the churches closed their doors against them. They preached in the streets in vain. The men of Aberdeen would not sign the Covenant. In the neighbourhood signatures were obtained amongst families which, like the Forbeses, were jealous of Huntly's power. Their example and the pressure of military force brought in a few subscribers. Two ministers appended their names with a protest that they remained loyal and obedient to the King; and the reservation was accepted, not only by Montrose, but by Henderson and Dickson as well.[2]

July 20. Montrose at Aberdeen.

July 29.

Such a reservation, to be differently interpreted in different mouths, would probably have been accepted

July 27. Hamilton's instruction.

---

[1] *Gordon*, i. 49.
[2] *General Demands concerning the Covenant.* Aberdeen, 1662. *Spalding*, i. 93.

VOL. I.   M

by all Scotland. No such simple means of saving his own dignity would commend itself to Charles. After consultation with Hamilton, he gave way so far as to authorise the meeting of an Assembly and a Parliament. Hamilton was to do his best to obtain as much influence for the Bishops in the Assembly as he possibly could. He was to protest against any motion for the abolition of their order, but he might consent to any plan for making them responsible for their conduct to future Assemblies. If this were objected to, Hamilton was 'to yield anything, though unreasonable, rather than to break.'

Difficult as it would probably be to obtain the consent of Scotland to this compromise, it was made more difficult by a gratuitous obstacle of Charles's own invention. The Covenant was neither to be passed over in silence nor explained away. It was to be met by the resuscitation of a Confession of Faith which had been adopted by the Scottish Parliament in 1567, and which, though strongly Protestant in tone, naturally passed entirely over all controversies of a later date. To this Confession Charles now added clauses binding those who accepted it to defend 'the King's Majesty's sacred person and authority, as also the laws and liberties of the country under his Majesty's Sovereign power.' This document was to be circulated for subscription in Scotland, not in addition to, but in substitution for, the National Covenant. All ministers expelled for refusing to sign the National Covenant were to be restored to their parishes. All ministers admitted to a parish without the intervention of the Bishop were to be expelled.[1]

With these instructions Hamilton started once more for Scotland. On August 10 he reached Edin-

[1] *Burnet*, 65.

burgh. He found himself at once involved in a controversy on the constitution of the Assembly which he had come to announce. What Charles proposed was an exclusively clerical Assembly, in which the Bishops should, if possible, preside. The Covenanting leaders would not hear of the arrangement. They were hardly likely to forget how Spottiswoode had threatened the ministers with the loss of their stipends at the Perth Assembly, and they knew enough of what was passing in London to distrust the King's intentions. Whether there be truth or not in the story which tells how Scottish grooms of the bed-chamber rifled the King's pockets after he was in bed, so as to learn the contents of his secret correspondence,[1] there can be no doubt that his projects were known in Scotland even better than they were known in England. Hamilton's efforts to divide the King's opponents served but to weld them together in more compact unity. When he talked to the nobles of the folly of reimposing on their own necks that yoke of Presbytery which their fathers had been unable to bear, he was told that Episcopacy was not the only means of averting the danger. Lay elders formed a part of the Presbyterian constitution, and under that name it would be easy for noblemen and gentlemen to find their way into the Church Courts, where they would have no difficulty in keeping in check any attempt at clerical domination. It is true that this prospect was not altogether pleasing to the ministers, and that many of them were somewhat alarmed at the growing influence of a nobility which would probably become lukewarm in the cause of

CHAP. IV.
1638.
Aug. 10.

His efforts to divide the Covenanters.

---

[1] It is in favour of this story that Henrietta Maria, after she left England in 1642, advised her husband to be careful of his pockets, where he then kept the key to the cypher used between them.

the Church as soon their own interests were satisfied. But the nobles told the clergy plainly, that if their support was wanted it must be taken on their own terms, and the chance that Charles would keep the engagements to which he had advanced with such hesitating steps was not sufficiently attractive to induce the clergy to abandon those protectors who had stood by them hitherto without flinching.

On August 13 Hamilton laid before the Privy Council his scheme for the pacification of Scotland. All extraordinary assemblies of the clergy and laity were to be broken up, and Bishops and expelled ministers were to be protected in their lawful cures. At the elections to the Assembly no layman was to have a vote, and the Council was 'to advise to give satisfaction anent the Covenant, or to renounce the same.' So unfavourable was the reception of these proposals, that Hamilton returned once more to England for further instructions; having first obtained from the Covenanters a promise that they would not proceed to any self-authorised elections till September 21, by which time he hoped to be back in Scotland.[1]

When, on September 17, Hamilton appeared for the third time in Edinburgh, he brought with him what must have seemed to Charles unlimited concessions. He was to issue a summons for the meeting of the Assembly and Parliament, and to content himself, as far as the elections to the former body were concerned, with coming as near as was possible to the forms observed in the preceding reign. He was to declare that the King absolutely revoked 'the Service Book, the Book of Canons, and the High

[1] *Baillie,* i. 98. *Spalding,* i. 98. *Burnet,* 69. *Large Declaration,* 111.

Commission,' that he suspended the practice of the Articles of Perth, and was ready to consent to their entire abolition, if Parliament wished him to do so. Episcopacy was to be limited in such a way that the Bishops in future would be responsible to the Assembly for their conduct.

The King's Covenant.

Charles did not stop here. It is true that he no longer directly asked for the surrender of the National Covenant. He abandoned also the idea of sending round for signature the Confession of 1567. But he seems to have thought it necessary to preserve his dignity by sending round for signature some document of his own. This time it was to consist of the Confession drawn up in 1580, which formed the basis of the National Covenant. Naturally, Johnston's additions were to be omitted, and they were to be replaced by a certain Covenant which had been drawn up in 1590, the signers of which had bound themselves to stand by the King in 'suppressing of the Papists, promotion of true religion, and settling of His Highness' estate, and obedience in all the countries and corners of the realm.'[1]

Sept. 22. Proclamation of the Assembly and Parliament.

On the 22nd the Privy Councillors, after some hesitation, signed the King's Covenant. The same day a Proclamation was made at the Cross. It began by announcing the concessions intended. It then called on the people to sign the new Covenant, not because any fresh attestation of their own faith was needed, but in order that the King might thereby assure his subjects that he never intended 'to admit of any change or alteration in the true religion already established and professed.' Finally, an Assembly was summoned to meet at Glasgow on November 21, and a Parliament on May 15.[2]

[1] *Burnet*, 75.   [2] Peterkin's *Records*, 81.

CHAP. IV.
1638.
Sept. 22.

Another Protestation.

By a few Scotsmen who, like Drummond of Hawthornden, had watched with anxiety the leagues of the nobles and the violence of the clergy, the Proclamation was hailed as a message of peace.[1] By the mass of Drummond's countrymen it was received with profound distrust. As its words died away, there followed another Protestation, more sharp and defiant than any before. Scotland had made up its mind to have no more to do with Bishops, whether their power were limited or unlimited. The introduction of a new Covenant without apparent reason was in itself certain to arouse suspicion. The question at once arose, for what purpose were their signatures demanded? The explanation given by the King was unintelligible. "If we should now enter upon this new subscription," said the Protesters—their words were in all probability the words of Henderson[2]— "we would think ourselves guilty of mocking God, and taking His name in vain; for the tears that began to be poured forth at the solemnising of the Covenant are not yet dried up and wiped away, and the joyful noise which then began to sound hath not yet ceased; and there can be no new necessity from us, and upon our part pretended, for a ground of urging this new subscription, at first intended to be an abjuration of Popery, upon us who are known to hate Popery with an unfeigned hatred, and have all this year bygone given large testimony of our zeal against it. As we are not to multiply miracles on God's part, so ought we not to multiply solemn oaths and covenants upon our part, and thus to play with oaths as children do with their toys without necessity."[3]

Why should another Covenant be signed?

---

[1] Drummond's *Irene*. Works, 163.
[2] This is the suggestion of Prof. Masson, *Life of Milton*, ii. 33.
[3] Peterkin's *Records*, 86.

Together with the controversy about the King's Covenant appeared another controversy more serious still. Charles thought he had done much in offering to place the Bishops under limitations. He was told that all such questions were beyond his competence. The Assembly would deal with them as it saw fit. It, not the King, was divinely empowered to judge of all questions relating to the Church.

CHAP. IV.
1638.
Sept. 22.
Is not the Assembly supreme?

Such was the declaration of war—it was nothing less—issued by the Scottish Covenanters. At the heart of the long appeals to Scripture and to Presbyterian logic lay the sense of National independency. Episcopacy was a foreign substance, which had never been assimilated by the living organism into which it had been introduced by force and fraud.

The Protestation a declaration of war.

The attempt to procure signatures to the King's Covenant was almost a total failure. Loyal Aberdeen and its neighbourhood produced 12,000 signatures; only 16,000 more could be obtained from the rest of Scotland. A mad woman named Margaret Michelson, who went about saying that she was inspired to declare that the National Covenant came from Heaven, and that the King's Covenant was the work of Satan, was very generally regarded as a prophetess.[1]

Few sign the King's Covenant.

In the face of such evidence of popular feeling, it hardly mattered much under what system the votes in the election of members of the Assembly were recorded. The Covenanters, however, treated it as a matter of course that an Act passed by an Assembly held in 1597 was to be accepted as the constitutional rule, all later acts being held to have been null and void. Hamilton's efforts to introduce jealousy between the gentry and the clergy were without effect. The constituencies in each Presbytery were composed

The electoral machinery.

---

[1] *Burnet*, 81. *Gordon*, i. 131.

CHAP. IV.
―――
1638.
Sept. 22.

of the minister and one lay elder from each parish. By this constituency three ministers were chosen to represent the Presbytery, whilst the gentry of the same district returned a lay elder to represent themselves. Edinburgh was separately represented by two members, and the other boroughs by one member apiece.

Strength of the Assembly.

It would have puzzled the sharpest logician to give any satisfactory reason why a body, brought into existence by this particular kind of electoral machinery, should be held to speak with Divine authority, rather than a body brought into existence in some other way. But there could be no doubt that it could speak with a national authority as no merely clerical assembly could have spoken. Whatever Scotland was, in its strength and its weakness, in its fierce uncompromising dogmatism, in its stern religious enthusiasm, in its worldly ambition and hair-splitting argumentativeness, in its homely ways and resolute defiance of a foreign creed and of a foreign worship, was reflected, as in a mirror, in the Assembly which was now elected in the teeth of the King's Commissioner.

Charles resolves to take up the challenge.

Charles could hardly avoid taking up the glove thrown down. To allow that he had neither part nor lot, either in the constitution of the Assembly or in the decisions to which it might come, would be to acknowledge that the kingly authority was no more than a cypher in Scotland; and he knew instinctively that if he gave way in Scotland he would soon be called upon to give way in England as well. The only question now was on what ground the challenge was to be accepted. The Scottish Bishops, knowing what was before them, advised that the very meeting of the Assembly should be prohibited.

Hamilton argued, that if this were done, the Covenanters would allege that the King had never seriously intended that any Assembly should meet at all; and Charles was of the same opinion as Hamilton.

Hamilton's plan was, that the Assembly should be allowed to proceed to business. His first care would be to lay before it the scheme of modified Episcopacy which had been foreshadowed in the late Proclamation. If this were rejected, as it would certainly be, and if the Bishops were summoned as culprits to the bar, he would then dissolve the Assembly and declare those who concurred in this course to be traitors to the King.[1] The Bishops, on their part, would be ready with a Declinator, denouncing the Assembly as unconstitutionally elected, and as disqualified, in any case, from passing sentence upon Bishops.

At last, the position taken up by Charles was clearly marked. There was no thought now of gaining time by spinning out negotiations which were to come to nothing. If the Scots would have accepted Charles's offer of limited Episcopacy, and have left the question of sovereignty untouched, he would probably have been content to see his concessions put in force, however unpalatable they were to himself. He knew well, however, that the question of sovereignty was at stake, and he doubtless felt the less anxiety on the score of the largeness of the concessions which he had made, because he believed that they were certain to be rejected. "Your commands," Hamilton had recently written to him, "I conceive, chiefly tend at this time so to make a party here for your Majesty, and once so to quiet this mad

[1] Hamilton to the King, Oct. 22. *Hamilton Papers*, 46.

*1638.
Oct. 22.*

Certainty of resistance.

people, that hereafter your Majesty may reign as king, and inflict the due punishment on such as have so infinitely offended against your Majesty's sacred authority."

The Scottish leaders, if they knew what was passing in the King's mind, as there can be little doubt that they did, had every reason to make the breach irreparable. They were not likely to have much difficulty with their followers. Large bodies of men, when once they are set in motion, acquire a momentum of their own, and every scrap of news which reached them from England confirmed them in the belief that the King meditated an attack upon Scotland, whether his terms were accepted or not.

Signs of war.

It was known that Hamilton had purchased from Mar the command of Edinburgh Castle; and that it was only owing to the strict watch kept upon it by the citizens that it had not been provided with those warlike stores without which its garrison would be unable to stand a siege. It was known, too, that a trusty officer had been despatched to take charge of Dumbarton, that preparations had been made for holding Berwick and Carlisle in force, and for creating a magazine of military stores at Hull. There had also been widely circulated a forged speech, which the Duke of Lennox was said to have delivered in defence of his native country, in the English Privy Council, from which the inference was drawn that the English Council entertained designs hostile to Scotland.

*Oct. 24.
The Bishops cited before the Assembly.*

As had usually happened in the course of these distractions, the Covenanters took the aggressive. On October 24, they appeared, in due legal form, before the Edinburgh Presbytery, to charge the pre-

---

[1] Hamilton to the King, Oct. 15. *Hamilton Papers*, 42.

tended Bishops with having overstepped the limits of their powers, and even with acts of dishonesty and profligacy, and requested the Presbytery to refer their cases to the Assembly. As might have been expected, this request was at once complied with, and the accusation was ordered to be read publicly in all the churches of Edinburgh.[1]

CHAP. IV.
1638.
Oct. 22.

The step thus given induced Charles to resort to threats. "You may take public notice," he wrote to Hamilton, "and declare that, as their carriage hath forced me to take care to arm myself against any insolence that may be committed, so you may give assurance that my care of peace is such that all those preparations shall be useless, except they first break out with insolent actions." As for the threatened proceedings against the Bishops, 'it was never heard that one should be both judge and party.' The very legality of the constitution of the Assembly was at issue, and that was no matter to be determined by the Assembly itself. He was still ready to perform everything that he had promised, and was prepared to summon 'a new Assembly upon the amendment of all the faults and nullities of this.'[2]

Nov. 17.
The King announces that he is preparing for war.

The Assembly, too, might well have asked whether Charles himself was not a party rather than a judge. It preferred action to recrimination. On November 21, it met in the Cathedral of Glasgow, the only one amongst the Scottish cathedrals which had been saved from destruction and decay by the affectionate reverence of the townsmen, and which had survived to witness the new birth of Presbytery. In spite of Hamilton's efforts to take the lead into his hands, the Assembly remained master of itself. The speech

Nov. 21.
Meeting of the Assembly.

[1] *Large Declaration*, 209.
[2] The King to Hamilton, Nov. 17. *Burnet*, 99.

CHAP. IV
1638.
Nov. 21.

which he had prepared for the occasion remained unspoken.¹ His demand that the question of the elections should be immediately taken up, was promptly refused. His proposal that the Bishops' Declinator should be read was received with contempt. The Assembly asserted its right to exist by proceeding to the choice of a Moderator.² That Moderator was Alexander Henderson. The clerk was Johnston of Warriston.

Nov. 22.
Hamilton's report.

The question being thus decided against him, Hamilton's only object was to put off the evil hour of dissolution as long as possible. The account which he gave the King was gloomy beyond measure. "Yesterday, the 21st," he wrote, "was the day appointed for the downsitting of the Assembly. Accordingly we met, and truly, sir, my soul was never sadder than to see such a sight; not one gown amongst the whole company, many swords but many more daggers—most of them having left their guns and pistols in their lodgings. The number of the pretended members are about 260; each one of these hath two, some three, some four assessors, who pretend not to have voice, but only are come to argue and assist the Commissioners; but the true reason is to make up a great and confused multitude, and I will add, a most ignorant one, for some Commissioners there are who can neither write nor read,³ the most part being totally void of learning, but resolved to follow the opinion of those few ministers who pretend to be learned, and those be the most rigid and seditious Puritans that live. What, then, can be expected but a total disobedience to authority, if not a present

---

¹ Compare *Burnet*, 94, with *Baillie*, i. 124.
² Answering to the Speaker in the English House of Commons.
³ This probably refers to some of the lay members of the Assembly.

rebellion? Yet this is no more than that which your Majesty hath had just reason this long time to look for, which I would not so much apprehend if I did not find so great an inclination in the body of your Council to go along their way; for, believe me, sir, there is no Puritan minister of them all who would more willingly be freed of Episcopal governance than they would, whose fault it is that this unlucky business is come to this height."[1]

1638. Nov. 22.

By general confession, Hamilton played well the part which he had undertaken. His attempt to get up a clerical movement against the lay elders failed entirely. On the 27th, the Assembly declared itself duly constituted, and set aside three scantily signed petitions against the lay elders as unworthy of notice.

His conduct in the Assembly.

Nov 27. The Assembly constituted.

Hamilton knew that the breach could not be averted much longer. "So unfortunate have I been in this unlucky country," he wrote to the King, "that though I did prefer your service before all worldly considerations . . . yet all hath been to small purpose; for I have missed my end in not being able to make your Majesty so considerable a party as will be able to curb the insolency of this rebellious nation without assistance from England, and greater charge to your Majesty than this miserable country is worth." In his annoyance at the approach of that open quarrel in which he expected to be the first to suffer, he dealt his blows impartially around. Everyone, excepting himself and the King, appeared to have been in fault. The Bishops had done things which were 'not justifiable by the laws.' 'Their pride was great, but their folly was greater.' Some of them were not 'of the best lives.' Others were 'inclined to simony.' He then, with characteristic confidence in schemes

Hamilton's account of the Assembly.

His attack on the Bishops.

[1] Hamilton to the King, Nov. 22. *Hamilton Papers*, 59.

1638.
Nov. 27.
His advice on the conduct of the war.

as yet untried, assured the King that success would be easily secured. By blockading the seaports he would ruin the commerce of the country. So far he was of one mind with Wentworth. But he believed, what Wentworth did not believe, that it was still possible to raise a force in Scotland to fight on Charles's side. Huntly, he argued, should be named as the King's Lieutenant in the North. Traquair or Roxburgh should hold the same authority in the South. There should be a Royal Commissioner—no doubt, himself—at the head of both. It would be difficult to carry arms and ammunition into Edinburgh Castle, but it would be easy to secure Dumbarton by sending soldiers from Ireland. "I have now only one suit to your Majesty," he ended by saying, "that if my sons live, they may be bred in England, and made happy by service in the Court; and if they prove not loyal to the Crown, my curse be on them. I wish my daughters be never married in Scotland."[1]

Nov. 28.
The Bishops' Declinator presented.

On the 28th, the day after this letter was written, the crisis arrived. The Bishops' Declinator was presented. Henderson put it to the vote whether the Assembly was a competent judge of their cause, notwithstanding their assertion to the contrary.

Question between Hamilton and the Assembly.

Before the answer was given, Hamilton rose. He read the King's offer, that all their grievances should be abolished, and that the Bishops should be responsible to future Assemblies. But he refused to acknowledge the legality of the Assembly before him. The only Assembly which he would acknowledge was one elected by ministers alone, and composed of ministers alone. In a long speech Henderson ascribed to the King very large powers indeed, even in ecclesiastical matters. The constitutional point raised by Hamilton

[1] Hamilton to the King, Nov. 27. *Hardw. St. P.*, ii. 113.

he altogether evaded. No Assembly likes to hear an attack on the basis upon which it rests. This one refused to re-open a question which it probably considered as settled by its previous rejection of the petitions against the lay elders. Hamilton pleaded in vain for further delay. "I must ask," said the Moderator, "if this Assembly finds themselves competent judges." A warm debate ensued. "If the Bishops," said Loudoun, "decline the judgment of a National Assembly, I know not a competent judgment seat for them but the King of Heaven." "I stand to the King's prerogative," replied the Commissioner, "as supreme judge over all causes civil and ecclesiastical, to whom I think they may appeal, and not let the causes be reasoned here."

No common understanding was any longer possible. After a few more words, Hamilton declared the Assembly to be dissolved in the King's name, and left the church. As soon as he was gone, the Assembly resolved that it was entitled to remain in session in spite of anything that had been done. Its first act was to pass a vote claiming competency to sit in judgment on the Bishops.

At the moment of Hamilton's departure an incident occurred from which the Assembly must have derived no slight encouragement. Argyle, like Huntly, was a potentate exercising almost royal power. He could bring 5,000 Highlanders into the field. Like Huntly, he came of a family which had long kept up its attachment to the Papal Church, and his father; who had lately died, had been for many years in the military service of the King of Spain in the Netherlands. During his father's absence he had exercised over the clan the authority which he now bore in his own name. Throwing off his father's religion, he adapted himself to the habits and the ideas of the inhabitants of the Southern Lowlands. He was often to be seen in Edinburgh, and he took his place as a member of the Privy Council. He thus early became a national, rather than, like Huntly, a local politician. As a nobleman, he shared in the jealousy of the Bishops which was common to his class. But he was politic and wary, not willing to commit himself hastily to any cause, and tied to more than ordinary caution by his rank as a Privy Councillor. He was ambitious of power, and unscrupulous in his choice of means. Unlike the other noblemen of the time, he was absolutely without personal courage. He could not look upon a hostile array without being overcome by sheer terror. Something of this feeling was manifested in his political career. He had the sure instinct which led him to place himself on the side of numbers, the pride, too, of capacity to grasp clearly the ideas of which those numbers were dimly conscious. In times of trouble, such capacity is power indeed. Then, if ever, the multitude, certain of their aim, uncertain of the means by which that aim is to be reached, look for the guidance of one in whose mental power they can repose confidence, and whose constancy they can trust. Such a man was Argyle. It is probable enough that there was no conscious hypocrisy in the choice which he was now to make. He would hardly have maintained himself in power so long as he did, if he had not shared the beliefs of those around him. He was probably as incapable of withstanding a popular belief as he was of withstanding an army of his foes. At all events, the time was now come for him to declare himself. When Hamilton swept out of the church, followed by the members of the Privy Council, Argyle alone remained behind. He took the part of the many against the few. "I have not striven to blow the bellows," he said, "but studied to keep matters in as soft a temper as I could; and now I desire to make it known to you that I take you all for members of a lawful Assembly, and honest countrymen."

CHAP. IV.
1638. Nov. 28.

Till December 20 the Assembly remained in session. As a matter of course, it swept away the Service Book, the Canons, and the Articles of Perth. It received with boundless credulity every incredible charge reported on the merest hearsay against the Bishops. It declared Episcopacy to be for ever abolished, and all the Assemblies held in Episcopal times to be null and void. It re-established the Presbyterian government, and ejected those ministers whose teaching had not been consonant with Calvinistic orthodoxy.[1]

Dec. Further proceedings in the Assembly.

The challenge thus uttered by the Scottish Assembly was in the main the same as that which had been uttered by the English Parliament in 1629, and which was to be uttered again by it in 1640. The Assembly demanded that the religion recognised by the nation itself should be placed beyond all contradiction, and that neither the King nor anyone else should venture to modify its ceremonies or its creed. Many conditions were present in the North to make the outbreak occur in Scotland earlier than it did in England. Charles's attack upon the religion of Scotland had been more sweeping and more provocative than anything that he had done in England. The Scottish nation, too, was more ready to combine than the English nation was. Government in England was a present reality. In Scotland it was but

Comparison between the Scottish Assembly and the English Parliament.

---

[1] Peterkin's *Records*, 128. *Baillie*, i. 165. Hamilton to the King, Dec. 1; *Hamilton Papers*, 62.

VOL. I. N

the shadow of an absentee sovereign. In the people itself, the influence of the Calvinistic clergy produced a strange uniformity of thought and character. Even the noblemen appear to have been cast very much in a common mould. It is true that Argyle and Montrose stand out amongst their fellows with distinct characters. The rest are scarcely more than names. To pass from a history which tells of Wentworth and Northumberland, Cottington and Portland, Essex and Saye, to a history which tells of Rothes and Loudoun, Balmerino and Lindsay, is like passing from the many-coloured life of the Iliad to the Gyas and Cloanthus of the Æneid. The want of originality of character made combination the easier. It made it the easier, too, to place the real direction of the movement in the hands of the ministers. Whatever forces were behind, the revolution which had been effected was a Presbyterian revolution. The preacher was and remained the guide and hero of Scottish nationality. The preacher was strong because he appealed to an ideal conviction larger and nobler than his logic. Bishops were to be proscribed, not because particular Bishops had done amiss, but in the name of the principle of parity amongst all who were engaged in the ministration of the same truths. The influence of the King was to be set aside in the Church, not because Charles had been unwarrantably meddlesome, but because the Church knew but one Heavenly King. It is impossible to doubt that the Scottish people grew the nobler and the purer for these thoughts—far nobler and purer than if they had accepted even a larger creed at the bidding of any earthly king. Of liberty of thought these Scottish preachers neither knew anything nor cared to know anything. To the mass of their followers they were kindly guides, reciprocating in their teaching the faith which existed around them. But Scotland was no country for eccentricities of thought and action. Hardihood was there, and brave championship of the native land and the native religion. Spiritual and mental freedom would have one day to be learned from England.

CHAP. IV.
1638. Dec.

On January 15, Hamilton told, before the English Council, the story of his bootless mission. The discussions which followed were long and anxious. Charles inclined to continue the negotiation. Disaffection, as he well knew, was widely spread in England, and any attempt to levy money would be met by redoubled outcries for a Parliament.¹

1639. Jan. 15. Hamilton's relation.

Charles might wish for peace, but, unless he had been prepared to sacrifice all that he had ever counted worth struggling for, he could not avoid war. For him the saying attributed to his father, "No Bishop, no King," was emphatically true. He had not chosen Bishops in Scotland amongst men who were imbued with the religious sentiment around them. He had rather sought for those who would serve as instruments in imposing his own religious practice upon an unwilling people. It is true, that before the Assembly met at Glasgow he had surrendered all the original objects of contention. Liturgy and Canons, Articles of Perth, and irresponsible Episcopacy had been given up. It is true that between Charles's moderate Episcopacy, responsible to Assemblies, and the direct government of the Assemblies themselves, the difference does not seem

War inevitable.

---

¹ Salvetti's *Newsletter*, Jan. 15/25. Bellievre to De Noyers, Jan. 17/27, Jan. 31/Feb. 10. *Arch. des Aff. Etr.* xlvii., fol. 341, 351. Joachimi to the States General, Jan. 18/28, *Add. MSS.*, 17,677 Q. fol. 10. Giustinian to the Doge, Jan. 18/28, *Ven. Transcripts*.

to have been very great. But to a man like Charles the appearance of victory was of greater importance than victory itself. He could not yield honourably and gracefully as Edward I. and Elizabeth would have yielded. He therefore felt that all was lost if he acknowledged that he had yielded to force what he had not been ready to yield to argument. The danger would not be confined to Scotland alone. His authority in England rested not on armed force, but on traditional conviction that he was supreme over all causes ecclesiastical and civil. If the Scottish Assembly claimed for itself the supremacy in ecclesiastical causes, it would not be long before the same claim would be put forward by an English Parliament. The question between Charles and his subjects was no longer one of forms of prayer and of Church government. It had become one reaching to the very foundations of political order.

Nor was it only upon his relations with England that Charles was compelled to cast his eyes. He knew that his position in the face of the Continental Powers was seriously weakened by the Scottish troubles, and he believed that those troubles had been fomented by the French Government. His diplomacy had been as unsuccessful in the past year, on the Continent, as it had been in Edinburgh and Glasgow. His hopes of recovering the Palatinate for his nephew seemed as little likely to be realised as they had ever been. The meeting of Ambassadors at Hamburg, to which had been referred the conditions of the treaty which had been under negotiation at Paris in 1637,[1] was long delayed, and it was not till the summer of 1638 that Sir Thomas Roe was despatched to meet the plenipotentiaries of France and

[1] *Pers. Government of Charles I.*, ii., 333.

Sweden in that city. Roe soon found that he could accomplish nothing. Charles still asked for an engagement from France and Sweden, that they would make no peace without the full restoration of the Palatinate, and those Powers still refused to comply with his wishes unless he would bind himself to join them in war by land as well as by sea.[1]

With this result Richelieu was well satisfied. He knew that Charles, with the Scottish dispute on his hands, would be unable to take part against France. More than that he had long ceased to expect.[2]

Charles himself was less clear-sighted. He had already lent himself to schemes for placing his nephew at the head of an army in the field at the very moment when he was looking in vain for the means of levying an army against the Scots. Charles actually sent the young man 30,000*l.* to raise troops, and Charles Lewis used the money to buy the allegiance of the garrison of Meppen. The Imperialists in the neighbourhood took the garrison by surprise, and occupied the town without any serious resistance. In the summer the young Prince started from the Netherlands, at the head of a small force, to join the Swedes. The Swedes were not anxious for his assistance, and left him unaided in the face of the enemy. He himself escaped to Hamburg, but his brother, Prince Rupert, with Lord Craven and others of his principal officers, were taken prisoners. Charles, however, did not relax his efforts. He kept up for some time a negotiation with Richelieu, with the object of inducing the Cardinal to share with him the expense of procuring the services of a

[1] Roe's Despatches, *S. P. Germany.*
[2] Chavigny's Despatches, *Bibl. Nat.* Fr. 15,915.

small army under General Melander, which was at that time waiting to sell itself to the highest bidder. Richelieu, however, preferred to acquire the army for himself, and Charles was doomed to a fresh disappointment.[1]

Charles's relations with Spain.

Earlier in the year, as soon as Charles had discovered that no very zealous assistance was to be expected from Richelieu, he turned in the direction of Spain. Under the name of a private merchant, he sold 3,000 barrels of powder to the Government of the Spanish Netherlands, and lent the services of his fleet to convey them safely to Dunkirk.

Secret negotiation at Brussels.

Then followed a long secret negotiation, carried on at Brussels through Gerbier, with the Princess of Pfalzburg, a sister of the exiled Duke of Lorraine, with the sanction of the Cardinal Infant. The scheme of an alliance with Spain split on much the same rock as that on which the conference at Hamburg had split. The Spaniards required that Charles should immediately declare war against France, and Charles required that the Emperor and the Spaniards should immediately deliver up to his nephew so much at least of the Palatinate as was actually in their hands.[2] In the Council of State at Madrid, Olivares scornfully asked how it was that Charles, who had his hands full at home, could talk of affronting France and Holland. No doubt, he added, the whole negotiation was mere trickery.[3]

Charles and Cardenas.

Charles had much to do to conceal from the

---

[1] Despatches in *S. P. Holland* and *Germany*. Chavigny to Bellievre, Nov. 12, Dec. 14. *Bibl. Nat.* Fr. 15,915, fol. 208,230.

[2] Some notices of this negotiation are in the *Clarendon St. P.* A full account may be derived from Gerbier's own despatches. *S. P. Flanders*.

[3] Consulta of the Council of State, Dec. $\frac{14}{24}$. *Simancas MSS.*, Est. 2521.

world the fact, that all through the summer and autumn of 1638 he was simultaneously offering his alliance to France and to Spain. A despatch written by Cardenas, the Spanish Resident in London, fell into the hands of the Swedes. It contained a statement that the Emperor was negotiating with the King of England, with the expectation that all difficulties about the Palatinate would soon be settled at a Conference at Brussels. Luckily for Charles, Cardenas knew nothing of the real negotiation in the hands of the Princess of Pfalzburg, and had only been informed of a project put forward without authority by Taylor, the English Resident at Vienna, and disavowed by Charles as soon as it came to his ears. Charles was therefore able with literal truth, though with no more than literal truth, to protest loudly to the world that he had been grossly calumniated, and that Taylor had acted in defiance of his instructions.[1] Cardenas was suspended from all intercourse with the Court,[2]

---

[1] Windebank to Hopton, Dec. 27, 1638. Windebank to Taylor, Jan. 11. Taylor's Relation, Apr. 4, 1639, *Clarendon MSS.*, 1161, 1170, 1218. Writing to Gerbier, Windebank blames him for not at once disavowing the story. "This," he adds, " you might safely have done without fearing to be guilty of Sir Henry Wotton's definition of an ambassador, seeing you know there is no direct treaty at all between His Majesty and them, and that all that has been done hath been by way of proposition moving from that side and managed by second hands, His Majesty neither appearing nor being engaged nor obliged to anything; and to this purpose His Majesty hath answered the French Ambassador; namely, that some propositions have been made to him from that side; but hath absolutely disavowed any formal or direct treaty at all, or that ever any letters to this purpose have passed between himself and them; and this, besides that it is a truth, His Majesty had reason to do, unless he were more sure of the success of that which hath been proposed from your parts, for by avowing that to be a treaty, he is sure to dissolve that with France, and so he may run hazard to lose both." Windebank to Gerbier, Jan. 4, 1639. *S. P. Flanders.*

[2] In the *S. P. Spain* is a copy of the intercepted despatch, together with the correspondence with Cardenas on the subject.

and Taylor was recalled and committed to the Tower.¹

Though neither France nor Spain entertained any hope of serious aid from Charles, there were many indirect ways in which his good will might be of use. Both Olivares and Richelieu, therefore, were anxious to be on friendly terms with the Queen. In March the Cardinal conceded to her the boon for which she had been so long begging, and released De Jars from captivity.² In April a heavier weight was thrown into the opposite scale. The Duchess of Chevreuse, gay, witty, and licentious, arrived to plot against the Cardinal from the secure distance of the English Court.

The arrival of the Duchess was the precursor of the arrival of another visitor of more exalted rank. The Queen Mother had long been weary of exile from France. All hopes of her restoration by the help of an insurrection of her partisans had long since passed away, and now that she had ceased to be serviceable to Spain, she was treated with cold courtesy at Brussels. The pension doled out to her was irregularly paid, and she looked back with fond regret to her old sumptuous life at Paris, where courtiers and artists had rivalled one another in doing her honour.

She could not believe that it was out of Charles's power to obtain for her permission to return. Charles, at her entreaty, put the question to the French Government. The response was unfavourable. Mary de Medicis attributed the failure to her presence on Spanish soil. Under the pretext of a visit to Spa,

---

¹ Windebank to Hopton, Sept. 29, 1639, *Clarendon St. P.* ii. 71.
² Clavigny to Bellievre, $\frac{\text{Feb. 24}}{\text{March 6}}$, March $\frac{9}{19}$, *Bibl. Nat.* Fr. 15,915, fol. 93, 97. See *Pers. Government of Charles I.*, ii. 197.

she left Brussels in the beginning of August, and crossed the frontier into the Dutch Netherlands. She was there received with every sign of respect by the Prince of Orange and the States General. Her presence soon caused a misunderstanding between the Dutch Government and the French Ambassador. The design of proceeding to England, which had probably been formed long before, took entire possession of her mind.

<small>CHAP. IV.
1638.
Aug. 4.
Crosses the Dutch frontier.
Proposes to visit England.</small>

Charles had always steadily refused her permission to land in his dominions. He knew that her mere presence would help to embroil him with France, and that the men whom she most trusted, Cogneux, Fabroni, and Monsigot, were steeped in intrigue, and were Richelieu's bitterest enemies. He therefore at once sent instructions to Boswell, his agent at the Hague, to remonstrate with her. Boswell's remonstrances were coldly received. At last he learned that she was making secret preparations for the voyage. He appealed to Fabroni, and Fabroni protested that there was no truth in the report. The next day the Queen Mother embarked for England.[1]

<small>Aug. 13. Charles remonstrates.
Aug. 30.
Sept. 24.
Sept. 25.</small>

On September 30 Monsigot presented himself before Charles to announce that his mistress was already on the way, and that, unless he turned her away from his ports, she would soon be on shore in England. Charles had not the heart to repel her, but he would willingly have seen her land without her disreputable train. Henrietta Maria's pleadings against this insult to her mother bore down his opposition, and orders were given that the mother of the Queen of England should be received with all

<small>Sept. 30. Monsigot's mission.</small>

---

[1] Coke to Boswell, Aug. 13; Boswell to Fabroni, Sept. 25; Boswell to Windebank, Aug. 9, Sept. 8, 26, 27, *S. P. Holland.*

the honours due to her exalted rank. No one, except her daughter, wished to see her in England. "I pray God," wrote Laud, "her coming do not spend the King more than . . would content the Swedes."[1] There was no remedy. Her arrival, said Windebank, "is so flat and sudden a surprisal as, without our ports should be shut against her, it is not to be avoided."

Mary de Medicis landed at Harwich on October 19. On her way to London she was received with every sign of a cordial welcome. The King met her at Chelmsford. As she passed through London, the Lord Mayor offered her his hospitality. The streets were lined with scaffoldings hung with rich cloths, and thronged by citizens ready to do honour to their guest, or at least to satisfy their own curiosity. At St. James's she was received by the Queen, who had parted from her thirteen years before. With motherly pride she presented her children to their grandmother. St. James's Palace was assigned to her as a residence.[2]

In vain Charles urged Lewis to allow his mother to return to France, on her engagement to meddle no more with politics. In vain did she entreat Bellièvre, the French Ambassador, to plead her cause with the Cardinal. The haughty widow of Henry IV. humiliated herself to no purpose. She was told that if she would betake herself to Florence a provision suitable to her rank would be bestowed upon her. In France she had always been troublesome, and she could not be admitted there. Such an offer was unac-

---

[1] Laud to Roe, Oct. 4, *Works*, vii. 486.

[2] Salvetti's *Newsletter*, Oct. $\frac{8}{18}$, Nov. $\frac{9}{19}$. La Serre *Histoire de l'Entrée de la Reine-Mère*. It is not necessary to believe all that the writer says about the enthusiasm with which the Queen was greeted. He says that the French Ambassador welcomed her, which is certainly untrue.

ceptable. Rather than revisit the home of her childhood, where she would find herself a stranger amongst strangers, she preferred to remain in England, a burdensome pensioner on Charles's bounty.[1]

The year 1638 did not end prosperously for Charles. His overtures had been rejected both by France and Spain. The Congress at Hamburg, without results for him, was not without results for others. A fresh compact was made between France and Sweden for a renewed attack upon the hereditary lands of the Emperor. Equipped with French subsidies, Bernhard of Weimar fell upon those Austrian lands upon the Upper Rhine, which barred the way of the French armies. Before the year came to an end he had won a great victory at Rheinfelden, and had forced the strong fortress of Breisach to surrender. To Richelieu, the surrender of Breisach brought the power of entering Germany at his pleasure. It implied, too, the power of cutting off supplies sent by land to the Spanish Netherlands. Richelieu felt that the great objects of his ambition were already within his grasp. A few months before, the birth of the Dauphin, who was afterwards Lewis XIV., had come to strengthen the basis of his power. It would be a son of the master whom he had served, who would be the next ruler of France, not his enemy Gaston, or any ally of the exiled Mary de Medicis.

The news of Bernhard's successes was almost as unwelcome at Whitehall as the news of Hamilton's failure at Glasgow. France was now strong in that very part of Germany from which the Palatinate might most easily be overawed. Nor was this all.

---

[1] Bellievre to Chavigny, Dec. $\frac{13}{23}$, *Arch. des Aff. Etr.* xlvii. 305. Memoir for Bellievre, Jan. $\frac{10}{20}$, *Bibl. Nat.* Fr. 15,915, fol. 258.

The danger by land was more than matched by the danger by sea. The French navy was growing in numbers and efficiency. One French fleet had burnt Spanish galleys in the Bay of Biscay. Another French fleet had repulsed Spanish ships in the Gulf of Genoa. It was by no means improbable that before long a triumphant French Armada would sail up the Channel to join the Dutch in the long-projected attack upon Dunkirk. No wonder Charles looked with wondering bitterness upon the swelling tide of Richelieu's success. No wonder that he fancied that he saw the hand of Richelieu in the Scottish troubles. Every loyal subject wished heartily that those troubles might be allayed. Till peace were established in Scotland, England could speak with but a feeble voice on the Continent. "The news of Scotland," wrote Roe, "is mortal to our reputation abroad. I hope it is not so ill as malignity spreads it."[1]

With the opening of the New Year, therefore, Charles had to face a Continental difficulty as well as a Scottish difficulty. Nothing would ever persuade him that the two were not far more closely connected than they really were. The Scottish resistance seemed to him so entirely incomprehensible, that he could not account for it, except on the supposition that Richelieu was at the bottom of the whole movement, stirring up rebellion in the North, in order to keep England from interfering on the Continent. In reality, Richelieu was doing nothing of the kind. Thoroughly convinced that Charles was rushing upon his own ruin, he did not think it worth while to interfere to stir the coals of an insurrection which was burning brightly enough without any aid from him. The very suspicion, however, was enough to

[1] Roe to Coke, Dec. 14; *S. P. Germany.*

increase Charles's anxieties. In one way or another, the Scottish troubles must be brought to an end, if his rule were not to become as despicable abroad as it was insecure at home.

    Step by step, therefore, pushed on by fate, which is but the consequence of past errors, Charles moved slowly and unwillingly towards war. Even before Hamilton's arrival, Sir Jacob Astley, a veteran who had served long in the Netherlands, was sent down to the North to muster the trained bands, and to bring them to due efficiency.[1] It was, indeed, officially stated that the object of these precautions was resistance to a possible invasion,[2] but it was hardly likely that such an announcement would be seriously believed. On January 17, the Committee on Scottish Affairs recommended the King to select from the trained bands a force of 30,000 men. It was arranged that the King should go to York in April, to treat or fight as occasion might serve, and that Newcastle and Hull should be placed in a state of defence.[3] Arms and munitions of war were brought over from the Continent in large quantities.

    Men and arms alone were not enough. "If money is to be found; and the Puritans kept quiet," wrote a disinterested onlooker, " all will go well."[4] Whatever the Puritans might do at some future time, they showed no signs of stirring now. For the navy, of course, ship-money was still available; yet, either because the excitement roused by the result of Hampden's trial had alarmed the Court, or because, in view of the probability that money would be

---

[1] Astley to Windebank, Jan. 4, 11, *S. P. Dom.* ccccix. 24, 65.
[2] The King to the Lords Lieutenants, Jan. 11, *Ibid.* ccccix. 59.
[3] Minutes of the Committee, Jan. 17, *Ibid.* ccccix. 106, 107
[4] Salvetti's *Newsletter*, $\frac{\text{Jan. 25}}{\text{Feb. 4}}$.

needed for land-service, it was thought wiser to decrease the burdens caused by the fleet, as much as possible, no writ of ship money was issued at the usual time in the autumn of 1638. When January came, the writs were indeed sent out, but only 69,000*l.* was asked for: about a third of the amount levied in former years. It was calculated that this would be sufficient to fit out the eighteen vessels which it was proposed to despatch to the coast of Scotland under Pennington's command.[1]

It was less easy to find means for the equipment and payment of the army. Early in the year, calculations were made of the expense which would be entailed by the army of 30,000 men whom it had been originally intended to place on the borders. Such an army, it appeared, could only be maintained at the rate of 935,000*l.* a year.[2] So large an expenditure was beyond Charles's means, and he therefore resolved to content himself with a smaller force. One scheme there was which recommended itself as as in some small measure an alleviation of the burden. By their feudal tenures, the nobility were bound to follow the King to war when his banner was displayed before him. It was true that many years had passed since the fulfilment of this duty had been required; but the King, who had replenished his exchequer by enforcing the antiquated obligation to take up knighthood, might very well replenish his army by enforcing the antiquated obligation to personal service. Every Peer of the realm was therefore

[1] Order in Council, Jan. 23, *S. P. Dom.* cccix. 194.

[2] *S. P. Dom.* ccccxv. 119. Mr. Hamilton dates this paper conjecturally in March. The project had been abandoned by that time, and it can hardly have been drawn up much later than the end of January. In his Preface he speaks erroneously of the number of 30,000 being that which actually marched.

directed to appear in person in defence of the borders, bringing with him such a following as his dignity required. It was gleefully calculated at Whitehall, that in this way the Royal camp would receive an accession of at least 1,200 horse without any payment whatever.[1]

Early in February, orders were given for the levy of 6,000 foot and 1,000 horse, to form the nucleus of the larger force which was to gather round the Royal standard. To these were to be added 4,000 of the trained bands of Yorkshire, Durham, and Northumberland. Charles would thus, after taking account of the cavalry furnished by the nobility, have an army of about 12,000 men, disposable for service in the field. For garrison duty at Berwick the Earl of Lindsey was to bring 2,000 men from Lincolnshire, and the Earl of Cumberland was to command at Carlisle with a force of 800 soldiers, of whom 300 were to be supplied from Wentworth's Irish levies. A little army of 5,000 men from the Eastern Counties were to follow Hamilton on shipboard, to be landed at Aberdeen, to join Huntly in the North. Taken altogether, the forces at the King's disposal might be reckoned as not far short of 20,000 men.[2]

Such a force would probably have been insufficient for the work in hand, even if Charles had been assured of national support. Of this, however, there was no sign. The nobility, indeed, had either obeyed his summons, or had sent money in lieu of service in cases of sickness or old age. Wentworth, detained in Ireland by his official duties, had directed his

[1] The King to Lord Grey of Werk, Jan. 26. Northumberland to Conway, Jan. 29, *S. P. Dom.* cccx. 24, 80.

[2] The details will be found in the accounts of the Treasurer of the Army, *Audit Office Declared Accounts*, Bundle 301, Roll 1148. Hamilton's men are there given as 4,500. Hamilton himself reckons them at 5,000, perhaps counting officers, artillerymen, and supernumeraries.

steward to pay 2,000*l.* to the King as soon as he appeared in the North. The Catholic Marquis of Winchester sent 500*l.* On the other hand, the Puritan Lord Brooke, when summoned to attend the King, replied that he 'did not apprehend himself obliged to any aid of that nature but by Parliament.'[1] And the equally Puritan Lord Saye returned a somewhat similar answer. The letter of the law was, however, clearly against them, and on second thoughts they expresssed their readiness to attend His Majesty, at least within the realm of England.

For the army thus constituted it was necessary to provide commanders. The general-in-chief was to be the Earl of Arundel, a stately nobleman, who was a Catholic by conviction, and who therefore hated the Presbyterian Scots, but who had never looked on the face of war. It had been originally intended to confer the command of the horse upon the Earl of Essex, who had seen some service in the Netherlands.[2] But the Queen begged this post for her favourite, the Earl of Holland, the most incompetent of men, and Essex had to content himself with the less brilliant office of second in command of the entire army. The seeds of jealousy were thus sown before a single regiment was formed. Arundel vowed that he would throw up his command rather than see Holland in a post of such authority, and it was only upon the warm intercession of the King that he was induced to withdraw his resignation.[3]

Even if Charles succeeded in filling up his ranks

---

[1] Minutes by Nicholas, Feb., *S. P. Dom.* cccxiii. 117.

[2] His service in the Palatinate, of which historians are fond of talking, was next to nothing.

[3] Northumberland to Wentworth, Jan. 29, *Straf. Letters*, ii. 276. The King to Arundel, Feb. 9, *S.P. Dom.* cccxii. 74. Con to Barberini, Feb. $\frac{1}{11}$, *Add. MSS.* 15,392, fol. 39.

to the number of 30,000—which was in those days considered to make up the largest force which could safely keep the field without a failure of supplies, unless it was intended, like the hordes of Wallenstein, to subsist upon organised plunder—his army would leave much to be desired in point of training. A body of veterans, if such a body could be found, would form a nucleus round which the raw English levies would soon acquire the consistency of a disciplined force. Such veterans were to be found in Flanders, and even in the summer of 1638 a proposal had been made to the Spanish Government for the loan of a body of troops. On that occasion Cardenas had been instructed to refuse the request. So incurable was the distrust which Charles had sown around him, that Olivares feared lest a victory in Scotland might be followed by a league between England and France, in the same way that Richelieu feared lest it might be followed by a league between England and Spain.[1]

The scheme, dropped for a time, was revived a few months later. In January 1639, a certain Colonel Gage, a Catholic officer in the Spanish service, communicated to the English Government his belief that the Cardinal Infant might be induced to supply Charles with a veteran force for his Scotch campaign, if he were allowed to raise from year to year a large number of recruits in England and Ireland by voluntary enlistment. A special emissary was accordingly sent to Brussels to carry on the negotiation. The Cardinal Infant received him politely, but assured him that, menaced as he was by French armies, he could not spare a single man.[2]

1638.

1639. Jan. Gage's proposal.

Feb. The Spaniards cannot be spared.

[1] Philip IV. to Cardenas, Sept. $\frac{3}{13}$, 1638. *Simancas MSS.*, Est. 2575.
[2] Col. Gage to G. Gage, $\frac{Jan. 26}{Feb. 5}$. Instructions to Col. Gage, Feb. 5.

VOL. I.   O

1639.
Feb.

Scottish soldiers from the German War.

Charles was thus saved from the consequences of the most ruinous step which he had hitherto contemplated. It can hardly be doubted that if these Spanish regiments had set foot in England, the whole country from the Cheviots to the Land's End would have broken out into instant rebellion.

Trained and war-worn troops, the value of which had been thus recognised by Charles, were not wanting to Scotland. The very poverty of the Scots, through no prevision of their own, had made them strong. For many a year, a stream of needy, stalwart adventurers had been flowing over from Scotland into Germany to be converted into hardy warriors by Gustavus Adolphus and his lieutenants. Many a man had returned, bringing with him his share of the plunder of Germany, together with an enthusiasm for the Protestantism which had been to him a war cry leading to fortune, as well as a strengthening faith in the hour of peril. Small as the population of Scotland was, when the hour of battle came, she would be able to oppose to the loose ranks of untrained peasants which were all that Charles could bring into the field, an army which comprised at least a fair proportion of practised soldiers.

The command of the Scottish army.

No special credit is due to the Covenanting leaders for being ready to make use of the instrument of war which circumstances had placed in their hands. But credit is due to them for avoiding the fault into which a proud and high-spirited nobility is most apt to fall. Very early they resolved that no Rothes or Loudoun should contest, as Essex and Holland were contesting, for those posts of military

Col. Gage to Windebank, Feb. $\frac{18}{28}$. G. Gage to Windebank, $\frac{\text{Feb. 23}}{\text{March 5}}$. *Clarendon St. P.* ii. 21.

trust to which they were unequal. The professional army of Scotland was to have a professional commander.

Alexander Leslie.

The leader of whom they were in search was found in Alexander Leslie, an illegitimate son of a Fifeshire laird. Deformed in person, and of low stature, he had served with credit in the German wars, and, if he had not gained high renown as a strategist, he was skilled in the arts by which recruits are trained into soldiers, and posts are occupied and held. In the spring of 1638, when he was in command of a force in the Swedish service in Pomerania, he visited Scotland in order to fetch away his wife and family. On his way he was presented to the King in London, and told Roe that, if his present masters could spare him, he would be happy to undertake the command of the army which it was at that time proposed to raise for the Elector Palatine.[1] Thrown into the midst of the excitement then spreading over his native country, he may even in the spring of 1638 have seen his way to a position which promised more than the service of the feeble Charles Lewis. It is not probable that he was himself very enthusiastic in the cause of the Covenant, or in any other cause whatever. For that very reason he was the better fitted to take the command of an army in which there were many enthusiasts. No doubt he entered into communication with Rothes, the head of the family of Leslie; and, whether any actual offer of command were made to him at this

1638. April. His visit to Scotland

---

[1] Roe to Elizabeth, March 22; Elizabeth to Roe, Apr. 2, *S. P. Germany.* Zonca to the Doge, Apr. 6, *Ven. Transcripts.* This puts an end to the story which has been copied from Spalding by most writers, that Leslie came home with the intention of settling in Scotland. On the fable of his inability to write, see Masson's *Life of Milton,* ii. 55.

time or not, Rothes was not likely to forget so useful a kinsman.

Leslie returned to the Continent. Before the end of the year he was again in Scotland, slipping through the watch of the English cruisers in a small bark. He was able to gladden the hearts of his fellow-countrymen by the announcement that he had induced large numbers of Scots arriving in Germany to take the Covenant, and that he had procured large stores of military supplies for the use of the Scottish army at home.[1] From time to time arms and powder were conveyed across the sea. Some of these supplies were intercepted by Charles's agents, but the greater part was safely landed. Soon after the conclusion of the sittings of the Assembly of Glasgow, Leslie was invested with the rank of general. Active preparations for defence were made on every side. "We are busy," wrote a Scotchman in February, " preaching, praying, and drilling ; could His Majesty and his subjects in England come hither, they will find a harder welcome than before, unless we be made quit of the Bishops."[2]

On February 14 the Covenanters brought matters to a crisis. They appealed from the King to the English people. They were loyal, they said, to their sovereign, and most anxious to remain on good terms with their brethren in the South. All the mischief which had happened had been the fault of some 'Churchmen of the greatest power in England.' These men had introduced innovations into their own Church, had fined and banished those who strove to resist the Church of Rome, and had finally interfered with the Scottish Church in order to create a

[1] *Baillie*, i. 111.
[2] Craig to Stewart, Feb. 12, *S. P. Dom.* ccccxii. 103.

precedent for similar work in England. Was the English nation willing to fight in such a cause? Already Papists—Arundel, whose secret convictions were well known, was clearly pointed out—were placed in command of the army preparing against Scotland. If war there was to be, it would be war for the re-establishment of the Bishops. If an English Parliament were convened, it would approve the equity and loyalty of the Scots.[1]

Charles was stung to the quick. The appeal to an English Parliament was specially annoying, and the assertion that he was showing undue favour to the Catholics would be widely circulated in England. He had long been contending against the belief that Laud was a friend of the Papacy in disguise, and, in order to refute it, he had recently directed the Archbishop to publish his narrative of the Conference in which, fifteen years before, he had upheld the doctrines of the English Church against the Jesuit Fisher. The book appeared on February 10, only to be received with jeers by Catholic and Puritan.[2] Laud could no longer count upon equitable consideration. At this very moment he was exposing himself to fresh obloquy by an unwise Star Chamber prosecution, directed against his old antagonist, Bishop Williams. Certain letters, written by a schoolmaster named Osbaldiston, were found in Williams's house at Buckden. In these letters an unnamed personage was irreverently styled 'the little urchin,' and 'the little meddling hocus-pocus.' There can be no reasonable doubt that Laud was intended. Williams suggested that the words referred to one Mr. Spicer. Williams

[1] *Rushworth*, ii. 798.
[2] Laud's Diary, Feb. 10, *Works*, iii. 231. Con to Barberini, Feb. 22/March 4, *Add. MSS.* 15,392, fol. 52.

was, however, condemned to pay a fine of 5,000*l.* to the King, and 3,000*l.* to the Archbishop, for having these letters in his possession. Osbaldiston, who was present in Court, slipped away as soon as he heard how matters were likely to go, and eluded all pursuit. He left behind him a written explanation that he had fled beyond Canterbury.[1]

Charles was able to fine and imprison his English subjects. The Scots were beyond his reach. On February 27 he published a proclamation in reply to the Scottish manifesto. It was untrue, he said in effect, that the religion of Scotland was attacked. It was perfectly safe in his hands. The Scots were aiming at the destruction of monarchical government. They had been tampering with his English subjects, and were now preparing to invade England, in order that their leaders might repair their broken fortunes by the plunder of the South.[2] If he was now compelled to levy an army, it was not merely to vindicate his rights in Scotland. The very safety of England was at stake. "The question," he said, "is not now whether a Service Book is to be received or not, nor whether episcopal government shall be continued or Presbyterial admitted, but whether we are their King or not." This proclamation was appointed to be read in every parish church in England.[3] It was speedily followed by the *Large Declaration*, as it was called, a portly volume in which the whole story of the misdeeds of the Scots was set forth at length from the King's point of view. The writer, a Scotchman, named Dr. Balcanqual, had accompanied Hamilton to

---

[1] *Rushw.* ii. 803.

[2] Charles had said much the same thing of Eliot, when he described him as 'an outlaw desperate in mind and fortune.'

[3] *Rushw.* ii. 830.

Glasgow as his chaplain. He now received the Deanery of Durham as the reward of his advocacy.

In one point at least Charles was undoubtedly right. The coming war would be a struggle for supremacy. Monarchy, as it had been hitherto understood, was now challenged by the principle of national sovereignty clothed in ecclesiastical forms. The issue thus raised could hardly be fought out in Scotland alone. As the Scottish manifesto declared, the future of England was involved in the strife which was now opening in the North.

CHAPTER V.

THE MARCH TO THE BORDERS AND THE PACIFICATION OF BERWICK.

CHAP. V.
1639. March.
Plan of the campaign.

WAR was now universally recognised as inevitable. The plan of campaign adopted by Charles was to a great extent the same as that which had been suggested by Wentworth. Carlisle and Berwick were to be firmly held, and an army on the borders was to protect England from invasion. Pennington's ships were to hover about the Firth of Forth to cut off the petty commerce which enriched Fife and the Lothians. The great blow, however, was to be struck, not at Leith, but at Aberdeen. Hamilton was to carry a force of 5,000 men to Huntly's support. As soon as he arrived, the two marquises would move southwards together, collecting as they went those scattered bodies of loyalists who were supposed to be burning to throw off the yoke of Covenanting tyranny.[1] From Hamilton's point of view, it was necessary that he should appear at the head of a Scottish party. To land simply in command of an English force was a course reconcileable neither with his feelings nor with his interests. He could not treat Scotland, as Wentworth treated it, as a mere land of rebels.

The Covenanters seize the castles of Edinburgh and Dumbarton.

In the midst of Charles's deliberate preparations, the Covenanters suddenly assumed the offensive. The walls of the castles of Edinburgh and Dumbarton were strong, but their garrisons had no heart to fight against their countrymen. At Edinburgh the outer

[1] *Burnet*, 113.

gate was burst open with a petard, and the walls were scaled, whilst the soldiers within looked on in stupefied amazement. The strongest fortress in Scotland was 'won without a stroke.' At Dumbarton the Governor was so much at his ease that he took some of his men with him to perform their devotions in a church outside the fortifications. He and his men were seized, and the rest of the garrison capitulated on the following day.[1] Stirling was still in the friendly keeping of the Earl of Mar.

At Dalkeith, Traquair had hoped to make a stand. The regalia of Scotland were there, and powder and arms had been stored up in the cellars for the use of that Royalist army which was to be raised in the Southern counties as soon as the King reached the Borders. Unluckily for the scheme, the place was not defensible by any means at Traquair's disposal. The Covenanters from Edinburgh climbed over the walls, and bore off the crown and sceptre with every sign of reverence.[2] Other fortified houses belonging to the loyal nobility were easily reduced to submission, and before the end of March Nithsdale's castle of Caerlaverock was the only defensible position untaken to the south of the Tay. For Charles the result was no mere military disaster. Nowhere amongst his few followers in the Southern Lowlands had there been found that desperate fidelity which springs from devotion to a great cause cheerfully embraced. The King who in time of danger is unable to awaken enthusiasm is lost already.

Worse news still came from Aberdeen. All through February, Montrose had been busy, levying men and money in his native Forfarshire. Once he dashed northwards as far as Turriff, to rally the gentry of

[1] *Baillie*, i. 195. [2] *Rushw.* ii. 906.

the district, who were good Covenanters because they feared Huntly. In March he had sterner work before him. On the 16th Huntly received a commission of Lieutenancy from the King, and the next day a large consignment of arms followed. He was ordered to take the aggressive.[1] Neither Charles nor Hamilton had any notion of the value of time in war, and they seem to have fancied that the Covenanters would be as slow in their preparations as they were themselves.

On the 25th Huntly was at Inverury at the head of 5,000 men. The Covenanters, he was told, were in full march to the North. Without succour from England, he was no match for the enemy. Amongst the gentry of the neighbourhood, the Frazers and the Forbeses, the Covenanting army was sure of a welcome. If Huntly had been a Montrose, he would have struck one stroke for the King in spite of the odds against him. Huntly was not a Montrose. He called a council of war. On its advice, he dismissed his troops and left Aberdeen to its fate.[2]

In the town everything was in confusion. Sixty of the principal citizens, accompanied by the greater number of the Doctors, shipped themselves to offer their services to the King. Others took refuge in friendly houses in the neighbourhood. On the 30th Montrose marched into Aberdeen with Leslie at his side, and 6,000 men at his heels. His allies from the country round made up 3,000 more. The young commander had a keen eye for the value of a symbol or a flag. He heard that the Gordons had adopted a

---

[1] *Gordon*, ii. 213. *Burnet*, 113.

[2] Gordon's story that Hamilton sent a direct message to Huntly to dismiss his troops may, I think, be rejected. There may have been orders not to fight till Hamilton arrived. We have no actually contemporary evidence, and must be content with probabilities.

red ribbon as a mark of loyalty. Montrose bade his men sling blue scarfs over their shoulders, or to tie bunches of blue ribbons on their bonnets. Montrose's whimsies, as they were called, were soon to become famous when the blue bonnets crossed the border. He did not neglect more serious work. Leaving a garrison behind him, he pushed on for Inverury, where he quartered his men on the opponents of the Covenant. Meal chests were broken open and cattle slaughtered. Houses standing empty were stripped of their contents. The language was enriched with a new verb 'to plunder'[1] imported by Leslie and his followers from the German war, as the synonymous verb 'to loot' has, in our days, been imported from the plains of Northern India.

March 30. Montrose's blue badges.

Despairing of aid from the South, Huntly sought an interview with Montrose. On April 5 a compromise was arrived at. Huntly was to throw no hindrance in the way of any of his followers who were pressed to sign the Covenant. Those of them who were unwilling to do so, and especially the numerous Catholics amongst them, were to enter into an engagement to maintain the laws and liberties of Scotland. On these conditions they were to be left without molestation as long as they remained quiet. Huntly himself was allowed to return to Strathbogie.[2]

April 5. Pacification of the North.

As far as the mass of the population was concerned, the compromise thus arrived at was eminently wise. No possible good could have arisen to

---

[1] Latham's *Johnson* gives the word on Fuller's authority as having been introduced in 1642. Gordon, however, says of this expedition, 'this they called for to plunder them' (ii. 229). It is used in a MS. letter of Sir H. Vane in 1640.

[2] *Spalding*, i. 160. *Gordon*, ii. 224. The evidence of the latter is worth more than usual here, as his father was engaged in the negotiation.

the national cause from the compulsory signature of the Covenant by friend or foe. It does not follow that it was equally wise to leave Huntly and his sons at liberty to form a centre of resistance as soon as pressure was withdrawn. So, at least, thought the Northern Covenanters, whose quarrel was rather with the Gordons than with Episcopacy. On the plea that without his aid it was impossible to arrive at a permanent settlement, the Marquis was invited to Aberdeen under a safe-conduct signed by Montrose and the other leaders, assuring him full liberty to return home as soon as the conference was over.

On the 12th Huntly was at Aberdeen. The next day, Montrose's language was that of a man seeking for a pretext to excuse in his own eyes a breach of his plighted word. He began by preferring unexpected demands. Would Huntly pay the expenses of the Covenanting army? Would he seize certain Highland robbers in the neighbourhood? Would he give the hand of friendship to his brother's murderer, Crichton of Frendraught? The last request could only be made to be refused. Between Crichton and Huntly lay the bitter memory of the night when the young Lord Meldrum, coming on an errand of mercy, was decoyed into the Tower of Frendraught only to be awakened by the roaring flames. Montrose's request was met, as it could not but have been met, with an unhesitating refusal. "My Lord," said Montrose, "seeing we are all now friends, will ye go South to Edinburgh with us?" After some further conversation, Huntly asked a plain question: Was he to go as a captive, or of his own free will? "Make your choice," was Montrose's reply. In that case, said Huntly, he would rather not go as a captive. The form of liberty made little difference to the fact of compulsion. Montrose may have been, as has been suggested, overruled by the Committee by which he was controlled; but whether this were the case or not, he had played but a mean and shabby part.

It had been intended that Huntly should have been accompanied by his two eldest sons—Lord Gordon and Lord Aboyne—who alone of his numerous family had reached man's estate. Aboyne asked leave to go home and fetch money for his journey; and Montrose, ashamed perhaps of his treatment of the family, gave the required permission on promise of a quick return. Aboyne, regardless of an engagement made to one whose faith had not been kept, took the opportunity to place himself beyond the reach of pursuit. His father and elder brother were conducted to Edinburgh. There Huntly was pressed to take the Covenant. "For my own part," he replied, "I am in your power, and resolved not to leave that foul title of traitor as an inheritance upon my posterity. You may take my head from my shoulders, but not my heart from my Sovereign."[1]

On March 30, the day on which Montrose entered Aberdeen, the King rode into York.[2] Already as he had journeyed northwards he had been met by bad news from Scotland. He would soon learn that Montrose had brought ruin upon his whole plan of operations. The party which Hamilton had promised him in Scotland was incapable of affording any serious assistance. Charles must fall back on Wentworth's plan now. If Scotland was to be conquered, it must be conquered by a purely English force, and he already knew that if it was comparatively easy to

---

[1] *Gordon*, ii. 232. *Spalding*, i. 168.
[2] Coke to Windebank, March 31, *S. P. Dom.* ccccxv. 78.

raise the troops which he required, it was a task of enormous difficulty to pay them.

CHAP. V.
1639. Feb. The City asked for money.

The first impulse of every Government in financial straits was to apply to the City of London. In February the citizens had therefore been asked for a free contribution. After a month's delay it was found that no more than 4,800*l.* had been paid, in spite of the personal entreaty of the Lord Mayor and Aldermen. A fresh and more urgent appeal in March produced a bare 200*l.* in addition. The whole amount was so small that it was contemptuously refused.[1]

April 9. A general contribution demanded.

In spite of this discouraging experience, the demand for a free contribution was extended to the whole country. In order to increase the chance of a favourable response, a proclamation was issued by which a considerable number of the new monopolies was revoked. Several, however, remained in force, and amongst these were some of the most obnoxious.[2]

March. Sale of the Mastership of the Rolls.

To provide for immediate necessities, the Mastership of the Rolls had been put up to auction. Sir Charles Cæsar bade higher than his competitors, and obtained the prize for 15,000*l.*[3]

April. Ship money comes in slowly.

It was a bad omen for the success of the general contribution, that ship money was coming in more slowly than ever. Though only 69,000*l.* had been required this year, on April 13 the payments had not exceeded 17,000*l.*[4]

At the beginning of April, therefore, Charles

---

[1] *Common Council Journal Book,* Feb. 16, March 15, 21, xxxviii. 208*b.*; 229; 297. Rossingham's *Newsletter,* Apr. 2. *Add. MSS.* 11,045, fol. 9.

[2] *Rushw.* iii. 910, 915.

[3] Garrard to Conway, March 28, *S. P. Dom.* ccccxv. 65. Rossingham's *Newsletter,* Apr. 2, *Add. MSS.* 11,045, fol. 9.

[4] Account of the Treasurers of the Navy, Apr. 13. *S. P. Dom.* ccccxvii. 90.

found himself at York with an insufficient army, and with very little assurance that he would be able to find money to pay even that army for more than a limited time. As the news of the disaster in Scotland dropped in, the cry of treachery was lightly raised. Charles himself imagined that the hand of Richelieu was to be seen in all that had occurred. Others threw the blame on the Scots themselves. When the capture of Edinburgh Castle was announced, Dorset told Hamilton in full Council that he deserved to lose his head as a traitor. Nothing but treason could be accepted as the explanation of Huntly's tame surrender of Aberdeen. Traquair had no sooner set foot in York, than he was placed under arrest for the loss of Dalkeith, though he was set free after a short detention. At the English Court it was impossible to judge fairly of the difficulties of Scottish loyalists abandoned to themselves amidst the waves of a great national movement, because it was not the fashion at the English Court to believe that there was any national movement in Scotland at all. Treachery undoubtedly existed; but it was the treachery of the Scottish gentlemen of the bedchamber who listened to Charles's unguarded talk, and forwarded his secrets to their countrymen across the border. In this way the Scots received intelligence of every decision almost as soon as it was taken.[1]

From Ireland, too, the news was not encouraging. Charles had confidently looked to the Earl of Antrim to land 10,000 men in the Western Highlands in order to overpower Argyle. Wentworth called

---

[1] Con to Barberini, $\frac{March\ 29}{Apr.\ 8}$, *Add. MSS.* 15,392, fol. 100. Smith to Pennington, Apr. 4. Arundel to Windebank, Apr. 4, *S. P. Dom.* ccccxvii. 26, 29. Rossingham's *Newsletter*, Nov. 23, *Add. MSS.* 11,05, fol. 14.

CHAP. V.
1639. April.
Wentworth's view of the situation.

Antrim before him, cross-examined him as to his means and intentions, and reported to the King that the Earl had neither 10,000 men at his disposal, nor the capacity to guide such a force if it were entrusted to his charge.[1] Wentworth's view of the situation was very much what it had been the year before. He knew, what Charles did not know, that it was impossible to improvise an army. He considered that Charles's officers were as inexperienced as his men. Looking at Arundel and Holland, he found it hard to understand that men were 'born great captains and generals.' He did not think that they were likely to become so on a day's warning. The best thing he thought would be for the army to keep the Scots in check on the borders, attending to its own drill and discipline, whilst the fleet blockaded the Scottish ports. If Berwick and Carlisle were well secured, it might 'keep our blue bonnet to his own peck of oatmeal—which they say the lay elder is to provide every soldier of, with a satchel to put it in—without tasting of our better fare, lest he might grow too much in love with it.' Such a plan would doubtless require more money than the King had at his disposal. It could not be, however, that Englishmen would grudge five or six months' service at their own cost. When the winter came it would be necessary 'to think of a constant revenue,' or, in other words, to summon Parliament.[2] If only Englishmen had felt towards the Scottish insurgents as Wentworth felt, there could be no question of the wisdom of his advice.

[1] Wentworth to Windebank, March 20, *Straf. Letters*, ii. 300.
[2] He had already written: "For Parliament I see not how that can be this summer, it being resolved His Majesty will be at York so early in the spring." Wentworth to Northumberland, Feb. 10, *Straf. Letters*, ii. 279.

Charles was too impatient for immediate success to be guided by such counsels. The news of the surrender of Aberdeen reached him on April 4. If it was useless to send Hamilton to Aberdeen, he might be sent elsewhere. Nothing could eradicate from Charles's mind the notion that, if he could only pierce through the hostile crust, he would find a loyal Scottish nation beneath. Hamilton was therefore to betake himself with his three regiments to the Firth of Forth, to make one more appeal to the people of Scotland against their leaders. It would be long before Charles could be brought to open his eyes to the fact that he was contending against Scotland itself.

CHAP. V.
1639.
April 4.
Hamilton to go to the Firth of Forth.

On April 7, therefore, a new proclamation was drawn up to enlighten the eyes of the misguided peasants and tradesmen of Scotland. In it Charles assured his subjects of his intention to stand by the promises made in his name at Glasgow. Nineteen of the leaders—Argyle, Rothes, Montrose, Leslie, and others—were excepted from pardon, though a promise was added that if they submitted within four-and-twenty hours after the publication of the proclamation, their cases should be taken into favourable consideration. After that time had elapsed, a price would be set on their heads to be paid to any one who put them to death. A free pardon should be granted to all others who had participated in rebellion. More than this, all vassals and tenants of persons in rebellion were to keep their rents in their own hands, one-half to be paid to the King, and the other to be retained by themselves. All tenants of rebels taking the King's side were to receive a long lease of their lands from the Crown at two-thirds of their present rent. Disloyal tenants of a loyal land-

April 7.
The new proclamation.

lord were to be expelled from their holdings. In one respect, this proclamation was modified before it was finally issued. The Scots about the King remonstrated against the clauses offering a reward for assassination, and he therefore substituted for them a general threat that all rebels not laying down their arms within eight days would be held to be traitors, and as such to have forfeited their estates and goods. To Hamilton Charles explained his reason for the alteration. "As for excepting some out of the general pardon," he wrote, "almost every one now thinks that it would be a means to unite them the faster together, whereas there is no fear but that those who are fit to be excepted will do it themselves by not accepting of pardon, of which number I pray God there be not too many."[1]

On the 15th Hamilton was at Yarmouth, prepared to take on board his men. He complained bitterly of the rawness of the levies provided for him by the magistrates. Of the whole number no more than 200 had ever had a gun in their hands. The muskets provided were not of the same calibre. The men, however, were strong and well clothed, but it could not be expected that they would be fit to take the field with less than a month's training.[2]

At York the impression was gaining ground that the conquest of Scotland was not to be effected by proclamations. On April 19 tidings came that the Scottish army on the Borders would soon be 10,000 strong. Another report declared that Leslie had threatened to meet the King on the Borders to parley

---

[1] Draft Proclamation, Apr. 7, enclosed by Hay to Windebank, Apr. 15. Proclamation, Apr. 25, *S. P. Dom.* cccxvii. 94, i., cccxviii. 50. The King to Hamilton, Apr. 5, 7, 10, *Burnet,* 119.

[2] Hamilton to the King, Apr. 15, 18, *Ham. Papers,* 72, 73.

with him at the head of 30,000 men. Charles's own forces were now marching in. There had been some disorders on the way. The Essex men had murdered a woman and had plundered houses as they passed. At Boston a pressed man sent his wife with one of his toes in a handkerchief as evidence that he could not march.[1] There was certainly no enthusiasm for the war. But neither was there any distinct animosity against the cause for which the war was fought. Ploughmen and carters would far rather have remained at home. But the stratum of society from which they came was not stirred very deeply by the Puritan movement. Amongst the trained bands of the northern counties there were even observable some sparks of the old feud with Scotland which had flamed up in many a Border conflict in the olden days. The mass of the army was listless and undisciplined, but it is not altogether impossible that good officers might after a time have succeeded in inspiring it with something of the military feeling.[2]

CHAP. V.
1639.
April.

Charles had, however, taken care to gather round him elements of hostility to his enterprise. Dragged against their will to the Borders, and long deprived of the part in the Government which they held to be their due, the English nobles bore no good will to a war which, if it were successful, would place them more completely than ever at the feet of their sovereign. If Charles had been quicksighted to perceive that

Disaffection of the English nobles.

---

[1] Lindsey to Windebank, Apr. 6, 7. Windebank to Read, Apr. 19. Norgate to Read, Apr. 19, *S. P. Dom.* cccxvii. 41, cccxviii. 78.

[2] I have come to this conclusion after a study of all the contemporary letters to which I have had access. As long as it was believed that the King had 30,000 men with him on the Borders from the first, his inactivity needed the active disaffection of the army to explain it. Now that it is known that he could put less than 12,000 into the field, such an explanation is unnecessary.

P 2

concession in Scotland would bring with it concession in England, they were no less quicksighted to perceive that the overthrow of the Scottish Covenanters would draw with it the erection of an absolute monarchy in England. The first test of their feeling was a proposal of a military oath binding them to fight in the King's cause 'to the utmost hazard of their life and fortunes.' They asked whether these words bound them to place their whole property at the King's disposal. The obnoxious words were accordingly changed for 'the utmost of my power and hazard of my life.' To this all consented except Saye and Brooke. These two Puritan lords flatly refused to take even the modified oath. They were committed to the custody of the Lord Mayor of York.[1]

Saye and Brooke were subsequently permitted to retire to their homes. The King was not without hope that some legal means of punishing them might be found. But the law officers of the Crown advised him that they had not committed a punishable offence. They suggested, however, a means of meeting the difficulty. It was probable, they thought, that the two lords had arrived at York without proper military equipment. In that case a fine might legally be imposed upon them. Charles thought the suggestion a good one; but, as nothing was done, it is not unlikely that inquiry only served to demonstrate that Saye and Brooke had taken good care to comply with the letter of the law.[2]

The two lords found no imitators at York. But the King soon discovered that the nobility had come rather as spectators than as actors. Amongst them Arundel

---

[1] Rossingham's *Newsletter*, Apr. 30, *S. P. Dom.* cccexviii. 99.
[2] Windebank to the King, May 21, *Clar. St. P.* ii. 45.

stood almost alone in urging him to carry on the war with vigour. On the 24th a letter, written on the 19th, was handed to Essex from the Covenanters. They protested that they cherished no design of invasion. They wanted only to enjoy their liberties in accordance with their own laws.[1] Essex handed the letter unopened to the King; but, as the messenger had brought with him an open copy, its contents were soon known. Arundel said that it was 'full of insolence;' but this was far from being the general opinion. The Knight Marshal, Sir Edmund Verney, thought that it was 'expressed with a great deal of modesty,' and Sir Edmund Verney was a typical personage. Attached to the King by long service and ancestral loyalty, he was ready to do whatever duty might require, and to fight, if need be, against the Scots. But he had no heart in the quarrel, no confidence in the undisciplined mob which his master called an army. Laud's proceedings in England he thoroughly disliked, and he could take no pleasure in a war which had been brought about by very similar proceedings in Scotland. For him, as for multitudes of his countrymen, the war, in spite of all that Charles might say about its political character, was *Bellum episcopale*, a war waged to restore Bishops to their misused authority. He had heard a Scotchman say, as he wrote in one of his letters to his son at home, that 'nothing will satisfy them but the taking away all Bishops.' 'I dare say,' he added, 'the King will never yield that, so we must be miserable.'[2]

On May 1 Charles advanced to Durham. The Scottish Royalist lords who had fled before the Covenanters were summoned to hear the proclamation read,

---

[1] The Covenanters to Essex, Apr. 19, *S. P. Dom.* cccexviii. 9.
[2] Verney to R. Verney, Apr. 25, May 5, *Verney Papers*, 225, 231.

CHAP. V.
1639.
May 1.

Its reading refused.

Scottish shipping seized.

Hamilton in the Firth of Forth.

Leith fortified.

Popular resistance.

and were ordered to return to their estates and to disperse copies amongst their friends in Scotland. Special orders were sent to Sir James Balfour, Lion King-at-Arms, to read it at the Cross at Edinburgh, and to depute heralds to read it publicly in every shire. Charles was not long in discovering that he had reckoned on more obedience than he was likely to find. Not a single Scotchman would take upon himself the odium of reading such a proclamation.[1]

The attempt to put pressure on the Scots by the interruption of their commerce had already been made. Scottish shipping arriving in England was arrested. Hamilton on his voyage northwards seized so many Scottish vessels as to be unable to man them, and contented himself afterwards with disarming those which he overtook.[2] On May 1 he had sailed up the Forth. Leith was now strong enough to resist attack. Every hand that could be spared had been busily employed in working at the fortifications. Women hurried down from Edinburgh to carry earth and stones. Hamilton's own mother appeared with a pistol in her hand, and vowed that she would be the first to shoot her son if he landed to attack the followers of the Covenant. Nor had he much more chance of military success in the open country. The men of Fife and the Lothians turned out in overwhelming numbers to defend their homes, and boastfully sent back, as unnecessary, a reinforcement of twelve hundred men which had been sent to their aid by the Western shires.[3] Nothing was wanting to raise the zeal of the defenders of their country. Preachers assured them that the cause of national

[1] Order in Council, May 1, *S. P. Dom.* ccccxx. 1.
[2] Hamilton to the King, Apr. 29, *Ham. Papers*, 76
[3] *Baillie*, i. 201.

resistance was the cause of God. The women of Scotland spoke with no uncertain voice. Mothers bade their sons go forth and quit themselves well in the quarrel which had been forced upon them. Wives cheerfully surrendered their husbands to the uncertainties of war; whilst every youthful volunteer knew well that it would fare ill with him if, after stepping aside from the conflict, he dared to pour his tale of love into the ear of a Scottish maiden. What had Hamilton to oppose to this band of brothers fighting in what they deemed the holiest of causes? His men were utterly undisciplined, and they had no heart in the cause for which they had been sent to fight. He landed them on the two islets Inchkeith and Inchcolm, and there he did his best to turn them into soldiers, whilst he attempted to negotiate with the hostile multitudes on shore.[1]

CHAP. V.
1639. May 1.

Whatever hopes he brought with him were soon at an end. "Your Majesty's affairs," he wrote on the 7th, "are in a desperate condition. The enraged people here run to the height of rebellion, and walk with a blind obedience as by their traiterous leaders they are commanded; and resolved they are rather to die than to embrace or accept of your proffered grace in your last most gratious proclamation. You will find it a work of great difficulty and of vast expence to curb them by force, their power being greater, their combination stronger, than can be imagined." He himself could do little for a long time to come. If the King was in no better condition, he might 'think of some way of packing it up.' The Scots seemed ready 'to offer all civil obedience.' If the King was able to 'suppress them

May 7. Hamilton's despair.

[1] De Vic to Windebank, May 7. Norgate to Read, May 9, 16, *S. P. Dom.* ccccxx. 77, 121, ccccxxi. 34.

CHAP. V.
1639.
May 7.

in a powerful way,' he would do his part, 'which will only be the stopping of their trade, and burning of such of their towns as' are 'upon the coast.' Even this he could not promise to do for any length of time, as his provisions would soon be exhausted.[1]

May 8. Aboyne offers to rouse the North.

Before this lugubrious despatch reached him, Charles had been listening to young Aboyne, who had come to offer to rouse the North if only money and arms were placed at his disposal. Charles sent him on to the Forth, directing Hamilton to give him what assistance he could in men, but to be careful not to engage him in further expense. He calculated that he had money enough to keep on foot his existing force till the end of the summer. More than this he could not do.[2]

May 9. Verney's opinion of the position

Others around him were not even so sanguine as this. "Our army," wrote Verney, "consists of two thousand horse and twelve thousand foot, and that is the most, and more by some reasonable proportion both of horse and foot than we shall have with us, or that will come to us, unless Marquis Hamilton's forces come to us. Our men are very raw, our arms of all sorts naught, our victual scarce, and provision for horses worse; and now you may judge what case we are in, and all for want of money to help us till we may be better men, or to bring more men to us. I will write to you again as soon as I hear what the Scots will do in obedience to the proclamation, which certainly will come to nothing." [3]

Rumours from Scotland.

The proclamation indeed had already come to nothing, but only the vaguest possible rumours of the state of the country across the Borders reached

[1] Hamilton to the King, May 7, *Ham. Papers*, 78.
[2] The King to Hamilton, May 13, *Burnet*, 136.
[3] Verney to R. Verney, May 6, *Verney Papers*, 232.

the King's ear. Some said that the Scotch were armed to the teeth. Others declared that their leaders had failed to raise the necessary supplies for the maintenance of an army. "Though many come from those parts," wrote Coke to his brother-secretary, " yet we find so much variety amongst their reports that we know not whom to credit, or what to expect."[1]

CHAP. V.
1639. May 9.

Already, therefore, Charles was hesitating between negotiation and war. On May 14 he signed a fresh proclamation, in startling contrast with the one which had threatened death and confiscation a month before.[2] He now assured his Scottish subjects that he would not think of invading Scotland if only civil and temporal obedience were secured to him. They must, however, abstain in their turn from invading England; and, to give him assurance of this, they must not approach within ten miles of the Border. If this condition were violated, his general would proceed against them as open traitors.[3]

May 14. Issue of a second proclamation.

It was Charles's habit to couch his demands in general terms, the intention of which was seldom defined even in his own mind. The requirement of civil and temporal obedience was perfectly compatible with a reassertion of all the demands which his Commissioner had made at Glasgow. But it was also compatible with much less; and on the very day on which this proclamation was drawn up, Hamilton was writing a despatch in which he urged his master to content himself with very much less. If the Scots would lay down their arms, surrender the King's castles, express repentance for their faults, and promise to respect his Majesty's civil authority, they

Its intention uncertain.

Hamilton's proposed surrender.

---

[1] Windebank to Windebank, May 8. Coke to Windebank, May 9, *S. P. Dom.* ccccxx. 106, 120.   [2] P. 209.
[3] Proclamation, May 14, Peterkin's *Records*, 220.

might then be allowed to express their objections to Episcopacy in Parliament, when these objections, as well as those which had been produced at the Glasgow Assembly, might, 'as their desire shall seem just or unjust, receive a ratification or denial.'[1]

Such a concession cost Hamilton nothing. He was quite as ready to put himself forward, in 1639, as the vindicator of the Royal authority, by taking the initiative in throwing over modified Episcopacy, as he had been to throw over absolute Episcopacy in 1638. It is quite possible, too, that he had taken care again to sound the Covenanting leaders as to their acceptance of a scheme which he now regarded as the only chance of restoring the kingly authority in any shape whatever. By such a course he might gain friends on both sides, as he had attempted to do in the previous year. Such at least, in the absence of positive evidence, is a probable explanation of the increasing rumours that he was playing a double part.

For the present, Charles evaded an absolute decision. He instructed Hamilton to go on with the negotiation on the basis which he had laid down, and to abstain from any immediate attack, unless a Scotch army should march to the Borders in such strength as to make it absolutely necessary that a diversion should be created. He did not say, and in all probability he did not know, whether he meant Hamilton's negotiation to be carried on seriously, or merely with the object of gaining time till his own preparations were ready.[2]

How inadequate those preparations were, he was himself now painfully conscious. In spite of his

---

[1] Hamilton to the King, May 14, *Ham. Papers*, 80. *Burnet*, 131.
[2] The King to Hamilton, May 17. Note by the King, May 16, *Burnet*, 131.

acknowledgment that he had not money to keep on foot additional troops, he wrote to order the levy of a reinforcement consisting of 4,000 foot and 300 horse. All his hope of supporting them when they arrived lay in the prospect of a favourable response to his demand of a general contribution for the war, and as yet no signs had appeared that such a response would be given. Fictions, however, cost nothing, and Windebank was directed to terrify the Scots by spreading rumours that this levy of 4,300 would consist of no less than 14,000 men.[1]

The quality of Charles's army was not such as to make amends for the deficiency of its numbers. "If the Covenanters meant foul play," wrote an official attached to the Court, "they might make foul work; for our people are not together, and are most unready and undisciplined, as every one says here. The Scotch Bishops are as detested here as by their own, who have expelled both their persons and order. The tales they told at London, that the Scots would disband and run away at our approach in the North, are every day disproved more than other, for they are 40,000 strong at least, and may go where they please, and do what they list. I think that no man, who loves the honour of his prince and safety of his country, but must be sensible of the loss and danger of both by this fatal business, wherein all men are losers, but the King most."[2]

In spite of these alarms, Charles announced his intention of advancing in person to Berwick. Bristol, who had retained in his old age that habit of looking facts in the face which in earlier life had

[1] The King to Windebank, May 17, *Clar. St. P.* ii. 42.
[2] Norgate to Read, May 16, *S. P. Dom.* cccexxi. 34.

CHAP. V.
1639.
May 22.

ruined his prospects at Court, said plainly that it would be folly to trust the person of the King so near the enemy with a dispersed and undisciplined army. The military leaders concurred with Bristol. But there are moments when there is no choice between rashness and irremediable disaster, and Charles, who, irresolute as he was in the face of the necessity of decision, was no coward to abandon the post of danger, firmly persisted in his resolution.[1]

Risk incurred.

Whether necessary or not, the resolution was hazardous in the extreme. If Leslie had not around him the 40,000 men with which he was credited at Newcastle, he had at least at his command a well-appointed force of half that number, against which Charles could at this time bring no more than at the utmost 15,000 men. So gloomy did the situation appear, that on the 22nd Charles wrote to Hamilton to be ready at a moment's notice to bring back his forces from the Firth to join the army on the Borders.[2]

Hamilton ordered to be ready to return.

May 21.
Hamilton's conference with the Covenanters.

Before these orders reached him, Hamilton had penned another despatch even more despondent than the last. He had been engaged in conferences with the Covenanting leaders, and had taken upon himself to explain the meaning of the civil obedience required by the King's latest proclamation. His Majesty, he said, was not bound to relinquish his negative on the acts of an ecclesiastical assembly, but he was 'confident, that whatsoever should be agreed on by such an assembly, called by his Majesty's command, and when the members should be legally chosen,[3] his

[1] Mildmay to Windebank, May 24, *S. P. Dom.* ccccxxi. 169.
[2] The King to Hamilton, May 22, *Burnet*, 133.
[3] This hints at the abolition of the lay elders as electors.

Majesty would not only consent unto them, but have them ratified in Parliament.'[1]

Hamilton's letter to the King is so involved as to give rise to the suspicion that he wanted to frighten Charles into the acceptance of these terms. The Scots, he said, would admit of no peace 'unless it be the ratification of their mad acts made in the late pretended General Assembly.' They were resolved to force a battle. The best thing would therefore be for him to send two out of his three regiments to reinforce the Royal army, keeping only one to burn villages on the Firth. Above all things, the King should avoid an encounter. If he kept quiet, the rebels could not keep their forces long together. On the other hand, they might pass round his army and cut him off from his base of supplies at Newcastle. If his Majesty were 'well-strengthened with foot,' this might be hindered. "They find," he went on to write, "they are not able to subsist, and therefore take this desperate course; for already they are pinched by stop of trade, and see in fine they must be miserable. Now, hoping in the weakness of your Majesty's army, they intend to venture that which shortly, themselves acknowledge, they must lose, and, for ought I can learn, will either make themselves a commonwealth or a conquered kingdom."

Hamilton at least did not wish to see Scotland either a commonwealth or a conquered kingdom. At the moment he would certainly have preferred to

---

[1] Account of the conference by De Vic, *Burnet*, 133. The paper is not dated; but there is mention of conferences in a letter of May 24 (*S. P. Dom.* ccccxxi. 176): and it is about this time that Burnet places it. The conference cannot have taken place after Hamilton received orders, on the 22nd, to be ready to return, as he states that he will be found where he is 'a month hence.'

appear as the champion of Monarchical government in the State and of Presbyterian government in the Church, an arrangement which would at least have the advantage of securing to him both his Scottish estates and the Royal favour. If this interpretation be the right one, his concluding paragraph can only be regarded as an awkward attempt to appear as if he shared his master's probable indignation. He was quite ready, he said, to begin hostilities as soon as he was ordered to do so. He had no hope of any treaty now, and had only engaged in one at all in order to amuse the Scots.[1]

One suggestion at least in this letter took immediate effect. On the 23rd orders were sent to Hamilton to send the two regiments, numbering 3,000 men, to Holy Island. These instructions were at once executed, and on the 28th the much-needed reinforcement arrived off the coast of Northumberland.[2] Hamilton himself remained to seize Scottish merchantmen, and to threaten more damage than he was able to do.

On the day after the order to send the regiments had been despatched, news reached Newcastle[3] which must have made the King wish that he had larger forces to leave in Hamilton's hands. In the North, Huntly's friends had risen against their Covenanting neighbours, had fallen upon a body of them at Turriff on the 14th, and had driven them out of the place. The Trot of Turriff, as this first skirmish of the long Civil War was called, inspirited the victors to follow up their advantage, and the Gordons pushed on to occupy Aberdeen,

---

[1] Hamilton to the King, May 21, *Ham. Papers*, 83.
[2] Note by the King, May 23, *Burnet*, 133. De Vic to Windebank, May 26, *S. P. Dom.* cccexxii. 28, 62.
[3] Mildmay to Windebank, May 24, *Ibid.* cccexxi. 169.

where they lived at free quarters on the few partisans of the Covenant in the place. Their triumph did not last long. On the 24th they were driven out by the Earl Marischal. On the 25th Montrose was back again with a strong force to occupy the town. Acts of pillage were committed by the soldiery; but Montrose refused to give up to a general plunder even that hostile city which, as the Presbyterians were never tired of asserting, had earned the fate of Meroz in refusing to come to the help of the Lord against the mighty.

CHAP. V.
1639.
May 15 The Gordons at Aberdeen.
May 25. Montrose occupies the town.

It was long before the news even of the Trot of Turriff reached Hamilton's fleet. It was unknown on the 29th, when Aboyne arrived with a number of Scottish lords sent by the King to get what help they could. Hamilton had now only one regiment left, and, even if he wished to help Aboyne, it was little indeed that he could do. If the King, he wrote, would send 5,000 men, and money to pay an equal number of Scots, something might be done. He himself, as the King well knew, had neither the men nor the money. Two days later Hamilton had heard of the rising in the North. He sent off Aboyne without delay, and he asked the King to despatch the force which he had mentioned in his last letter. Of this force he wished to take the command in person. With ten or twelve thousand pounds he could do much.[1]

May 29. Aboyne with Hamilton.

May 31. Hamilton asks for an army.

Charles would have been sorely puzzled to spare such a sum from his meagre resources. Yet, difficult as his position was, he was not despondent. His last proclamation had received an answer which can hardly have been to his mind. The Scots declared themselves quite ready to keep the prescribed distance of ten

May 25. The Scottish answer to the last proclamation.

[1] Hamilton to the King, May 29, 31, *Ham. Papers*, 89, 90.

miles from the Borders, if he would on his part withdraw his army and his fleet.[1] Leslie in the meanwhile had taken up his post at Dunglas, between Berwick and Dunbar, ready for peace or negotiation.

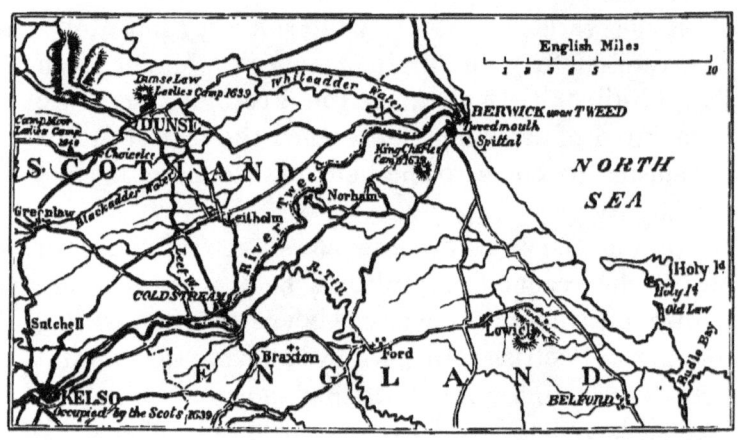

May 28. Charles at Berwick.

For negotiation as between equal and equal, Charles was not yet prepared. As he rode into Berwick on the 28th he could witness the landing of Hamilton's men,[2] and he felt himself safer than before.

May 30. The King in camp.

On the 30th he left Berwick for the Birks, a piece of ground on Tweedside, about three miles above the town, and took up his quarters under canvas in the midst of his soldiers. Once at the head of his men, he fretted at the tame submission which so many of his counsellors recommended. All that day he was on horseback, riding about to view the quarters of the men. Raw and untrained as they were, these hasty levies warmed with the prospect of a combat. "One thing," wrote an onlooker, "I must not conceal, which I care not if all Europe knew, that no nation

[1] The Scottish Nobility to Holland, May 25, Peterkin's *Records*, 222.
[2] Borough to Windebank, May 28, *S. P. Dom.* ccccxxii. 63.

in the world can show greater courage and bravery of spirit than our soldiers do, even the meanest of them, in hope of fight, which they extremely desire; upon the first intimation of the Scots' approach, and their dislodging and new camp upon the face of the enemy, they cast up their caps with caprioles, shouts, and signs of joy, and marched by force in the morning to their new station with fury."[1]

<small>CHAP. V.
1639.
May 30.</small>

At the head of such men Charles might well believe that in time everything would still be possible. In the immediate present very little indeed was possible. He could not send his enthusiastic but undisciplined levies to storm Leslie's camp at Dunglas. He would therefore make one more effort to win over the Scottish peasants in his vicinity by those tempting offers of a diminution of rent which had been embodied in his proclamation,[1] and which, as he believed, needed only to be heard to be accepted with joy. As an Edinburgh preacher expressed it, he was eager to address the humble Scottish Covenanter in the words of the Satanic temptation: "All these things will I give thee, if thou wilt fall down and worship me."[2]

Charles determined that the first experiment should be made at Dunse. No lesser personages than Arundel and Holland, the commander of the whole army and the General of the Horse, were to be the bearers of the King's gracious declaration to the peasant, and of his fierce denunciation of the landlord. When Arundel rode into Dunse in the early morning, not a man was to be seen. The women came out into the street, threw themselves on their knees, as their grandmothers had doubtless done to the leaders of many a Border foray, cursing

<small>May 31. Arundel sent to Dunse.</small>

<small>June 1.</small>

---

[1] Norgate to Windebank, May 28, *S. P. Dom.* ccccxxii. 62.
[2] *Newsletter*, May 24, *Ibid.* ccccxxi. 171.

VOL. I.   Q

Leslie and beseeching the English general 'for God's sake not to burn their houses, kill their children, nor bring in popery, as Leslie had told them the King meant to do.' Arundel spoke them fairly, assuring them of his protection, and ordering that the proclamation should be read in their hearing. When the ceremony was over, a few men stole out of their hiding-places, and a market was soon established. Arundel did his best to create a good impression in the country by directing his men to pay for everything that they took, and the Scotchmen took good care to ask exorbitant prices for the stock of milk and oaten cakes which was all that they possessed.

Of such services Charles's army was not incapable. But it had no confidence in its leaders, no habitual restraint under the rules of military life. The men fired off their guns at random in the camp. Officers complained of bullets perforating the canvas of their tents. Even the King's pavilion was pierced by a shot. For all this he was strangely confident. He refused, indeed, Hamilton's request for men for a great expedition to the North, but he refused it on the ground that he was himself on the point of assuming the aggressive. Not a few of the Lords beyond the Border had already been gained over to his side, and it would be a shame to be idle. "Wherefore now," he ended, "I set you loose to do what mischief you can do upon the rebels for my service with those men you have, for you cannot have one man from hence."[1]

The numbers of Charles's army had lately been considerably increased. With the new reinforcements and with the regiments returned from the Firth, he

---

[1] Borough to Windebank, June 3, 7. Windebank to Windebank, June 3. Norgate to Read, June 3, *S. P. Dom.* ccccxxiii. 12, 13, 16. The King to Hamilton, June 2, *Burnet*, 138.

could now reckon upon 18,000 foot, and 3,000 horse.[1] But the very improvement in one respect brought with it a fresh danger in another. The larger the army grew, the more difficult it was to maintain it. Before the end of May the Lord Treasurer and the Chancellor of the Exchequer had lost all hope. The revenue, they declared, was completely exhausted. Cottington averred that even before the King left London he had in vain 'searched every corner from whence any probability of money could be procured.' The only chance of finding pay for the army lay in that general contribution which had been demanded in April. The Council had long ceased to be sanguine of a favourable reply. "Hitherto," wrote Windebank, "we have very cold answers, which, though they be not direct refusals, are almost as ill; for they bring us no relief nor no hope of it. Some petty sums, and those very few, have been offered. So that my lords begin to apprehend this will be of little consideration, and to use compulsory means in these distempered times my lords are very tender, and apprehend it may be of dangerous consequence."[2]

It was hard to say what answer could be made to this. By leaving just claims unpaid, and by anticipating the revenue to the extent of about 150,000$l.$, the army had hitherto been kept on foot, though its expenditure after the late reinforcements might be approximately reckoned at the rate of 750,000$l.$ a year. As to the general contribution of which

---

[1] The account given by *Rushworth* (iii. 926) is, after deducting the Carlisle garrison of 1,300 men, in exact figures 18,314 foot and 3,260 horse. It is shown by comparison with the account of the treasurer of the army (see note at p. 191) to belong to the first days of June. Some of the forces mentioned are not borne on the Treasurer's accounts, and were probably paid from special funds in Charles's hands.

[2] Windebank to the King, May 24, *Clar. St. P.* ii. 46.

1639. June.

The general contribution.

Windebank spoke so despondingly, it was found at the end of July, when money ceased to come in, to have amounted in all to 50,000*l.* Of this 15,000*l.* were produced by the sale of the Mastership in Chancery to Sir Charles Cæsar.[1] Of the remaining 35,000*l.*, 2,200*l.* came from a nobleman too sickly to follow the King in person, and 24,395*l.* were paid by the clergy, the class of all others most deeply interested in the King's success, and most amenable to pressure from above. The whole amount contributed by the laity of England barely exceeded 8,400*l.*, and the greater part even of this was provided by judges and other legal officials, who were almost as amenable to pressure as the clergy. The unofficial contributions certainly did not exceed 3,000*l.*, if indeed they reached anything like that sum.[2]

The Catholic contribution.

One source of supply, indeed, was still open. The Queen had urged the Catholics to testify their gratitude by a donation to the King in his time of need. She did not find them in a liberal mood. They counted the reduced fines which they were still forced to pay, as so much injustice, and they had some suspicion that the Puritans might after all get the upper hand. Walter Montague, too, who was employed as the Queen's Agent in the matter, was not much more popular with the old Catholic families than hot-headed converts usually are with those whose religion is inherited from their ancestors. But a demand made by the Queen was hardly to be rejected, and,

---

[1] I have no absolute evidence of this; but I find that Uvedale, the Treasurer of the Army, paid into the exchequer a sum of 15,207*l.* 7*s.* on March 30. Two days after we learn from Garrard of Cæsar's payment. Unless there had been something to conceal, Uvedale would have kept this money in his own hands, and it does not appear how it reached him.

[2] *Breviates of the Receipt.*

after a long discussion, they agreed to present the King with 10,000*l.* at Midsummer, and a similar sum at Michaelmas.¹ Such a sum would not support the army much more than a week. Another plan of the Queen's did not achieve even this amount of success. She proposed that the ladies of England should combine to present the King with a substantial token of their regard.² Either the ladies took no great interest in the Royal cause, or their purses were too much under the control of their husbands to open readily. No money reached the King from this quarter.

1639.
Proposed ladies' contribution.

In this stress the King wrote to his Council in London to send him 10,000*l.* at once, and to require the Lord Mayor and Aldermen to provide a loan, as a matter in which his Majesty would take no denial.³

June 4.
The City to be applied to for a loan.

Charles's power of making use of the army which he found it so difficult to maintain was soon to be brought to the test. On the 3rd news came into the camp that a considerable Scottish force had established itself at Kelso—an indication that the Scots considered themselves released by Arundel's raid upon Dunse from any obligation to keep within the limit of ten miles from the Border which had been imposed upon them by the King. Orders were therefore given

June 2.

June 3.
The Scots at Kelso.

¹ Con's letters are full of this affair. Compare *Rushworth*, ii. 820 The letter printed at p. 821, as a letter from the Pope to his Nuncio, is an evident forgery, as it states that the Catholics had been offering men for the Northern expedition, which is untrue. Rossetti, writing on $\frac{\text{Jan. 22}}{\text{Feb. 1}}$, 1641 (*R. O. Transcripts*), says that a forged letter, said to be brought by him to Toby Matthew, was printed about this time, and I suspect that this is the one.

² Rossingham's *Newsletter*, *Add. MSS.* 11,045, fol. 9.

³ Windebank to the King, June 8. The King's letter is not preserved, but it seems to have reached London on the 6th, and so to have been written on the 2nd. According to Salvetti, orders were given to levy ten or twelve thousand men (Salvetti's *Newsletter*, June $\frac{14}{24}$), but this is doubtless only the echo of the false rumour which Windebank was to give out. See p. 219.

to Holland to take with him 3,000 foot and 300 horse to drive them out.

The day was hot and dusty, and the infantry straggled along weary and footsore. Yet their officers believed that, inexperienced as they were, they would have acquitted themselves well if they had come to blows.[1] That day no opportunity was given them to display their courage. Riding hastily forward at the head of his horse, Holland found himself face to face with a Scottish force advancing to meet him. His men perhaps exaggerated the numbers of the enemy as six, eight, or even ten thousand, and it was averred by some that an additional force of 3,000 Highlanders was lying in ambush armed with bows and arrows.[2] Holland at first proposed to fall back on the infantry, and to make the attack with both arms. But he soon discovered that he was far outnumbered, and preferred to send a trumpeter to the Scots to ask them what they were doing within the ten miles limit. The Scots asked him scornfully in return, what he was doing in their country. He had better be gone, or they would teach him the way. There was nothing for it but to retreat to the camp beyond the Tweed.[3]

Holland was but a carpet knight, and contemporaries and posterity have combined in jeering him on his failure. Yet it may be doubted whether the most practised soldier would have acted otherwise. He was entrusted with a reconnaissance in force, and

---

[1] Dymocke to Windebank, July 5, *S. P. Dom.* ccccxxv. 21.

[2] Account of the Campaign, Bodl. Lib. *Rawlinson MSS.* B. 210. These are the only archers I know anything about. Mr. Peter Bayne says there were some on the King's side, but gives no reference.

[3] Coke to Windebank, June 4. Mildmay to Windebank, June 4. Norgate to Read, June 5. Weckerlin to Conway, June 6, *S. P. Dom.* ccccxxiii. 21, 22, 29, 49.

finding the enemy too strong to be prudently attacked, he brought his men back in safety. In any ordinary army such a proceeding would be taken as a matter of course. But Charles's was not an ordinary army. It had nothing but its reputation to subsist on, and its reputation was not enough to endure even an apparent check.

In fact, it was not merely the retreat which spread alarm in the camp. Men began to ask one another how it was that the Scots had been prepared to meet Holland's movements. A suspicion arose, which was probably justified by fact, that every movement of the English army was known to Leslie, whilst the manœuvres of the Scottish army were covered by a wall of impenetrable darkness. "The truth is," wrote Verney to his son, "we are betrayed in all our intelligence, and the King is still made to believe in a party that will come to him, but I am confident he is mightily abused in it, for they are a people strangely united. . . . I think the King dares not stir out of his trenches. What counsels he will take, or what he will do, I cannot divine; but if this army be lost that we have here, I believe the Scots may make their own conditions with England, and therefore I could wish that all my friends would arm themselves as soon as they could. We want money to exercise our army, and the strength we have here will only defend ourselves. I do not conceive it of force to do any harm to them, so we daily spend our money and our honour together." [1]

The day which witnessed Holland's retreat brought still more alarming tidings. Leslie, it was said, had broken up his camp at Dunglas, and was in full march to the Border. In hot haste a messenger was

[1] Sir E. Verney to R. Verney, June 4, *Verney Papers*, 243.

despatched to Hamilton, bidding him to desist from all warlike operations, and to come in person to Berwick to advise the King. His Majesty, he was told, was now resolved to keep on the defensive.[1]

The resolution thus taken was not altogether voluntary. Before leaving him at Whitehall, Hamilton had warned Charles that Englishmen would not fight in this quarrel, and Charles now ruefully acknowledged that the prediction had proved true.[2] Above all, the English nobility had no wish to prolong the war. Even those who had no sympathy with Puritanism were deeply aggrieved by their systematic exclusion from all posts of influence, and they had no desire to aid the King to a triumph which would make the prospect of a Parliament more distant than ever. Others again were loth to strike a blow against the opponents of Episcopacy in Scotland, whilst Bishops in England were exercising powers so unwonted and so harsh. The common soldiers, too, when once the excitement of impending combat was removed, sunk into listless dissatisfaction. Their condition at the Birks was not one of comfort. They were left all night to lie on the bare ground, with such shelter from the wind as they could make by throwing up walls of turf, and laying branches of furze across them. Not a tree was to be found for many miles to offer timber for the construction of huts. The Tweed, where they were, was too salt to drink, and beer was sold at 3*d*. the quart—a price equivalent to at least a shilling now. The smallpox broke out amongst these ill-cared-for troops, and carried off its victims. The deserters were numerous. The chief employment of those who remained was the

---

[1] Vane to Hamilton, June 4 (misprinted July), *Burnet*, 139.
[2] *Burnet*, 140.

chase after the vermin by which their persons were infested, and which were known as Covenanters in the rude language of the camp.

On June 5, when the discouragement caused by Holland's failure was at its height, Leslie appeared on the scene. The army from Dunglas, some 12,000 strong, tramped into Dunse, the little town where Arundel had read the King's proclamation to the women less than a week before. Leslie at once took up his position on Dunse Law, an isolated hill which rose just in sight of the King's camp, eleven or twelve miles distant. Charles received the intelligence with his usual imperturbability. Stepping in front of his tent he examined through a telescope the dark figures swarming on the hill. "Come, let us go to supper," he said at last; " the number is not considerable."[1]

Counting the troops at Kelso and the neighbouring villages, Leslie had an army of 20,000 men upon the Borders. In mere numbers the King's forces had a slight superiority, but the Scots made up in the quality of their men for the numerical deficiency. There was no lack in their camp either of money or provisions. The taxation levied by the Tables had been on the whole cheerfully paid, and the rents of those who refused to take the Covenant had been seized for the use of the defenders of the country. The voluntary contributions of the citizens of Edinburgh did the rest. The 'stout young ploughmen' who had come forth to fight round the banners which bore the rallying cry, "For Christ's Crown and Covenant," were well pleased to satisfy their hunger on the wheaten bread and the legs of lamb which 'was a dainty world to the most of them.' Not everything,

[1] Account of the campaign, Bodl. Lib. *Rawlinson MSS.* B. 210. Weckerlin to Conway, June 6, *S. P. Dom.* ccccxxiii. 49.

indeed, in this Covenanting army was to the mind of the pious ministers who had left their parishes to fan the flame of zeal amongst the soldiers. In that army were to be heard the singing of psalms and the fervent accents of prayer. But there was also to be heard the sound of 'swearing and cursing and brawling.'[1] If piety was not everywhere to be found in Leslie's camp, there was at least military discipline. The Scottish nobility set an excellent example of subordination. Englishmen who carried messages from Hamilton's fleet to the Covenanting leaders remarked with surprise that high-born nobles sat uncovered in the presence of the dwarfish and deformed man whom they had chosen to be their master in the art of war.[2] Baillie, who had come to act as chaplain to the host, was unable to restrain his admiration. "Our soldiers," he wrote, "grow in experience of arms, in courage, in favour daily; every one encouraged another, the sight of the nobles and their beloved pastors daily raised their hearts, the good sermons and prayers, morning and even, under the roof of heaven, to which their drums did call them for bells; the remonstrances, very frequent, of the goodness of their cause, of their conduct hitherto by a hand clearly Divine; also Leslie's skill and fortune, made them all so resolute for battle as could be wished. We were feared that emulation among our nobles might have done harm when they should be met in the fields; but such was the wisdom and authority of that old, little, crooked soldier, that all, with an incredible submission from the beginning to the end, gave over themselves to be guided by him as if he had been great Solyman. Certainly, the obedience of our nobles to

---

[1] *Baillie*, 212.
[2] De Vic to Windebank, May 23, *S. P. Dom.* ccccxxii. 28.

that man's advices was as great as their forbears' wont to be to their King's commands; yet that was the man's understanding of our Scots' humour, that gave out, not only to the nobles, but to very mean gentlemen, his directions in a very homely and simple form, as if they had been but the advices of their neighbour and companion; for, as he rightly observed, a difference would be used in commanding soldiers of fortune, and of soldiers volunteers, of which the most part of our camp did stand."[1]

1639. June 6.

What had Charles to bring against this combination of military discipline and national and religious enthusiasm? Brave as his English followers individually were, Leslie, if he had chosen to attack them in their bivouac at the Birks, would have driven them like chaff before the wind. But there were shrewd heads in the Scottish camp, who knew better than to court the perilous victory. They were now contending with Charles. If English soldiers were driven in headlong rout, and if the tramp of a Scottish army were heard on English soil, it might very well be that they would have to contend with an insulted nation. In Parliament or out of Parliament, supplies would no longer be withheld, and the invaders would meet with a very different force from that which was now before them.

The Scots shrink from invading England.

Whilst the Scots were in this frame of mind,[2] one of the King's Scotch pages visited their camp and recommended his countrymen to open a negotiation. They at once sent the Earl of Dunfermline to request the King to appoint Commissioners to treat, and to

The offer to negotiate.

---

[1] *Baillie*, i. 213.

[2] As early as the beginning of the month there had been talk of a negotiation, but the King would admit of no treaty unless his houses and castles were first given up. Widdrington to Lord Fairfax, June 3, *Fairfax Correspondence*, i. 367.

assure the English nobility that they had no wish to throw off their allegiance to the Crown. Charles laid it down as a condition of the negotiation that they must first read his proclamation denouncing their leaders as traitors. As usual, they were perfectly ready to give obedience in the letter. A few of the very men who were denounced assembled in a tent to hear the proclamation read. On them the threat of the confiscation of their lands was not likely to make much impression. Yet with this hollow form Charles was forced to content himself. The disposition to avoid a battle, which had long prevailed amongst the men of rank in the English camp, had now spread to the common soldiers. They had learned by this time that money was running short, and they knew by experience that bread and beer were growing scarce. "A great neglect there hath been," wrote one who was on the spot, "in those who had the charge of providing for the soldiers, for they have wanted exceedingly since their coming, yet have been very patient, but now there is strange doctrine spread in the camp and swallowed by the officers and soldiers, so that it is time to make an end of this work. The clergy that are in this camp doth carry themselves so indiscreetly, as also the Scottish Bishops and clergy here, that I assure you they do much hurt his Majesty's affairs by their violence." Bristol bluntly spoke out what was doubtless in their thoughts. Most of the Lords, he said, were resolved to petition for a Parliament. The Lords, indeed, disclaimed any such intention. But the unspoken thought was, we may well believe, in the minds of all of them.[1]

On the afternoon of the 7th Hamilton appeared in Charles's camp. He had to tell how Aboyne had

[1] Mildmay to Windebank, June 10, *S. P. Dom.* cccexxiii. 67.

reached Aberdeen, and had driven the Covenanting forces to retire by his mere presence in the roads. But he could not say that this diversion was likely to be of any permanent benefit to the Royal cause. Aboyne had written to him urgently for supplies. Even if he had had supplies to give, he was already on his way to Berwick by the King's orders before he received the letter.[1]

CHAP. V.
1639. June 2. Aboyne at Aberdeen.
June 7. Hamilton is unable to support him.

Hamilton had every reason to be satisfied with the temper of his Royal master. The negotiation which had already been informally opened on the Borders was merely a continuation of that which had been set on foot by himself. He would now be present to watch over its progress. The day after the illusory reading of the Proclamation at Dunse, Dunfermline returned to ask for a safe conduct for the Scottish negotiators. Hamilton was there, to whisper that it would be wise to consent to the abolition of Episcopacy, and even to the Covenant itself. In time the discontented nobility would be gained over by favours, and better times would come.[2]

The negotiation on the Borders.

Hamilton's advice.

Such advice was too consonant with Charles's nature not to find entrance into his mind. He may not have intended foul play. But he was not likely frankly to acknowledge errors of which he was perfectly unconscious. He doubtless believed firmly that the Presbyterian experiment would before long prove intolerable, and he did not wish to bar the door against the restitution of the more perfect system. A man of a larger mind might have felt in

[1] *Burnet*, 140. *Spalding*, i. 200. Spalding charges Hamilton with having deserted Aboyne in defiance of orders from the King. This is plainly a mistake. Even when Aboyne was in the Forth, Hamilton had but one regiment with him.

[2] *Burnet*, 140.

precisely the same way. But he would have declared openly what his hopes were, and in so doing he would have inspired confidence where Charles only inspired distrust.

June 11. Opening of the conference.

On the 11th the conference was opened in Arundel's tent between six Commissioners from the Scots and six Commissioners from the King. Scarcely had the negotiators taken their places, when Charles himself stepped in. He assumed that tone of superiority which was natural to his position. He was there, he said, to show that he was always ready to listen to his subjects, and he expected them to act as was becoming to subjects.

The King appears to take part in the negotiation.

From this position he never departed. He had come not as a diplomatist but as a judge. "I never took upon me," he said, "to give end to any difference but where both parties first submitted themselves unto my censure, which if you will do, I shall do you justice to the utmost of my knowledge, without partiality." "The best way," he said afterwards, "were to take my word, and to submit all to my judgment."

His dialectical skill.

In the discussion which followed, Charles showed great dialectical skill. He seized rapidly on the weak points of the Scottish case, and exposed them without ostentation or vindictiveness. The strength of the Scottish case lay outside the domain of dialectics. All sorts of questions might arise about the composition of the Assembly, about the vote of the lay elders, and about the pressure exercised by the Tables at the time of the election. The arguments by which the Scots were ready to prove that the decisive authority in ecclesiastical matters resided in the Assembly which had met at Glasgow were neither more nor less convincing than the arguments by which Charles was ready to prove that it resided in himself. The true answer for the Scots to have made would have been, that whatever might have been the legality of the forms observed, the Assembly had had the nation behind it. This, however, was precisely what the Scottish Commissioners never thought of saying, and by leaving it unsaid they left the honours of the dispute with Charles.

CHAP. V.
1639. June 11.

What was wanting to the Scots in argument was amply made up to them by the presence of Leslie's army on Dunse Law. Whether the Scottish nation had the right to settle its own affairs in the teeth of Charles might be open to argument. It was clear enough now that it was strong enough to do so. Charles's own army was no more ready for battle than it had been before, and every day brought him worse news from the South. Without fresh supplies of money his army would soon dissolve from want of pay, and he had not much hope left that those supplies would be forthcoming.

The military position.

Windebank's report of a fresh attempt to obtain a loan from the City was most discouraging. The Council, indeed, had been busily employed in forcing all Scotchmen resident in England to take an oath, of Wentworth's invention, binding them to renounce the Covenant.[1] Oaths, however, brought no money into the Exchequer. On the 7th the Lord Mayor, having been summoned by the Council, appeared with such a scanty following of Aldermen, that he was ordered to go back and to return on the 10th with all his brothers. When the Aldermen at last made their appearance, they were told that the King expected from them a loan of 100,000*l.* The

June 7. The Lord Mayor before the Council.

June 10. A loan demanded.

---

[1] *Council Register,* June 5. Rossingham's *Newsletter,* June 18, *Add. MSS.* 11,045, fol. 29.

CHAP. V.
1639.
June 10.

war was even more unpopular in London than in other parts of England. Trade was suffering, and the recent confiscation of the Londonderry charter was rankling in the minds of the Aldermen. They replied that it was impossible to find the money. The Council told them that it must be done. Cottington said they ought to have sold their chains and gowns before giving such a reply. They were ordered to appear once more on the 12th with a final answer.

Windebank's advice.

Even within the Council there were signs of dissatisfaction at this high-handed course. Coventry and Manchester sat silently by whilst threats were used. "The rest," wrote Windebank, "are of opinion that either your Majesty should command the City to furnish 6,000 men at their own charge for the reinforcing your army, or else send for six or eight Aldermen to attend you in person at the camp, which the other two lords do not like, but hold dangerous in these times; and in case the City should refuse the former, they know not how they can be compelled to it. I am humbly of opinion that both should be done, and if the former be refused, the chief officers of the City are answerable for so high a contempt: if the latter, the Aldermen whom you shall summon to attend are finable."[1]

The Queen proposes to visit Berwick.

Whilst Windebank was suggesting counsels so wild as these, the Queen was trembling lest the two armies should come to blows. At the suggestion of the adventurous Duchess of Chevreuse, she proposed to hasten to the camp that she might adjure her husband not to expose his person to the risks of war.[2]

---

[1] The King to the Lord Mayor and Aldermen, June 4, *S. P. Dom.* ccccxxiii. 20. Windebank to the King, June 8, 11, *Clarendon St. P.* ii. 53, 54.

[2] Con to Barberini, June $\frac{14}{24}$, *Add. MSS.* 15,392, fol. 176.

The contents of Windebank's despatch saved Charles from this embarrassing proof of wifely affection. On the 12th he learned that the Lord Treasurer had scraped together 20,000*l.* for the needs of the army.[1] By the 15th he must have known that nothing was to be had from the City,[2] and on that day he despatched an answer to the Scots in which he practically accepted their terms. There was still some haggling over details, and it was not till the 17th that his answer assumed its final shape.[3] On the 18th the treaty was signed.

CHAP. V.
1639.
June 10. Deficiency of supplies. The Scottish terms accepted.

June 18. Signature of the Treaty of Berwick.

By this treaty the Scots engaged to disband their troops, to break up the Tables and all unlawful committees, and to restore the royal castles to the King's officers. In return Charles engaged to send back his soldiers to their homes, and to issue a declaration in which he was to assure his subjects that, though he could not ratify the acts of the pretended Assembly of Glasgow, he was pleased that all ecclesiastical matters should be determined by Assemblies, and all civil matters by Parliaments and other legal judicatories. On August 6 a free General Assembly was to be held at Edinburgh, and on August 20 a Parliament was to follow. In this Parliament, in addition to other acts, an act of pardon and oblivion was to be passed.[4]

The pacification of Berwick came just in time to save from extinction the last remnants of a Royalist party in the North. On the very day on which the treaty was signed, Montrose fell upon Aboyne at the

The war in the North.

---

[1] Note by the King, June 12, *Clarendon St. P.* ii. 54.
[2] Windebank's letter of the 11th must have reached him by that date.
[3] Compare the first draft (*S. P. Dom.* cccxxiii. 107) with the final treaty, *Burnet*, 141.
[4] *Rushw.* iii. 944.

VOL. I.   R

CHAP. V.
1639.
June 18.

Bridge of Dee close to Aberdeen. Aboyne's Highlanders withdrew in terror before the mother of the musket, as they styled Montrose's cannon. But the men of Aberdeen and the Royalists of the Northern Lowlands held out firmly, and it was not till the afternoon of the second day that the position was forced.[1]

June 19. Storming of the Bridge of Dee.

The storming party was led by Middleton, a rude soldier for whom a strange destiny was reserved. He lived to receive an Earldom without any special merits of his own, to preside over the execution of Argyle, and over the reverent consignment to Christian burial of the shrivelled remains of the body of Montrose.

Montrose again spares Aberdeen.

For the third time the Covenanting army entered Aberdeen. Montrose had brought with him orders to sack the town. He disobeyed the pitiless injunction, and Aberdeen was saved.

Satisfaction in England at the news of the Treaty.

All further hostilities were stopped by the news from Berwick. In England the utmost satisfaction was expressed. It was known that the peace had been to a great extent the work of the English nobility,[2] and few were aware how powerfully the King's financial difficulties had contributed to the result.

[1] It is generally supposed that Colonel Gun, who had been sent with Aboyne by Hamilton, was a traitor, and helped on the defeat. We have not his defence, and he may have been simply a methodical soldier, unused to Montrose's dashing ways. He had been recommended by Elizabeth for service, which would hardly have been the case unless he bore a good reputation abroad. Hamilton's double-dealing naturally brought suspicions upon him of any kind of villainy. See *Baillie*, i. 186. *Gordon*, ii. 269. *Spalding*, i. 209.

[2] "Il Conte di Olanda ... parla ... con grand' avantaggio delle ragioni che mossero li Scozzesi all' armi in modo che bisogna attribuire le buone conditioni date al loro non tanto all' affetto del Rè verso la patria, quanto all' inclinatione della nobiltà Inglese alla causa loro, essendo vero che eccettuato il generale et il Conte di Bristo, ... quasi tutti gli altri hanno favito alle pretensioni de' Scozzesi vergognosamente." Con to Barberini, July 5/15, *Add. MSS.* 15,392, fol. 191.

For Henrietta Maria the mere cessation of danger to her husband was enough, and those who looked in her beaming face could see her happiness there.[1]

CHAP. V.
1639. June.

The King's sister Elizabeth had reasons of her own for being equally well satisfied.[2] She fondly hoped that something would at last be done for the Palatinate. So assured were Leslie and the Covenanting leaders that all danger was past, that they offered to provide ten or twelve thousand Scottish soldiers for the service of the Elector Palatine. Charles was merely to furnish ships to transport them to the Continent, and to provide them with provisions till they reached their destination. Immediately on the signature of the treaty, Charles assured Leslie that he would agree to these terms. Before long, however, Leslie came to the conclusion that such conditions were insufficient. He required that Charles should ask the Scottish Parliament to provide pay for the army, and this request Charles refused to make.[2]

Project of sending a Scottish army to Germany.

By this time indeed the prospect of a good understanding had already been clouded over. In accepting the King's declaration the Scots had been guided rather by their wishes than by their intelligence. Two capital points had been entirely passed over. Nothing was said in it either of the constitution of the future Assembly, or of the course to be pursued if the Assembly came to resolutions obnoxious to the King. With a man of Charles's character, ever ready to claim all his formal rights, such omissions were likely to lead to serious consequences. The Scots had probably taken it for granted that he was merely seeking a decent veil to cover the reality of his defeat. They

Vagueness of the declaration.

---

[1] Con to Barberini, $\frac{\text{June 11}}{\text{July 1}}$, *Add. MSS.* 15,392, fol. 182.

[2] Elizabeth to Roe, July 2, 11. Cave to Roe, July 11, *S. P. Germany.* Salvetti's *Newsletter*, July $\frac{5}{15}$.

CHAP. V.
1639. June.

Ecclesiastical difficulties.

asserted that he had used words which implied as much, having assured them that 'he would not pre-limit and forestall his voice, but he had appointed a free Assembly which might judge of ecclesiastical matters, the constitutions whereof he would ratify in the ensuing Parliament.'[1] The accuracy of the paper which contained these words was indeed denied by the King, but it is not probable that it was substantially untrue. The difficulty vanishes if we suppose that the King regarded the exercise of his veto as a most important part of the legislation of the Assembly, and that his subjects imagined that no such veto was to be heard of. Nor is it at all unlikely that Charles really believed that if the question of Episcopacy were seriously discussed, his views of the matter would gain the upper hand.[2]

Political difficulties.

The ecclesiastical difficulty was dangerous enough. The political difficulty was still more dangerous. With the best possible intentions, the Scottish people could not restore that fabric of ancient authority which had crumbled in the dust. If Charles was ever to exercise power in Scotland again, he would have to toil painfully at its reconstruction. Either he must throw himself, as the too subtle Hamilton recommended, on the side of a nobility which was certain to have cause enough of discontent under the sway of the Presbyterian clergy; or else, as Montrose not long afterwards advised, he must accept the ecclesiastical settle-

[1] Peterkin's *Records*, 230.

[2] Rossingham, who picked up the news floating in the camp, tells us that 'There was much ado whether there should be Bishops, yea or no. The King pressed to have Bishops, and the Scotch Commissioners .... most humbly presented it to His Majesty that the order of Bishops was against the law of the land which His Majesty had promised to maintain; wherefore at last, as I hear, His Majesty was graciously pleased to have that about the Bishops to be disputed in their next Assembly.' *Newsletter*, June 25, *Add. MSS.* 11,045, fol. 31*b*.

ment now proposed as final, in order to win back the good will of the nation itself by trying to promote its welfare within the lines of its own conceptions. Charles would hear nothing of either plan. He claimed authority as a right, not as the ripe fruit of helpful labour. He could not understand that resistance to himself had given rise to a new political organisation which could not at once drop out of remembrance for any words which might be inserted in a treaty. He looked for reverence and submission where he should have looked for an opportunity of renewing that bond between himself and his subjects, which, through his own fault, had been so unhappily broken.

CHAPTER VI.

THE ASSEMBLY AND PARLIAMENT OF EDINBURGH.

<small>CHAP. VI.
1639.
June 24.
Hamilton at Edinburgh.
The Castle surrendered.</small>

THE full difficulties in the way of the execution of the Treaty of Berwick did not immediately appear. On June 24 Hamilton received the keys of Edinburgh Castle, and installed General Ruthven, a stout soldier and a firm Royalist, as its governor. It was difficult to make the policy of surrender intelligible to the Edinburgh citizens. When Hamilton visited the Castle he was followed by four or five hundred persons who jostled him in an unseemly manner. Scornful cries of " Stand by Jesus Christ " were raised, and the Lord Commissioner was branded as an enemy of God and his country.[1]

<small>Charles at Berwick.</small>

Charles was still at Berwick. He intended to preside in person over the Assembly and Parliament which he was about to summon. Before long he saw reason to change his purpose. The first serious offence came from himself. On July 1 a Proclamation ordering fresh elections for an Assembly which was to meet at Edinburgh was read at the Market Cross. It invited all Archbishops and Bishops to take their places there. As might have been expected, the Proclamation was met by a Protestation. Once more the two parties stood opposed in mutual defiance.[2] Charles might have argued that Episco-

<small>July 1.
Bishops summoned to the Assembly.</small>

---

[1] *Burnet*, 144. Norgate to Read, June 27, 30, *S. P. Dom.* ccccxxiv. 77, 96.
[2] Proclamation and Protestation, July 1, Peterkin's *Records*, 230.

pacy was not as yet legally abolished, and that the presence of the Bishops was necessary to the fair discussion which he contemplated. He did not understand that he was called on to sanction the results of a revolution, not to preside over a Parliamentary debate.

CHAP. VI.
1639.
July 1.

If the Proclamation took for granted the illegality of the acts of the Glasgow Assembly, the Protestation took for granted their legality. The feelings of the populace were expressed in a rougher fashion. Aboyne, who unwisely ventured to show himself in the capital, was chased through the streets by an angry mob. Traquair's coachman was beaten. His Treasurer's staff was broken, and his coach pierced with swords. One of the judges, Sir William Elphinstone, was struck and kicked.[1]

July 3. Riot at Edinburgh.

Charles's displeasure may easily be imagined. But he was even less prepared to carry on war now than he had been in June. Hamilton told him plainly that the Scots would have no Bishops. If he meant to force Episcopacy on the nation, he must summon an English Parliament, and be prepared for all the consequences which might flow from that step.

July 5. The King's displeasure.

Charles was the more angry because he discovered that a paper had been circulated in Scotland, purporting to be a report of conversations held with himself, in which he was said to have consented tacitly to abandon the Bishops. Possibly the account may have been too highly coloured. Possibly, too, his own recollection may have fallen short of his actual words. At all events, he believed himself to have been foully misrepresented. His feeling was rather one of astonishment than of anger. "Why,"

July 6. Believes himself to have been misrepresented.

---

[1] *Baillie,* i. 220. Borough to Windebank, July 5, *S. P. Dom.* cccexxv. 22.

he complained to Loudoun, " do you use me thus ? "¹ Yet, if he had no choice but to give up the Bishops, he could not bring himself to pronounce the fatal words. The intention of appearing in person at Edinburgh was abandoned. Hamilton, too, had no mind to expose himself again to obloquy. He resigned his Commissionership, and Traquair was appointed in his room.²

If the Covenanters complained of Charles for his continued support of the Bishops, Charles had to complain of them that in some respects the Treaty of Berwick had not been put in execution. The Tables had not been at once dissolved. Hindrances had been placed in the way of the entrance of stores into Edinburgh Castle. A regiment was still kept on foot under Colonel Monro, and the fortifications of Leith were not demolished. Leslie still behaved as if his commission as general retained its force. Charles accordingly sent for the Covenanting leaders to confer with him at Berwick. Those for whom he sent did not all obey the summons. Argyle sent a hollow excuse. The Edinburgh citizens prevented others from setting out on what they believed to be a perilous journey. Six only of the number, Rothes and Montrose amongst them, appeared at Berwick.³

During the days of this visit to Berwick, Hamilton had been busy. He was authorised by a special warrant to enter into communication with the Covenanters in order that he might learn their plans. He was to gain their confidence by speaking as they spoke, and that he might do this fearlessly he was

---

¹ Unsigned Letter, July 11, *S. P. Dom.* ccccxxv. 51.
² Burnet, 144, 146.
³ De Vic to Windebank, July 15. Borough to Windebank, July 21, *S. P. Dom.* ccccxxv. 77, ccccxxvi. 22.

exonerated from all penalties to which he might make himself liable by traitorous or seditious expressions.¹

Into the dark mysteries of Hamilton's intrigues, it is impossible to enter further. As matters stood, no real understanding was possible. Between the King and Rothes there was a bitter personal altercation. Charles twice called the Earl to his face an equivocator and a liar. To the King's demand that all that could be said in favour of Episcopacy should be freely urged at Edinburgh, Rothes replied that if his countrymen were not allowed to rid themselves of the Bishops at home, they would be forced to open an attack upon the Bishops of England and Ireland.² On the 21st Rothes and his companions were sent back with orders to return on the 25th, together with those who had been detained in Edinburgh. On the 25th Dumfermline, Loudoun, and Lindsay arrived alone. They promised to dismiss the troops and pull down the fortifications of Leith. But mutual confidence was altogether wanting, and Charles informed them that he had given up his intention of appearing at Edinburgh in person.³

The Covenanters believed that Charles was still hankering after the restoration of Episcopacy. They were not altogether in the wrong. In the instructions given to Traquair, on the 27th, Charles declared that he had commanded the Bishops to absent themselves from the Assembly, and that he was ready to agree to the abolition of Episcopacy if it were not declared to be positively unlawful, but only 'contrary to the constitution of the Church of Scotland.' Such a reservation might appear to be no more than the

---

¹ Warrant, July 17, *Hardw. St. P.* ii. 141.
² Rothes to Murray, Aug., *Ham. Papers*, 98.
³ De Vic to Windebank, July 16, *S. P. Dom.* ccccxxvi. 50.

satisfaction due to a scrupulous conscience. There can be little doubt that it was more than that. Unless we are misinformed, Traquair told the King that in the absence of the Bishops the proceedings in Parliament would be null and void, and that he would therefore be able, without violation of the law, to re-introduce Episcopacy whenever he felt himself strong enough to do so.[1]

There can be little doubt that the prospect thus opened was pleasing to Charles. On August 3 he was once more at Whitehall. There he was surrounded by those counsellors who were most hostile to the Scots. "For the Scottish business," Laud wrote to Roe, "'tis true I sent you the happy word of peace, but what the thing will be in future I know not. Had I liked the conditions at the very first, I would have been as ready to have given you notice of them as of the peace itself. But I knew they would come soon enough to you, and I had no great joy to express them. 'Tis true that things were referred to a new Assembly and Parliament, but in such a way as that, whereas you write that the perfection of wisdom will consist in the conduct of them, there will certainly be no room left for either wisdom or moderation to have a voice there; but faction and ignorance will govern the Assembly, and faction, and somewhat else that I list not to name,[2] the Parliament; for they will utterly cast off all episcopal government, and introduce a worse regulated parity than is anywhere else that I know. How this will stand with monarchy, future times will discover; but,

---

[1] This rests on Burnet's testimony. He had many documents before him which are now lost, and his care in giving the substance of those which have been preserved speaks in his favour.

[2] "Treason" is probably meant.

for my own part, I am clear of opinion the King can have neither honour nor safety by it; and considering what a faction we have in England which leans that way, it is much to be feared this Scottish violence will make some unfitting impressions upon both this Church and State, which will much concern the King both in regard of himself and his posterity to look to." [1]

Charles's first act after his return was one of defiance to the Scottish leaders. He found that the report which they had issued of his conversations with them at Berwick was circulating in England. He ordered that it should be burnt by the public hangman? [2] His next step was to direct the Scottish Bishops to draw up a protest against the legality of the approaching Assembly and to place it privately in Traquair's hands. "We would not," wrote the King to Spottiswoode, "have it either read or argued in this meeting, when nothing but partiality is to be expected, but to be represented to us by him; which we promise to take so into consideration, as becometh a prince sensible of his own interest and honour, joined with the equity of your desires; and you may rest secure that, though perhaps we may give way for the present to that which will be prejudicial both to the Church and our own Government, yet we shall not leave thinking in time how to remedy both." [3]

Charles, in short, was to cozen the Scots by appearing to yield everything, whilst he was secretly preparing an excuse which would justify him in his own eyes in taking back all that he had yielded,

---

[1] Laud to Roe, July 26, *Works*, vii. 583.
[2] Act of State, Aug. 4, *S. P. Dom.* ccccxxvii. 14.
[3] The King to Spottiswoode, Aug. 6, the Bishops' Declinator, Aug. 10, 11. *Burnet*, 154.

whenever he was strong enough to do so. He was too conscientious to tell a direct falsehood, but he was not conscientious enough to abstain from conveying a false impression. The student of these transactions may perhaps be able to comprehend the meaning of that dark saying of Luther: "If thou sinnest, sin boldly."

Of all this as yet, the Scottish people knew nothing. They believed that they had at last attained the object of their desires. On August 12 the Assembly was opened in due form by Traquair at Edinburgh. No public notice was given of the Bishops' protest. On the 17th Episcopacy and all its attendant ceremonies were swept away as ruthlessly as they had been swept away at Glasgow. Old men who had known the evil days shed tears of joy as they looked upon 'a beautiful day, and that under the conduct and favour of' the King. "Blessed for evermore," cried one of those who was present, "be our Lord and King Jesus, and the blessing of God be upon his Majesty, and the Lord make us thankful." When Traquair signified his assent to the Act in his master's name, the enthusiasm of the assembly knew no bounds. "We bless the Lord," said Dickson, the Moderator, "and do thank King Charles, and pray for the prosperity of his throne and constancy of it so long as the sun and the moon endure."

Before the Assembly dispersed, it showed its renewed loyalty by adding a Royalist explanation to the Covenant, and then asked that every Scottish subject might be called on to subscribe it in this amended form. To this, too, Traquair gave his assent.[1]

Against this unwarrantable interference with the conscience of individual Scots, Traquair raised no

---

[1] Peterkin's *Records*, 204. *Burnet*, 157.

protest. Before the Assembly separated, however, he protested, as Charles had directed him to do, that the King would not engage to call Assemblies annually, and that he would not accept the abolition of Episcopacy as 'unlawful within this kirk,' unless the illegality were defined as arising merely from its being 'contrary to the constitution thereof.' Otherwise Charles might be urged to draw the inference that what was unlawful in Scotland was unlawful in England as well.[1]

1639. Aug. 30.

Parliament met on August 31. A constitutional question of the highest importance was immediately raised. The absence of the Bishops brought with it not merely the loss of fourteen votes to the King, but it disarranged the artificial machinery by which the nomination of the Lords of the Articles had been left practically in the hands of the Crown. This Committee, having complete authority over the amendment and rejection of Bills, whilst the mere final vote of Aye or No upon the Bills in the form in which the Lords of the Articles passed them, was all that was left to Parliament as a body, was of far more importance than Parliament itself. It was evident that in some way or other it must be extensively remodelled, and that on the mode in which it was remodelled the future constitutional influence of the Crown would to a great extent depend.

Aug. 31. The Lords of the Articles to be reconstituted.

For the present Parliament a temporary compromise was arrived at. Traquair selected eight members of the nobility, and was wise enough to choose a majority of the eight from the supporters of the Covenant. These eight then chose eight from the estate of the Barons or country gentlemen, and eight from the estate of the Burgesses.

[1] Peterkin's *Records*, 235.

CHAP. VI.
1639.
Sept.

A permanent arrangement was more difficult to hit upon. Looking forward, as he did, to the ultimate restoration of Episcopacy,[1] Charles would gladly have seen the fourteen Bishops replaced by fourteen ministers,[2] whom he doubtless hoped ultimately to convert into Bishops. It was not likely that such a proposal would obtain any support whatever. It was obnoxious to the ministers, who had no wish to see some of their number elevated above the rest; and it was equally obnoxious to the nobility, who had no wish to share their power in Parliament with any of the clergy. Charles was therefore obliged to fall back upon a plan supported by a party amongst the Covenanters, of which Montrose was the leading spirit, which urged that the place of the Bishops should be taken by a body of fourteen laymen to be appointed by the King, and who, if, as must be supposed, they were to play the same part in the selection of the Lords of the Articles that had formerly been played by the Bishops, would have restored to the Crown the control of that important Committee.[3] The re-

[1] "Il Rè sta tuttavia di buon animo, sperando che le cose possino passare per adesso in qualche maniera tollerabile con pensiero poi al sua tempo d'accomodarle a modo suo." Con to Barberini, Aug. $\frac{16}{26}$, *Add. MSS.* 15,392, fol. 223.   [2] Instructions to Traquair, *Burnet*, 150.
[3] The vague statements in Airth's letter (Napier, *Memoirs of Montrose*, i. 226) may be elucidated from Rossingham's *Newsletter* of Oct. 7, *Add. MSS.* 11,045, fol. 61. "There is no agreement concerning the third estate yet. . . . The King hath a party in the Parliament that pleaded hard for the King that he may not lose the Bishops' fourteen voices, and therefore there hath been some propositions how to supply this third estate by introducing fourteen laymen to supply the Bishops which are included, but it does not take, many objections being urged against it. . . . The Earl of Montrose, the Lord Lindsay, two very active Covenanters, are body and soul for His Majesty in Parliament, in that particular of settling the third estate; so are divers others of the known Covenanters." This letter does not say that the fourteen were to be chosen by the King, but, if they were to be a substitute for 'The Bishops' voices,' this must have been intended.

mainder, and, as it proved, the majority of the Covenanters, and especially the Barons and the Burgesses, were anxious to diminish the powers of the Lords of the Articles, and to make them a more exact representation of the House itself.

<small>CHAP. VI.
1639.
Sept.</small>

The parties thus formed were of permanent significance in Scottish history. Montrose and his friends wished to break with Episcopacy for ever. They were jealous of the popular movement which had made Episcopacy impossible, and they sought in the Crown a counterpoise, and more than a counterpoise, against the power which would be acquired by any members of their own order who chose to rest upon popular support. As might have been expected, Montrose's conduct exposed him to general distrust. The popular feeling was alarmed, and took expression in a placard which was affixed to his door: "*Invictus armis, verbis vincitur.*" It could not be, it was thought, that the hero of the Covenant should have adopted the cause of the enemy of the Covenant, unless he had been beguiled by flattering words at his interview with Charles at Berwick.

<small>Formation of parties. Montrose's policy.</small>

In this charge there was doubtless much injustice. But it was not entirely unjust. Montrose could not understand, as Wentworth could never understand, how hard it was to work successfully for Charles. He presupposed that Charles intended to make a fresh start, and would reconcile himself to Scottish Presbyterianism. On October 1 Charles wrote to Traquair, announcing that though he had consented to the abolition of Episcopacy, he would not consent to any act rescinding the existing laws by which Episcopacy had been established. "We cannot," he wrote, "consent to the rescinding any acts of Parliament made in favour of Episcopacy; nor do we conceive

<small>Oct. 1. Charles refuses to rescind the acts in favour of Episcopacy</small>

that our refusal to abolish those acts of Parliament is contradictory to what we have consented to, or that we were obliged to. There is less danger in discovering any future intentions of ours, or, at the best, letting them guess at the same, than if we should permit the rescinding those acts of Parliament which our fathers with so much expence of time and industry established, and which may hereafter be of so great use to us."[1]

Surely, in vain the net is spread in the sight of any bird. The King's refusal to consent to a rescissory Act was an advertisement to all Presbyterians that they had nothing to expect from him. Montrose's political design was rendered hopeless from the beginning.

Argyle's policy.

Montrose's opponents found a leader in Argyle. With the eye of a statesman, he perceived that the political meaning of the Presbyterian victory lay in the increased weight of the middle classes. Their ideas had prevailed in the Church, and their ideas must prevail in the State. The constitution of the Lords of the Articles must be made to give expression to this all-important fact. Montrose might try to support the nobility upon the unsafe foundation of the Royal power; Argyle would fall back upon the leadership of the middle classes.

It was difficult to carry the change which Argyle advocated through the Lords of the Articles, as they had been selected by Traquair. In the end it was voted by a bare majority of one, that each estate should in future choose its own Lords of the Articles. In this way the Barons and Burgesses would be represented by sixteen votes, the nobility by only eight, and the King by none at all. No Reform Bill in our own days has ever brought about anything approach-

[1] The King to Traquair, Oct. 1, *Burnet*, 158.

ing to the political change which was the result of this decision.[1] Henceforth the business of Parliament was to pass into the hands of a body fairly representing Parliament itself, whereas it had hitherto been in the hands of a body craftily contrived to represent the King.

The legislative changes proposed by the Lords of the Articles were as distasteful to Charles as the constitutional changes. Episcopacy was to be abolished as 'unlawful within this Kirk,' and the Bishops were to be deprived of their votes in Parliament. A general taxation was to be levied to cover the expenses of the late war; and not only were the few Royalists in the country to be called on to pay their share of the burden of a defence which Charles styled rebellion, but that defence was expressly said to have been entered on for the sake of the laws and liberties of Scotland. The command of the castles of

[1] Rossingham's *Newsletter*, Oct. 28, *Add. MSS.* 11,045, fol. 68. In an earlier letter of Oct. 21 the political situation is more fully depicted: "The Barons allege great mischiefs arise in their not choosing their own Commissioners for the Articles, so do the Burgesses, and the Nobility are divided about it. The Commissioners for the shires gave instructions to the Commissioners for the Articles requiring such things as quite overturn the very constitution of all future Parliaments, besides that they would choose the clerk of the Parliament, as all inferior judicatories do, which the King hath ever made choice of. Then they would have all the Bills and Supplications given to the Lords of the Articles by any member during the sitting in Parliament, that they may be read and answered accordingly; for they allege that the Lords of the Articles receive and reject what they please, to the great grievance of the whole kingdom, which they desire should be amended for time to come. Another of their propositions is that there be no public conclusion of any article which is to be passed or not passed for a law at the day of voicing; that before the conclusion a copy of every such article be given to every estate to be advised on by them with the representative body, that they may be more maturely advised on before the day of voicing, and that on the day of voicing, after one article is read, any member of Parliament may reason for it or against it, which hath not been the custom ever heretofore in that kingdom."

Edinburgh, Stirling, and Dumbarton was to be entrusted to none but Scottish subjects, and though these governors were still to be selected by the King they were not to be admitted to exercise their authority until they had been approved by the Estates.[1] Taken as a whole, the new legislation implied that Parliament and not the King was to be the central force in Scotland. Before the end of October Charles had made up his mind to resist. It was not the government of the Church alone that was at stake. Civil obedience, he held, was no longer to be had in Scotland. He sent orders to Traquair to prorogue Parliament till March. Traquair was met by the assertion that the King had no right to prorogue Parliament without its own consent. So strong was the opposition, that Traquair consented to a short adjournment to November 14, to give him time to consult Charles afresh. Two lords, Dumfermline and Loudoun, were despatched to England to plead the cause of Scotland before the King.[2]

The day of the adjournment was signalised by a distribution of favours amongst those who had taken Charles's part. Hamilton's brother became Earl of Lanark; Lord Ogilvy was created Earl of Airlie; Lord Dalziel appeared as Earl of Carnwath. Amongst the newly-created lords was Ruthven, the Governor of Edinburgh Castle, who was now to assume the title of Lord Ettrick.[3] It was impossible for Charles to signify more clearly that opposition to the national will was the surest road to such honours as he had it in his power to distribute. He had done all that

---

[1] *Acts of Parl. of Scotl.* (new edition), v. 595. *Rushw.* iii. 1040. *Gordon*, iii. 64.

[2] Sir T. Hope's *Diary*, 110. Lockhart to Traquair, Nov. 8, *Hailes' Memorials*, 76. *Spalding*, i. 230, 235. *Balfour*, ii. 361. Rossetti to Barberini, Nov. $\frac{1}{11}$, *R. O. Transcripts*. Salvetti's *Newsletters*, Nov. $\frac{1}{11}$, $\frac{8}{18}$, $\frac{15}{25}$.
[3] Balfour's *Annals*, ii. 362.

could be done to arouse suspicion. He had done nothing whatever to increase his chance of being able to carry his intentions into effect.

<small>CHAP. VI.
1639.
Oct. 31.</small>

Charles's misfortunes never came alone. The same want of perception of the conditions of action which had baffled him in Scotland baffled him in his dealing with the Continental Powers. The year had been a year of gloom for him in every direction. Early in the spring he had learned from Roe that there was no likelihood that any such treaty as that which he had sent him to negotiate would ever be obtained.[1] Before long the Swedish General Baner, careless of the fortunes of the Elector Palatine, was pushing forward in triumph through Thuringia, if a commander can be said to triumph who marches forward unchecked through scenes of havoc and desolation. "It is no more war, but spoil," wrote the English Ambassador, "without difference of friend or foe, and therein also I give it a civil name. . . Men hunt men as beasts for prey in the woods and on the ways." Charles indeed was hopeful, but his hopefulness was not for Germany or for humanity. The one thing he cared for, amidst these horrors, was to regain the Palatinate for his nephew. He assured his sister that when he had gained that victory in Scotland to which he was at that time looking forward with confidence, his power to assist her son would be as free as his will. Disappointed of aid from Sweden, Charles turned his eyes wistfully to Bernhard of Weimar. Like Charles Lewis, Bernhard was a dispossessed prince. Like Charles Lewis, he had good cause to be jealous of the French Government. He knew that, if he had won victories by Richelieu's aid, Richelieu coveted for his master the cities and lands of Alsace which had been

<small>Charles's relations with the Continental Powers.</small>

<small>Feb.</small>

<small>Baner in Thuringia.</small>

<small>Bernhard of Weimar,</small>

[1] See p. 180.

the spoils of victory. Charles Lewis, therefore, invited Bernhard to make common cause with him against their common enemies. Bernhard naturally replied by asking what assistance the Elector could give. Could he, for instance, supply a force of 4,000 men, and a round sum of money with which to support them? Such assistance it was beyond the power of Charles Lewis to give, and he soon began to suspect that Bernhard was more anxious to win territory for himself than for others.[1]

The young man's suspicions were never put to the test. Bernhard crossed the Rhine at the head of a well-appointed army, with the fairest expectations of success. In a few days he was stricken down by mortal sickness, and before June was over he was dead.[2]

With Bernhard's death passed away the last chance of checking the advance of French authority towards the Rhine. Everything concurred to inspire Charles with animosity against France. He was firmly convinced that Richelieu was at the bottom of the Scottish troubles. He therefore once more sought the alliance of Spain. It may indeed be doubted whether Charles was likely to receive more help from Spain than he had received before, but it is certain that Spain had more need of Charles than it had had before. Now that the Rhine valley was closed by Bernhard's victories against the passage of Spanish troops, the freedom of the navigation of the Channel was more important than ever. Reinforcements and supplies must come in that way from Spain to Flanders, or they would hardly come at all.

[1] Elizabeth to Roe, Feb. 25, *S. P. Holland*. Roe to Coke, Jan. 29, Feb. 6. The Elector Palatine to Roe, Apr. 16, June 7, *S. P. Germany*.
[2] June $\frac{28}{\text{July 8}}$.

Early in the summer it was known in England that English ships had been chartered to bring troops from Spain to Dunkirk, and that Tromp, the new Dutch admiral, was cruising off Portland to intercept them. As the vessels came up they were boarded by the Dutchmen. The English sailors were treated with all possible courtesy, but the Spaniards were carried off. To Northumberland and Pennington this appeared to be no more than a fair exercise of the rights of war. Charles was of a different opinion. He directed Pennington to maintain his sovereignty in the Channel. A small band of Spanish soldiers which had taken refuge in the Western ports was allowed to march on foot to the Downs, whence it was safely conveyed to a Flemish harbour.[1]

Chap. VI.
1639. June. Spanish soldiers in English ships.
July. Seized by Tromp.

Against these proceedings Joachimi, the Dutch Ambassador, protested. After some hesitation Charles proposed a compromise. He could not, he said, admit the right of search claimed by the Dutch, but he would prohibit his subjects from convoying soldiers if the States General would prohibit their subjects from selling their assistance to their own enemies in the Mediterranean. Charles possibly imagined that the Dutch habit of bargaining even with an enemy was too ingrained to be got rid of, and intended his compromise merely as a polite form of refusal. The progress of events was too rapid for any agreement on the subject.[2]

Aug. Compromise proposed by Charles.

[1] Hopton to Windebank, May 8, *S. P. Spain*. Povey to Pennington, June 3. Carteret to Pennington, June 3. Smith to Pennington, June 8. Pennington to Windebank, July 13. Northumberland to Windebank, July 15. Windebank to Pennington, July 16, *S. P. Dom.* ccccxxiii. 17, 18, 56, ccccxxv. 61, 78, 81. Cardenas to Salamanca, June $\frac{14}{24}$, $\frac{June\ 28}{July\ 8}$, July $\frac{8}{15}$, $\frac{19}{29}$. Cardenas to the Card. Infant, July 1, *Brussels MSS. Sec. Exp.* cclxxix. fol. 243, 301, 309, 325, 292.

[2] Northumberland to Pennington, Aug. 11, *S. P. Dom.* ccccxxvii.

CHAP.
VI.
───
1639.
July.
The Spanish fleet at Corunna.

All through the summer, a great Spanish fleet had been gathering at Corunna. Thirty huge galleons and thirty-six transports, eight of the latter being the property of English owners, were preparing to convoy to Flanders 10,000 soldiers and a large quantity of money. Magnificent as these preparations were, the Spanish statesmen had no longer the confidence in their naval power which had inspired their predecessors in the days when the Armada was launched against Elizabeth. They knew that their ships were ill-found and ill-provided, and that their seamen were no match for the sailors of the Dutch Republic. They humbled themselves to apply to Charles for a convoy.[1]

Charles offers to protect.

When the application was made, Charles was in the heat of his controversy with the Dutch about the right of search. He ordered Pennington to protect the Spaniards from all attack.[2]

40. Joachimi to the States General, Aug. $\frac{16}{20}$. The Prince of Orange to the States General, $\frac{Aug. 28}{Sept. 7}$, *Add. MSS.* 17,677, Q. fol. 75, 79.

[1] *Rushw.* (iii. 973) has printed a paper which he supposed to contain an account of this fleet, but an inspection of the number of the ships and the names of the commanders shows that it can have nothing whatever to do with it. The mention of the Archduke settles its date as belonging to the lifetime of the Archduke Albert. I strongly suspect that it refers to the expedition planned against Algiers in 1619. See *Prince Charles and the Spanish Marriage,* i. 274.

[2] "Muy contento estoy del buen suceso que ha tenuto la diligencia que per orden de su Mag^d hize con este Rey, para que su Armada franqueasse el Canal con fin de que la gente que havia de venir de España en los vajeles de Dunquerque pueda con mayor seguridad hazer su viaje, a que oy me respondio el Sñr Windevanch que su Mag^d de la Gran Bretaña havia dado orden a su Vizalmirante sali con los vajeles de su Armada que han venido de Escocia, y que limpiase el Canal sin consentir en el desorden ni hostilidad alguna, y que ya ha salido a executarlo." Cardenas to Salamanca, Aug. $\frac{2}{12}$, *Brussels MSS. Sec. Esp.* cclxxx. fol. 16. Windebank tried afterwards to shuffle out of this engagement. "It is very true," he wrote, "that Don Alonso gave some intimation .... that some vessels were preparing in Spain for transportation of forces into Flanders, and desired his Majesty would not take apprehen-

Thus encouraged, the great fleet sailed from Corunna on August 26.[1] On September 1 the eight English transports with 2,000 men on board put into Plymouth. The inhabitants of the Western Port were startled by the news that a fleet of huge galleons would soon be in the offing. Their thoughts recurred to the day on which Drake and Hawkins finished their game of bowls on the Hoe; and when they saw the Spanish hulls rising above the horizon, they believed for the moment that the unwelcome visitors would soon be in the Sound. If the Spanish Admiral, Oquendo, had any such intention, it was soon abandoned. On the 6th his course was waylaid by the Dutch Vice-Admiral with seventeen ships. All the next day a running fight was kept up as he made his way to the eastward. On the evening of the 7th the two fleets were off Dungeness, the smaller Dutch squadron keeping well to windward. Tromp, who was blockading Dunkirk, heard the sound of the firing, and on the 8th he joined his Vice-Admiral with fifteen sail.[2] That day there was a fierce battle between Dover and Calais. One Dutch ship blew up. Of the Spanish galleons three were sunk and one taken.[3] Before nightfall the Spaniards had fired away all their powder, and Oquendo did not venture to pursue his course to Flanders. With the shattered remnants of his fleet he put into the Downs for shelter, with Tromp following hard behind him.[4]

sion of it, but that they might have a friendly reception . . . . but he spoke not of so great a number nor such a strength." Windebank to Hopton, Sept. 29, *Clar. St. P.* ii. 71.

[1] Hopton to Cottington, Sept. 2, *S. P. Spain.*
[2] Account of the action, *Nalson,* i. 258. Aitzema, *Saken van Staet en Oorlogh,* ii. 609. Oquendo to Cardenas, Sept. $\frac{12}{22}$, *Brussels MSS. Sec. Esp.* cclxxx. fol. 86.
[3] According to other accounts, two were taken and one sunk.
[4] Manwood to Suffolk, Sept. 1, *S. P. Dom.* ccccxxviii. 52. Cave to

1639.
Sept. 9.
The Spaniards in the Downs.

The Spanish Admiral met with a rough greeting from Pennington. The English Vice-Admiral bade him lower the golden standard of Spain in the presence of his Majesty's flag. He had no choice but to obey. Pennington then insisted that Tromp, who was pressing on to follow up his victory, should abstain from hostilities and keep to the southern part of the anchorage, whilst the northern part was assigned to the Spaniards. Three days after his arrival, Oquendo took advantage of the distance which separated him from the enemy, to send off to Dunkirk, under cover of the night, fifteen of his smaller vessels laden with soldiers.[1]

Sept. 12.

Appeal to Charles.

Oquendo and Tromp appealed, through their respective ambassadors, to Charles. Then ensued an auction, the strangest in the annals of diplomacy, in which Charles's protection was offered as a prize to the highest bidder. As a prelude to the main bargain, Charles was not ashamed to make a hucksterer's profit out of the distress of the fugitives who had taken refuge in his port. Cardenas applied to the Master of the Ordnance, the Earl of Newport, for permission to purchase gunpowder from the King's stores. Newport told him that he might have the powder, if he were willing to give a handsome present in addition to the regular price. Cardenas remonstrated. "The King of Spain," replied Newport, "is very rich, and it is of no importance to him how much he gives for the powder of which he is so

---

Roe, Sept. 23, *S. P. Germany.* Rossingham's *Newsletter,* Sept. 9, Add. MSS. 11,045, fol. 53. Cardenas to Windebank, Sept. $\frac{10}{20}$. Cardenas to the Card. Infant, Oct. $\frac{4}{14}$, *Brussels MSS. Sec. Esp.* cclxxx. fol. 106, 129. Salvetti's *Newsletter,* Sept. $\frac{13}{23}$. Windebank to Hopton, Sept. 29, *Clar. St. P.* ii. 71.

[1] Oquendo to Cardenas, Sept. $\frac{9}{19}$. Cardenas to the Card. Infant, Sept. $\frac{13}{23}$, *Brussels MSS. Sec. Esp.* cclxxx. fol. 88, 78.

greatly in need." In the end, Cardenas was forced to pay 5,000*l.* to the King, and 1,000*l.* to the Earl, beyond the value of the powder. Those who are aware of this incident will not find much difficulty in understanding how it was that Lady Newport found her husband's religion unsatisfactory.[1]

Before the powder could be conveyed on board, fresh difficulties had to be met. Charles, indeed, appeared willing to concede all that the Ambassador could demand. He would allow the Spaniards to sail two tides before Tromp was permitted to leave the Downs, so as to enable them to reach Dunkirk without further opposition.[2] Suddenly, however, Charles altered his tone. Northumberland informed Pennington that the delay of two tides was never granted to so large a fleet. At the same time an embargo was laid upon all vessels in the Thames, in order that they might be pressed into the King's service for the purpose of strengthening Pennington's fleet, and a special prohibition was issued against the employment of any English ship in carrying troops to Flanders.[3] These measures, however, which were taken upon the advice of the Privy Council, were but the screen behind which was concealed a secret negotiation with Spain. Windebank told Cardenas, that as long as his master did so little for the Elector Palatine he must not expect many courtesies in England. Then came a formal demand for money. If the King of Spain would give 150,000*l.* his ships

---

[1] Cardenas to Salamanca, Sept. $\frac{13}{23}$, $\frac{20}{30}$, *Brussels MSS. Sec. Esp.* cclxxx. fol. 97, 107. Order to Newport, Sept. 20, *S. P. Dom.* ccccxxviii. 113.

[2] Joachimi to Van Tromp, Sept. $\frac{14}{24}$, *Add. MSS.* 11,677, Q. fol. 39.

[3] Northumberland to Pennington, Sept. 16, *S. P. Dom.* ccccxxviii. 93. Joachimi to the States General, Sept. $\frac{16}{26}$, *Add. MSS.* 17,677, Q. fol. 94.

should be placed in safety. The next day Cardenas told Windebank that he had suggested to his master the payment of 100,000*l.*, but that he might as well have asked for a million. It would have been as easy to procure the one sum as the other.[1]

The King proclaimed his intention of enforcing strict neutrality. He told Joachimi that not an English ship or an English man should render assistance to either side. There was a talk of compelling both fleets to put to sea together to try their fortune there.[2] There was no doubt which of the two would gain the mastery. Tromp had been heavily reinforced from Holland, and by the end of September he mustered some eighty sail, well manned and supplied. His crews were full of warlike ardour. Pennington would be hard put to it if he were called on to defend the helpless Spaniards against so overpowering a force. In the meanwhile the King's directions grew more contradictory than ever. Northumberland was fairly puzzled. To a friend of Pennington's, who begged for more precise orders, he replied 'that he had often pressed his Majesty to declare his resolution, but never could get any.'[3] Northumberland was not in the secret. He did not know that Charles was only waiting for the answer from Madrid to his demand for 150,000*l.* as the price of his assistance.

The French Ambassador, Bellievre, had been no less active than Cardenas. He had waited, indeed, till Tromp's reinforcements arrived, before he broached

---

[1] Cardenas to the Card. Infant, Sept. $\frac{20}{30}$. Cardenas to Salamanca, Sept. $\frac{20}{30}$, *Brussels MSS.* cclxxx. fol. 98, 107. Windebank to Hopton, Sept. 29, *Clar. St. P.* ii. 71.

[2] Joachimi to the States General, Sept. $\frac{19}{29}$, $\frac{Sept. 21}{Oct. 1}$, *Add. MSS.* 17,677, Q. fol. 103.

[3] Smith to Kensington, Sept. 30, *S. P. Dom.* ccccxxix. 83.

the subject. Then he commenced operations by winning the Queen over to his side. How he accomplished this feat is a mystery which he did not care to reveal. In the beginning of the month Henrietta Maria was a passionate supporter of Spain. At the end of the month she was a passionate supporter of France. She told Bellievre that the Spanish offers were magnificent, and that he must be prepared with offers more magnificent still. The King had assured her that his intention was to convoy the Spanish fleet to a place of safety. So well did she play her part, that a few hours later Charles declared himself ready to abandon the Spaniards to Tromp if the French Government would place his nephew at the head of the army which had been commanded by Bernhard of Weimar. Bellievre urged the Queen to ask that the Elector might carry with him ten or twelve thousand English troops in Charles's pay. Charles had no money to spare, and he answered that the utmost he could do would be to send over six thousand men to be paid out of the French treasury. In return, Lewis was to bind himself to make neither truce nor peace without comprising the rights of the Elector. Charles was ready to promise that he would conclude nothing with Spain till a fortnight had elapsed, in order to allow time for the consideration of his terms in France.[1]

Charles could hardly have made a proposal to which Richelieu was less likely to consent. Ever since Bernhard's death he had been engaged in winning over the officers of his army by lavish offers of money. During the whole of September, the negotiation had been going briskly on, and on the 29th, the very day on which Bellievre's despatch left

[1] Bellievre to Bullion, Sept. 29 / Oct. 9, *Arch. des Aff. Etr.* xlvii. fol. 558.

England, the articles were signed by which the colonels of the army sold themselves and the strong places of Alsace and the Breisgau to the King of France.[1]

Since the beginning of August, Charles Lewis had been in England urging his uncle to obtain for him the command of this very army. So little did Charles understand the realities of his position, that he fancied that the Elector had but to present himself at Breisach to be received with enthusiasm as the successor of the great Duke. On October 4 the helpless young man sailed from the Downs disguised as Lord Craven's valet, hoping to make his way through France to Alsace.[2] For a few days Charles fancied himself master of the situation. He had but to choose between a gift of 150,000*l*. from Spain, and a binding promise from France, to support vigorously his nephew's claims in the Palatinate, whilst in any case the young Elector was to put himself without trouble at the head of the finest army in Europe.

In the meanwhile Cardenas was playing his own game. His negotiation for the purchase of gunpowder had given him some insight into Newport's character, and he now concluded a bargain with the Master of the Ordnance for the transport of the Spanish soldiers to Dunkirk at the rate of thirty shillings a head, in direct defiance of the King's prohibition. It was Newport's business to send boats laden with munitions to Pennington's fleet in the Downs, and he now promised that these boats should

---

[1] Molitor, *Der Verrath von Breisach*, Jena, 1875.
[2] Bellievre to Chavigny, Oct. $\frac{8}{14}$, *Arch. des Aff. Étr.* xlvii. fol. 572. Memoir for Bellievre, *Bibl. Nat. Fr.* 15,913, fol. 381. Pennington to Suffolk, *S. P. Dom.*, Oct. 5, ccccxxx. 35, i.

be placed at Oquendo's disposition as soon as they had accomplished their legitimate task. It is true that nothing was done by Newport to carry out this promise, and it is possible that, on second thoughts, he considered it to be too audacious to be put in practice. That such a bargain should ever have been contemplated, however, is sufficient evidence of the low tone of morality which prevailed at Charles's Court.

CHAP. VI.
1639.
Oct. 4.

A day or two later Cardenas reported home that he had gained a step with Charles. Orders had been given to Pennington to protect Oquendo from any hostile attacks as long as he remained in the Downs.[1] If, indeed, the ambassador had been allowed to read the despatch in which these orders were conveyed, he would hardly have been as sanguine as he was. "I have made his Majesty acquainted with that part of your letter," wrote the Lord Admiral to his subordinate, "which concerns your demeanour between the Holland and the Spanish admirals, unto which his Majesty's answer is this, that you are to let the Holland admiral know that his Majesty is now celebrating the feast of St. George at Windsor, but within four days will return to London, and is then resolved to appoint a short time for both fleets to depart the Road; and upon the assurance which the Holland Ambassador hath given his Majesty, he rests confident that in the meanwhile no acts of hostility will be committed by them in that place. This being done, you are to send to the Spanish admiral to inform yourself in what state they are to defend themselves, and to resist that great force of the Hollanders which now threatens them. If, when the

Oct. 8.
The Spaniards to be protected.

Pennington's instructions.

[1] Cardenas to Salamanca, Oct. $\frac{1}{11}$. Cardenas to the Card. Infant, Oct. $\frac{11}{21}$, *Brussels MSS. Sec. Esp.* cclxxx. fol. 129, 147.

CHAP.
VI.
———
1639.
Oct. 8.

Hollanders assault the others, you see the Spaniards defend themselves so well that, with the help of those few ships that are with you, they shall be able to make their party good—which the King, upon the reports of some, is well inclined to believe—then are you to give them your best assistance, otherwise you must make as handsome a retreat as you can in so unlucky a business." As far as any inference can be drawn from directions so incoherent, it would seem that Charles, at the moment, hoped more from France than from Spain. "More particular instructions," added Northumberland, "I cannot get for you, which you must manage to your best advantage."[1]

The King's message to Cardenas.

To do Charles justice, he did not leave Cardenas entirely in the dark. He sent Endymion Porter to tell him that 'the King hath showed his care of the Spanish fleet with all the kindness that could be expected, and that, if the wind sit where it doth, it will be impossible for his ships to come to protect them against the Hollander; but his Majesty will do the best he can. Howsoever, he would have the Spaniards prepare themselves for the worst, for they cannot imagine but that he will have to limit a time for their abode in his port. In the mean time, he shall keep them from hostility, if it be possible, and his Majesty hath given the best order he can to that purpose.' Cardenas was also to be told 'how great a prejudice it would be to the King if they should fight in the harbour, for if any ships should miscarry, and be sunk there, it would be the ruin of the best harbour in the kingdom.' "But," reported Porter, "it seems the Spaniard regards nothing but his own accommodation, nor will they look about them until the King assign him a day to set sail, the which will

[1] Northumberland to Pennington, Oct. 8, *S. P. Dom.* cccxxx. 47.

be required from him; and when they are out of the port they must trust to their own force, for his Majesty will protect them no farther."

CHAP. VI.
1639.

If, in short, the Spaniards were to be sunk, they ought to oblige the King by choosing deep water to be sunk in. Charles, however, was prepared to face even the disagreeable alternative of a combat in the Downs. On the 10th Suffolk was directed, as Lord Warden of the Cinque Ports, to provide board and lodging for any Spaniards who might take refuge on shore, in case of a fight, at least as long as they were able to pay for his hospitality.[1]

Oct. 10. A conflict expected.

A man who is so uncertain of his intentions, as Charles had shown himself to be, ceases to have the power of making his intentions respected. On the 12th Cardenas was occupied with Windebank in drawing up an engagement, by which a considerable sum of money was to be secured to Charles in return for his protection, when unexpected news arrived from the Downs.[2] The reply of the French Government to Charles's overtures was written on the 8th. Of his demand, that his nephew should be placed in command of Bernhard's troops, it took no notice; but it distinctly asserted, that if France was to enter into any engagement with respect to the Palatinate, the six thousand men offered in return must be paid by Charles as well as levied. If he allowed the Spanish fleet to escape, the statesmen of Madrid would laugh at him as Gondomar had laughed at his father.[3]

Oct. 12. Offers of Cardenas.

Oct. 8. The French reply.

Richelieu had long ago taken the measure of Charles's capacity for aid or resistance. He did not

Reinforcements for Oquendo.

[1] Porter to Windebank, Oct. 9. Windebank to Suffolk, Oct. 10 *S. P. Dom.* ccccxxx. 57, 60.
[2] Cardenas to the Card. Infant, Oct. $\frac{12}{22}$, *Brussels MSS. Sec. Esp* cclxxx. fol. 152. Gage to Windebank, Oct. $\frac{19}{28}$, *Clar. St. P.* ii. 79.
[3] Memoir to Bellievre, Oct. $\frac{8}{18}$, *Bibl. Nat. Fr.* 15,995, fol. 373.

wait, as Cardenas was obliged to wait, for Charles's resolution. There can be little doubt that Tromp acted under advice from the Cardinal. Whether this were so or not, the Dutch admiral knew that his enemy was growing stronger under his eyes. Thirty sloops arrived from Dunkirk laden with reinforcements for Oquendo. In the evening of the 10th the barrels of powder, which had been purchased at so exorbitant a price, were at last alongside his ships. The night, however, was closing in, and the Spaniards did not venture to bring them on board by the light of a candle.[1]

But little of that powder ever reached the holds of the Spanish ships. Tromp knew that there was no time to be lost. He had a hundred armed vessels with him now, besides fire-ships ready to be let loose on the disabled foe. On the evening of the 10th a shot, accidentally fired from on board a Spanish vessel, had killed a Dutch sailor. Tromp charged the Spaniards with a breach of the peace. In the morning of the 11th, whilst the Spanish powder was still in the boats, Tromp ranged up alongside of his outnumbered and unprepared antagonists. At eight, Pennington was roused by the boom of cannon-shot sounding out of the fog which lay heavily on the water. It was impossible for him to know which fleet had been the first to fire, and he tried hard to persuade himself that the Spaniards had been the aggressors. He knew that he could do but little good by thrusting himself between the Dutchmen and their prey, whilst the orders which he had received had been too incoherent to justify him in exposing his men to slaughter in a cause so unpopular. In an

---

[1] Pennington to Northumberland, Oct. 11, *S. P. Dom.* ccccxxx. 77. Salvetti's *Newsletter*, Oct. $\frac{18}{28}$.

hour's time the firing came almost to an end. Some twenty Spanish vessels had run ashore to escape from their pursuers. The rest made off towards the South Foreland, chased by the Dutch. By this time Pennington had placed himself to windward, and after firing some shots at the victorious Dutch ships, returned to protect the stranded vessels, one of which was already blazing, and to seize upon two of Tromp's ships which had run ashore in the fog. Of the remaining Spaniards not a few were taken or sunk. The rest—numbering, according to various accounts, from ten to eighteen—reached Dunkirk in safety.[1]

CHAP. VI.
1639.
Oct. 11.

Charles was highly indignant. His golden dream of a choice between 150,000*l.* from Spain, and the command of Bernhard's army for his nephew, had vanished in the smoke of Tromp's guns. His boasted sovereignty of the seas had been flouted in his very harbour by the audacious Netherlanders. Yet it was not in his power to take revenge. The barrenness of the Exchequer, which had checked his march across the Tweed, would hardly allow him to embark upon a war with the Dutch. He ordered Pennington to get off the stranded Spanish vessels and to convoy them to Dunkirk. More than that he could not do.[2]

The King's displeasure.

Damaging as was the true story of the fight in the Downs to Charles's reputation, it was concealed from the eyes of his subjects. But its place was taken by a cloud of rumour no less damaging. Oquendo's fleet, it was believed, had been intended to land troops not in Flanders, but in England. Men sapiently in-

Rumours about the Spanish fleet.

---

[1] Relation by Pennington and others, Oct. 11. *Newsletter*, Oct. 12, *S. P. Dom.* cccсxxx. 74, cccсxxxi. 4. Account of the action, *Nalson*, i. 258. Extract from a letter, *S. P. Flanders. Rushw.* iii. 969.

[2] Salvetti's *Newsletter*, Nov. $\frac{1}{11}$.

VOL. I.   T

formed one another that the Governor of the Isle of Wight—the heir of Lord Treasurer Portland, who was himself suspected to be a Catholic in disguise—had shot away all his powder as a salvo at the drinking of healths, with the evident intention of leaving the island without the means of resistance; and that the arms of the county of Kent had been, with a similar intention, exhausted in supplying its trained bands on the Borders. The Governor of Dunkirk, it was said, had been so astonished at the arrival of the first shiploads of escaped soldiers, for which he was entirely unprepared, that he had at first refused them admission. From all this it was easy to conclude that England had been saved by the gallant Dutchmen from a grave peril—a peril all the more dangerous because the invaders, unlike the invaders of 1588, had the Sovereign of England on their side.[1] Unfounded as the suspicion was, it cannot be said to have been absurd. Only a few months before, Charles had been planning how to obtain the services of 6,000 Spanish veterans for his war against the Scots, and the notion was already ripening in the minds of Englishmen, that an attack on Scotland was equivalent to an attack on England.

Another disappointment was in store for Charles. His nephew had made his way in disguise through Paris, and had reached Moulins on the road to Breisach. He was there arrested and detained, on the plea that he carried no passport. He was taken to Vincennes and kept in strict custody. To Charles,

---

[1] *Rushw.* iii. 969. Examination of Dominey, Sept. 16, *S. P. Dom.* cccexxviii. 94. Salvetti, in his *Newsletter* of Oct. $\frac{4}{14}$, says that the idea was spread by the French and Dutch Puritan faction, and speaks of it as an 'artifizio che se bene non ha colpito in quelli che governono, ha nondimeno intossicato talmente il popolo che malamente si può loro ridurre a credere il contrario.'

the imprisonment of his nephew was scarcely less offensive than Tromp's attack in the Downs, but he was equally powerless to avenge it.

Wentworth as Charles's counsellor.

With Scotland in all but open insurrection, and with his maritime supremacy set at nought in his own ports, Charles felt the need of a counsellor who could reveal to him the secret of success. That counsellor he hoped to find in Wentworth. It happened that the Lord Deputy was at the time in England. He had long been exposed to petty annoyances from Irish officials and English courtiers, and though, whenever he stood at bay, he had no difficulty in routing his enemies, he was unable to shake them off entirely. One case in which he was concerned had been brought to an issue in the preceding May. In November 1634 a man named Robert Esmond had been summoned before Wentworth in Dublin for having refused to carry on board his vessel some timber belonging to the King. Wentworth was in an ill temper, shook his cane at Esmond, and after having, according to some accounts, actually struck him, committed him to prison. After a short imprisonment the man, who had long been suffering from consumption, was allowed to go at large, but he died a few days after his release.

His case against Crosby and Mountnorris.

The moment at which this unlucky affair occurred was one in which Wentworth had surrounded himself with bitter enemies. Crosby had just been ejected from the Privy Council, and Mountnorris was at the height of his feud with the Lord Deputy. Crosby and Mountnorris busied themselves with the collection of evidence to prove that Esmond's death had been caused by the severity of the blows administered to him, with the intention of bringing a charge against the Deputy before the King. Wentworth, as usual, anticipated the blow, and accused Crosby and Mountnorris and some of their confederates, before the English Court of Star Chamber, as the propagators of scandalous falsehoods to his discredit.

At last, in May 1639, the case was ready for a hearing. The evidence that Wentworth had not actually touched the man was extremely strong. Mountnorris escaped punishment through defect of proof, but Crosby and others were sentenced to various fines.[1]

It was not the only case in which Wentworth was at this time involved. In the first years of his government he had found a strong supporter in the Chancellor, Lord Loftus. In 1637 the two men were deadly enemies. According to Wentworth's story, the Lord Chancellor, having covenanted to settle certain estates on his eldest son upon his marriage, had broken away from his word. He was summoned before the Irish Privy Council, and, answering insolently, was placed under restraint. What justification Loftus may have had cannot now be ascertained. He fell back on his political friends at Court, and by their intercession he obtained leave from Charles to cross St. George's Channel, that he might plead his own cause in England. From that moment his fault must have assumed a peculiar heinousness in Wentworth's eyes. The permission given him was a direct challenge to the policy of "Thorough." A highly-placed offender was, it seemed, to be permitted to set at nought the judgment of the Irish

---

[1] The account in *Rushw.* (iii. 888) is very incomplete. It may be supplemented by a fuller, but also incomplete, account in the *State Papers* (*Dom.* cccxx. 36), and by a statement by Lord Esmond (*S. P. Ireland*, Undated). It was given in evidence, that Esmond when in prison distinctly denied that he had been struck by Wentworth.

Privy Council because Arundel and Holland, and all the courtiers who had a grudge against the Lord Deputy, had placed themselves on his side. Wentworth took the daring step of vindicating the King's authority against the King himself. He resolved that if Loftus went to England he should not go as Chancellor. Acting upon instructions which had not hitherto been put in force, he summoned him before the Council, and took the Great Seal out of his hands.[1]

For many months Charles hesitated between the pleadings of the courtiers and Laud's advocacy of Wentworth. Wentworth lashed himself into rage at the obstacles raised against him. He declared the Chancellor to have been guilty of the worst oppres-

---

[1] The King to Wentworth, Apr. 9. Wentworth and the Irish Council to the King, Apr. 20. Wentworth to the King, Apr. 22, 168, *Straf. Letters*, ii. 160. I have said nothing in the text about the alleged intrigue between Strafford and Lady Loftus. Clarendon's assertion is no evidence, and Sir G. Radcliffe's testimony, coming from a friend so intimate, is conclusive. "He was defamed for incontinence, wherein I have reason to believe that he was exceedingly much wronged. I had occasion of some speech with him about the state of his soul several times, but twice especially, when I verily believe he did lay open unto me the very bottom of his heart. Once was when he was in a very great affliction upon the death of his second wife; and then for some days and nights I was very few minutes out of his company. The other time was at Dublin, on a Good Friday, his birthday, when he was preparing himself to receive the Blessed Sacrament on Easter Day following. At both these times I received such satisfaction as left no scruple with me at all, but much assurance of his chastity." *Straf. Letters*, ii. App. 435. Strafford's own language, too, in speaking of the lady is inconsistent with the charge, whilst the respectful admiration which it reveals would account for the rise of scandalous rumours. "We have sadly buried my Lady Loftus, one of the noblest persons I ever had the happiness to be acquainted with; and as I had received greater obligations from her ladyship than from all Ireland beside, so with her are gone the greatest part of my affections to the country; and all that is left of them shall be thankfully and religiously paid to her excellent memory and lasting goodness." Strafford to Conway, *Ibid.* ii. 381.

sion in the exercise of his office, and to be unworthy of serving the Crown in any capacity whatever. His opponents naturally set down his indignation to mere passion. At last Charles decided substantially for Wentworth. He allowed, indeed, the Chancellor to come to England to plead his cause. But he forced him first to submit to the decree of the Irish Council against him, pending the result of his appeal. Wentworth was allowed to visit England to conduct his case in person. The English Council declared itself to be convinced by the arguments of the Deputy, and ordered that Loftus should be prosecuted in the Star Chamber. It is possible that the Chancellor deserved his fate, but the decision of a body composed as the Privy Council was could carry little weight.[1]

Sept. 22. Wentworth in England.

Wentworth had arrived in London on September 22. From that time he became, what he had never been before, the trusted counsellor of Charles, so far at least as it was possible for Charles to trust any one. During the fourteen months which followed he was the great minister, striving with all the force of his iron will to rescue his master from the net in which his feet were inextricably entangled. To some extent the blame of failure must lie with the King himself. Charles was not easy to save. He was too inconsistent in carrying out a settled policy, too readily inclined to listen to personal claims and personal attachments, to be able to cut his way sternly and ruthlessly through opposing ranks. But, after all, the main cause of failure lay in Wentworth himself. His want of sympathy with his generation is fatal to his claim to the highest statesmanship. He could criti-

---

[1] The King to Wentworth, July 23. Wentworth to Conway, Aug. 13, *Ibid.* ii. 372, 381. Salvetti's *Newsletter*, $\frac{\text{Sept. 27}}{\text{Oct. 7}}$. *Council Register*, Oct. 13.

cise incisively the organised ecclesiastical democracy of the Scottish Assembly, but he had nothing to substitute for it which could give him any hold on the hearts of the Scottish people. For the Scottish people, indeed, he took but little thought. It was enough for him if he was able to subdue them, and in order to subdue them it was necessary to rally Englishmen round the throne. In truth, he knew England hardly better than he knew Scotland. He could not comprehend how honest men could look on the Scottish resistance from a point of view different from his own. If Englishmen would but open their eyes to the foulness of that mad rebellion, they would rejoice to be the rod in the King's hand to exercise righteous judgment on his enemies.

During the first few weeks of Wentworth's sojourn in England, disaster had followed disaster. The lesson which Wentworth saw in the disgrace of the conflict in the Downs, and in the scornful imprisonment of the Elector by Richelieu, was the necessity of showing a firm front to the Northern traitors, whose rebellion had made it impossible to avenge such insults. On November 7 two commissioners from the Scottish Parliament, the Earls of Loudoun and Dunfermline, arrived in London to ask that the acts of the Scottish Parliament might receive confirmation by the King.[1] The question was referred to a committee of eight Privy Councillors which had recently been formed for consultation on the affairs of Scotland. Of that Committee, the Junto, or Committee of eight, as it was frequently called, Wentworth was the ruling spirit. Its other members were Laud, Hamilton, Juxon, Northumberland, Cottington, Windebank, and

[1] *Guthry*, 69.

Vane.¹ From such a committee the Scottish demands were not likely to meet with much consideration. By a considerable majority of its members, Charles was urged to send Loudoun to prison, on the ground that he had circulated that account of the King's conversation at Berwick which had been burnt as false by the hangman in England.² With this recommendation Charles did not comply; but he ordered Loudoun and Dunfermline to return at once, on the ground that their commission had not been signed by Traquair. He declined, in short, to treat with the Parliament of Scotland as an independent body.³

The dismissal of the Commissioners had been anticipated by an order to Traquair to prorogue the Parliament—not, as had been before intended, to March, but to June 2. This time the prorogation was accepted at Edinburgh, though not without a protest. Parliament separated, after appointing a committee to sit in its absence to consider the answer which Loudoun and Dunfermline were at that time expected to bring back from London.

This contemptuous rejection of the Scottish demands at the instance of a committee of which only one member was of Scottish blood, was certain to irritate the Scottish national feeling. "The Scots," wrote an Englishman who made it his business to collect information on passing events, "have lately declared their great jealousies that the kingdom of Scotland is designed to be made a province of England, and to be governed by orders and directions from the Council of England, which they protest against, that they will never consent unto it, but to be governed by their own laws formerly made, and hereafter to be made, in their

---

¹ Cardenas to Salamanca, Nov. 1/11, *Brussels MSS. Sec. Esp.* cclxxx. 200. ² Salvetti's *Newsletter*, Nov. 15/25. ³ *Spalding*, i. 235.

own Parliament, and by themselves, but to be confirmed by his Majesty."[1]

Wentworth's advice had at last been taken. Lest every movement in opposition to Charles's government in England should find encouragement and support in Scotland, Scotland must be ruled directly from England. Proudly and unhesitatingly, Wentworth stepped forward towards the end which he had long foreseen to be the only alternative which it was possible for the King to adopt. Of the loyalty of England he still believed himself to be secure. The order to prorogue the Scottish Parliament had been despatched on November 8. On the 10th it was decided that ship money should be collected, not at the reduced rate of the preceding year,[2] but at the full amount of the earlier assessments. Ship money alone, however, would not suffice to conquer Scotland. On the 27th Traquair, who had returned from Edinburgh,[3] told before the Committee of eight, the long story of Scottish disobedience. That Scotland must be coerced, was accepted as a necessity. But there were long debates as to the best means of effecting this object. Some of the members of the Committee talked, as Privy Councillors had talked twelve years before, of establishing an excise by prerogative. Others suggested that the precedent of ship money should be applied to the land forces, and that each county should be required to support a certain number of soldiers. Wentworth's voice rose clearly above this Babel of tongues. He insisted that a Parliament, and a Parliament alone, was the remedy fitted for the occasion. Laud and Hamilton gave him their support. He

---

[1] Rossingham's *Newsletter*, Nov. 12, *Add. MSS.* 11,045, fol. 72.
[2] See p. 190.
[3] Rossingham's *Newsletter*, Dec. 3, *Add. MSS.* 11,045, fol. 78.

carried his point with the Committee. What was of more importance, he carried it with the King.

It is not to be imagined for a moment that Wentworth had any intention of lowering the flag of the monarchy in the presence of the representatives of the nation. What he proposed was but an experiment and nothing more. "The Lords," as Windebank expressed it, "being desirous that the King and his people should meet, if it were possible, in the ancient and ordinary way of Parliament, rather than any other, were of opinion his Majesty should make trial of that once more, that so he might leave his people without excuse, and have wherewithal to justify himself to God and the world that in his own inclination he desired the old way; but that if his people should not cheerfully, according to their duties, meet him in that, especially in this exigent when his kingdom and person are in apparent[1] danger, the world might see he is forced, contrary to his own inclination, to use extraordinary means rather than, by the peevishness of some few factious spirits, to suffer his state and government to be lost."[2]

On December 5 the discussion was transferred to the Council itself. Traquair made a formal report of his mission. He painted the disobedience of the Scottish Parliament in the blackest colours; all the blacker perhaps because he knew that he was regarded at Court as an accomplice of the Covenanters, and that it was reported that he had said at Edinburgh that his Majesty desired but the shadow, but would be content to quit the substance. Wentworth's advice was unanimously accepted by the Council. Those members who were in any way favourable to

[1] In the old sense of 'evident.'
[2] Windebank to Hopton, Dec. 13, *Clar. St. P.* ii. 81.

the Scots were also those who desired most heartily to see another Parliament at Westminster.

Before giving his formal consent to the proposal, Charles requested the Council to advise him on the financial situation. It was certain that no further help was to be expected from the City. The loan which had been demanded in the summer had been absolutely refused, and repeated pressure had only produced an offer of 10,000*l.* as a gift: an offer which was at first rejected as insufficient, and only accepted when it became evident that no more was to be had.[1] The King now asked the Councillors whether, 'if the Parliament should prove as untoward as some have lately been, the Lords would not then assist him in such extraordinary ways in the extremity as should be thought fit.' They unanimously voted in the affirmative. On this the King announced that Parliament should be summoned for April 13, and that Wentworth should first proceed to Ireland to hold a Parliament at Dublin, which would doubtless set a good example to the English Parliament which was to follow.[2] It is impossible not to recognise the hand of Wentworth here. It was no mere financial operation that was in question. Parliament was to be made to feel that the King did not rely on its vote alone. Before the Council broke up, it was resolved that its members should at once offer a loan to the King. Wentworth led the way with 20,000*l.* Coventry, Manchester, and Newcastle followed with 10,000*l.* apiece. The whole loan was fixed at 300,000*l.* In a few days the subscriptions amounted to 150,000*l.*, and 50,000*l.* more were gathered before Christmas.[3]

1639.
Dec. 5.
The Councillors' loan.

[1] Rossingham's *Newsletter*, Aug. 6, 13, *Add. MSS.* 11,045, fol. 43, 45.
[2] Windebank to Hopton, Dec. 13, *Clar. St. P.* ii. 31.
[3] The King to the Lords of the Council, Dec. 6, *S. P. Dom.* ccccxxxv. 37. Rossetti to Barberini, Dec. $\frac{29}{30}$, *R. O. Transcripts.*

1639.
Dec. 5.
The Scots invited to give satisfaction.

Wentworth's next care was to preserve the appearance of magnanimity. The Scots were not to have it in their power to say that the King had refused to listen to them. In spite, therefore, of the dismissal of Loudoun and Dunfermline, Traquair was directed to return to Edinburgh, and to inform the Committee left behind by the Parliament, that if they still wished to send a deputation to the King they were at liberty to do so.

Reception of the news in England.

In England the unexpected announcement of a Parliament was received with joyful surprise. The surprise was not accompanied with any feeling of gratitude to the King. The very precautions which had been taken were certain to arouse suspicion. It might reasonably be argued that if Charles had purposed a thorough reconciliation with his people, he would not have thought it necessary to fortify himself with the Privy Councillor's loan. Graver rumours too were floating in the air. It was whispered that the army was to be raised, not to fight the Scots, but to intimidate Parliament. The members would be called on to deliberate amidst the clash of arms, and would be called upon to vote away under durance the ancient liberties of Englishmen. Any one who ventured to raise his voice against the Court would pay for his audacity with his head.[1] It is easy to say that such suspicions were unfounded and un-

Suspicious of the King's intentions.

Aerssens to the Prince of Orange, Dec. $\frac{19}{29}$, *Arch. de la Maison d'Orange-Nassau*, Ser. 2, iii. 155. The payments cannot be traced on the Exchequer Books, as they were secured as anticipations on payments hereafter to be made by the subscribers, and anticipations do not appear on these books. Wentworth's money, for instance, was secured out of the Northern Recusancy fines, of which he was the collector, and which he would keep in his own hands till the 20,000*l.* had been paid off. There is, however, a complete list of the payments in *S. P. Dom.* cccliii. 75.

[1] Bellievre to Chavigny, Dec. $\frac{10}{20}$, *Arch. des Aff. Etr.* xlvii. 650.

reasonable, but it is impossible to deny that it was natural that they should be entertained.

Both Charles and Wentworth underestimated the strength of the opposition against their policy too much, to make them even think of recurring to violence. Nor is it at all likely that even those who felt most bitterly against the Government were aware how strong was their position in the country. In the seventeenth century, when Parliament was not sitting, our ancestors were a divided people. Each county formed a separate community, in which the gentry discussed politics and compared grievances when they met at quarter sessions and assizes. Between county and county there was no such bond. No easy and rapid means of communication united York with London, and London with Exeter. No newspapers sped over the land, forming and echoing a national opinion from the Cheviots to the Land's End. The men who grudged the payment of ship money in Buckinghamshire could only learn from uncertain rumour that it was equally unpopular in Essex or in Shropshire. There was therefore little of that mutual confidence which distinguishes an army of veterans from an army of recruits, none of that sense of dependence upon trusted leaders which gives unity of purpose and calm reliance to an eager and expectant nation.

If the sense of union was wanting to the opponents of the existing political system, it was still more wanting to the opponents of the existing ecclesiastical system. Disinclination to pay money which is not regarded as legally due is a very simple feeling. The dislike felt for Laud's ecclesiastical policy was by no means so simple. Many persons wished to see the Prayer Book replaced by the unceremonial worship

CHAP. VI.

1639. Dec. The Opposition not conscious of its strength.

The ecclesiastical opposition.

CHAP.
VI.
1639.
Dec.

of New England or Geneva. A larger number wished to retain the Prayer Book with certain alterations. Others again would leave the Prayer Book itself untouched, but would interpret the rubrics as they had been interpreted in the days of their boyhood, when the Communion table stood in the centre of the church. Behind all these there was a body of resistance not called forth by any ecclesiastical or religious feeling whatever, but simply arising from the dissatisfaction of the gentry with the interference of the clergy.

Laud's report.

How widely spread the latter feeling was, neither Charles nor Laud had any notion. Laud's certificate of the condition of the Church during the past year was written in a cheerful tone.[1] The Bishop of Peterborough had stated that few of the laity were factious, excepting where they were misled by the clergy. "This," noted Laud, "is too true in most parts of the kingdom." If Laud had been right in this, his task would not have been as hopeless as it was. A little more care in weeding out clergymen of the wrong stamp, and a steady persistence in scrutinising the character of candidates for ordination, would have reduced England to the proper ecclesiastical pattern.

The Ecclesiastical Courts.

Nor was evidence wanting which might seem to encourage a hopeful view. During the last months of 1639 and the first months of 1640, the Act Book of the High Commission Court only records the deprivation of one clergyman, and that for open and unblushing drunkenness.[2] The books of the Officials' Court of the Archdeaconry of Colchester tell much

---

[1] *Works*, v. 361.
[2] Sentence on Rawson, Feb. 6. High Commission Book, *S. P. Dom.* ccccxxxiv. fol. 92.

the same tale. It is true that many persons were summoned before it for absenting themselves from church; but their excuses and promises of amendment were readily admitted, and the time of the Court was mainly occupied with those cases of immorality which would have been even more severely visited by the Puritan clergy than by the Laudian Courts. Amongst the charges brought were complaints against persons who behaved indecently in church, who refused to bow at the name of Jesus, who worked in the fields on saints' days, and even on one occasion on the day of Gunpowder Plot. Women were reprimanded for chattering or sewing in church, and more frequently for refusing to appear veiled when returning thanks after childbirth: a practice on which Laud insisted with unusual vehemence, and to which they objected strongly, apparently from the imaginary resemblance of the required veil to the linen sheet worn in penance by the unchaste. The fines imposed were small, and penalties infrequent, but they undoubtedly caused considerable irritation whenever they were inflicted.[1]

The dissatisfaction called forth amongst the Puritan clergy was suppressed rather than overcome. Hundreds unwillingly administered the Communion at the rails. In one part of England the ill-feeling of the clergy was peculiarly strong. Wren had lately been removed from Norwich to Ely, and the Puritan diocese of Norwich was handed over to

The diocese of Norwich.

---

[1] The Act Books are kept in a room over the porch of the parish church at Colchester, and are in the charge of the registrar. I have to thank the Rev. Sir J. Hawkins, Bart., and F. T. Veley, Esq., for their kind assistance in helping me to see these books at a time when the illness of the late registrar made it difficult for me to procure access to them in the ordinary way. Extracts from the books are given by Archdeacon Hales, in his *Series of Precedents and Proceedings*.

Montague, the chief mover in the scheme for the reconciliation of the Churches of Rome and England. Yet even Montague was deceived by the external signs of quiet. "This diocese," wrote Laud in his report, "my lord the Bishop assures me is as quiet, uniform, and conformable as any in the kingdom, if not more; and doth avow it that all which stood out in Suffolk as well as Norfolk at his coming to that see, are come over, and have now legally subscribed and professed all conformity, and, for aught he can learn, observe it accordingly. Yet his lordship confesses that some of the vulgar sort in Suffolk are not conformable enough, especially in coming up to receive at the steps of the chancel where the rails are set; but he hopes by fair means he shall be able to work upon them in time."

Indictment of a minister.

Some, indeed, whether of the vulgar sort or not does not appear, attempted a counter-stroke. They indicted at the assizes a minister who had declined to administer the Communion to them in their seats. The Judges, as might have been expected, refused to interfere in a matter purely ecclesiastical, but the attempt was significant of the spreading feeling that the institutions of the Church ought to be brought into closer harmony with the religion of the laity.

Aug. Spread of the sects.

The sullen ill-feeling of the gentry and middle class gave encouragement to the wilder and more vehement Puritanism of those whom Laud contemptuously styled the vulgar sort. The excitement amongst these men was evidently rising. The Archbishop was forced to confess that even in his own diocese the Church Courts were unable to keep down the Separatists and the Anabaptists, and that if they were to be got rid of it would be necessary to force them to abjure the realm.[1] In London one of these

[1] *Works*, v. 361.

men died in prison. His corpse was followed by two hundred members of his own sect. To questioners who inquired the name of the deceased, they answered fiercely, that he 'was one of the Bishop's prisoners.' When they reached the burial-ground 'they, like so many Bedlams, cast the corpse in, and, with their feet instead of spades, cast and thrust in the mould till the grave was almost full; then they paid the grave-maker for his pains, who told them that he must fetch a minister; but they said he might spare his labour.'[1]

The feeling engendered by such manifestations in the minds of the supporters of established order was one of angry vexation at the presence of an unpalatable evil against which it was impossible to guard. Even the Privy Council was at one moment carried away so far as to meditate an act of abnormal cruelty. In July information was brought to Laud that a certain stonemason of Dover, named John Trendall, had refused to take the Oath of Supremacy, and had expounded the Scriptures in his own house. Further, he had denied that the Lord's Prayer ought to be used, had expressed disapproval of the Creed, and had kept away from church on the ground that it was against his conscience to worship under the authority of the Bishops. Laud referred the matter to the Council, and, after consultation with the Attorney and Solicitor General, the Council actually applied to Archbishop Neile, who had been Bishop of Lichfield at the time when Wightman and Legate were burnt in his diocese in 1611, to certify them of the nature of the proceedings in their case.[2]

[1] Memorandum to Dr. Alsop, Aug. 31, *S. P. Dom.* ccccxxvii. 107.
[2] The Mayor and Jurats of Dover to Laud, July 27. Examination of Trendall, July 27, *S. P. Dom.* cccxxxii. 27 i. 27 I. i. *Council Register*, July 31, Aug. 2.

Neile was not content to give a simple answer to the question put to him. He not only gave a full narrative of the circumstances attending the execution of the two heretics, but he declared his conviction that the punishment of the two men 'did a great deal of good in this Church.' "I fear me," added the Archbishop, "the present times do require like exemplary punishment."[1]

By the time that Neile's report arrived, the Council had returned to a better frame of mind. Trendall was ordered to take the Oath of Supremacy, and this time he did not refuse. Subsequently he was sent to give an account of himself before the High Commission. At first he refused to acknowledge the jurisdiction of the Court; but, as its records are silent on his subsequent fate, it is probable that he gave way and was released.[2] At all events, there was no longer any thought of sending him to the stake, and there is reason to believe that he became a Puritan minister under the Long Parliament and lived on into the reign of Charles II.[3]

Little did Charles imagine that such men as Trendall would be a power in England before many years were over. If he felt any apprehension for the coming Parliament, it was of a different kind. Whatever that apprehension may have been, he looked with confidence to Wentworth to overcome opposition in England as he had formerly overcome opposition in

---

[1] Neile to Laud, Aug. 23. Becher to Mottershed, Nov. 9, *S. P. Dom.* ccccxxvii. 78, ccccxxxii. 27.

[2] *Council Register,* Aug. 18. Day to Coke, Aug. 25, *S. P. Dom.* ccccxxvii. 80. The extracts from the High Commission Book are in Mr. Hamilton's Preface.

[3] A petition from a John Trendall to Charles II., asking not to be turned out of his cure, has recently been discovered by Mrs. Everett Green.

Ireland. At last he was prepared to confer upon his faithful Minister that token of his confidence which he had twice refused before. On January 12 Wentworth received the Earldom of Strafford, and a week later he exchanged the title of Lord-Deputy of Ireland for the higher dignity of Lord-Lieutenant, which had last been borne by Devonshire when he lived in England and governed Ireland by a deputy.

Before the new Earl left England arrangements were made for levying the army which was to march against Scotland in the summer. According to the scheme adopted by the Council of War, it was to consist of 23,000 men.[1] This time there was to be no attempt to save a few thousand pounds by calling upon the peers to serve at their own expense. Neither Arundel nor Essex nor Holland were to receive a command. The Lord-General was to be the Earl of Northumberland, in whom Strafford placed his confidence. Another friend of Strafford's, Lord Conway, the son of the Secretary of Charles's earlier days, was to command the Horse. Strafford himself was to serve as Lieutenant-General under Northumberland, and to take the field with a force of 8,000 men, which were to follow him from Ireland. Sir John Conyers, a military man of reputation in the Dutch service, was to take the command of the garrison at Berwick.[2] With such appointments there was likely to be less personal rivalry between the superior officers than in the preceding year.

Civil offices which fell vacant about this time were less wisely filled. On January 14 the death of Lord Keeper Coventry deprived Charles of the services of

[1] Resolutions at the Council of War, Jan. 10, *S. P. Dom.* ccccxli. 83.

[2] Cave to Roe, Jan. 10. Northumberland to Conyers, Jan. 12, *S. P. Dom.* ccccxli. 92, 110 i.

the most prudent amongst his counsellors. As a lawyer of the old school, he was on the side of the prerogative against the new ideas of Parliamentary supremacy, but he had always shrunk from the extravagant applications of his own theory which were urged upon him by men of observation inferior to his own. Only a few months had passed since he had opposed in Council the wild projects suggested for the support of the army; and, if a not improbable report is to be trusted, he conjured the King on his death-bed to endure patiently any opposition which might arise in the coming Parliament, and to 'suffer it to sit without any unkind dissolution.'[1] Charles showed how little he appreciated the advice given him by appointing Finch as his successor, who, as Speaker, had been held down in the chair in 1629, and who, as Judge, had passionately advocated the King's claim to ship money in its most extreme form.

Another vacancy had to be filled up about the same time. Sir John Coke's tenure of the Secretaryship had long been regarded as uncertain. He was growing too old for his work. Other causes besides his age affected his position. Many counted him a Puritan, or, in other words, an opponent of the existing ecclesiastical system. He was suspected of drawing a pension from the Dutch Government, and since the attack in the Downs all friends of the Dutch Government were in ill odour at Whitehall.[2] In November Strafford had been favourable to his removal, and had supported the claims of Leicester, the Ambassador at Paris, to the vacancy which would be created. Leicester was married to Northumberland's sister, and, like Northumberland, he belonged to that section of the nobility which was distinctly Protestant without

[1] *Hacket*, ii. 137. [2] Salvetti's *Newsletter*, Jan. 17/27.

being Puritan, and which was disposed to support the King against rebellion, without favouring an arbitrary exertion of the prerogative. Strafford was well aware of the importance of conciliating this class of men, and he had special reasons for favouring Leicester. Leicester's cause was pleaded by his wife's sister, Lady Carlisle. Lady Carlisle had now been for many years a widow. She had long been the reigning beauty at Court, and she loved to mingle political intrigue with social intercourse. For politics as a serious occupation she had no aptitude; but, in middle age, she felt a woman's pride in attaching to herself the strong heads by which the world was ruled, as she had attached to herself in youth the witty courtier or the agile dancer. It was worth a statesman's while to cultivate her acquaintance. She could make him a power in society as well as in Council, could worm out a secret which it behoved him to know, and could convey to others his suggestions with assured fidelity. The calumny which treated Strafford, as it afterwards treated Pym, as her accepted lover, may be safely disregarded. Neither Strafford nor Pym was the man to descend to loose and degrading debauchery. But there can be no doubt that purely personal motives attached her both to Strafford and Pym. For Strafford's theory of Monarchical government she cared as little as she cared for Pym's theory of Parliamentary government. It may be, too, that some mingled feeling may have arisen in Strafford's breast. It was something to have an ally at Court ready at all times to plead his cause with gay enthusiasm, to warn him of hidden dangers, and to offer him the thread of that labyrinth which, under the name of 'the Queen's side,' was such a mystery to him. It was something, too, no doubt, that this advocate was not a grey-haired statesman, but a woman, in spite of growing years, of winning grace and sparkling vivacity of eye and tongue.

The Queen supports Leicester.

The Queen, too, was enlisted on Leicester's side, probably through Henry Percy, Northumberland's brother, who was also a brother of Lady Carlisle and Lady Leicester, and who stood high in her favour.

Leicester rejected.

Yet, in spite of his wife's pleading, Charles would not hear of her candidate. Whatever the cause may have been, Northumberland singled out Laud as the author of the mischief. "To think well of the Reformed religion," he wrote, "is enough to make the Archbishop one's enemy."[1]

Vane proposed.

A new combination was now proposed. At Hamilton's suggestion the Queen put forward Vane. Strafford knew him as an inefficient self-seeking courtier. He had also given Vane personal offence, which he was not likely to forget. Though the estate of Raby was in Vane's possession, Strafford had chosen the barony of Raby to give a subsidiary title to his earldom.[2] Rather than see Vane in office, Strafford urged that Coke should be retained. He was borne down by the influence of Hamilton and the Queen, and on February 3 Vane became Secretary of State.[3] Vane's son had been brought, in the preceding spring, to some outward show of conformity, and, as Joint Treasurer of the Navy, was engaged, amongst other occupations, in reckoning up the payments of ship money as they came slowly in.

Feb. 3. Becomes Secretary.

---

[1] Northumberland to Leicester, Nov. 21, Dec. 13, *Sydney Papers*, 618, 623.

[2] Cave to Roe, Feb. 7, *S. P. Dom.* cccxliv. 54.

[3] Clarendon's account is borne out by Rossetti's despatches.

CHAPTER VII.

THE SHORT PARLIAMENT.

IT was not likely that Charles would even attempt to remove the real obstacles to a good understanding between himself and his people. He could hardly, however, venture to face a Parliament without liberating Valentine and Strode, the two of the companions of Eliot's imprisonment who still remained in custody. They had been the confessors, as Eliot had been the martyr, of the Parliamentary faith. After a seclusion from the world of almost eleven years they stepped forth into freedom.[1]

Whilst Charles was calculating the chances of a Parliamentary grant for his Scottish war, the Queen was, naturally enough, alarmed at the probability that Parliament would ask for a renewal of the persecution of the Catholics. Con, who had pleaded their cause with her so successfully, had left England in the preceding autumn, and had died soon after his arrival in Rome. His successor was an Italian prelate, the Count Rossetti. Rossetti's first impression of England had been one of amazement at the liberty enjoyed by the Catholics, and more especially at the language of Windebank who, though ostensibly a Protestant, spoke to him 'like a zealous

CHAP. VII.
1640. Jan.
Release of Valentine and Strode.

1639. The Queen anxious about the Catholics.

Aug.

Rossetti at Court.
Sept.

---

[1] Rossingham's *Newsletter*, Jan. 24, *Add. MSS.* 11,045, fol. 87. I was quite unaware, when I wrote my last volumes, that their imprisonment had not come to an end, as has been supposed by others, much earlier.

Catholic,' and offered to give him every information of which he might stand in need.¹ As soon as he heard of the approaching meeting of Parliament, he appealed to the Queen for protection against the very probable demand of the Commons for his own dismissal. The Queen carried his representations to her husband, and returned with comforting assurances. Charles had told her, that if the point were raised he would reply that her right to hold correspondence with Rome was secured by her marriage treaty. "This," she explained to Rossetti, "is not true, but the King will take this pretext to reduce to silence any one who meddles with the matter."² Before long this precious scheme broke down. The necessary secrecy was not observed, and the project reached the ears of Coke. Coke, who was out of humour at his own dismissal, went about assuring all who would listen to him that the treaty did not contain a word about a correspondence with Rome. Another scheme which presented itself to the Queen's mind was still more unwise. Many of the Catholic Peers were prevented from taking their seats in the House of Lords by their refusal to take the Oath of Allegiance. It was now suggested that the Lords had no right to impose this qualification, and it was hoped that in this way the Catholics would be better represented in Parliament than had hitherto been the case. Yet the Queen could not but feel that, even if she had her wish in this matter, the prospects of the Catholics were very unfavourable. She applied to Strafford for help. Strafford answered civilly, but his civil answers did not

---

¹ Rossetti to Barberini, Sept. $\frac{6}{16}$, *R. O. Transcripts*.

² "Il che se bene non è vero, vuole nondimeno valersene il Rè per pretesto per ribattere chiunque sarà per trattarli di questo fatto." Rossetti to Barberini, $\frac{\text{Dec. 27}}{\text{Jan. 6}}$, *Ibid.*

inspire confidence. He was always an enigma to the Queen and her friends. Rossetti was not quite sure whether he was a Protestant or a Puritan, but was inclined, on the whole, to regard him as a Puritan.[1] If he meant, as he probably did, that Strafford had no wish to favour the Catholics, he was doubtless in the right.

So slight were Charles's hopes of a successful issue of the Parliament which he had summoned, that he was already looking abroad for the support which was likely to fail him at home. Since the sea-fight in the Downs and the detention of the Elector Palatine, he was more alienated from France than before, and more convinced that Richelieu was at the bottom of his Scottish troubles. His relations with the States General were equally unsatisfactory. Aerssens, indeed, had arrived on a mission of explanation; but his explanations consisted simply in an assertion that Tromp had been doing good service to Charles by destroying the fleet of the common enemy; and that, at all events, he had only followed the precedent set by Charles himself in 1627, when he seized a French ship in the neutral harbour of the Texel.[2] Charles showed his displeasure in his reception of a proposal made to him at this time for a marriage between his eldest daughter Mary and the only son of the Prince of Orange. He told Heenvliet, the confidential agent of the Prince, that if he asked for his second daughter, Elizabeth, he might take the request into consideration. As the child was only four years old, the change was not likely to give satisfaction at the Hague.[3]

---

[1] Rossetti to Barberini, $\frac{\text{Jan. 24}}{\text{Feb. 3}}$, $\frac{\text{Feb. 28}}{\text{March 9}}$, March $\frac{13}{23}$, *R. O. Transcripts*.

[2] Aerssens and Joachimi to the States General, Dec. $\frac{19}{29}$, *Add. MSS.* 17,677, fol. 146. *England under Buckingham and Charles I.*, ii. 150.

[3] Heenvliet to the Prince of Orange, $\frac{\text{Dec. 27}}{\text{Jan. 6}}$, Jan. $\frac{3}{13}$, Groen van Prinsterer, *Archives*, Ser. 2, iii. 159, 169.

Charles had, in fact, another alliance in view. That veteran intriguer, the Duchess of Chevreuse, had suggested that Charles's eldest son and daughter should be united to the daughter and the son of the King of Spain. It was known that a new Spanish Ambassador, the Marquis of Velada, would soon be in England to join Cardenas in urging Charles to revenge the insult which had been offered him by the Dutch. Sir Arthur Hopton, the English agent at Madrid, was instructed to hint that if Velada brought proposals for a new Spanish marriage, they would be favourably received.[1] It was not, indeed, likely that the overture would be really made. As usual, Charles took care to make the Spaniards understand how little his alliance was worth. Hopton was to say that his master found 'himself in a great strait' in consequence of the occurrence in the Downs. It would be as dangerous to show 'a sense equal to the affront' as to show 'none at all.' If he demanded reparation from the States, there would be no course open to him, in the probable event of a refusal, short of a declaration of war; and, as matters stood, a declaration of war was simply impossible. What he wanted, in short, was that Philip should help him out of his present difficulty, on the understanding that Charles would help him in turn when he was in more prosperous circumstances.

The reply made by Olivares was not encouraging. He would hear nothing of an alliance unless Charles would actually declare war against the Dutch. In that case the old secret treaty, negotiated by Cottington for the partition of the Netherlands, should be revived, and Charles might choose any part of the

---

[1] Aerssens to the Prince of Orange, $\frac{\text{Dec. 31}}{\text{Jan. 10}}$, Groen van Prinsterer, *Archives*, Ser. 2, iii. 165.

Dutch territory which suited him best. If this offer were accepted, the King of Spain would do that which had been asked in vain in the preceding summer. He would lend Charles eight or ten thousand veterans in exchange for the same number of recruits. On the subject of the marriage Olivares was extremely reserved.

<small>CHAP. VII.
1640. Feb.</small>

In reporting this conversation Hopton warned Charles that he had little to expect from the Spaniards. They had now but few ships and less money. Their habit was to promise mountains and perform molehills.[1]

<small>March 12.</small>

These overtures to Spain were perhaps to some extent owing to Charles's prior conviction that the Scottish troubles were the result of Richelieu's intrigues. As a matter of fact, Richelieu had taken no part in them. It is true, indeed, that in May 1639 a certain William Colvill had been instructed by the Covenanting leaders to visit the Hague and Paris, in order to ask for the mediation of the States General and the King of France, whilst another agent was to go with a similar object to the Queen of Sweden and the King of Denmark. Scruples, however, against the propriety of asking for foreign intervention prevailed; and, though the letters which these agents were to have carried were written, they were not despatched.[2]

<small>1639. May. Relations between Scotland and France.</small>

In proposing to make application to France, the Scots did but revive the old policy of their ancestors.

[1] Windebank to Hopton, Feb. 7. Hopton to Windebank, Feb. 18, March 12, *Clarendon MSS.* 1,351, 1,353, 1,362.

[2] *Baillie*, i. 190. Draft to the King of France, *Hailes's Memorials*, 60. The letter ultimately written is printed in *Rushw.* iii. 1,119. In Mazure's *Hist. de la Révolution*, ii. 405, where it is also printed, it is followed by an instruction which is of a later date, and has no connection with the abortive mission of 1639.

CHAP. VII.
1639.
May.

The memory of the ancient league had not died away. Scottish archers still guarded the person of the King of France, and Scottish visitors to Paris in need of protection were in the habit of going straight to Richelieu's Scottish chaplain Chambers, seldom troubling themselves to pay even a visit of ceremony to the English Ambassador. Even in our days it has sometimes happened that a Scotsman can procure unwonted attention in Paris by the mere mention of his nationality.

Bellievre advocates intervention.

The policy of giving active assistance to the Covenanters had a warm advocate in Bellievre. He had long ago entered into communication with their leaders, and had sent emissaries to Scotland to watch the course of affairs. When Dunfermline and Loudoun arrived in London at the end of the year, they sent to the Ambassador to ask for French support in case of need. In return, they were ready to engage to make no further treaty with Charles in which their alliance with France was not recognised, as well as to stipulate for the admission of Scots to the Committee of Foreign Affairs,[1] where they would be in a position to give warning of anything which might be contemplated to the prejudice of that alliance.

Dec.
Offers of Dunfermline and Loudoun.

Richelieu refuses to accept them.

Bellievre would gladly have fallen in with this proposal. Richelieu would not hear of it. All through the summer he had been warning the Ambassador that it would be unwise to enter into any engagements with the Scots. The sagacious Cardinal

[1] This proposal was based on a suggestion made by Bellievre in the autumn. Ranke, who was the first to tell the story, missed the point of this demand by translating the 'Conseil des Affaires Etrangères' by the Privy Council. A man might be a Privy Councillor, and know nothing of importance.

held that Charles would ruin himself without any effort on the part of France. He now positively ordered Bellievre not to meddle in the affairs of Scotland. It was probably in consequence of this rebuff that Bellievre was recalled at his own request. Early in January he returned to Paris.[1]

In the beginning of February Traquair arrived in London, bringing with him the Scottish Commissioners who had been deputed to lay the case of their countrymen before the King. By neither side could it be seriously expected that any good would result from their mission; and Charles was more especially distrustful because Traquair had come into possession[2] of the letter which the Covenanters had intended to send to France by Colvill in the preceding spring. When Charles saw it he was confirmed in all his suspicions. Now, he thought, he would be able to prove to all men that religion had been but the pretext under which the Scots had cloaked deliberate treason.

Nor were the Scots more hopeful of a satisfactory issue. They did not, indeed, break out into open resistance, and they even allowed a hundred English soldiers to enter the Castle of Edinburgh as a reinforcement of Ettrick's scanty garrison.[3] Yet they knew that they must be prepared for the worst, and, on the day after the soldiers entered, Colvill was despatched to France with a second letter asking for the mediation of Lewis in the name of the ancient league.[4]

---

[1] Chavigny to Bellievre. Lewis XIII. to Bellievre, Apr. $\frac{5}{15}$, Dec. $\frac{20}{30}$, $\frac{Dec. 30}{Jan. 9}$, *Bibl. Nat.* Fr. 15,915, fol. 302, 393, 398. Bellievre to De la Barde, $\frac{June 27}{July 7}$, *Arch. des Aff. Etr.* xlvii. 510.

[2] *Balfour*, iii. 76.

[3] Ettrick to the King, Feb. 18, *S. P. Dom.* ccccxlix. 58.

[4] The Covenanters to Lewis XIII., Feb. 19, *Bibl. Nat.* Fr. 15,915, fol. 410. The instructions printed by *Mazure*, ii. 406, refer to this mission.

To this letter Montrose's signature was appended. If he was tending towards Charles, he had not yet gone over to him altogether. It was necessary to keep up appearances, and in December he had been compelled by popular clamour to refuse an invitation to Court which had reached him from Charles himself.[1] Yet it would probably be unjust to ascribe his conduct simply to a wish to keep up appearances. It may very well be that Charles's reluctance to throw the Bishops frankly overboard had its effect upon Montrose as well as upon others. How much Charles's hesitation on this point contributed to give strength to his political opponents is evident to all dispassionate inquirers. Sir Thomas Hope was one of the most fanatical of the Covenanters. "My lord," he said one day to Rothes, who had assured him that the King meant to restore the Bishops, "let no reports move you, but do your duty. Put his Majesty to it, and if it be refused then you are blameless. But if on these reports ye press civil points, his Majesty will make all Protestant princes see that you have not religion for your end, but the bearing down of monarchy."[2] If Charles expected to derive any strength from the monarchical sentiment which was still living in Scotland, he must agree quickly with the Presbyterians.

Unluckily for Charles, it was to England rather than to Scotland that he was looking for help. In his discussions with the Scottish Commissioners he showed no alacrity to win the hearts of Scotsmen by any plain declaration on the subject of Episcopacy. After some preliminary fencing, he took up the position that 'the supreme magistrate must have authority

---

[1] Montrose to the King, Dec. 26, Napier, *Memoirs of Montrose*, i. 228.   [2] Hope's *Diary*, Jan. 14, 115.

to call assemblies and to dissolve them, and to have a negative voice in them as is accustomed in all supreme powers of Christendom.'[1] He truly felt that the proposed Acts contained nothing less than a political revolution. But he had nothing positive to offer. Even when the Commissioners observed that, after all, the Bills had not yet passed the Articles, and were consequently still open to revision, he made no attempt to seize the opportunity by announcing his readiness to assent to the Bill for repealing the Acts by which Episcopacy had been legalised. No wonder the Commissioners were left under the impression that his reservation of the negative voice implied a purpose to restore Episcopacy at the first favourable opportunity.[2]

These discussions, meaningless in themselves, were carried on in the midst of warlike preparations. On February 24 arrangements were made for pressing 30,000 foot from the several counties south of the Humber,[3] the northern shires being excused as having borne the burden heavily in the last campaign. At Edinburgh an appeal to arms was no less imminent. On the 25th some ill-built works which had been erected as a defence to the castle, fell down, and the population of the town refused to allow Ettrick to carry in the materials needed to repair the damage. A few days later the Earl of Southesk, Sir Lewis Gordon, and other noted Royalists were seized and imprisoned.[4] The struggle for sovereignty in Scotland was evidently about to recommence.

One gleam of hope shone upon Charles's path. On March 16 Strafford crossed the Irish Sea, suffering, as

[1] *Rushw.* iii. 1,035.   [2] *Ibid.* iii. 994, 1,018.
[3] Nicholas's *Minutes*, Feb. 24, *S. P. Dom.* ccccxlv. 6.
[4] Ettrick to the King, March 2, 11, 25, *Ibid.* ccccxlvii. 6, 89, ccccxlviii. 81. *Spalding*, i. 260.

he was from his old disease, the gout. "Howbeit," he gaily wrote as he was preparing to embark, "one way or other, I hope to make shift to be there and back again hither in good time, for I will make strange shift and put myself to all the pain I shall be able to endure before I be anywhere awanting to my master or his affairs in this conjuncture; and therefore, sound or lame, you shall have me with you before the beginning of the Parliament. I should not fail, though Sir John Eliot were living."[1]

Meeting of the Irish Parliament.   Strafford kept his word. On the 18th he landed in Ireland. The Parliament had been already two days in session. A body so equally divided was always at the disposal of a strong ruler. With his little phalanx of officials well in hand, he could throw the majority in the House of Commons on which side he pleased. In 1634 he had thrown it on the side of the colonists of English birth. In 1640 he threw it on the side of the native Irish. Predisposed by their religious ties to dread the victory of the Covenanting Scots, the Irish Catholics would be ready to follow Strafford at least so long as he could convince them of his power. When he left England he had intended to ask for six subsidies, a grant which was estimated as equivalent to 270,000*l*. On the recommendation of the Council, however, he contented himself with asking for four, or 180,000*l*., on condition that the Commons would supplement it by a declaration that, if more were required, more should be given.[2]

[1] Strafford to ——? March 16, *Straf. Letters*, ii. 303. The editor gives this letter as written to Secretary Coke, though Coke was no longer Secretary. I suspect Conway to have been the man.
[2] The King to Strafford, March 2, 3. The Irish Council to Windebank, March 19, 23, *Straf. Letters*, ii. 391, 394, 396, 397. Cromwell to Conway, March 31, *S. P. Dom.* ccccxlix. 47.

The demand was made on the 23rd. Never was there a greater appearance of unanimity. Abhorrence of the Covenanters expressed itself in every word which was uttered. The King was thanked for not having taken what he needed by a simple act of the prerogative. He was assured that his Irish subjects would supply his needs if they left no more than hose and doublet to themselves. When the vote was taken, not a single negative was heard. Hands were stretched aloft and hats flung into the air in a burst of enthusiasm. Those who witnessed the scene declared that if one part of the assembly was more vehement than another, it was that in which the native Irish were to be found.

<small>CHAP. VII.
1640.
March 23.
Four subsidies voted.</small>

This exuberant loyalty found full expression in a declaration by which the grant was accompanied.[1] Its phrases sound unreal enough now. Yet they were doubtless not altogether unreal to those who uttered them. The zeal of the Irish Catholics, at least, was quickened by a lively anticipation of future favours. If they took the lead in the overthrow of the King's enemies, what could possibly be denied them?

In Strafford's eyes the declaration was a simple act of confidence in himself. The Irish, he wrote, would be as ready to serve with their persons as with their purses. By the middle of May he would be ready to take the field at the head of an army of 9,000 men, if only money were sent from England to enable him to make the first payments before the subsidies began to come in.[2] The Session was speedily brought to an end, and the Lord-Lieutenant recrossed the sea in hope to be as successful at Westminster as he had been at Dublin.

<small>March 24. An Irish army to be levied.</small>

---

[1] *Journals of the Commons of Ireland*, i. 141.
[2] Strafford to Windebank, March 24, *Straf. Letters*, ii. 398.

The English elections were held in March. The returns were not to the satisfaction of the Court. Suspicion was doing its work among the electors and the elected. Men spoke of the cavalry which was being raised for the Northern war as if it were intended to keep Parliament in check. When the members arrived in London, it was evident that they did not quail before the danger. Their talk was of limitations to be placed on the prerogative, and of calling in question the Ministers by whom it had been unduly exalted. The work of the Long Parliament was already in their minds.[1] On the other hand, counsellors were not wanting to urge Charles to be prepared to resort to force, and, in the belief of those who were likely to be well informed, he cherished the idea as at least a possible resource in the not improbable event of a refusal of supplies.[2] As if to give warning of coming danger, he appointed a considerable number of Catholics as officers in his new army, whilst all who were tainted with Puritanism were sedulously excluded.[3]

It was no immediate blow that Charles contemplated. He placed great confidence in the effect likely to be produced even upon the new House of Commons by the revelation which he had in store for them. On the back of the letter which Traquair had brought him was an address *Au Roi*. It was evident to Charles not only that the Scots had committed treason in addressing Lewis as their King, but that every reasonable person was certain to come to the same conclusion. The opinion of the House of Commons would in this way be gained over to his side.

---

[1] Salvetti's *Newsletter*, March $\frac{20}{30}$.
[2] Giustinian to the Doge, March $\frac{13}{23}$, March $\frac{20}{30}$, *Ven. Transcripts*.
[3] Rossetti to Barberini, $\frac{\text{March 27}}{\text{Apr. 6}}$, *R. O. Transcripts*.

A copy of the letter was first sent to the King of France.[1] Lewis, of course, disavowed having ever seen it before; and, as the letter which he had seen was a different one, he was able to make this disavowal with at least literal truthfulness. Richelieu congratulated himself that he had kept clear of all negotiation with the Scots. "By this event," he wrote, "M. de Bellievre will see that we have been more prudent than he."[2]

CHAP VII.
1640.
April 11. The letter communicated to Lewis.

Of those whose signatures were appended to the letter, one only was in Charles's power. Loudoun was one of the Scottish Commissioners in London. He was at once committed to the custody of one of the sheriffs, and the other Commissioners shared his fate, though they had nothing to do with the letter. It is probable that Charles's real motive is to be found in his anxiety to cut off all communication between them and the members of the English Parliament.

Committal of Loudoun.

In spite of the hopes which he founded on the effect of the letter which he had in his hands, Charles was depressed and anxious. The Privy Councillor's loan had been all too little for his needs. In vain he called on the citizens to lend him 100,000*l.* at eight per cent. for the necessary defence of the realm. Two days before the date appointed for the meeting of Parliament, the Lord Mayor and Aldermen were summoned before the Council. Manchester assured them not only that they were sure to have the money repaid, but that they ought to be grateful to the King for offering such advantageous terms. The citizens were not to be persuaded by his eloquence.[3]

The City refuse to lend money.

Parliament was opened on April 13. The new

[1] The King to Leicester, Apr. 11, *Sydney Letters,* ii. 645.
[2] Richelieu to Chavigny, $\frac{\text{Apr. }24}{\text{May }4}$, *Avenel,* vi. 689.
[3] Rossingham's *Newsletter,* Apr. 14, *S. P. Dom.* ccccl. 88.

Lord Keeper, who had recently been raised to the peerage as Lord Finch of Fordwich, set forth at length the disloyalty of the Scots, dwelt upon their unnatural conduct in opening negotiations with foreign States, and pointed out that, now that Ireland had been civilised, Scotland was the only quarter from which England was open to attack. It was in defence as much of his subjects as of himself, that the King had been compelled to raise an army. For the payment of that army money was urgently needed. In order to anticipate any dispute about tonnage and poundage, a Bill had been prepared, in which those duties would be granted from his Majesty's accession. When this and a Subsidy Bill had been passed, Parliament would have some time to devote to the consideration of grievances, and, if the season of the year did not allow sufficient opportunity, another Session should be held in the following winter.

As soon as the Lord Keeper had finished his speech, the King called on him to read the intercepted letter. "The superscription," said Finch, "is this— *Au Roi*. For the nature of which superscription, it is well known to all that know the style of France that it is never written by any Frenchman to any but to their own King ; and therefore, being directed *Au Roi*, it is to their own King ; for so in effect they do by that superscription acknowledge him."

As the letter itself bore no intimation of any such acknowledgment, the whole evidence of treasonable intention lay in the superscription ; and it is needless to say that this evidence was far too flimsy to support the weight which it was intended to bear.[1] Even if

---

[1] No doubt, *Au Roi* was not in any proper sense a direction. Several letters would be included in one packet, and marked *Au Roi, Au Cardinal*, &c., for the mere instruction of the bearer.

the superscription had been treasonable, there was nothing to connect it with any one of those by whom the letter had been signed. On the 14th Loudoun was examined. He asserted that he was completely ignorant of the French language, but that, so far as he knew, the letter was harmless. At all events, it had never reached its destination.

CHAP. VII.
1640.
April 14. Loudoun examined.

The King had gone too far to draw back. On the 16th the letter was read by Windebank in the House of Commons. It made no impression whatever there. The Commons were far more interested in noting that Finch had not had even a passing word to spare for the all-important subject of ship money.[1]

April 16. The Commons proceed to business.

The intercepted letter was therefore simply ignored by the Commons. Harbottle Grimston, the member for Colchester, was the first to break the ice.[2] He argued that, bad as a Scottish invasion might be, the invasions made upon the liberties of the subjects at home were nearer and more dangerous. Not only ought these grievances to be remedied, but an example ought to be made of those men with whom they had originated.[3]

Grimston's speech.

Grimston was an excellent specimen of that great middle party, on whom devolved the burden of maintaining in its essential parts the old constitution of the country. Born the second son of a baronet, he devoted himself in early manhood to the study of the law. On his elder brother's death he gave up his

Grimston a type of a party.

[1] Rossingham's *Newsletter*, Apr. 14, *S. P. Dom.* ccccl. 88. The scanty notices of this Parliament which are to be found in Rushworth may be largely supplemented from Rossingham's letters and notes. There is also a separate set of notes in *Harl. MSS.* 4,931, fol. 47, and there are special reports of speeches amongst the State Papers.

[2] This phrase, used by Clarendon of Pym is here restored to Grimston, to whom it properly belongs. Clarendon's account of this session is nearly worthless.

[3] *Rushw.* iii. 1,128.

profession as standing no longer in need of its emoluments. Soon afterwards he met and admired the daughter of Croke, the judge, who was to render good service to the State by his judgment in Hampden's case. He found that the old lawyer would not hear of a son-in-law who had turned aside from the legal plough, and, to gain a wife, young Grimston returned to the practice of the law. In 1638 he was appointed Recorder of Colchester, and he now sat in the Commons as member for that borough. He lived long enough to be able to boast that he had refused to take the Solemn League and Covenant, and that he had stood up alike against Cromwell and against Laud. He was a fitting Speaker of that Convention Parliament which recalled Charles II. without sharing in the violent intolerance of its successor, the Long Parliament of the Restoration, and he died at an advanced age two years before the accession of James II. Pious without fanaticism, and charitable without ostentation, he was naturally distrustful of all that was new and unexpected, and in this he did no more than reflect those conservative instincts which in every nation stand in the way of too rapid change.[1]

Grimston was followed by Seymour, in a speech more especially directed against the ecclesiastical grievances. After that Rudyerd discoursed, in his usual benevolent way, on the virtue of moderation, and proved decisively that he had grown neither wiser nor more resolute since he sat in the Parliament of 1628. As far as we know, no one rose in defence of Charles's government.

Whilst the tide was thus running strongly against Charles's system in the Commons, it received an unexpected blow in the Upper House. At the end of

[1] Collins' *Peerage*, viii. 214.

the sitting, Laud moved, as usual, that as the following day was appointed for the sitting of Convocation, the House should adjourn over it, on account of the enforced absence of the Bishops. Saye objected, on the ground that the presence of the Bishops was unnecessary to give validity to the proceedings of the Peers. Laud modestly answered that he asked for the adjournment not of right, but of courtesy. Finch came to the support of the Archbishop, stating that he was himself out of health, and that it would be difficult for him to attend, upon which the adjournment was voted solely on account of the Lord Keeper's inability to be present. It was evident that the Bishops were as unpopular amongst the Lords as they were amongst the Commons. "The Lower House," was Northumberland's comment on that day's proceedings, "fell into almost as great a heat as ever you saw them in my Lord of Buckingham's time, and I perceive our House apt to take fire at the least sparkle."[1]

The next day petitions from several counties, complaining of grievances of every kind, were presented to the Commons. The courtiers described them as the Scottish Covenant 'wanting only hands.'

If the petitions wanted hands, Pym gave them a voice. He spoke for nearly two hours, a length to which the Commons of those days were unaccustomed. The speech itself, sustained as it was by the fervour of strong conviction, had nothing of the poetic imagination for which members of earlier Parliaments had never looked in vain to Eliot or Wentworth. Those who sympathised with Pym most thoroughly feared lest his long argumentative reasoning should strike coldly upon the ears of his hearers. When he sat down, they knew that their fears had been un-

[1] Northumberland to Conway, Apr. 17, *S. P. Dom.* ccccl. 101.

founded. The general sense of the House was expressed by cries of "A good oration."[1]

The House was in the right. Pym's speech was one of those which gain immeasurably by subsequent study. Its greatness consists far more in what the speaker left unspoken than in what he said. Others could have summed up the well-known catalogue of grievances as well. The words of the petitions were too distinct to allow much room for addition. That which marks Pym from henceforth as a leader of men is the moderation combined with firmness with which every sentence is stamped. It was easy enough to start with an assurance that the King would be strengthened rather than weakened by granting the relief demanded. The Scotch Covenanters had done as much as that. But it was not easy to say things which must have been diametrically opposed to all the King's ideas, and yet so to say them as to give as little offence as possible to men who had no sympathy with fanaticism or violence. It may possibly have occurred to Pym's hearers—it will certainly occur to his readers—that the cause which Pym and Eliot had alike at heart had gained not a little by the sad fate which had condemned the stainless martyr to an early grave.

The first words with which Pym touched on the great question of Parliamentary privilege showed how thoroughly he was in accord with Eliot's principles. The 'powers of Parliament,' he said, 'are to the body politic as the rational faculties of the soul to a man.' The whole spirit of the coming revolution, at least on the political side, was to be found in these

---

[1] "The best feared it would scarce have taken because it was so plain; but at the end of it all cried out, A good oration." *Harl. MSS.* 4,931, fol. 47.

words. They made, indeed, the task of this Parliament hopeless from the first. It was the contention of Charles against the Scots that he, and no assembly, civil or ecclesiastical, was the soul of the body politic. What would it advantage him to receive subsidies and to gather armies to impose his authority on Scotland, if he were compelled to yield at Westminster all that he claimed at Edinburgh. It was therefore to the nation rather than to Charles that Pym's appeal was addressed. If once this first principle were admitted, all the rest of his argument would follow. The complaint was justified, that the events of the last day of the Session of 1629 and the treatment of the imprisoned members had been distinct violations of the privileges of the House, and even that the sudden and abrupt dissolution of Parliaments before their petitions were answered was 'contrary to the law and custom.'[1]

On turning to the ecclesiastical grievances, Pym stepped upon more uncertain ground. Till the question of Church government were solved in the sense of religious liberty, there could be no permanent solution of the constitutional problem. Yet for Pym or for any other man to solve it yet was altogether impossible. The sense of irritation which had been roused by Laud's unwise proceedings had been conducive to a temper predisposed to treat Laud and his allies as the enemies of the Church and country. It might have been expected that, after the occurrences of the last eleven years, Pym would have called for measures far more stringent than had satisfied the last Parliament. Exactly the contrary was the case.

---

[1] The ground on which the Scots had opposed the prorogation of their Parliament was that the matters were still dependent before the Lords of the Articles, and therefore neither accepted nor denied.

In 1629 Eliot led the House in asking for the proscription of all but Calvinistic opinions. In 1640 Pym after speaking of the danger from Popery, touched lightly upon the support which had been given in public to 'the chiefest points of religion in difference between us and the Papists.' Abstaining from any attempt to set up a new doctrinal test, he commented less upon the opinions of his opponents than upon their ceremonial innovations. He spoke of 'the new ceremonies and observances, which had put upon the churches a shape and face of Popery,' of the introduction of 'altars, images, crucifixes, bowings and other gestures,' the preferring of the men who were most forward in setting up such innovations, and the discouragement of the 'faithful professors of the truth.' Matters of small moment had been taken hold of 'to enforce and enlarge those unhappy differences,' and 'to raise up new occasions of further division.' Then, too, there had been 'the over rigid prosecution of those who' were 'scrupulous in using some things enjoined,' which were yet held by those who enjoined them to be in themselves indifferent. Pym's remedy for the mischief lay at least in the direction of liberty. "It hath ever been the desire of this House," he said, "expressed in many Parliaments in Queen Elizabeth's time and since, that such might be tenderly used. It was one of our petitions delivered at Oxford to his Majesty that now is; but what little moderation it hath produced is not unknown to us all. Any other vice almost may be better endured in a minister than inconformity." That there might be no doubt to what he referred, he enumerated the cases in which punishment had been inflicted 'without any warrant of law.' Men, he said, had been brought to task for refusing to read the Declaration of Sports, for not removing the Communion table to the east end, for not coming to the rails to receive the Sacrament, for preaching on Sunday afternoons instead of catechising, and even for using other questions than those which were to be found in the authorised Catechism. Finally, there had been abuse in the exercise of ecclesiastical jurisdiction.

<small>CHAP. VII.
1640.
April 17.</small>

It cannot be denied that to grant Pym's demands would have broken up the Church system of Charles and Laud. But though some of the more extreme ceremonial forms would undoubtedly have been proscribed, the whole tone of his speech was in favour of a liberal and comprehensive treatment of the Church question. The unnecessary restrictions upon conscientious religion held far the largest space in his argument. Even when Pym spoke of practices to which he took objection, it was the compulsion even more than the practices which he held up to animadversion.

Finally, came the long enumeration of the political grievances. The enforcement of tonnage and poundage, and impositions without a Parliamentary grant, which had been the subject of contention in preceding Parliaments, was naturally placed first. Pym distinctly asserted that in attacking these he had no wish to diminish the King's profit, but merely to establish the right in Parliament. Then came the grievances of the past eleven years—the enhancement of the customs by the new book of rates, the compositions for knighthood, the monopolies in the hands of the new companies, the enforcement of ship money, the enlargement of the forests, the appeal to obsolete statutes against nuisances in order to fill the exchequer, whilst no attempt was made to abate the nuisances themselves; and last of all, those

<small>The civil grievances.</small>

military charges which were now for the first time treated as a grievance. Pym gave a history of the way in which these last charges had grown. Coat and conduct money, or the expenses of clothing newly raised levies, and of taking them to the place of rendezvous had originally been borne by the Crown. Elizabeth in her need had sometimes asked the counties to advance the money till she was able to repay it. By degrees the exception had become the rule, whilst the engagement to repay the advance had ceased to be observed. New customs were already springing up. Not only were men pressed against their will, but the counties were compelled to furnish public magazines for powder and munitions, to pay certain officers, and to provide horses and carts for the King's service without any remuneration whatever.

As Pym knew, the strength of the King's authority lay in his being able to fall back upon the Courts of Law. As yet no one was prepared to strike at the root of the evil. Pym contented himself with protesting against 'extrajudicial declarations of judges,' made without hearing counsel on the point at issue, and against the employment of the Privy Council and the Star Chamber in protecting monopolists. Many of the clergy had thrust themselves forward to undertake the defence of unconstitutional power. It was 'now the high way to preferment' to preach that there was 'Divine anthority for an absolute power in the King' to do what he would with 'the persons and goods of Englishmen.' Dr. Mainwaring had been condemned in the last Parliament for this offence, and he had now 'leapt into a Bishop's chair.'

Then, returning to the point from which he

STRENGTH OF PYM'S POSITION.

CHAP. VII.
1640.

started, Pym pointed to the source of all other grievances in 'the long intromission of Parliaments, contrary to the two statutes yet in force, whereby it is appointed there should be Parliaments once in the year.'

April 17. The intromission of Parliaments.

How then was the mischief to be remedied? Here Pym refused to follow Grimston. He refrained from requiring that any individual minister should be called to account. Let them ask the Lords to join in searching out 'the causes and remedies of these insupportable grievances,' and in petitioning the King for redress.[1]

The remedy.

Such a speech, so decisive and yet so moderate, carried the House with it. It laid down the lines within which, under altered conditions, the Long Parliament afterwards moved. It gave no offence to the hesitating and timid, as Eliot had given offence by summoning the King's officers to the bar, and by his wild attack upon Weston. It seemed as if both Houses had agreed to follow Pym. The next day the Lords called in question the appointment of Mainwaring to a Bishopric, whilst the Commons placed Grimston in the chair of a Committee of the whole House, sent for the records of the case of Eliot and his fellow-prisoners, and appointed a Select

April 18. Proceedings in both Houses.

---

[1] I cannot agree with Ranke in holding that the draft in the State Paper Office is more accurate than that given by Rushworth. It leaves out all about the privileges of Parliament. The printed speech in the King's Pamphlets, used by Mr. Forster, is not perhaps to be taken as being literally Pym's as it was spoken. There was no thorough system of shorthand in those days. But it has every characteristic of Pym, and most probably was corrected by him, or by some one present on the occasion of its delivery, and I have quoted from it as from something better than "a later amplification." The report given in *Rushw.* iii. 21, is, as Mr. Forster has pointed out, another report of this speech. But Mr. Forster was wrong in saying that Pym did not speak on Nov. 7.

Committee to draw up a narrative of the proceedings against them. Before the House rose, it had ordered that the records of the ship-money case should also be brought before it.

The feeling against the Bishops was perhaps even stronger in the Lords than in the Commons. There was more of personal jealousy there, as there had been among the nobility of Scotland. It was in the House of Lords that, for the first time since the days of Lollardism, the old constitutional doctrine, that lay peers, the clergy, and the Commons were the three estates of the realm was brought in question. The Bishops were distinctly told that the three estates were the King, the Barons, and the Commons. "The Bishops then, it was said, would make four estates or exclude the King."[1]

The words thus defiantly spoken did not touch the Bishops alone. The notion that Parliament was the soul of the body politic, had been welcomed by the Lords. The King was no longer to reign supreme, summoning his estates, as Edward I. had summoned them, to gather round his throne. He was to be no more than a first estate, called on to join with the others, but not called on to do more. To such a pass had Charles brought himself by his resolution to walk alone. The time was not far off when even so much participation would be denied him.

On the 21st the feeling of the Peers was even more strongly manifested. Bishop Hall had recently attracted attention to himself by publishing, at Laud's instigation, a work entitled 'Episcopacy by Divine Right,' in which he had argued that the primitive character of Episcopacy stamped it with Divine autho-

[1] *Harl. MSS.* 4,931, fol. 47.

rity.[1] He now rashly spoke of Saye as one who 'savoured of a Scottish Covenanter.' He was at once ordered to the bar. "If I have offended," he said, "I cry pardon." The words were received with a shout of "No ifs," and Hall was forced to beg pardon in positive terms.

<small>CHAP. VII.
1640.
April 21.</small>

In the meanwhile, the Lower House was busy with its grievances. Preparations were made to petition the King on the breach of privilege in 1629, and to draw up a statement of the case against the Crown on ship money and the impositions.

<small>The Lower House busy with grievances.</small>

On this, both Houses were summoned to Whitehall. In the King's presence, Finch explained the absolute necessity of a fleet, and declared that the King 'was not wedded to this particular way' of supporting it, and that if the Houses would find the money in some other manner, he would readily give his consent to the change. Then, after holding up the example of the fresh Parliament as worthy of imitation, Finch turned to the Lords. His Majesty, he said, did not doubt 'that, if the House of Commons should fail in their duty,' the Lords would concur with him to preserve himself and the nation.

<small>Finch explains that the King will accept any other way of supporting a navy.</small>

The appeal to the Lords was followed by an appeal to a body upon which the Commons looked with no slight jealousy. On the 22nd, at Laud's

<small>April 22. Subsidies voted in Convocation.</small>

---

[1] Professor Masson is rather hard upon Hall all through this affair (*Life of Milton*, ii. 124). It should be remembered that the book was intended not as a private venture of Hall's, but as a manifesto of the English Church. It was therefore perfectly reasonable that Laud, being invited to comment, should do as he was asked. After all, the comments were merely those which would suggest themselves to a mind rather more resolute and thorough than that of Hall, and Hall did himself no discredit by accepting them. There is nothing in them in the slightest degree discordant with Hall's own system, which may be seen briefly in a paper of propositions sent by him to Laud (Laud's *Works*, iv. 310).

request, Convocation unanimously granted six subsidies from the clergy.[1] These subsidies would, in the usual course, require the confirmation of Parliament before they could be levied, but it was natural that the Commons should not be very well pleased with the contrast between the alacrity of the clergy and their own deliberate hesitation.

The next day, accordingly, the House went into Committee on the message delivered by the Lord Keeper, and resolved to demand a conference with the Lords. "Till the liberties of the House and kingdom were cleared, they knew not whether they had anything to give or no."[2]

When the news of this resolution reached the King, he was at supper. He rose angrily from the table, and summoned the Council to meet at once. That evening he had his sternest counsellor once more by his side. In spite of gout, Strafford had come back from Ireland. He found that his opponents at Court had taken advantage of his absence to complain of him as the main author of the summoning of so untoward a Parliament.[3] He little heeded their words. He fiercely urged that Charles should go down to the House of Lords the next morning before the message of the Commons had been delivered, and should urge the Peers to declare that it was right that the satisfaction to be given to the King should precede the presentation of grievances.[4]

Strafford's advice was taken, and at the opening of the next morning's sitting, Charles appeared in the Upper House. This time he spoke with his own

---

[1] *Nalson*, i. 36.
[2] *Harl. MSS.* 3,931, fol. 47, 6.
[3] Rossetti to Barberini, $\frac{\text{Apr. 24}}{\text{May 4}}$, *R. O. Transcripts*.
[4] Montreuil to Bellievre, $\frac{\text{Apr. 30}}{\text{March 10}}$, *Bibl. Nat. Fr.* 15,995, fol. 81.

mouth. The Commons, he said, had put the cart before the horse. His necessities were too serious to admit of delay. If the Commons would trust him, he would make good all that Finch had promised in his name, and hear their grievances in the winter. In the other alternative, he conjured their lordships not 'to join with them, but to leave them to themselves.'

In an attack upon the Bishops, the Lords were ready to go at least as far as the Commons. But they were too accustomed to support the Crown to fall into opposition on such an appeal as this. In a House of eighty-six, of which eighteen were Bishops, sixty-one voted that the King's supply ought to have precedency of grievances. The minority of twenty-five contained the names of Hertford and Southampton, who afterwards took the side of the King in the Civil War, as well as those of Bedford, Essex, of Brooke and Saye.[1]

Strafford had done neither the King nor the Lords service in thus thrusting the Upper House forward in opposition to the Lower. What he did amiss sprang from his fundamental misconception of the situation. Like Wellington in 1831 and 1832, he saw the constitution threatened by a change which would shift completely, and for ever, the basis of power. Believing in his heart that this change would be prejudicial to the country, he was ready to resist it with every instrument that came ready to his hand. Like Wellington, he would appeal first to the House of Lords in the hope that the voice of the Lords would serve

CHAP. VII.
1640. April 24.

The Lords support the King.

---

[1] The minority were Rutland, Southampton, Bedford, Hertford, Essex, Lincoln, Warwick, Clare, Bolingbroke, Nottingham, Bath, Saye and Sele, Willoughby of Parham, Paget, North, Mandeville, Brooke, Robartes, Lovelace, Savile, Dunsmore, Deyncourt, Montague of Boughton, Howard of Escrick, and Wharton. Note by Windebank, *S. P. Dom.* ccccli. 39.

CHAP. VII.
1640.
April 24.

as a rallying cry for the well-affected part of the nation. But there can be little doubt that he would have refused to be controlled by any numerical majority whatever, and would have fallen back upon an armed force if necessary, to beat down a resistance which he believed to be destructive of all that was most valuable in the country.

It was a fatal mistake, fatal if only because it was out of Strafford's power to keep erect that mingled system of law and prerogative which stood for the English constitution in his eyes. If the Commons persisted in their opinion, the only choice would be between a military despotism and the supremacy of the Lower House. If Pym could not in the face of Charles call back into existence the whole of the Elizabethan constitution, he was at least standing up in defence of its nobler and better part. The claim of Englishmen to determine their own policy, and not to be the humble recipients of bounties at the good pleasure of the King and the Bishops, was the question at issue. Pym might not produce a complete and perfect work. He might sometimes be harsh in his judgments and defective in penetrating motives; but, for all that, it was the voice of Pym and not the voice of Strafford which appealed to the memories of the great England of the past, and which reached across the gulf of time to do, as Eliot would have said, the work of posterity, and to call into being the greater England of the future.

April 27
The Commons declare this a breach of privilege.

Strafford had to content himself with the approbation of the Court. Charles said openly that he trusted him more than all his Council. Even the Queen was won. She told him [1] that she esteemed him the most capable and faithful servant her

[1] Montreuil to Bellievre, $\frac{\text{Apr. 30}}{\text{May 10}}$, *Bibl. Nat. Fr.* 15,995, fol. 81.

husband had. The Commons were not likely to regard his performances in the same light. For a moment, perhaps, the thought of averting a collision gained the upper hand. Might it not be possible to vote money to the King with the proviso that it should not be used against the Scots? Pym had little difficulty in showing the absurdity of the proposal; and the House, recovering its balance, took up as a breach of privilege the suggestion about supply which had been made by the Peers, and demanded reparation of the Lords. Before the question, thus raised, came to an issue, Charles learned how little he could count even upon the Upper House on ecclesiastical matters. It needed his special intervention to hinder the Lords from passing a fresh censure on Mainwaring.[1]

On the 29th the Lords resolved to maintain their position. But the resistance of the Commons had not been without its effect. This time the King's majority had dwindled from 36 to 20. The resolution of the Upper House let loose men's tongues. For the first time in English history its composition was unfavourably canvassed. In that House, it was said, 'there were few cordial for the Commonweal;' its members spoke 'so cautelously as doth not become a free Commonwealth.' The votes of the Bishops and the Councillors were at the King's disposal. It was

---

[1] "'The House begins to proceed to censure Mainwaring; but the King sent word that they should desist, or not censure him so far as to make him incapable of his Bishopric.

"The Archbishop affirmed that, if the Parliament did deprive a man of his Bishopric, it was in the King's power to remit that censure. Some said that he pleaded his own case.

"My Lord Saye spoke nobly for the kingdom, but he had many adversaries. He answered the Lord Keeper, the Archbishop, &c., but none was found a match for him but the Deputy of Ireland." *Harl. MSS.* 4,931, fol. 48.

well known that a heavy pressure had been put on the Lords by the King. Carlisle and others acknowledged that they had voted against their consciences. Holland had been urged to speak on behalf of the King. He had given a silent vote and had retired to Kensington in disgust. Newport, on the other hand, declared that he had been so agitated as to vote against the King by mistake. "They of the Upper House," it was bitterly said, "were fully fitted for slavery."[1]

On May 1 the first division of the Session was taken in the Commons. Pym stated that Dr. Beale, the Master of St. John's at Cambridge, had asserted, in a sermon, that the King had power to make laws without the help of Parliament, and moved that he should be sent for to account for his words. An amendment that the evidence should first be referred to a Select Committee was lost by a majority of 109. It was impossible to have a plainer indication of the temper of the Commons on ecclesiastical matters.[2]

That same day news arrived from Scotland which made Charles more impatient than ever for an immediate grant of money. The first blood in a new civil war had been shed at Edinburgh. The citizens had thrown up a work opposite the Castle Gate, and Ettrick had replied by firing upon them with his cannon. Four of the townsmen had been slain and some houses injured.[3]

Upon this the King himself intervened, asking for an immediate answer to his request for money. In the Lords, Strafford distinctly announced that a

[1] *Harl. MSS.* 4,931, fol. 486. Montreuil to Bellievre, Apr. 30/May 10, *Bibl. Nat. Fr.* 15,995, fol. 32.

[2] *Commons Journals,* ii. 18. Rossingham's *Newsletter,* May 4, *S. P. Dom.* cccclii. 20.

[3] Rossingham's *Newsletter,* May 5, *Add. MSS.* 11,045, fol. 114.

refusal would be followed by a dissolution, and there can be little doubt that Vane conveyed the same intimation to the Commons. The House went at once into Committee, and broke up at the unusually late hour of six in the evening without coming to any conclusion.

Though no vote was taken, the general feeling of the House was to be ascertained without difficulty. The impression left by the debate was that the Commons would have been quite ready to leave to some future time the discussion of their ecclesiastical grievances, and of that invasion of their privileges which they held to have taken place in 1629. But they were unwilling to vote money until the question of arbitrary taxation had been fully cleared up. It must be finally settled, they thought, that the King had no right to take what they were prepared voluntarily to offer. Not only must the money required for the navy be levied by a Parliamentary grant, but the money needed for the army as well. The military charges, especially coat and conduct money, must no longer be fixed upon the subject by the sole authority of the King.[1]

The next day was a Sunday. At the Council Board Strafford recommended the King not to allow ship money to stand in the way of a reconciliation with the Commons. Charles consented that the ship money judgment should be carried before the House of Lords upon a writ of error, where it would undoubtedly be reversed. No better way of making the concession could possibly be devised. On another point Strafford found him less yielding. When Vane argued that no less than twelve subsidies, or about 840,000*l.*, should be fixed as the price of

[1] Rossingham's *Newsletter*, May 5, *Add. MSS.* 11,045, fol. 114.

CHAP VII.
1640.
May 3.

so great a concession, Charles seemed inclined to agree with him. Strafford, in the very spirit of Bacon, urged that there should be no haggling in the matter. He told the King, 'that the said offer to the Commons' House ought not to be conditional,' but that he should 'put it upon their affections for supply.' Charles answered, hesitatingly, that he feared less would not serve his occasion. Before Strafford's repeated warnings, however, he gave way at last and consented to be satisfied with eight.[1]

Vane gains over the King.

Strafford's urgency was entirely thrown away. It was impossible to rely upon Charles for any steady and consistent policy. It is exceedingly probable—though no evidence of the fact exists—that after the Council was dismissed, Vane drew away the King from the conciliatory attitude recommended by Strafford. At all events, he was able to appear in his place in Parliament the next morning to deliver a message, distinctly asking for twelve subsidies as the price of the abandonment of ship money.

May 4.
Twelve subsidies demanded.

The debate in Committee.

The House was again in Committee. Hampden asked that the question might be put whether the King's request, 'as it was contained in the message,' should be granted. Edward Hyde—then, as ever, anxious to step forward as the mediator between extreme opinions—asked that the question should be simply whether supply should be given at all.[2] He

[1] The only distinct information we have is from Strafford's interrogatories (Whitaker's *Life of Radcliffe*, 233). It is evident that they do not all relate to the same discussion. The last five interrogatories are plainly connected with the later Council, at which a dissolution was resolved on.

[2] So far, I suppose, we may trust Clarendon (ii. 72). His account of this Parliament, however, is so inaccurate that I dare not use his narrative of the debate. His memory only served him to show the figure of Vane as frustrating an agreement which, but for Vane's delinquencies, would have been brought about by himself.

might reasonably expect that many members who would vote in the negative on Hampden's motion, would vote in the affirmative on his.

<small>CHAP. VII.
1640.
May 4.</small>

The debate which followed only served to bring out the difficulties of an agreement in a stronger light than Strafford had supposed to be possible. The dread of an early dissolution, indeed, had great effect. As far as the amount of the subsidies was concerned, those who most strongly objected to even a tacit acknowledgment of the legality of ship money, were prepared to vote at least six subsidies; and Strafford, at all events, was ready to advise the King to accept the offer. Glanville, the Speaker of the House, a lawyer of no mean repute, inveighed bitterly against taxation by prerogative. The judgment of the Exchequer Chamber, he said, 'was a senseless judgment.' All the arguments contained in it 'might easily have been answered.' If it were allowed to stand upon record, 'after ages would see the folly of their times.' It was 'against law, if he understood what law was.'[1] Yet even Glanville recommended that supply should be given. An understanding would doubtless have been come to on the basis laid down by Strafford, if there had been no other question but that of ship money before the Committee. As the debate went on, however, greater prominence was given to the demand for the abolition of the military charges which had been mooted on the preceding Saturday. One of the members for Yorkshire, Sir William Savile, said that his constituents would not care how many subsidies were voted if only they were relieved of ship money. He was at once contradicted by Bellasys, the other member for the same

<small>Demand for the abolition of the military charges.</small>

---

[1] The last sentence is from Clarendon. The rest from *Harl. MSS.* 4,931, fol. 49.

CHAP. VII.
1640.
May 4.

county, who, some years before, had suffered imprisonment for his insolence to Strafford. The men of Yorkshire, he now said, 'required to be eased of coat and conduct money, and other such military charges.' Unless their representatives brought them that relief they dared not return home. Another Yorkshire man, Sir John Hotham, put the case as strongly as possible. Ship money, he said, had cost the country but 12,000*l.* The military charges cost it 40,000*l.* Others again attacked the whole system of impressment which Selden had attacked in 1628.[1]

Vane insists on the acceptance of the King's terms.

Such speeches, received with evident approbation by the House, drew forth a fresh declaration from Vane. He rose to state that the King would accept nothing less than the twelve subsidies which he had demanded in his message. Upon this the Committee broke up without coming to a resolution, postponing further consideration of the matter to the following day.

It is incredible that Vane should thus have acted without express authority from Charles.[2] The ques-

---

[1] Rossingham to Conway, May 12, *S. P. Dom.* ccccliii. 24.

[2] ...irely omitting the matter of the military charges Clarendon ...hole affair to a personal question. My account is founded ...letely independent statements. There are amongst the State papers ... notes (*S. P. Dom.* cccl. 94) which I believe to have been drawn up by Rossingham for circulation amongst his correspondents. In these we are told that 'the sense of the House was that not only ship money should be abolished, but also all military taxes or other taxes for the future, by what name or title soever it might be called, should be provided against before that twelve subsidies were granted, so that no positive answer was this day given to his Majesty.' Northumberland, in a letter to Conway, of May 5 (*Ibid.* ccclii. 33) is equally explicit. "The King," he wrote, "did yesterday offer the House of Commons to relinquish absolutely the shipping money if they would at this time supply him with twelve subsidies. This gave them not satisfaction. They desired to be also eased of the military charge, as they termed it, which was from the pressing, coating, and conducting of soldiers. Innovations in religion they likewise insisted much upon. Other grievances they

tion of the military charges affected the King far more deeply than even the question of ship money. Charles knew well that whether ship money were levied by the prerogative or not, England could no longer endure to be without a navy. At that very moment Barbary pirates were cruising off the mouth of the Channel, scuttling English ships and dragging English sailors into a miserable captivity. But if the Commons could not refuse to supply the Government with a navy, they might very well refuse to supply it with an army. If Charles assented to their present demand, the machinery by which he had been in the habit of collecting a military force, would be hopelessly disarranged. Nor was this all. Though it does not seem that any word of direct sympathy with the Scots was spoken in that day's Committee, it must have been evident to the Privy Councillors present that the war itself found but little support amongst the members of the House. Already, indeed, the leaders of the popular party had opened communications with some of the Scottish Commissioners, asking them to lay the grievances of their countrymen before the Commons. To this the Commissioners had replied that, as their lives were now at the King's mercy, they could not venture to take such a step, but that if the House of Commons, after reading their printed Declaration, chose to send for them and to inquire into the truth of its allegations, they would be ready to reply to any questions which might be asked. The English leaders, in fact, had accepted this proposal, and had fixed the 7th as the day

CHAP. VII.

1640.
May 4.
Bearing of this demand.

Proposed petition against the war.

trenched upon, but these were the main ones they complained of; and had they been well advised I am verily persuaded they might in time have gained their desires, but they in a tumultuous and confused way went on with their businesses, which gave so great offence unto his Majesty, that this morning he hath dissolved the Parliament."

on which the Scots' Declaration should be discussed. The debate of the 4th, however, changed their plans. After Vane's threatening language it was impossible to doubt that a dissolution was imminent. That evening, therefore, it was resolved that Pym should bring forward the subject as soon as the House met on the following morning. A petition, it would seem, was to be drawn up to beg the King to come to terms with the Scots, and it is probable that the Lords were to be asked to concur in this petition.[1]

The Council summoned.

Some one who could not be trusted was present at this meeting. That very evening the King received intelligence of Pym's plan of operations. He at once summoned the Privy Council to meet at the unusual hour of six on the following morning. He sent for the Speaker and forbade him to take his place, lest the dreaded petition should be voted before he had time to intervene.[2]

May 5. The Council votes for a dissolution.

When the Council met the next morning the King announced his intention of proceeding to a dissolu-

[1] Heylyn's statement (*Cyprianus Angl.* 396) that the Commons 'came to a resolution of yielding somewhat towards his Majesty's supply, but in the grant thereof blasted his Majesty's expedition against the Scots,' only puts the intention into positive terms. "Our Parliament," writes a Scotchman in London, "hath yet settled nothing. They are this day about to petition his Majesty to hearken to a reconciliation with you, his subjects in Scotland." Johnstoun to Smith, May 5, *S. P. Dom.* cccclii. 46. A few days later we hear that the members of the dissolved Parliament spoke freely of their disinclination to grant money for a Scottish war, and said that the cause of the Scots was in reality their own. Salvetti's *Newsletter*, May $\frac{8}{15}$. The greater part of what I have stated is drawn from an anonymous deposition and a paper of interrogatories founded on it (*S. P. Dom.* cccclii. 114, 115). We there learn that 'it was otherwise resolved on Monday night that the next morning the book should have been produced, as he conceived, by Mr. Pym, who should have spoken then also in that business.' Mr. Hamilton is to be congratulated on this important discovery, which first appeared in his Calendar for 1640.

[2] "Lest that they should urge him to prefer any petition to the Upper House." *Harl. MSS.* 4,931, fol. 49.

tion. Strafford, who arrived late, begged that the question might first be seriously discussed, and that the opinions of the Councillors, who were also members of the Lower House, might first be heard. Vane declared that there was no hope that the Commons 'would give one penny.' On this the votes were taken. Northumberland and Holland were alone in wishing to avert a dissolution.[1] Supported by the rest of the Council the King hurried to the House of Lords and dissolved Parliament.

The Short Parliament, for by that name this assembly is known in history, had sat for three weeks. As far as actual results were concerned it accomplished nothing at all. For all that, its work was as memorable as that of any Parliament in our history. It made England conscious of the universality of its displeasure. Falkland, we are told, went back from this Parliament full of dissatisfaction with the Court,[2] and doubtless he did not stand alone. The chorus of complaint sounded louder when it was echoed from Cornwall to Northumberland than when it seemed to be no more than a local outcry. Nor was this Parliament more memorable for the complaints which it uttered than for the remedies which it proposed. The work which it assigned to itself was of no less import than that to which the Long Parliament subsequently addressed itself. Its moderation consisted rather in the temper in which it approached its labours, than in the demands which it made. What it proposed was nothing short of a complete change in the relations between the King and the nation. It announced through the mouth of Pym that Parliament was the soul of the Commonwealth, and there

---

[1] Laud's *Works*, iii. 284. Whitaker's *Life of Radcliffe*, 233.
[2] *Clarendon*, vii. 222.

CHAP. VII.

1640.
May 5.
A dissolution unavoidable.

were some amongst its members who sought for that soul in the Lower House alone.

It was impossible that such a body should long have escaped a dissolution. From the very first the resolution had been taken at Court to break up the Parliament unless it would give its support to the war. When it laid hands upon fleet and army, and seemed likely to give its voice for peace, the moment foreseen in Charles's Council had arrived. It needed all Hyde's bland conviction that contradictory forces were to be reconciled by his own lawyer-like dexterity to throw the whole blame of the dissolution upon Vane. Oliver St. John understood better what the facts of the case really were, when he said 'that all was well, and that it must be worse before it could be better; and that this Parliament would never have done what was necessary to be done.' St. John knew full well what he wanted. Hyde never knew what he wanted beyond some dream of his own, in which Charles and Laud were to come to a happy compromise with all moderate men, and tyranny and sedition were to be renounced as equally impracticable.

Strafford's view of the situation.

Strafford, at least, had no notion of coming to a compromise with a Parliament which was bent on peace with Scotland, and which was determined to place the whole military force of the Crown at its own disposal. The knowledge of Pym's intercourse with the Scots, which he doubtless acquired in the course of the day, changed his longing for conciliation to bitter hostility. The King, he thought, might leave his subjects to provide support for the navy, but he could not safely depend on them for the very existence of an army. If Charles gave way now, a modification of the whole constitution of England would be the result. The English Parliament would claim all the rights which the Scottish Parliament had asserted. The country, he may well have thought, would be handed over to the persuasive rhetoric of factious adventurers. The functions of government would be at an end. He saw all the weak points of the Parliamentary system without seeing any of its strong ones. He had no belief in the possibility that a better organisation might arise out of the chaotic public opinion of his day. The secret of the future, the growth of cabinet government, was a veiled mystery to him as it was to the rest of his generation.

In conversation with his friends he made no secret of his conviction that the summoning of Parliament had been an experiment to which he indeed had heartily desired success, but that it had been nothing more than an experiment. The King's cause, he said to Conway, 'was very just and lawful, and if the Parliament would not supply him, then he was justified before God and man if he sought means to help himself, though it were against their wills.[1] Much the same language had been used by him to Ussher whilst he was still in Ireland. The crisis which he then contemplated had now arrived. It was absolutely necessary for the common safety that the King should ward off the approaching danger from Scotland in spite of the refusal of the House of Commons to support him.[2]

As soon as the King returned to Whitehall, a meeting was held of that Committee of eight which had been appointed in the preceding winter to take special cognisance of Scottish affairs. Charles asked the advice of this select body on the course which it

[1] *Rushw. Straf. Trial*, 536. [2] *Ibid.* 535.

1640.
May 5.
Vane argues for a war of defence.

now behoved him to take. Vane argued, not without support, that to defend England against invasion was all that was now possible.[1] Strafford was too clear-sighted not to perceive at once the hopelessness of such a course. Only a fierce blow, sharp and decisive, would save the King now. England would never bear the long contribution of enforced supplies to an inactive army on the Borders. Let the City, he said, be required to lend 100,000*l*. to the King. Let ship money be vigorously collected. This would suffice for a short campaign, and it was clearly his opinion that a few months of invasion would bring Scotland to its knees. "Do you invade them," was his closing admonition.[2]

Strafford supports an aggressive war.

[1] This rests on Vane's own evidence. *Rushw. Straf. Trial*, 546.

[2] I have no hesitation in accepting the form of Vane's notes printed in the *Hist. MSS. Commissioners' Report*, iii. 3, against that given by Whitelocke. All external evidence is in favour of a copy found in the House of Lords, and the internal evidence goes in the same direction. The heading which appears in Whitelocke's copy might easily have been added; but it would be difficult to account for the presence of Northumberland's speech, or the characteristic saying of Strafford's about Saul and David in the House of Lords' copy while they are absent from Whitelocke's, unless the former were taken as genuine. Clarendon's account agrees with neither, and was doubtless given merely from memory, like his account of the debates in the Short Parliament. The existence of a copy amongst the State Papers corresponding with that in the House of Lords is in itself almost decisive, as it is hardly to be imagined that both the King and the peers would content themselves with anything but a real copy.

The notion that Vane's paper was stolen, and therefore could not have found its way into the House of Lords, will not bear the test of investigation. According to Lord Bute's MS., Whitelocke states that 'this and all the rest of the papers concerning the charge against the Earl were entrusted to the care and custody of Whitelocke, the chairman of the Close Committee, and being for a time missing at the Committee, and because the Earl answered so fully, some were jealous of Whitelocke that he had let see it, the better to make his defence and to oblige the Earl.' He then goes on to show, not very conclusively, that Digby and not himself was the culprit. As, however, the reply of Strafford referred to was on April 5, and the paper was produced in the Commons on the 10th, it is plain that it cannot have been actually lost at the time referred

Northumberland took up the word. In the morning he had voted against the dissolution, and he now gave his reasons for wishing the King to hold his hand. He belonged to a class of politicians whom enthusiastic partisans always despise at their peril. He was not in the habit of thinking deeply on any subject, and had taken the command of the army, as he had before taken the command of the fleet, without any strong persuasion of the righteousness of the cause for which he was about to draw his sword. Personally he admired Strafford, and he liked his own position as a great nobleman at Court. He felt no attraction towards the aggressive Puritanism of the Commons; but he had an instinctive feeling that to enter on a war without the support of the Commons, was a rash and headlong proceeding, which would probably end in disaster. How, he asked, could they 'make an offensive war' if they had no better means at their disposal than those which Strafford had just recited. They were in a difficulty whether 'to do nothing or to let them alone, or go on with a vigorous war.'

CHAP. VII.
1640. May 5. Northumberland's objection.

Strafford's fierce, resolute spirit waved the objection haughtily away. "Go on vigorously," he cried,

Strafford's reply.

to, and it is not unlikely that Whitelocke's account of the matter being written down long after the event was not altogether correct. It certainly differs considerably from that given in D'Ewes's *Diary*. No one need be surprised that the paper in the House of Lords is in a clerk's hand, as both the original paper and the younger Vane's copy had been previously destroyed. I fancy that Whitelocke's copy was merely one set down from memory by some one who had only heard it read.

It is of course quite a different question whether the notes, granting them to be Vane's, were really trustworthy. Vane had reason to bear hard upon Strafford; but there is something very characteristic in each utterance, and I am ready to accept the paper as substantially correct, though it is impossible to say more than this. Verbally accurate they do not even profess to be. The question of the Irish army will be discussed subsequently.

and we can fancy how his eyes flashed as he spoke, "or let them alone." The broken, disjointed notes are all that remain to us. "No defensive war; loss of honour and reputation. The quiet of England will hold out long. You will languish as betwixt Saul and David. Go on with a vigorous war, as you first designed, loose and absolved from all rules of government; being reduced to extreme necessity, everything is to be done that power might admit, and that you are to do. They refusing, you are acquitted towards God and man. You have an army in Ireland you may employ here to reduce this kingdom. Confident as anything under heaven, Scotland shall not hold out five months. One summer well employed will do it. Venture all I had, I would carry it or lose it. Whether a defensive war as impossible as an offensive, or whether to let them alone."

Opinions of Laud and Cottington.

Strafford's vehement words were echoed by Laud and Cottington. "Tried all ways," said the Archbishop, "and refused all ways. By the law of God and man you should have subsistence, and ought to have it, and lawful to take it." Cottington followed with an argument that, as the Scots were certain to enter into leagues with foreign Powers, an attack upon them was in reality 'a defence of this kingdom.' "The Lower House," he added, "are weary both of King and Church.[1] All ways shall be just to raise money for this unavoidable necessity, therefore to be used, being lawful." Strafford again struck in. Commissions of array were to be put in execution. Those to whom they were issued would be bound to bring the men to the Borders at the charge of the

[1] Ranke (*Eng. Transl.* ii. 196) speaks of this as a mere party statement. It is, however, quite true that the Commons wanted to get rid of kingship, as Charles and Cottington understood kingship.

counties. "If any of the Lords," he added, "can show me a better way, let them do it." To this some one feebly answered that the town was 'full of nobility, who' would 'talk of it.' "I will make them smart for it," was Strafford's contemptuous reply.

Eleven months afterwards, when the notes which were taken by Vane of these speeches were laid before the Long Parliament, opinion fixed upon the words relating to the employment of the Irish army in England as the most offensive to English feeling. Strafford then asserted that, as far as his memory served, he had never said anything of the kind; and Northumberland, Hamilton, Juxon, and Cottington, the only witnesses whom it was then possible to produce, gave similar evidence. No such project, they added, had ever been in contemplation.

On the other hand, there is strong reason to believe that the charge did not arise from Vane's hostile imagination, or from more deliberate falsification. The suspicion was certainly abroad only two days after the meeting of the Committee. "The King of England," wrote Montreuil, who had been left by Bellievre to act as French Agent till the appointment of an Ambassador, "thinks of making use of the 10,000 Irishmen as well to bring to terms his English subjects as for the Scottish war."[1] There is

[1] Montreuil to Bellievre, May $\frac{7}{17}$, *Bibl. Nat.* Fr. 15,995, fol. 84. In the following August Strafford was authorised to command an 'army or armies both to resist and withstand all invasions, tumults, seditions, conspiracies, or attempts that may happen in our Kingdoms of England and Ireland, or our Dominion of Wales, to be made against our kingdom, state, safety, crown, or dignity, and also to be led into our kingdom of Scotland.' Strafford's patent, Aug. 3, *Carte MSS.* i. fol. 247. These words, however, as Strafford afterwards stated, were merely copied from Northumberland's patent, which is printed in *Rymer* xx. 364. The only difference between the parallel passages is the insertion of Ireland as a sphere of action, which would not be fitting in Northumberland's case,

CHAP. VII.
1640.
May 5.

at least a strong probability that this language was inspired by some knowledge of Strafford's speech in the Committee. It is at least certain that in the formal document in which the command of the Irish army was subsequently conferred upon Strafford, the contingency of its employment against rebellion in England was specially provided for.

and the verbal substitution of the word 'kingdom' for 'person.' Probably this was a set form. I have sought in vain for Arundel's patent given in 1639. It seems never to have been enrolled. Even the Privy Seal is not to be found at the Record Office. Strafford's argument at his trial that no Irish army was in existence is worthless. There was always a small army, and the new one was to have been ready by May 18.

In Vane's notes the sentence about the quiet of England is followed by: "They refusing," i.e. the English, "you are acquitted before God and man;" and it seems to me likely enough that this outburst about the Irish army may have sprung to Strafford's lips at the bare thought of English refusal, though it was not quite in accord with what he had said before. The acquittal before God and man referred to acquittal for conduct towards the English, and the words about the Irish army would naturally also apply to the English. But I wish to be clearly understood as not giving any positive opinion on the matter. Vane's jottings will not bear dogmatism on either side. In fairness to those who accept an interpretation different from my own, I should add an extract from a letter written by Windebank to the King, after his flight in 1641. "I have received a signification of your Majesty's pleasure to declare and test fy (upon my allegiance to your Majesty) whether in a debate in Council at a Committee about a defensive and offensive war with the Scots, I do remember that the Lord Lieutenant of Ireland did say to your Majesty that, having tried the affections of your people, you were absolved from all rules of government, and were to do everything that power would admit, since your subjects had denied to supply you, and that in so doing you should be acquitted both of God and man, and that your Majesty had an army in Ireland, which you might employ to reduce this kingdom to obedience; to which, upon my allegiance to your Majesty, I do most humbly make this direct, clear, and true answer (which your Majesty may well remember) of that which passed in debate from time to time in Council at the Committee about a defensive and offensive war with the Scots, I do not remember that my Lord Lieutenant of Ireland did say to your Majesty the words above mentioned, or any other to that purpose, being confident that in a business so remarkable, and of so great moment, I could not but have remembered them if they had been spoken. And, further, I do not remember that ever I so much as heard the least speech that the army in Ireland was to

Yet, in spite of this, it may be reasonably doubted whether any deliberate purpose of preparing for an Irish occupation of England was ever entertained. Not only does no trace remain of any counsels, save those already mentioned, in which such a design formed a part, but everything that we learn of Strafford and Charles induces us to believe that neither of them had any real expectation that such a course would be necessary. To the end Strafford underrated the forces opposed to him. He believed that, apart from the ambition of the House of Commons,

<small>CHAP. VII.
1640.
May 5.
Strafford probably had formed no determinate plan.</small>

<small>be employed to reduce the kingdom of England to obedience; and either I misunderstood the sense of the Committee from time to time, or else the consultations of the Committee concerning the disposing and employing of the Irish army did ever bend wholly another way." Windebank to the King, May 16, 1641, *S. P. Dom.*

This letter, like the evidence of the other members of the Committee given at the trial, asserts far more than the mere transference of the proposed employment of the Irish army from England to Scotland. It asserts that the writer had no recollection of the whole passage which preceded the words about Ireland. Is his inability to recollect all this to make us give up Vane's notes altogether? The passage quoted from Montreuil shows at least that the proposal to attack Ireland was talked of at this time. But, leaving this out of the question, it is impossible not to lay weight on the fact that Charles saw the notes before the meeting of the Long Parliament. The elder Vane stated in the House of Commons, April 12, 1641, according to D'Ewes, that Charles had sent for these notes and had ordered them to be burnt. According to the *Verney Notes* (37) Vane said that he had himself 'moved the King to burn the papers, and the King consented to it.' Whichever of these two accounts is right, it is clear that Vane spoke of the King's knowledge of the notes as something beyond question. And it is also certain that, as far as we know, Charles never denied the statement. This would imply that they really were taken at the time, for the King's use. Private notes, forged, to be subsequently flung at Strafford, would not come to the knowledge of the King. Is it not incredible that the whole of the passage from the assertion that the King was loose and absolved from all rules of Government down to the sentence about Ireland, should have been put in without ground, when Vane must have known that the King might call for the notes at any moment? Verbal inaccuracies there must have been, and perhaps misapprehension of the drift of a sentence, but surely not the pure invention of whole sentences. Yet that is what the argument from the want of memory of the members of the Committee really comes to.</small>

the real England was on his side, and would rally round him as soon as it learnt how grossly deluded it had been. With these feelings he was not likely to plan an Irish invasion of England. But it does not follow that he did not contemplate it as a distant possibility. Pushed hard in the discussion in the Committee to justify his confidence, he might fall back upon the forces in Ireland as a convincing proof that alarm was needless, just as he would have the clause relating to England inserted in his patent in order to provide for all eventualities, without expecting those eventualities to occur.

Even Vane's paper of notes conveys the impression that the thought of employing this Irish army for the repression of resistance in England did not enter largely into Strafford's plans. His words point to no knot worthy of such a solution. He had been arguing that the Scots would be overpowered in a single campaign, and that the quiet of England would hold out long. It was only as the refusal of the Commons presented itself to his thoughts that he flashed out into threats of this last resource. Nor is it likely that he at all understood what his countrymen would think of such a threat. To him the thought of an Irish army conveyed no impression which was not satisfactory. The small force which was already in existence was distinguished for its discipline and good behaviour. He had every reason to believe that the larger force which he now contemplated would be distinguished by the same qualities. He did not realise the feeling of horror which the very notion of an Irish army conveyed to the mass of Englishmen. Pride of race and pride of religion combined in regarding the mere suggestion of the introduction of such a force as a deadly insult. The English people resented it as the Americans resented the employment of Indians against them in 1776, and as the Germans resented the employment of Turcos against them in 1870. To bring over Irishmen to crush their liberties was in their eyes to let loose a horde of pitiless Popish savages upon the sober Protestant, God-fearing population of England. To have planned such an atrocity was sufficient to exclude the contriver from the courtesies of civilised existence.

That the suggestion of bringing over the Irish army, when once it came to be known, added bitter intensity to the feeling of hatred with which Strafford was now beginning to be regarded, is beyond dispute. That hatred dates from the day of the dissolution of the Short Parliament. From thenceforth the name of Strafford, of black Tom Tyrant, as he was sometimes called, was coupled with that of Laud in the popular imagination, as the bulwark of arbitrary and despotic government.

The popular imagination was in the main right. No doubt Strafford would have rejected the charge. It was the Commons, he thought, who had failed to do their duty. The case was one in which, as he afterwards expressed it, the King might 'use as the common parent of the country what power God Almighty hath given him for preserving himself and his people, for whom he is accountable to Almighty God.' This power, he then added, could not 'be taken from him by others; neither, under favour, is he able to take it from himself.'[1] Somewhere or another in every Constitution a power must be lodged of providing for extreme necessities, irrespective of the bonds of positive law, and this power had, at least for some generations, been lodged in the Crown.

[1] *Rushw. Straf. Trial*, 559.

What Strafford failed to see was that the King had brought that power into contempt by constantly using it to provide for necessities which were not extreme. Men were slow to believe that a special emergency existed when that emergency had been appealed to to justify an unparliamentary government of eleven years. Strafford was undoubtedly in earnest in desiring to put an end to this evil system. If he had no wish to anticipate the constitution of the eighteenth century, he at least wished to bring back the Constitution of the sixteenth. It was precisely this which he was powerless to do. If his master had returned victorious from the Northern war at the head of a devoted army, no result but the establishment of a military despotism would have been possible for him. Against this the great national party, with Pym at its head, now numbering the vast majority of educated Englishmen, raised its voice. They were no reformers, no followers of new ideas, by which the lives of men might be made brighter and happier than of old. They wished to worship as their fathers had worshipped, to believe as their fathers had believed, and to live as their fathers had lived. They did not wish to be harassed by constant changes, of which they did not understand the import, and of which they mistrusted the tendency. To them Parliaments were not an instrument of improvement, but an instrument to avert unpopular alterations. Parliamentary supremacy would give full expression to the inertia which appeared to Strafford to be the most dangerous quality of human society. To Strafford, the active-minded reformer, impatient of restraint, the very thought of Parliamentary supremacy was abominable. He did not, could not, rise up into the knowledge that acceptance of the limitations imposed by the national temper was the only condition under which permanent reforms could ever be accomplished. He did not even acknowledge to himself that the national temper was truly reflected in the Parliament which had been so recently dissolved.

CHAPTER VIII.

PASSIVE RESISTANCE.

<small>CHAP. VIII.
1640.
May 5
Strafford and Pym.</small>

On May 5 two systems of government entered upon the final struggle for supremacy in England. Each of these systems had its own representative leader. The voice of Pym was silenced for a time. It was for Strafford to do what in him lay to encourage his fainting allies, to stand forward as the saviour of monarchical government in its hour of trial.

<small>The King's Declaration.</small>

At once a Declaration was issued in the King's name for general circulation. Subjects were reminded that of old time it had been held to be the duty of Parliament to support their kings in time of war, not to abuse their power of control over supplies to extort the surrender of the rightful prerogatives of Sovereigns.[1] Orders were also issued to the Lords Lieutenants to postpone the departure of the new levies till June 10, so as to gain a little time for financial preparation.[2] The studies of Lords Saye and Brooke, of Pym, Hampden, and Earle, were searched, doubtless in the belief that evidence would be secured of criminal intelligence with the Scots. No compromising matter was discovered, and no further proceeding was taken. Three other members did not escape so easily. Crew, the Chairman of the Committee on Religion, was sent to the Tower for refusing to deliver up the petitions entrusted to his charge. Sir John Hotham and Henry

<small>Measures of the Government.</small>

<small>May 8
Members of Parliament in prison.</small>

---

[1] *Rushw.* iii. 1,160. [2] *Ibid.* iii. 1,170.

Bellasys were questioned about their speeches on the military charges. Both declared that they neither 'could nor would remember' words which they had spoken in Parliament. Both were committed to prison on the ground that they had given undutiful answers to the Council; and in this way, at least, the appearance of an attack on the Privileges of Parliament was avoided.

The Council then turned its attention to the financial difficulties of the Crown. Sheriffs, who had been remiss in the collection of ship money, were subjected to stern questioning by the Attorney-General, and orders were sent to the Deputy-Lieutenants to see that coat and conduct money was duly paid.[1]

On the 7th the Lord Mayor and Aldermen were summoned before the Council. The King told them that he expected from them a loan of 200,000*l*. If they did not provide the money, 'he would have 300,000*l*. of the City.' They were to return on the 10th with a list of such persons in their several wards as they believed to be capable of bearing their part of the loan, rated according to their means. On the appointed day they came without the list. Strafford lost his temper. "Sir," he said to the King, "you will never do good to these citizens of London till you have made examples of some of the Aldermen. Unless you hang up some of them, you will do no good with them."[2] The King ordered the Lord Mayor Garway to resign his sword and collar of office; and though, at the intercession of the bystanders, he relented and restored them, he committed to prison four of the Aldermen—Soames, Rain-

---

[1] *Rushw.* iii. 1,167. Rossingham's *Newsletter*, May 12, *S. P. Dom.* cccliii. 24. Rossetti to Barberini, May $\frac{8}{18}$, *R. O. Transcripts.*

[2] *Rushw. Straf. Trial*, 586.

CHAP. VIII.
1640.
May 10.
Imprisonment of four Aldermen.

ton, Geere, and Adkins—who had been specially firm in their refusal. One of them, Alderman Soames, gave particular offence. "I was held an honest man whilst I was a commoner," he told the King to his face, "and I would continue to be so now I am an Alderman." The other Aldermen professed their readiness to give in the names of the richer citizens, though they objected to rate them according to their means.[1]

Strafford and the Spanish alliance.

From the London citizens Strafford turned to the Spanish Court. He had always supported an alliance with Spain, and the recent occurrence in the Downs had strengthened him in his desire to break the maritime superiority of the Dutch. For the present, however, the conflict for empire must be waged in Scotland, and it was to gain the money rather than the fleets of Spain that his efforts were directed. There were now no less than three Spanish ambassadors in England. The Marquis of Velada and the Marquis Virgilio Malvezzi[2] had come to the assistance of Cardenas, who, though he had been re-admitted to his right of audience, was in no good odour at the English Court. So great a diplomatic display was regarded by Charles as a sign that the new ambassadors were instructed to accept the proposals of marriage, of which he had communicated hints to Olivares a few months before.[3] On this point, however, the ambassadors remained obstinately silent. They declared that the object of their mission was solely to treat of a league against the Dutch. Before

Spanish ambassadors in England.

---

[1] Salvetti's *Newsletter*, May $\frac{8}{18}$. *Council Register*, May 10. Rossingham's *Newsletter*, May 12, *S. P. Dom.* ccccliii. 24. Rossetti to Barberini, May $\frac{15}{25}$, *R. O. Transcripts.*

[2] This visit explains Milton's reference to him as 'their Malvezzi, that can cut Tacitus into slivers and steaks.' *Ref. of Church Gov.* Malvezzi must have been a well-known personage in London.

[3] P. 298.

the dissolution, Commissioners, of whom Strafford was the leading spirit, had been appointed to negotiate with them on this subject. At once it appeared that there was a radical difference of opinion between the two parties. The Spaniards insisted that, by accepting the secret treaty of 1630, the English Government should bind itself to an open rupture with the States General with a view to the ultimate partition of the territory of the Republic. The English diplomatists preferred to start from Necolalde's articles of 1634, which would not involve an avowed breach with the Dutch.

Under ordinary circumstances this radical difference of opinion would probably have brought the negotiation to an end. But on May 10, the day of the imprisonment of the Aldermen, Strafford discovered how very doubtful was the prospect of obtaining any considerable sum of money from the City. The next morning, he visited the Ambassadors in person. His master, he told them, was ready, as soon as it was in his power, to join them in that league against the Dutch, which was the object of their wishes. But it was not in his power to do so as long as Scotland was unconquered. To conquer Scotland a large sum of money was needed. Why should not the King of Spain lend 300,000*l.* for that purpose? As soon as Scotland was subdued war should be declared against the Dutch. Even for the present the English fleet could be used in conveying supplies to Flanders, and in protecting Dunkirk against a siege. Permission, too, would be given for the levy of 3,000 Irishmen for the Spanish service. The King of Spain should have ample security for the repayment of the loan, and, even if that failed, Philip might easily recompense himself by the seizure of the property of English merchants whose vessels happened at the time to be in Spanish harbours.¹

The end of his tragic struggle against the world must have been drawing very near before even Strafford could have ventured on so audacious a proposal as this. The days which followed must have been for him the saddest in his life, far sadder than those in which, after the lapse of a year, he stood proudly conscious of the rectitude of his cause on the scaffold on Tower Hill. In vain was the iron will and the ready wit given him if he could not breathe his own hardihood into the breast of the man without whom he was as powerless as an infant. In the very crisis of the struggle Charles hesitated and drew back. Strafford stood alone as the champion of the cause of monarchy.

It was not entirely without reason that Charles was terrified. On the 6th papers were posted up calling on the apprentices to join in hunting 'William the Fox' for breaking the Parliament.² Three days later a placard was placed up in the Exchange inviting all who were faithful to the City, and lovers of liberty and the Commonwealth, to assemble in St. George's Fields in Southwark, on the early morning of the 11th. Warned in time, the Council ordered that St. George's Fields should be occupied on the 11th by the Southwark Trained Bands.³ The apprentices were not so easily baffled. They waited quietly till the Trained Bands had retired in the evening. A little before midnight a mob of some five hundred persons, for the most part journeymen and appren-

---

¹ Windebank to Hopton, May 11, *Clar. St. P.* ii. 83. Velada to the Cardinal Infant, Apr. $\frac{12}{22}$, May $\frac{2}{12}$, $\frac{8}{18}$. Velada to Philip IV, May $\frac{11}{21}$, $\frac{13}{23}$, $\frac{15}{25}$, $\frac{16}{26}$, *Brussels MSS.* Secr. d'Etat Esp. cclxxxiv. fol. 153, 201, 214, 248, 258, 268, 276.

² Laud's *Works*, iii. 284.

³ *Rushw.* iii. 1173.

tices, answered to the summons. In this class the general dislike of Laud was sharpened by its own special grievances against the new monopolies.[1] With a drum beating in front, the rabble took its way to Lambeth. Laud, warned in time, had placed his house in a state of defence, and had crossed the river to Whitehall for safety.[2] The rioters, finding that their prey had escaped them, retired with threats of returning to burn down the house. Next morning the Council gave directions that watch should be kept by night as well as by day, and that the Trained Bands of Middlesex and Surrey should be called in to help in preserving order. Several persons were arrested on suspicion. Insulting placards continued to be posted in the streets, threatening an attack on the apartments of the Queen's mother at St. James's, and calling on the mob to pull down her chapel and do what mischief they could to her priests. Others urged that Laud should be dragged out of Whitehall and murdered. One went so far as to announce that the King's palace was to let. Nor were these tumults confined to the mob alone. At Aylesbury some soldiers mutinied against their officers, and twenty-two houses were burnt down before the disturbance was quelled. In Kent the yeomen and farmers who had been pressed declared that they were not bound to go beyond the limits of their county, and left the ranks in a body. On the night of the 14th the Court was startled by a fresh outrage. The prisons in which the rioters were confined were broken open by a mob, and the prisoners were set at liberty. It was plain that something must be done if the country was not to lapse into an-

[1] Joachimi to the States General, May 21/11, *Add. MSS.* 17,677 Q. fol. 190.   [2] Laud's *Works*, iii. 284.

archy. Orders were given to the Deputy-Lieutenants and the Justices of the Peace of several counties who happened to be in London, to return home to preserve order. Doubts, however, were freely expressed whether the guardians of the peace could be depended on. It was said that they had been sent from London to keep them from the temptation of imitating the Covenanting Tables. The support of the lower ranks was still more doubtful. The recent imprisonment of the Aldermen had been felt by the City as an insult. The freeholders and farmers of Middlesex and Surrey had no love for Laud. They were heard to mutter that if they must fight they would rather fight against the Government than for it. The defence of the Queen's mother was especially distasteful. It was known that she had urged her daughter to use her influence with the King during the sitting of the late Parliament, and it was taken for granted that this influence had been used to hasten the dissolution. For the first time in the reign the name of Henrietta Maria herself was drawn into the political conflict.[1] It could not well be otherwise. It had been so natural for her to take the part of her husband's Roman Catholic subjects; so natural, too, for her to urge their cause in contemptuous disregard of a public opinion, of which she neither understood the meaning nor estimated the weight. Yet, when all allowance has been made for the ignorance of a woman and a foreigner, it is difficult to speak with patience of the rash act of which Henrietta Maria, if not Charles himself, was now

[1] Laud's Diary, *Works*, iii. 235. *Rushw.* iii. 1,173. Rossetti to Barberini, May $\frac{15}{25}$, *R. O. Transcripts*. Salvetti's *Newsletter*, May $\frac{15}{25}$. Giustinian's Despatch, May $\frac{15}{27}$, *Ven. Transcripts*. Rossingham's *Newsletter*, May 19, *Sloane MSS.* 1,467, fol. 198. Deputy-Lieutenants of Kent to the Council, May 11, *S. P. Dom.* ccccliii. 11.

guilty. At the height of the alarm Windebank appeared before Rossetti, conjuring him to write to Rome for help in money and men. The Pope, it was probably thought, would be ready to assist a King who had given some protection to the Catholics against subjects who were exposing them to danger and persecution.[1]

CHAP. VIII.
1640.
May 14.

Whilst overtures so ruinous were being made to Rome, other voices were raised at Whitehall in condemnation of Strafford. Why, it was asked, had he brought things to such a pass without sufficient forces at his disposal to compel submission.[2] The attack on the prisons brought matters to a crisis. Six thousand foot were ordered up from the Trained Bands of Essex, Kent, and Hertfordshire. It was impossible to fall back thus on popular support without conceding something to the popular agitation. On the 15th, the day after the attack on the prisons, Hotham and Bellasys, together with the four Aldermen, were set at liberty, though the latter were required to enter into bond to appear in the Star Chamber when called on. The next day, when the Lord Mayor and Aldermen repeated their refusal to

Strafford blamed.

May 15. Fresh precautions.

Concessions made.

[1] Rossetti's letter of May $\frac{15}{25}$ is not to be found amongst the Record Office Transcripts, but its purport is clear from Barberini's reply of June $\frac{20}{30}$, and from Rossetti's answer to Barberini of Aug. $\frac{20}{30}$. Windebank is directly stated to have made the overture. It is impossible that he should have done so without orders from the Queen or the King. That the Queen knew of this seems made out, by the fact that Rossetti as a matter of course communicated Barberini's reply to her, and also by the part she subsequently took in pressing for similar help in the course of 1641. On the other hand, the long conversation with Windebank, related in the last-named letter, turns so entirely on the King's proceedings, that it seems very likely that the secretary was originally commissioned by him. Indeed, if the Queen had opened the negotiation without her husband's knowledge she would hardly have employed a Secretary of State.

[2] Montreuil's Despatch, May $\frac{14}{24}$, *Bib. Nat. Fr.* 15,995, fol. 87.

rate any man to the loan, they were sent away without further reproaches. On the 17th the Sheriffs of London were ordered to make a bonfire of a large number of Roman Catholic books which had recently been seized. Even a party of young lawyers, who had drunk confusion to the Archbishop, were dismissed by the Council on the plea, suggested to them by Dorset, that they had been really drinking confusion to the Archbishop's foes. There was even talk of taking up again the dropped negotiation with Scotland. With the exception of Loudoun, the Scottish Commissioners were set at liberty.[1] Traquair was asked whether he would undertake a mission to Edinburgh to preside over the Parliament which was to meet in June. On Traquair's refusal, Hamilton was requested to go. The King, however, proposed to delay Hamilton's journey, and to prorogue the Scottish Parliament for another month on the characteristic ground that by the middle of July he would know whether he was to have a loan from Spain which would enable him to make war on Scotland.[2]

Such was the end of Charles's first attempt to do all that power would admit. Though a list of names of those qualified to lend was sent in by the Aldermen, the project of forcing a loan from the London citizens was tacitly abandoned. Efforts would still be made to enforce the payment of ship money and coat and conduct money; but even if ship money and coat and conduct money were collected with more regularity than was likely to be the

---

[1] Montreuil's Despatch, May $\frac{21}{31}$, *Bib. Nat.* Fr. 15,995, fol. 87. *Ibid.* fol. 89. Giustinian's Despatch, $\frac{May\ 22}{June\ 1}$. *Ven. Transcripts. Council Register,* May 15. *Rushw.* iii. 1,180.

[2] Montreuil's Despatches, May $\frac{21}{31}$, $\frac{May\ 26}{June\ 7}$, *Bibl. Nat.* Fr. 15,995, fol. 89, 91. Giustinian's Despatch, $\frac{May\ 22}{June\ 1}$, *Ven. Transcripts.* Rossingham's *Newsletter,* May 26, *Sloane MSS.* 1,467, fol. 112, b.

case they would not pay the army in the field. By pressure upon official persons the loan which had been begun with the Privy Councillors was raised by May 15 to 232,530*l*.[1] But this sum had been already spent, and except in the very unlikely case of a loan from Spain no way appeared to meet the necessities of war. The feeling with which Strafford's violence was regarded by loyal but unenthusiastic subjects was well expressed by Northumberland. "The nature of most men," he wrote to Conway, who had already been sent to drill the cavalry in the North, "is not willingly to acknowledge an error until they needs must, which is some of our condition here at this time. We have engaged the King in an expensive occasion, without any certain ways to maintain it; all those that are proposed to ourselves have hitherto failed, and though our designs of raising this great army are likely to fail, yet are we loath to publish that which cannot many days be concealed. In plain terms I have little hope to see you in the North this year, which I profess I am extremely sorry for, conceiving it will be dishonourable to the King, and infamous for us that have the honour to be his ministers, when it shall be known that he shall be obliged to give over the design."[2]

Strafford was no longer at hand to inspire courage into the fainting hearts at Whitehall. For some days he had been absent from the Council table, suffering from an attack of dysentery. On the first news of the tumults, Bristol had sought him out, and had urged him to give his voice for another Parliament. To the calm, good sense of Bristol, the policy

---

[1] Account of the Loan, *S. P. Dom.* ccccliii. 14.
[2] Northumberland to Conway, May 18, *S. P. Dom.*

of adventure into which the King had been drawn, seemed devoid of all the higher elements of statesmanship. When, some months later, Bristol gave an account of his conversation with Strafford on this occasion,[1] he stated 'that he never understood by the discourse of the Earl of Strafford that the King should use any force or power of arms, but only some strict and severe course in raising money by extraordinary ways for his supplies in the present danger.' To Bristol's plea for another Parliament, he was entirely deaf. He did not, indeed, show any 'dislike of the said discourse, but said he held it not counsellable at that time, neither did the present danger of the kingdom which was not imaginary, but real and pressing, admit of so slow and uncertain remedies; that the Parliament, in this great distress of the King and kingdom, had refused to supply the King by the ordinary and usual ways, and, therefore, the King must provide for the safety of the kingdom by such ways as he should hold fit, and this examinant remembereth the said Earl of Strafford used this sentence, *Salus reipublicæ suprema lex*. This examinant likewise thinketh that at the same time the said Earl of Strafford used some words to this purpose, that the King was not to suffer himself to be mastered by the frowardness or undutifulness of the people, or rather, he conceived, by the disaffection of some particular men.' Bristol proceeded to depose that, according to the best of his memory, Strafford added, 'that when the King should see himself master of his affairs, and that it should be seen that he wanted not power to go through with his designs—as he hoped he would not do—then he conceived that' it would be advisable to call a

---

[1] The date is fixed as being not long after the dissolution, and also by the reference to the Lambeth tumults and the mutinies of the soldiers.

Parliament, 'and nobody should contribute more than himself to all moderate counsels.'[1]

When these words of high courage, worthy of a better cause, were uttered, Strafford's health was already giving way. The violence of the disease was doubtless aggravated by all that was passing around him. The scowling discontent of the gentry, the suppressed hatred of the London citizens, the growing detestation of the populace, coupling his name at last with that of Laud in their anger, might have been met calmly and defiantly, if the assailed minister had been sure of support from his Sovereign. Strafford knew that his adversaries were not inactive; that Holland, and Pembroke, and Dorset were sounding out his faults in Charles's ear;[2] that Privy Councillors, in spite of their oath of secrecy, had some days before betrayed to members of the House of Commons the resolution taken to dissolve Parliament before it was publicly announced;[3] and that the secret of his negotiation with Spain had been no better kept.[4]

The strain was too great for the weakly body in which that will of iron was enshrined. In Ireland, during his last visit, he had been racked by gout and dysentery. On his return he had been borne to London in a litter. When he found himself once more at the centre of affairs, he had shaken off his weakness. He had stepped without an effort into a commanding position in the Council. He had organised the House of Lords in resistance to the Commons. Then, when the Dissolution came, it was he who had taken the lead in the high-handed compulsion which

---

[1] Bristol's Deposition, Jan. 14, 1641, *Sherborne MSS.*
[2] Montreuil's *Despatch*, May 2¾/3¼, *Bibl. Nat.* Fr. 1,599, fol. 89.
[3] Form of oath, May 27, *S. P. Dom.* ccccliv. 11.
[4] Salvetti's *Newsletter*, May 8/18, 15/25. The security offered on the merchants' goods, however, seems to have remained a secret.

CHAP. VIII.
1640.
May.

was to gather up the resources of an unwilling nation to be used for purposes in which it took no pleasure. In a week after the Dissolution, the excitement of the conflict had told upon him, and he was again suffering. Then came the bitter disappointment of failure. On the 15th, the day on which the Aldermen were released, he was forced to receive the Spanish Ambassadors in bed.[1] Two or three days later, his life was in imminent danger. In some few the knowledge called forth expressions of bitter sorrow. One royalist poet, ignorant of what another year was to bring forth, called upon him to live not for his own sake, but for the sake of his country.[2] His personal friends were broken-hearted with grief. Wandesford, left behind as Lord Deputy to rule Ireland in his name, passed on the bitter tidings to Ormond. "The truth is," he wrote, "I am not master of myself, therefore I cannot enlarge myself much. If you did not love this man well of whom I speak, I would not write thus much."

May 24. His convalescence.

Then came days on which hope returned, and on the 24th the King visited him, to congratulate him on his convalescence. In the presence of the King, Strafford had no eyes for the vacillation of the man. To him Charles was still what Elizabeth had been to her subjects, the living personification of government, at a time when government was sorely needed. True to his ceremonious loyalty, the convalescent threw off his warm gown to receive his Sovereign in befitting guise. His imprudence went near to cost him his life. Struck down again by the chill, it was only after a week in which the physicians despaired of recovery,

---

[1] Velada to Philip IV., May $\frac{15}{25}$, *Brussels MSS.* Sec. d'Etat Esp. cclxxxiv. 258.

[2] This curious poem, probably the work of Cartwright, is in MS. in the library of Corpus Christi College, Oxford.

that hope could again be spoken of to his friends. It was not thus that he was to pass from this world of toil, of error, and of sin.[1]

CHAP. VIII.
1640.

Before Charles visited Strafford, he had already repented of his hesitation. The forces which he had called to his aid had been sufficient to prevent any repetition of the tumults. On the 20th it was resolved in Council that the proposed negotiation with Scotland should be abandoned. A violent attack written by Baillie, against Laud and his system,[2] which had just reached the King's hand, made him more than ever averse to an accommodation. But the difficulty of finding means to conduct the war was as insuperable as ever. By the end of the month the amount of ship money collected barely exceeded 20,000*l.*, less than one-tenth of the sum required,[3] and every letter to the Privy Council from the country carried news of the impossibility of obtaining more. Constables refused to assess, and even when this difficulty had been surmounted those who were assessed refused to pay. If distresses were taken, the articles seized were either rescued by violence, or were left on the hands of the officers because no one would buy them. In many parts of the country the levy of coat and conduct money was equally unpopular. Sometimes it was directly denounced as illegal, and, where that was not the case, payment was refused on the score of poverty.

May 20. The war with Scotland persisted in.

Difficulty of collecting ship money

and coat and conduct money.

Against this spirit of insubordination, the Council which met on the 20th took such measures as were in its power. A Special Committee was formed to watch

Measures of the Council.

[1] Wandesford to Ormond, May 26, 29, June 4, 7, *Carte MSS.* i. 197, 199, 200, 203.
[2] *Ladensium αὐτοκατάκρισις*, an answer to *Lysimachus Nicanor*, by whom the Covenanters were charged with Jesuitry. Rossingham's *Newsletter*, May 26, *Sloane MSS.* 1,467, fol. 112, b.
[3] Account of ship money, May 30, *S. P. Dom.* ccclv. 92.

over the enforcement of ship money,[1] and orders were given to prosecute in the Star Chamber those amongst the Sheriffs who were held to have been more than ordinarily remiss. Equal severity was to be used to gather in coat and conduct money; and five Deputy-Lieutenants of Hertfordshire, who had expressed themselves doubtfully as to the legality of the imposition, were summoned before the Board.[2] How much remained to be done may be gathered from the fact that, out of 2,600*l.* demanded from Buckinghamshire, only 8*l.* 10*s.* had been collected; and, though this was an extreme instance, other counties were not far in advance.[3]

May 21. The riots declared treasonable.

The day after these resolutions were taken, one of the leaders of the Southwark tumults was tried before a Special Commission. The judges laid it down that the disturbances amounted to High Treason, and supported their decision by a precedent from the reign of Elizabeth. The prisoner, a poor sailor, was therefore sentenced to be quartered, as well as hung, and the sentence was carried into execution at Southwark, though the authorities mercifully allowed him to hang till he was dead, before the hangman's knife was thrust into his body.

May 23. Execution of a rioter.

May 21. Torture and execution of Archer.

John Archer was less fortunate. His part had been to beat the drum in advance of the crowd which marched to the attack upon Lambeth. A glover by trade, he had been pressed into the King's service to go with the army as a drummer, and, for some reason or other, it was supposed that he could give information against persons in high position, who were believed to have instigated these tumults. Orders

---

[1] *Rushw.* iii. 1,184.
[2] Rossingham's *Newsletter*, May 26, *Sloane MSS.* 1,467, fol. 112, b.
[3] Crane to Crane, May 29, *Tanner MSS.* lxv. 78.

were accordingly given to put him to the torture. The last attempt ever made in England to enforce confession by the rack was as useless as it was barbarous. Archer probably had nothing to disclose, and he was executed without making any revelation.¹

CHAP. VIII.
1640.
May.

These stern measures were not without effect. For some time extraordinary precautions were needed. On the 27th a placard was fixed up in four places in the City, calling on the defenders of the purity of the gospel to kill Rossetti. The King was insulted even within the walls of his palace. Some one scratched with a diamond on a window at Whitehall: "God save the King, confound the Queen and her children, and give us the Palsgrave to reign in this kingdom."² Charles dashed the glass into fragments with his hand. But there was no further disturbance in the streets, and after some little time the Trained Bands summoned to the aid of the Government were sent home or countermanded, and the capital resumed its usual appearance.

The excitement dies out.

During these days of disturbance, Convocation had been busily at work, in spite of the Dissolution of Parliament. It was none of Laud's doing. The Archbishop shared the general opinion, that the end of the Parliament brought with it the end of the Convocation, and applied to the King for a writ to dismiss the ecclesiastical assembly. To his surprise, the King answered that he wished to have the grant of subsidies completed, and that the canons, the discussion of which had been begun, should be finally adopted. He had spoken to Finch, and Finch had

May 9
Convocation continues sitting.

¹ Warrant to torture Archer, May 21, *S. P. Dom.* ccccliv. 39. Jardine's *Reading on the Use of Torture*, 57, 108. Rossingham's *Newsletter*, May 26, *Sloane MSS.* 1,467, fol. 112, b.

² I retranslate from Rossetti's Italian. Rossetti to Barberini, $\frac{May\ 29}{June\ 8}$, *R. O. Transcripts.*

assured him that the continuance of a session of Convocation after the Dissolution of Parliament was not prohibited by law. Laud expostulated in vain. He was irritated that the King had conferred with the Lord Keeper, rather than with himself, in a matter which concerned the Church, and he had reason to fear that the proceeding would not be so well approved of by public opinion as it was by Finch. When the King's mind was made known in Convocation, some members of the Lower House expressed doubts of the legality of the course pursued, and Charles laid the question formally before a Committee of lawyers for their opinion.[1] The opinion of the lawyers coincided with that of Finch, and on the 15th, the day on which the King was giving in on everything else, it was announced to the two Houses that they were to meet on the next day for business.

On the 16th Convocation took into consideration a precedent of 1587, when their predecessors had granted a benevolence to Elizabeth in addition to the subsidy which had received Parliamentary confirmation. They, therefore, renewed their grant of 20,000*l.* a year for six years, only, instead of calling it a subsidy, they called it a benevolence, or free contribution.[2]

Having thus expressed their loyalty, the Laudian clergy published in seventeen new canons its manifesto to a disloyal generation. Those canons, indeed, were not wanting in that reasonableness which has ever been the special characteristic of the English Church.

---

[1] The Committee consisted of Finch, Manchester, Chief Justices Bramston and Lyttelton, Attorney-General Bankes, and Sergeants Whitfield and Heath.

[2] *Nalson*, i. 365. Laud's *Works*, iii. 285. Strype's *Life of Whitgift*, 1,497, iii. 196. Parliament was still sitting when this grant was made.

They do not simply fulminate anathemas. They condescend to explain difficulties, and to invite to charitable construction. The canon relating to the ceremonies began with a declaration that it was 'generally to be wished that unity of faith were accompanied with uniformity of practice . . . chiefly for the avoiding of groundless suspicions of those who are weak, and the malicious aspersions of the professed enemies of our religion.' It went on to say that the position of the Communion Table was 'in its own nature indifferent,' but that the place at the east end being authorised by Queen Elizabeth, it was fit that all churches 'should conform themselves in this particular to the example of the Cathedral or mother churches, saving always the general liberty left to the Bishop by the law during the time of the administration of the Holy Communion.' This situation of the holy table did not imply that 'it is or ought to be esteemed a true and proper altar, wherein Christ is again really sacrificed; but it is, and may be called an altar by us, in that sense in which the primitive Church called it an altar, and in no other.'

As this table had been irreverently treated, it was to be surrounded with rails to avoid profanation, and, for the same reason, it was fitting that communicants should receive at the table, and not in their seats. Lastly, the custom of doing reverence and obeisance upon entering and quitting the church was highly recommended, though in this the rule of charity was to be observed; namely, 'that they which use this rite, despise not them who use it not, and that they who use it not, condemn not those that use it.'

It can hardly be disputed that there is more of the liberal spirit in this canon than in the Scottish Covenant. It is fairly justifiable as a serious effort to

CHAP. VIII.
1640.
May.

find a broad ground on which all could unite. Its fault was, that it sought to compel all to unite on the ground which it had chosen. No doubt this was a common fault of the time. In the British Isles at least no one, with the exception of some few despised Separatists, had seriously advocated the idea that worship was to be tolerated outside the National Church. What was fatal to the canon on the ceremonies was that the worship which it advocated was not in any sense national. It approved itself to the few, not to the many, and the many who objected to it had other reasons for being dissatisfied with the authorities by whom it was imposed.

The Divine right of kings.

The canons were therefore at every disadvantage in comparison with the Covenant, as far as their subject matter was concerned. They were no less at a disadvantage in the sanction to which they appealed. The Covenant claimed to be, and in the main was, the voice of the Scottish Church and people. The canons were only, in a very artificial sense, the voice of the English Church, and they were in no sense at all the voice of the English people. They were therefore driven to magnify the authority of the King from whom alone Convocation derived its title to legislate. In the forefront of the argument, therefore, was placed the inculcation of the obedience due to kings. "The most high and sacred order of kings," it was declared in a canon ordered to be read in churches four times in every year, "is of Divine right." It was founded in the prime laws of nature, and clearly established by express texts both of the Old and New Testaments, that God had Himself given authority to kings over all persons ecclesiastical or civil. Therefore it was treasonable against God, as well as against the King, to maintain 'any independent coactive power either papal or popular,' whilst 'for subjects to bear arms against their kings, offensive or defensive, upon any pretence whatsoever,' was 'at the least to resist the powers which are ordained of God,' and such as resisted would 'receive to themselves damnation.'

In this language there was nothing new. It had been used in the sixteenth century to attack the claims of the Pope. It would be used again in the latter half of the seventeenth century to attack the claims of the Presbyterians. Where Laud erred was in failing to see that an argument always derives its practical force from the mental condition of those to whom it is addressed. The Divine right of kings had been a popular theory when it coincided with a suppressed assertion of the Divine right of the nation. Henry VIII. and Elizabeth had prospered not because their thrones were established by the decree of Heaven, but because they stood up for the national independence against foreign authority. Charles and Laud had placed themselves outside the national conscience, and their Divine right of kings was held up to the mockery of those to whom their assertions were addressed.

Nowhere was Laud's feeble grasp on the realities of life shown more than in the clause relating to taxation. It was the duty of subjects to give 'tribute and custom, and aid and subsidy, and all manner of necessary support and supply' to kings, 'for the public defence, care, and protection of them.' Subjects, on the other hand, had 'not only possession of, but a true and just right, title, and property to and in all their goods and estates, and ought so to have.' A more innocuous proposition was never drawn up, if it implied that the subjects were to be the judges

CHAP. VIII.
1640. May.

New import of the language used.

The question of taxation.

whether their money was needed for the public defence. If, on the other hand, it implied that the King was to be the judge, it erected a despotism as arbitrary as that which existed in France. What was the bearing of such high-sounding platitudes on the question really at issue—whether an invasion of Scotland was or was not necessary for the public defence and protection of Englishmen?

The etcetera oath.

In one point, at least, the new canons directly imitated the Covenant. It was impossible that the effective force of the oath which bound Scotsmen together could have escaped the eye of Laud. The Church of England, too, should have its oath, not enforced by lawless violence but emanating from legitimate authority. "I, A. B.," so ran the formula, "do swear that I do approve the doctrine and discipline, or government, established in the Church of England, as containing all things necessary to salvation, and that I will not endeavour by myself or any other, directly or indirectly, to bring in Popish doctrine contrary to that which is so established, nor will I ever give my consent to alter the government of this Church by archbishops, bishops, deans, and archdeacons, &c., as it stands now established, and as by right it ought to stand, nor yet ever to subject it to the usurpations and superstitions of the See of Rome."

Its unpopularity.

This oath, soon to be known to the world as the etcetera oath, was hardly likely to serve the purpose for which it was intended. The ridicule piled on the demand, that every clergyman, every master of arts who was not the son of a nobleman, all who had taken a degree in divinity, law, or physic, all registrars, actuaries, proctors, and schoolmasters, should swear to make no attempt to alter institutions, which the very framers of the formula omitted completely to specify, would have had little effect if the oath had in any way given expression to the popular sentiment. It is true that, even in this unlucky production, all was not amiss, and in these days we may contemplate with satisfaction the spirit which demanded no more than a general approval of the doctrine of the Church as containing all things necessary to salvation. After all, the main fault to be found with the oath is that it was intended to be imposed on those who did not want to take it; whilst the Covenant, at least in its earlier days, was intended to bind together, in conscious unity, those who approved more or less zealously of its principles.[1]

The very existence of this Convocation, after the Dissolution of Parliament, was in itself a special offence. It accentuated the distinction, already sharp enough, between the laity and the clergy. The clergy, it seemed, were to form a legislature apart, making laws in ecclesiastical matters, and even laying down principles for the observance of Parliaments in such essentially secular matters as the grant of subsidies. No doubt it was the Tudor theory, that Convocation was dependent on the King and not on Parliament, just as it was the Tudor theory that the Royal supremacy in ecclesiastical matters was vested in the Crown antecedently to Parliamentary statutes. The time was now come when the sufficiency of these theories to meet the altered circumstances of the time would be rudely put to the test.

Even in Convocation itself, the question was raised. Bishop Goodman of Gloucester, who had retained his bishopric in spite of his conversion to the Roman Catholic Church, took umbrage at a canon directed

[1] Canons, in Laud's *Works*, v. 607.

at those professors of his creed who were more honest than himself. 'He would be torn with wild horses,' he told Laud, 'before he would subscribe that canon.' When he reached the place of meeting his courage failed him. He fell back on a denial of the right of Convocation to make canons when Parliament was not sitting. Laud waved aside the objection and told him he was obliged to vote for or against the canons. On his refusal to do either, the Archbishop, with the consent of Convocation, suspended him from his office. In the end, Goodman gave way and signed the canons as they stood. As soon as the King heard what had passed he committed the Bishop to the Gate-House, to answer for his offence in entering into communications with Rome whilst he remained a Bishop of the English Church.

Dissolution of Convocation. Charles and Laud were, before all things, anxious to clear themselves from the stigma of friendliness to Rome. When Convocation was dissolved, on the 29th, the Archbishop protested that the King 'was so far from Popery that there was no man in England more ready to be a martyr for our religion than his Majesty.'[1]

April. Convention of Estates at Edinburgh. In such a case protests could avail little. They could not call out the national enthusiasm, without which Charles's cause was hopeless. Of such enthusiasm there was no lack in Scotland. A Convention of Estates, a kind of informal Parliament, had sat in Edinburgh in April. It had taken every precaution against surprise. Lord Eglinton was directed to watch the coast from the Clyde to the English Border against the landing of the Irish army.

---

[1] Laud's *Works*, iii. 287, vi. 539. Rossingham's *Newsletter*, June 2, 9. *Sloane MSS.* 1,467, fol. 117, 121. Identical canons were passed by the Convocation of York.

Argyle was naturally entrusted with the defence of the Western Highlands. As in the preceding year the main difficulty lay in Aberdeen. On May 5 the Earl Marischal marched in, imposed a fine on the Royalist town, and enforced the signature of the Covenant.[1] In Edinburgh, Ettrick had continued firing on the town from his impregnable position in the Castle, and had killed some thirty of the inhabitants in the streets.[2] An attempt was made to undermine his defences, but the rocks on which they were built were so hard that the project was soon abandoned. At sea Charles's cruisers were let loose on Scottish commerce, and a large number of vessels were brought as prizes into English harbours.

CHAP. VIII.
1640. May. The Earl Marischal in Aberdeen. Ettrick in Edinburgh Castle.

The Scottish Parliament had been prorogued to June 2. A decision would soon be taken upon the attitude to be observed towards the King. No doubt could be entertained what that decision would be. Every letter from the South brought confirmation of the belief that England was not with Charles. It was openly said at Edinburgh, that as soon as Parliament met the Castle would surrender, and 20,000 Scots would cross the Border to support the demands which had been made by their Commissioners.

The approaching session at Edinburgh.

In such a temper the Scots were not likely to respect the King's order for the prorogation of Parliament till the beginning of July, an order which, as they rightly judged, was only intended to gain time for the completion of the English military preparations. The Covenanting leaders consulted the principal divines and lawyers of their party on the course to be pursued, and received assurance that Parlia-

The King orders prorogation.

Opinions of the lawyers.

[1] *Spalding*, i. 267.
[2] The Marquis of Douglas to Guthrie, May 21. Ernley to Conway, May 22. Intelligence sent to Conway, May 25, *S. P. Dom.* ccccliv. 51, 75, 98.

ment might lawfully sit without the presence either of the King or his Commissioner.[1] They were even informed that a King who sold his country to a stranger, who deserted it for a foreign land, or who attacked it with an invading force, might lawfully be deposed.[2]

Startling as the question was, it was one which could not but force itself on the minds of the Scottish leaders. There was something ridiculous in the phrases of devoted loyalty with which they besprinkled a King whom they were preparing to attack with force of arms. Yet, illogical as their position was, it was not in their power to abandon it. To do so would be to introduce hesitation into the hearts of

---

[1] *Burnet*, 165. "The Scots estates," writes Mr. Burton, "did not admit the irresponsibility of the Sovereign. We have seen them bringing James III. to task, and the precedent was made all the more emphatic by the attempt of the lawyers of the 17th century to conceal it by mutilating the record in which it is set forth. The punishment of bad Sovereigns is a thing in which the literature of the country deals in a tone evidently directed towards practice. We find the estates of Scotland dealing with many things now deemed the peculiar function of the executive. They kept in their own hands the power of making peace and war. . . . We shall find that at the time we have now reached," *i.e.* the first years of Mary Stuart, "a critical question was standing over, Whether the Crown had a veto on the acts of the estates; in other words, Whether the consent of the Sovereign was necessary to an Act of Parliament, and down to the Union with England this question was not decided." *Hist. of Scotl.* iv. 93.

[2] The evidence for this is a deposition by Sir T. Steward that Argyle had said in his presence that at Edinburgh 'it was agitatt . . . whether or not ane Parliament might be holdane without the King or his Commissioner, and that a King might be depositt being found guilty of any of thir three: 1. *Venditio*, 2. *Desertio*; 3. *Invasio.*' Napier, *Memorials of Montrose*, i. 266. This seems to me credible in itself, and it is borne out by the deposition of John Stuart even before his recantation (*Ibid.* i. 297, 299). It is evident, too, from the following phrase in a letter from Johnston, immediately to be quoted, that something of the kind was in agitation. "Montrose did dispute against Argyle, Rothes, Balmerino, and myself, because some urged that, as long as we had a King, we could not sit without him; and it was answered that to do the less was more lawful than to do the greater." Napier, *Memoirs of Montrose*, i. 236.

their countrymen, when hesitation would have been ruinous, and would perhaps even raise qualms of conscience in their own bosoms. They therefore fell back on a technical informality in the manner in which the King's orders were presented to them. Montrose urged obedience on the ground that as long as they had a king they could not act without him. Argyle, Balmerino, Rothes, and Johnston significantly replied, 'that to do the less was more lawful than to do the greater.'[1] They held that it was better to act without their sovereign than to depose him.

 Montrose and his friends submitted. They were prepared to support the Royal authority if Charles showed himself ready to comply with the requirements of the Scottish nation. They were not ready to desert the cause which they had hitherto upheld in the face of a bearing so ambiguous as that of the King.[2] Charles had as yet given no engagement to

CHAP. VIII.
1640.
May.

June 2.
Session of Parliament.

Montrose's position.

---

[1] Napier, *Memoirs of Montrose*, i. 236.

[2] "But the members of the said Parliament," wrote Montrose in 1645, " some of them having far designs unknown to us, others of them having found the sweetness of government, were pleased to refuse the ratification of the Acts of the Assembly, with the abjuration of Episcopacy and Court of High Commission, introduced by the Prelates, unless they had the whole alleged liberty due to the subject, which was, in fact, intrenching upon authority, and the total abrogation of his Majesty's royal prerogative ; whereby the King's Commissioner was constrained to rise and discharge the Parliament, and was urged to levy new forces to suppress their unlawful desires ; and, fearing lest their unlawful desires and our flat refusal of his Majesty's offer conform to the conference foresaid, should have moved his Majesty to recal what he had condescended unto, to the prejudice of religion and liberties of the subject ; and, on the other hand, calling to mind the oath of allegiance and covenant subscribed for the maintenance of his Majesty's honour and greatness—wrestling betwixt extremities, and resolved rather to suffer with the people of God for the benefit of true religion than to give way to his Majesty in what then seemed doubtsome, and being most unwilling to divide from them we were joined with in Covenant, did still undertake with them " (Napier, *Memorials of Montrose*, i. 218). Whether this is a perfectly correct account of Montrose's state of mind five years before may perhap

CHAP. VIII.
1640.
June 2.

assent to the Acts abolishing Episcopacy. Nor were other causes wanting to determine Montrose's action at this juncture of affairs. Sharing, as he did, to some extent in Strafford's ideas on the place of monarchy in constitutional government, though laying more stress than Strafford did on the duty of kings to take into consideration the wishes of their subjects, he was more under the limitations of nationality than Strafford was. Monarchy was not to him an authority disposing of the forces of the three kingdoms for the coercion of any one which happened to resist the wisdom of the Government. It was a purely Scottish institution. Beyond Scottish territory and Scottish men his thoughts did not travel. Whether Charles were right or wrong he was to be resisted if he attempted to enforce his views by means of an army of English foreigners.

June 11.
The Acts passed.

Montrose, therefore, a half-hearted Covenanter it might be, was a Covenanter still. His fellow-countrymen became Covenanters, if possible, more resolutely than ever. The Scottish Parliament made short work of the questions at issue. It speedily converted into laws, as far as it was possible to do so without the Royal assent, all the Bills which had received the approbation of the Lords of the Articles

be doubted; but it is at all events significant that he expresses doubts whether the King might be induced to withdraw the concessions which he had made at Berwick. In writing to Charles in 1641 Montrose distinctly admits that the cause of the mischief was not to be sought only in the conduct of the subjects. They, he tells the King, are likely to fall from himself if, by removing the cause and by the application of wholesome remedies, it be not speedily prevented. "They," he goes on to say, "have no other end but to preserve their religion in purity and their liberties entire." He even speaks as if some moderate alteration in the Acts ought to satisfy the King. "Any difference that may arise upon the Acts passed in the last Parliament your Majesty's presence and the advice and endeavours of your faithful servants will easily accommodate" (*Ibid.* i. 268).

before the prorogation in November. On June 11 the new constitution—it was nothing less than that—was formally approved of, and Parliament separated, leaving behind it a numerous Committee of Estates, empowered to conduct the government of the country in its name.

Of these Acts an enthusiastic Covenanter declared that they exhibited 'the next greatest change in one blow that ever happened to this church and state these six hundred years by-past; for in effect it overturned not only the ancient state government, but fettered monarchy with chains, and set new limits and marks[1] to the same beyond which it was not legally to proceed.'[2]

If such was the view taken of these Acts at Edinburgh it was not likely that they would be acceptable to Charles. Yet it was hard to say what he could do. His army was still to be formed. Conway's 2,000 Horse at Newcastle was the only force as yet disposable against the enemy. Conway's account of their condition was most depressing. The pistols which had been sent down to them were absolutely unserviceable, and, as no money was to be had from London to meet the expense of repairing them, he had to give orders that twopence a day should be deducted from the pay of the troopers. A mutiny was the result; and Conway, who had scant time to think of the Petition of Right, ordered one of the ringleaders to be shot. The soldiers themselves were not such as to be easy of guidance. "I am teaching," wrote Conway, "cart horses to manage, and men that are fit for Bedlam and Bridewell to keep the ten commandments; so that General Leslie and I keep two schools. He hath scholars that profess to serve God, and he is instruct-

[1] *i.e.* boundaries.   [2] *Balfour*, ii. 379.

ing them how they may safely do injury and all impiety. Mine to the uttermost of their power never kept any law either of God or the King, and they are to be made fit to make others keep them."[1]

Almost as soon as the news of the determination of the Scottish Parliament to continue in session reached the King, a desperate effort was made to extract ship money from the city of London. On June 9 the Lord Mayor and Sheriffs were before the Council. The Lord Mayor was asked why he had not collected the money. He replied that he had done his best. "Why," asked the King, "did you not distrain?" The poor man pleaded that one of his predecessors was the defendant of an action brought against him in the King's Bench by the indefatigable Richard Chambers, for his conduct in collecting ship money, and that he did not wish to be in the same position. "No man," said Charles peremptorily, "shall suffer for obeying my commands." Lord Mayor Garway was hardly the man to hold out as Alderman Soames had held out in the case of the loan. He was himself one of the collectors of the new impositions, and had made good profit out of an unparliamentary levy. The next day, accompanied by the Sheriffs, he went from house to house to demand the money for the King. In the whole City only one man was found to pay it. The Lord Mayor then bade the Sheriffs to distrain the goods of the refusers. They told him that this 'was his business, not theirs.' Entering a draper's shop, he took hold of a piece of linen. The owner coolly asked to be allowed to measure the stuff before he parted with it. When he had ascer-

[1] Conway to Laud, May 20. Conway to Northumberland, May 20. Conway to the Countess of Devonshire, May 28, *S. P. Dom.* ccccliv. 30, 38.

GENERAL APATHY IN ENGLAND. 373

tained its length, he named the price of the goods, and said that he should charge it to his lordship's account.[1]

On the 11th the Common Council met to consider another demand which had been recently made upon them. They had been required to furnish 4,000 men to the army, and to comply with the usual requisition for coat and conduct money. After some discussion the meeting separated without returning an answer, and this postponement of a resolution was almost tantamount to a refusal.[2]

Such a rebuff left Charles almost as much irritated with the City as he was with the Scottish Parliament. The ease with which he had gained the mastery over the turbulent apprentices brought the notion into his head that it would be possible to use armed force to compel the City to minister of its fulness to the necessities of the State. In his eyes the refusal of ship money and of coat and conduct money was a distinct rejection of legal obligations, and compulsion would thus only be used to bring offenders upon their knees. Such fancies remained with Charles no more than fancies. To carry them out would take time, and it might be that, before he had effected his purpose, a Scottish army would cross the Borders to throw its sword into the scale. It would therefore be necessary to take up once more the scheme of a negotiation with the Scots. A peace with the northern kingdom might be patched up on the best terms which could be obtained, in the expectation that sooner or later an excuse would be given for recommencing the war with better chances, and for re-

CHAP. VIII.
1640.
June 11.
Coat and conduct money in the City.

June 12.
Charles thinks of using force with the City;

and of negotiating with the Scots.

[1] Rossingham's *Newsletter*, June 16, *S. P. Dom.* ccclvii. 36.
[2] The Council to the Lord Mayor, May 31, *Rushw.* iii. 1,188. *Common Council Journal*, xxxix. 97, *Corporation Records.*

CHAP. VIII.
1640.
June 1.
The second Session of the Irish Parliament.

ducing Scotland to the obedience which it owed to its rightful King.[1]

Before Charles could resolve to take one course or another, even worse news than that which had reached him from Edinburgh was spreading across the Irish Channel. The Parliament of Ireland met for its second Session on June 1. The enthusiasm, real or factitious, with which the subsidies had been granted in March had long since died away. Strafford was no longer in Dublin to warn and to encourage. Nor was the situation the same in June as it had been three months before. Not only was there a difference between the time of payment and the time of promise, but there was no longer reason to believe that the Irish who supported the King would be on the winning side. Nor was the House of Commons quite the same as it had been in March. An Irish House of Commons was a very artificial production. Care had been taken that neither the Roman Catholic

[1] This rests on the testimony of Rossetti. He would be well informed by the Queen of what was passing. After speaking of the guards placed by the King on Somerset House and St. James's, he says that this was done 'poiche avrebbe voluto, sotto questo colore di reprimere tali seditioni, unire insieme le sue forze per meglio tenere in offitio la città, e costringerla formatamente à dargli qual sussidio di danaro che per via parlamentaria non ha potuto ottenere. . . . Ma perchè per essere la stagione troppo inanzi, e questo dissegno del Rè solamente meditato, difficilmente o con molto progresso potrebbe effettuarlo in quest' anno, si è inteso di più che egli voglia pacificare in qualche buon modo gli Scozzesi per hora et intanto aggiustare le cose d'Inghilterra per non haver impedimento dietro le spalle, e provedersi di danari e d'altre cose necessarie per poter essere in termini à tempo più maturo di muoversi contro la Scotia, et per condurre S. M^{ta} più cautamente il tutto credessi che pensi di voler andare con aparecchio pacifico alle frontieri di quel Regno, accommodarsi in qual miglior modo che si potesse con li Scozzesi, e veder poi a suo tempo di ridurgli à perfetta obbedienza coll' armi.' He goes on to say that, in spite of the King's irritation about the news from Scotland 'nondimeno credesi che egli voglia per hora con l'arte più che con la forza procurare di ridurre a qualche quiete le cose.' Rossetti to Barberini, June $\frac{12}{22}$, R. O. Transcripts.

members nor the independent Protestant members should form a majority. By means of the knot of civilian and military officials the Government could convert either of these minorities into a majority, and it was, therefore, in the interest of both parties to court the good-will of that Government which could do so much to serve them or to injure them. For the moment, however, this source of authority was no longer available. Wandesford, the new Lord Deputy, was an honourable and loyal man, but he was not a Strafford. Even if he had been all that Strafford was, it is doubtful whether success would have been within his reach. Many of the official members were absent from their posts, actively employed in raising troops and in preparing for the coming campaign.[1]

CHAP. VIII.
1640.
June.

Protestants and Roman Catholics might be at issue on many points, but they were agreed in disliking to pay large sums of money. In 1634 the Lord Deputy had bethought himself of a new way of collecting the supplies voted. He and his Council came to the conclusion that each subsidy ought to be worth a certain sum, and this sum was then distributed amongst the counties, each county being left to assess its own share upon its inhabitants. This precedent had been followed by Wandesford. The Commons now drew up a declaration, in which they alleged that each man's property[2] should be rated to pay a certain proportion, whether the whole sum came up to the Deputy's expectations or not. The first subsidy voted might be gathered in as Wandesford had proposed, but the others must be collected 'in a moderate Parliamentary way.' To this demand Wandesford was forced to give his

Objections to the mode of levying subsidies.

June 13. Declaration of the Commons.

[1] Carte's *Ormond*, i. 99.
[2] *Irish Commons' Journals*, i. 146

CHAP. VIII.
1640.
June.
The Irish army.

Small value of the subsidies.

Proposed Genoese and French loans.

consent, and the Houses were then prorogued till October.[1] In spite of this rebuff Wandesford was still hopeful. The full value of the first subsidy would now be paid. The army, which was waiting for supplies, would be able to rendezvous at Carrickfergus by the end of July. By that time Strafford would be sufficiently recovered to cross the sea, and with him as their leader the long-expected blow would at last be struck.

The pecuniary loss to the Irish Treasury was even greater than the Lord Deputy anticipated. The first subsidy, indeed, collected on Strafford's plan brought in 46,000*l*. The second and third subsidies together brought in only half that sum. The fourth subsidy was never collected at all.[2]

It was as well that it should be so. Strafford's plan deserved to fail. To call upon Ireland, poor as it was, to bear a burthen out of all proportion to that which England had ever consented to bear, was to make a demand beyond the bounds of reason. Nor was it fair upon Ireland to place it thus in the forefront of the battle. Victorious or vanquished, she would but bring down upon herself the hatred of her more powerful neighbour.

Whilst Ireland was drawing back and Scotland was menacing, the English Government was in desperate straits for money. Early in June an agent

---

[1] In a subsequent petition of the Commons (*S. P. Ireland*, Bundle cclxxxvi.) it is said that estates were valued at the tenth part, and that they then paid 4*s*. in the pound in lands and 2*s*. 8*d*. in goods, and that this was higher than the rates used in England. This helps us to understand how a subsidy of nominally 4*s*. in the pound was borne.

[2] Wandesford to Ormond, June 7, 10, 12, 30, *Carte MSS*. i. fol. 203, 206, 209, 211. Radcliffe to Conway, July 4, *S. P. Ireland*, Bundle cclxxxvi.

of Cottington's offered the most advantageous conditions to the French Government in return for a loan, and at the same time an effort was made to obtain a similar advance from the financiers of Genoa. Neither attempt was successful. Richelieu had no wish to help Charles out of his difficulties, and the Genoese were hardly likely to be satisfied with any security which the English Government had in its power to give.[1] Another plan was to squeeze money out of the unfortunate Catholics. Orders were given to arrest all the priests who were to be found, as well as such of the laity as frequented the chapels of the Catholic ambassadors. The Queen's influence, however, was once more brought to bear upon her husband, and these proceedings were stopped on the understanding that the Catholics would follow the precedent of 1639 by making a voluntary contribution towards the expenses of the war.[2]

1640. June.

Attempt to get money from the Catholics.

Alarming news began to pour into Whitehall from those who were entrusted with the military preparations. There had always been a strong belief at Court that the opposition to the King was for the most part confined to the upper classes—at all events amongst the rural population. The theory was not entirely without foundation. Puritanism had no deep root in the minds of the agricultural poor. Country gentlemen and small freeholders might be averse to Laudian innovations in the Church and to unparliamentary exactions in the State, but the labourers and the small handicraftsmen of the country-side cared very little about the matter. They wanted to be let alone that they might be allowed to earn their

Condition of the army.

[1] Memorandum, June, *S. P. Dom.* ccclviii. 75. Montreuil's Despatch, June 4, *Bibl. Nat.* Fr. 15,995, fol. 93. Giustinian's Despatches, June $\frac{5}{15}, \frac{19}{29}$, *Ven. Transcripts.*
[2] Rossetti to Barberini, June $\frac{19}{29}$, *R. O. Transcripts.*

daily bread in peace. It was the great mistake of the Government to imagine that this passive submission could be easily converted into active loyalty, and that it was possible to pass over the opposition of the intelligent classes, because those classes were of necessity only a minority of the whole population. The moment the carters, the blacksmiths, and the labourers were ordered to put on a uniform and to march far away from their cottages and their families they would be full of dissatisfaction with the Government which tore them from their homes to expose them to danger, and perhaps to death, for a cause which inspired them with no interest whatever. Something of this feeling is sometimes manifested in modern armies whenever the reserves are called out for actual war. But in modern armies the feeling is always shortlived. Enthusiasm for the cause at stake, military habits created early in life, and, above all, the influence of a body of officers accustomed to command, and of comrades accustomed to obey, combine to create the military habit of discipline and obedience which has been for a time put off amidst the cares and emulation of civil life. To Charles's army all this was lacking. There was no enthusiasm whatever. In the new-levied ranks there were none but raw recruits, and the alienation of the country gentlemen made it impossible to appoint men whose local influence would inspire confidence, and in some way redeem their want of military knowledge. Officers who had served in Holland or Germany were mingled with officers who had never served at all. Scarcely one of either class had any knowledge of the men whom they were designed to lead. Fresh from Court they arrived to take the command of companies in which every soldier was in a state of irritation at having to serve at all, and in which not a single soldier had any reason to hold them in the slightest respect. Even in the preceding year something of this inconvenience had been felt. But in 1639 the bulk of the army had been drawn from the trained bands of the counties north of the Humber, who were consequently under the orders of the gentlemen of their own shires. In 1640 the trained bands were not called out at all, and the Northern counties were excused from a service to which they had contributed so much in the preceding summer. The pressed men of the shires south of the Humber, who formed the army of 1640, were both more indifferent to the chances of a Scottish invasion, which was not likely to reach their own homes, and were themselves drawn from a lower class.

Nor did the danger end here. The sixteenth century had left behind it as a legacy an indelible, if somewhat unintelligent, hatred of the Roman Catholic Church. With few exceptions, high and low were actuated by a common feeling of abhorrence. Charles, indeed, had himself a firm determination never to acknowledge the Papal claims; but in his dread of Puritan ascendency, he fancied that he could trust the Catholics, and that he could trust very few others. Even before the Short Parliament Rossetti boasted that many Catholics were placed in military commands from which Puritans were strictly excluded.[1] Charles forgot that such an arrangement would loosen still more the ties of discipline, already loose enough.

It is possible that if pay had been constant, such seeds of mischief might, not without much difficulty, have been eradicated. But the financial troubles of the Government made themselves felt everywhere.

[1] Rossetti to Barberini, $\frac{\text{March 27}}{\text{Apr. 6}}$, *R. O. Transcripts.*

CHAP. VIII.
1640.
June.

Want of discipline.

When at last, early in June, the men started on the march for the rendezvous at Selby, it was often with a feeling of doubt whether the money due for their services would ever really be paid.

Tales of disorder at once began to pour in from every side. In Wiltshire a company roved about stealing poultry and assaulting honest countrymen who refused to satisfy the demands of the soldiery. Another body of men in the same county were filled with the universal fear of Popish intrigue. They asked their captain whether he would receive the Communion with them. On his refusal, they told him 'that if he would not pray with them, they would not fight with him,'[1] and declined to follow him further. In Suffolk the deputy-lieutenants announced that the mutinous soldiers had threatened 'to murder them.' In the City of London, in Kent, Surrey, Essex, Herts, Buckinghamshire, and Bedfordshire, resistance to the levy was almost universal. On the 16th Northumberland complained that desertions were so numerous that scarcely half the numbers raised would appear at Selby.[2] Before long the Government and the country were startled by the news that an officer had been actually murdered by the Dorsetshire men at Faringdon. Lieutenant Mohun had given an order to the drummer. The boy refused to obey, and insolently raised his drumstick to strike him. Mohun drew his sword, and slashed at the drummer's wrist, almost slicing away his hand. The news quickly spread. Mohun was chased to his lodgings by the angry soldiers. His brains were dashed out with their clubs, and his

June 17. Murder of Lieutenant Mohun.

---

[1] J. Nicholas to Nicholas, June 1. Rossingham's *Newsletter*, June 8, S. P. Dom. cccclvi. 44.

[2] Deputy-Lieutenants of Suffolk to the Council, June 8, fol. 2. Northumberland to Conway, June 13, 16, *Ibid.* cccclvi. 45, 77; cccclvii. 5, 34.

body, after it had been dragged through the mire, was suspended to the pillory. The authors of the outrage dispersed in every direction. Many of them were subsequently captured and committed for trial, but the organisation of the force was hopelessly broken up.[1]

*CHAP. VIII.
1640.
June 17.*

Other regiments were nearly in as bad a condition. Lunsford complained that the Somersetshire men in his charge refused to obey his orders. "Divers of these," he wrote from Warwick, "in troops returned home, all in a forwardness to disband, and the counties rather to foment their dislikes than to assist in punishment or persuasions. Hues and cries work no effect. We want orders to raise the power of the countries, are daily assaulted by sometimes five hundred of them together, have hurt and killed some in our own defences, and are driven to keep together upon our guard."[2]

June 22. Desertion in Warwickshire.

Whilst the soldiers were thus breaking out into open mutiny, the Court of King's Bench, the great prop of Charles's government, was showing signs of uneasiness. When the counsel for Chambers, in his ship-money case, had been heard, Heath applied, on behalf of the defendant, to postpone his argument till after the Long Vacation, and the concession, though made by the Court, was only made with considerable hesitation. On another case of still greater importance, the judges were more peremptory. A Northamptonshire gentleman, named Pargiter, had been committed for refusing the payment of coat and conduct money. He applied for a writ of *habeas corpus*, and the Court, in accordance with the Petition

June 20. Case of Chambers.

Case of Pargiter.

The legality of coat and conduct money questioned.

---

[1] The Sheriff of Berks to the Council, June 20. Rossingham's *Newsletter*, June 23, *S. P. Dom.* ccclvii. 104.

[2] Lunsford to Northumberland, June 22, *S. P. Dom.* ccclvii. 91.

of Right, required that the cause of his committal should be signified. The counsel for the Crown asked for delay, and, though his request was not absolutely refused, he was told that cause must be shown before the end of the month.[1]

The difficulty of the Government.

This occurrence placed the Government in no slight difficulty. It seemed as if another monster trial, similar to that of Hampden, was inevitable. The lawyers of the Opposition would argue, with the sympathy of the nation again on their side, that coat and conduct money was an illegal exaction. The existing system was of such recent introduction, that this time the judges might possibly not be in favour of the Crown. It was certain that, whether the judges decided in favour of the Crown or not, very little money would be paid whilst their decision was pending. The prospect of meeting the Scots in the field with a sufficient army, bad as it was already, would be altogether at an end.

June 24. Proposed issue of Commissions of Array.

From this difficulty Charles was saved by his legal advisers. In the reign of Henry IV., it had been decided in Parliament that, when an invasion was impending, the King might issue Commissions of Array. All who were capable of bearing arms would be bound to march in person to the defence of the realm. Those who were incapacitated by age or infirmity would be bound to contribute both to the equipment of this force, and to its support till it passed the borders of the county in which it had been levied. After that, it would be taken into the King's pay.

The Attorney-General was therefore ordered to prepare such Commissions of Array. Not only had

---

[1] *Council Register*, May 22. Rossingham's *Newsletters*, June 16, 23, *S. P. Dom.* ccclvii. 36, 104.

Charles found a legal basis for the exaction which had been questioned, but he would be freed from the obligation of repaying the sums which had been expended in the counties.¹

There can be little doubt that this resolution was applauded by Strafford, who was now sufficiently recovered to take part in public affairs, though he did not sit in Council till some days later.² But, though he was glad to find that the law would cover strong measures, he was still of opinion that the crisis demanded strong measures whether the law would cover them or not. Conway, at Newcastle, was much vexed by Northumberland's anxiety to keep within the law. The Lord General had been especially alarmed by the intelligence that Conway had executed a mutineer by martial law. He consulted the lawyers, and the lawyers told him that both he and Conway must receive a pardon from the Crown if they wished to escape punishment.³ Conway complained to Strafford, as certain of his sympathy. How, he asked, could discipline be maintained on such conditions? A soldier was then in prison charged with a brutal murder. "If he be not executed by martial law, but that we turn him over to the law, it will utterly lose all respect and power. If martial law may be executed, let me know it; if it be not, and that the King cannot find a remedy for it, it will not be possible to keep the troops together." ⁴

---

¹ *Council Register*, June 24. *Rolls of Parliament*, iii. 526. Stubbs, *Const. Hist.* iii. 262.

² On July 5. Joachimi to the States General, July $\frac{15}{25}$, *Add. MSS.* 17,677, 2. fol. 216.

³ They held that martial law could still be exercised 'where an army is in a body drawn together and near an enemy,' which was not the case here.

⁴ Conway to Strafford, June 28, *S. P. Dom.* ccccli. 58.

Charles, as Strafford would have said, was lost by halting between Saul and David. He had neither the advantage of popular support nor of self-reliant dictatorship. In vain Conway pointed out the absolute necessity of fortifying Newcastle, and begged to be allowed to lay an imposition on the townsmen for the purpose. Northumberland hesitated in face of the obvious illegality of the proposal. It was, he said, a good work, but he doubted 'whether these distempered times' were 'proper for such a business.' "When all levies that have formerly been paid," he wrote to Conway, "are now generally refused, what hope is there of raising money by any such way till there come a fitter season? I will keep your proposition by me, and make use of it as I see occasion." The occasion never came till it was too late. To Northumberland, all the efforts made by his more warlike colleagues were hopeless from the first. "To your lordship," he went on to say, "I must confess that our wants and disorders are so great that I cannot devise how we should go on with our designs for this year. Most of the ways that we relied on for supplies of money have hitherto failed us, and for aught I know we are likely to become the most despised nation of Europe. To the regiments that are now rising we have, for want of money, been able to advance but fourteen days' pay, the rest must meet them on their march towards Selby, and for both horse and foot already in the North we can for the present send them but seven days' pay. We are gallant men, for this doth not at all discourage us. We yet make full account of conquering Scotland before many months pass."[1]

Amongst these gallant men who were not to be

[1] Northumberland to Conway, June 30, *S. P. Dom.* ccccli. 58.

discouraged was Windebank. To him all the disorder amongst the troops was but the work of a few evil-disposed persons in the higher ranks of society. "Some restiveness appears in some counties," he wrote, "in raising the forces, and sundry insolences are committed by the forces when they are levied, most of which have been redressed upon repair of the Lords Lieutenants in person to the counties, so that the people are not in themselves refractory, but when the Lords Lieutenants are well affected and diligent, the service succeeds without difficulty.'[1]

CHAP. VIII.
1640.
July 6.
Windebank's satisfaction.

The Secretary's optimism was not shared by Sir Jacob Astley, the veteran to whom was entrusted the task of receiving the recruits as they arrived at Selby. On July 9, he reported that 4,000 had then arrived, 'the arch knaves of the country.' He had only money enough to pay them for a week. Large numbers of them straggled over the country, beating their officers and the peasants. On the 11th, 2,000 more came in. Unless he had more money soon, he declared, the whole force would break up. The men came ill-clothed from their homes. Many had neither shoes nor stockings. The captains were constantly going to York to ask for money to pay their men, when they ought to have been drilling them, if they were ever to convert them into soldiers.

July 9. Astley's report.

July 11.

Whilst the English army was falling into a state of dissolution, the Scots were taking advantage of the time afforded them to master all resistance in the rear. This time the hand of the Committee of Estates was to fall heavily on the North. With them, as with Strafford, there was a firm resolve that all

The Scots determine to coerce the North.

---

[1] Windebank to Conway, July 6. Astley to Conway, July 9, 11, *S. P. Dom.* ccclix. 41, 64, 84.

VOL. I.   C C

should be done that power would permit. If the North could not be conciliated it must be coerced. Montrose's visionary notion that gentle treatment would avail must be laid aside.

This time the command of the force destined for the North was assigned to Monro, a rough soldier fresh from the school of violence which had been set up in Germany. On May 28 he joined the Earl Marischal at Aberdeen. The inhabitants were driven by military compulsion to sign the Covenant, those who refused being sent to Edinburgh as prisoners. A hundred and fifty of the stoutest men in the place were pressed into the army. The country around was subjected to visitation. The doors were broken open, the furniture was burnt, and the horses carried off.

The turn of the Gordons came in July. On the 5th Monro was in Strathbogie. Huntly had sought refuge in England, and his tenants paid the penalty. Their sheep and cattle were driven away, or restored only on payment of money, and heavy fines were imposed upon themselves. The unpaid soldiers lived at their ease at the expense of the inhabitants of the district.[1]

Further south, Argyle had his interests as a Highland chieftain to serve as well as his interests as a Covenanter. At Edinburgh he was the wily statesman directing every move of the game, whilst keeping himself studiously in the background, and not even taking a place in the Committee of Estates. In the Western Highlands he was the head of the Campbells, eager to push the authority of his family over an ever-widening circle of once independent clans. The character borne by the Campbells in the

[1] *Spalding*, i. 272–307. *Balfour*, ii. 381.

Highlands was not a good one. Their favourite tactics, it was said, had been to urge their neighbours to resistance against the king of the day, and then to obtain powers from the king to suppress the rebellion to their own profit. Each of the subdued clans was forced to forsake its own organisation, and to merge its very name in that of the Campbells.[1] The opportunity had now come for carrying out this process in the name not of the King but of the Covenant. Very few, if any, of the dwellers in those rugged glens cared for either King or Covenant. But where the influences of Argyle and Huntly met in the very centre of the Highlands, those who feared and detested Argyle were necessarily the partisans of Huntly and, in some sort, of the King.

The first act of the new Committee of Estates had been to issue to Argyle a commission of fire and sword against the Earl of Athol, the Earl of Airlie, and various Highland clans whom it was determined to reduce to submission. Argyle set out from Inverary on June 18, with a following of 4,000 Highlanders. Athol had but 1,200 to oppose to him. The two forces met near the spot on which Taymouth Castle now stands. Athol was inveigled by a promise of safe return to an interview with Argyle. Argyle tried to win him over by considerations of personal interest. He told him significantly that he had himself claims upon his lands, and that there had been a talk at the late Parliament of deposing the King, from which Athol was probably intended to infer that he might have a difficulty in making out his title to the satisfaction of a new and hostile Government. As Athol did not take the hint, he was seized, as Huntly had been seized the year before, and sent a prisoner

[1] Skene, *The Highlanders of Scotland*, i. 138.

CHAP. VIII.
1640.
July.
Airlie House capitulates to Montrose.

to Edinburgh, in defiance of the pledge given by his host.[1]

Argyle pushed on into Angus, the Forfarshire of modern geography. The Earl of Airlie was away with the King, but he had fortified his house, leaving it in the keeping of Lord Ogilvy, his eldest son. The news that Argyle and his dreaded Highlanders were on the march for the uplands which swell towards the Grampians from broad Strathmore struck terror into the hearts of Covenanter and anti-Covenanter. The gentry of Angus and Perthshire called on Montrose to provide a remedy. Montrose, it is true, had been one of those who had signed the terrible commission to Argyle.[2] But it was well understood that his heart was not with Argyle. He soon gathered the forces of the neighbourhood, obtained from Lord Ogilvy the surrender of the house, and placed in it a small garrison, to hold it for the Committee of Estates.

Argyle's ravages.

When Argyle arrived it seemed as if nothing remained to be done. The intervention of Montrose, however, goaded him into savage exasperation. He was too shrewd not to perceive that Montrose's policy of reconciling the King with the nation was thoroughly impracticable, and he had none of those generous instincts which lay at the root of Montrose's error. As Montrose was beyond his reach, he wreaked his vengeance on the property and tenants of the owner of the lands of Airlie. The 'bonnie house' was burnt to the ground. Another house belonging to the Earl of Airlie at Forthar shared the same fate. Plunder went hand in hand with destruction. The wild High-

---

[1] Sir T. Stewart's Deposition. Answers to J. Stewart's Deposition. Exoneration of Argyle. Napier's *Memorials of Montrose*, i. 257, 266; ii. 475.

[2] Commission, June 12, *Hist. MSS. Com. Rep.* iv. 491.

landers stripped the fields of sheep and cattle, and drove them off to stock the valleys of the Campbells in the West.¹

CHAP. VIII.
1640.

Having done his work on the edge of the Lowlands, Argyle turned his course homewards along the fringe of his own dominions. Braemar and Badenoch felt the terror of his coming. There was plundering and burning and slaying in those distant glens. The Camerons of Lochaber, on the other hand, were treated with special favour. They had grown weary of their dependence on Huntly, and were ready to transfer their allegiance to Argyle.²

July. Argyle in the Highlands.

For the immediate purposes of war, Scotland was now a realm at unity with itself. This time there was no risk of repeated diversions in the stricken North. In the South the Royalists were few and easily suppressed. The lands and houses of all who opposed the Covenant were taken by force. It was not long before Ettrick on the castled crag of Edinburgh was alone in upholding the banner of the King.

Condition of Scotland.

¹ *Gordon*, iii. 165. *Spalding*, i. 291. *Memorials of Montrose*, i. 256, 264, 330, 358. In a letter to Dugald Campbell, of Inverawe (*Notes and Queries*, 5th ser., ix. 364), Argyle gave the following instructions:—"See how ye can cast off the iron gates and windows, and take down the roof; and if ye find it will be longsome, ye shall fire it well, that so it may be destroyed. But you need not let know that ye have directions from me to fire it; only ye may say that ye have warrant to demolish it, and that to make the work short ye will fire it." This keeping back his own part in the matter is quite in character. I have not inserted Gordon's story about Argyle's expulsion of Lady Ogilvy from Forthar when near her lying-in, as it is stated in a letter from Patrick Drummond of Sept. 12 (*S. P. Dom.*) that Argyle accused Montrose of having suffered the lady to escape, which is inconsistent with Gordon's account.

² *Gordon*, iii. 163.

CHAPTER IX.

THE SCOTTISH INVASION.

CHAP. IX.
1640. June.
Argyle and Montrose.

STRONG for the present moment, Argyle was raising up enemies to give him trouble at some future day. His rival Montrose had one fatal weakness. The corner-stone of his policy was the chance that Charles would at last be frank and consistent. In reality, Charles was wavering from day to day. Before the end of June Hamilton had won him over to another attempt to conciliate Scotland. On the 27th Loudoun was set free and despatched with instructions which were vague enough in themselves, but which seem to have been explained to mean that Charles would now bind himself to carry out the Treaty of Berwick after the Scottish interpretation; and that, although he refused to acknowledge the validity of Acts of the late session, he would promise not to interpose his veto upon the Acts for the establishment of the Presbyterian Constitution, if they were presented to him in a regular manner. On the other hand, Loudoun was to do his best to prevail with his countrymen 'that the King's authority should not be entrenched upon nor diminished.'[1]

June 27. Liberation and mission of Loudoun.

As he passed through Durham, Loudoun gave out freely that he was carrying peace to Scotland.[2] When

---
[1] Instructions and Memorandum, June 26. Lanark to the Lords, June 26, *Burnet*, 170. Compare Giustinian's Despatch, July $\frac{3}{13}$, *Ven. Transcripts*.

[2] Duncon to Windebank, July 9, *S. P. Dom.* ccclix. 61.

he arrived in Edinburgh he found that the terms which he brought would no longer give satisfaction. The question which had come to an issue since he had been thrust into the Tower was whether or no the Parliament had the right of making laws in defiance of the King. On this the leaders declared themselves to have no intention of giving way.[1] During the first week in July, whilst Monro was harrying Strathbogie and Argyle was harrying Angus, Leslie was gathering the nucleus of an army, and preparing for the invasion of England.

A Scottish army could support itself, at least for a time, on taxes levied by the orders of the National Government, eked out by voluntary contributions and the confiscated property of the opponents of the Covenant. Charles had none of these resources. The Commissions of Array were now supported by fresh orders for the collection of coat and conduct money, and on July 5 the Attorney-General was directed to prosecute the Lord Mayor and Sheriffs for their neglect in the collection of this money. Some relief, indeed, had been obtained before the end of June by an advance made by the farmers of the customs of more than 44,000*l.*, and other loans obtained from officials and men of position had raised the sum obtained in this way to little less than 60,000*l.*[2] But the necessities of the army were too great to be permanently supplied thus, and if England was to be defended recourse must be had to one or other of those extraordinary measures which had been so often talked of.

The first plan attempted appears to have been

---

[1] The Lords, &c., to Lanark, July 7, *Burnet*, 172.
[2] Account of Loans, June 23, *Breviates of the receipt*.

CHAP. IX.
1640.
July 4.
Proposed seizure of bullion at the Tower.

suggested by Hamilton.[1] For some years the King had derived profit from a percentage upon the coinage of Spanish bullion, which he afterwards transported to Dunkirk. This bullion was now seized in the Tower, to the amount of 130,000*l*., on promise of repayment six months later.

July 6.
Protest of the Merchant Adventurers.

Such a blow startled every merchant in the City. Those who had money or stocks in foreign cities dreaded reprisals, which would put an end to commerce. The great Company of the Merchant Adventurers took the lead in protesting. They sent a deputation to call Strafford's attention to the mischiefs which were certain to result. Strafford told them bluntly that it was the fault of the City of London that the King had been brought to such a pass. The remonstrances of the merchants, however, were too well founded to be thus dealt with. The Council was told that if the King's faith were broken so flagrantly, all the profits which both he and his subjects had derived from making England the bullion-mart of Europe, would come to an end. At last a compromise was arrived at. The merchants agreed to lend the King 40,000*l*. on the security of the farmers of the customs, a security which they justly considered to be better than his own.[2]

July 11.
Proposed debasement of the coinage.

More than this was needed, and it was now proposed to find the necessary resources in a debasement of the coinage. The officers of the Mint were directed to produce shillings the real value of which would be

---

[1] The Spanish ambassadors give this as a rumour (Velada, Malvezzi, and Cardenas to the Cardinal Infant, July $\frac{18}{28}$, *Brussels MSS*. Sec. Esp. cclxxxv. fol. 32), but it is borne out by Strafford's disclaimer of having been the originator of the idea.

[2] *Rushw.* iii. 1,216. *Straf. Trial*, 589. Montreuil's Despatches, July $\frac{9}{15}$, $\frac{18}{28}$, *Bibl. Nat.* Fr. 15,995, fol. 97, 99. Salvetti's *Newsletter*, July $\frac{10}{20}$. Giustinian's Despatch, July $\frac{17}{27}$, *Ven. Transcripts*.

threepence each, and which were to bear as a motto in Latin the confident words, "Let God arise, let His enemies be scattered."[1] Of these coins the officers declared they would be at once able to turn out the nominal amount of 14,000*l.* a week, and after a little preparation they would be able to turn out 30,000*l.* a week. Strafford recommended that the soldiers should be paid, at least for some time, in good money, but that all other payments out of the Exchequer should be made in bad money.[2] As soon as the project was known there was a loud outcry. The citizens declared that nothing would induce them to accept the rubbish to which it pleased the King to give the name of shillings. The officers of the Mint asserted that their men would not work if their own wages were to be paid in the new coins. Strafford could but answer by threatening the workmen with the House of Correction. To the citizens he had already replied, by telling them that Frenchmen were worse dealt with than they, and that the King of France had recently sent round commissioners to search the books of the Paris merchants in order to levy contributions on them.[3]

Even in the Privy Council, the miserable scheme met with warm opposition. Sir Thomas Roe, who had recently been added to the Board, argued forcibly that it would be as disastrous to the Crown as to the people. Strafford had now ceased to have eyes for anything save the immediate present. He broke out into a rage, and rated Roe soundly for his meddling. The King announced that the debasement was unavoidable. The Attorney-General was directed to

[1] *Exurgat Deus, dissipentur inimici.*
[2] Notes of the proceedings in the Committee, July 11, *S. P. Dom.* ccclix. 77.
[3] *Rushw. Straf. Trial,* 596. Strafford here is described as sick, so that the question was probably first mooted earlier than it came openly forward.

draw up a proclamation on the subject, and orders were given to prepare the new dies at the Mint.¹

CHAP. IX. 1640. July 13. Northumberland's opinion.

Every day marked Strafford more clearly than before as the author or supporter of all violent and ill-considered actions. Men with less burning heat in the cause could see what he could not see. "The keeping of disorderly and new raised men," wrote Northumberland, whose languid interest in the struggle enabled him to cast his glances around him with the impartiality of a mere spectator, "and the coining of copper money, are shrewd signs that money is not so plentiful as it ought to be at the beginning of a war. . . . I pray God those that were the advisers of it do not approve themselves more ignorant in the ways of governing an army than they would seem to be."²

July 12. Murder of Lieutenant Eure.

The disorders of the men on the march were still continuing. On the 12th the Devon men halting at Wellington, in Somersetshire, murdered Lieutenant Eure, a Catholic officer, who refused to accompany them to church. The population of the town and neighbourhood sympathised with the perpetrators of the crime. Not a man would stir to arrest the murderers. Even the neighbouring magistrates gave no assistance. The appointment of Catholic officers had not been by any means the source of strength which Charles had expected it to be. An indefinable feeling of uneasiness and suspicion was spreading through the ranks of the ignorant peasants on whom Charles had rested his cause. At Daventry, five or six hundred Berkshire men broke out into mutiny. Some of them said they would not fight against the Gospel.

Mutiny at Daventry.

---

¹ Montreuil's Despatch, July $\frac{16}{26}$, *Bibl. Nat.* Fr. 15,995, fol. 99. *Rushw.* iii. 1,217. *Straf. Trials,* 591.

² Northumberland to Conway, July 13. Northumberland to Astley, July 14, *S. P. Dom.* cccclix. 97, cccclx. 3.

Others declared that they would not be commanded by Papists. The determination not to serve under Catholic officers threw whole regiments into disorder. In a force intended to serve under Hamilton on the east coast of Scotland, a full half of the officers were Catholics, and it was only by calling out the trained bands to seize the mutineers, and to thrust them into the House of Correction, that order was restored at all.[1]

Amongst men so ignorant and unruly it sometimes happened that a clever officer gained an ascendency which raised him above suspicion. Windebank's son heard that the men of his company had sworn to murder all Popish officers. He at once ordered them all to kneel down and sing psalms, told one of his subalterns to read some prayers, and ended the scene by serving out beer and cheap tobacco at his own expense. The plan was perfectly successful. "They all now," he wrote to his father, "swear that they will never leave me as long as they live, and indeed, I have not had one man run from me yet in this nine days' march; but other captains of our regiment which marched a week before us, are so fearful of their soldiers that they dare not march with them on the way; their soldiers having much threatened them, and have done much mischief in all places they come, by stealing and abusing every one, their officers daring not to correct them; but I thank God, I have all my men in so great obedience, that all the country as I go pray for me, saying they never met with so civil soldiers."[2]

---

[1] Gibson to Conway, July 14. Byron's relation, July 14. Byron to Conway, July 20. Deputy Lieutenants of Devon to the Council, July 21, *S. P. Dom.* ccclx. 5, 50, 52.

[2] F. Windebank to Windebank, July 19, *Ibid.* ccclx. 46.

CHAP.
IX.
___
1640.
July 11.
The King irresolute.

July 19.
News from Scotland.

July 23.
Cottington and Vane in the City.

The loan again refused.

The debasement of the coinage to proceed.

Under the evil news which came so thickly upon him, Charles's resolution waxed and waned from day to day,[1] whilst he was listening to counsellors of war or peace, as indignation or fear predominated in his mind. On the 19th news arrived from the North that the Scots contemplated the seizure of Newcastle. Once in possession of the collieries there, they would be able to dictate their own terms, as London could not endure the deprivation of the supply of coal.[2] Charles saw in this intelligence the means of working upon the Londoners through their interests. On the 22nd the Lord Mayor was ordered to summon a Common Council for the following day. On the 23rd Cottington and Vane appeared in the City, the bearers of a letter from the King, in which assurances were given that if the long-asked-for loan of 200,000*l.* were now agreed to, nothing more should be heard of the debasement of the coinage. Leaving the Common Council to discuss the demand, the Privy Councillors amused themselves by strolling through the Cloth Exchange at Blackwell Hall. The owners of cloth gathered quickly round them. They hoped, they said, that they were not to be compelled to sell, for copper, goods for which sterling silver had been paid. After a debate of an hour and a half Cottington and Vane were re-admitted, to be informed that the Common Council had no power to dispose of the money of the citizens.

Charles was highly displeased with the stiff-necked obstinacy of the City. He at once ordered the officers

---

[1] "Ad ogni modo provocata la M^{ta} sua dall' ardore della propria indignatione in vedersi ogni giorno più offesa da nuove cause, confusa nell' istessime risolutioni, viva piena di perplessità in appigliarsi all' ultimo partito, per non sapere il migliore." Rossetti to Barberini, $\frac{July\ 24}{Aug.\ 3}$, *R. O. Transcripts*.

[2] News from Scotland, July 17, *S. P. Dom.*

of the Mint to proceed with the coinage. A scheme was prepared by which it was hoped to obviate the worst consequences of that measure. For the sake of the poor, all payments below the value of half-a-crown were still to be made in good silver. One tenth of all payments above that sum were to be made in the new copper money. As soon as this arrangement was announced men engaged in business drily remarked that in that case there would be a general rise of 10 per cent. in their prices. Again, Charles hesitated, and the plan was once more thrown over for further consideration. He reaped all the unpopularity of his proposal without any of the advantages which he might have derived from prompt and unscrupulous action.[1]

Fresh efforts to obtain a loan from Spain.

Whilst Cottington and Vane were pleading to no purpose with the Londoners, Strafford was pleading equally in vain with the Spanish Ambassadors. Almost imploringly the proud and haughty minister adjured the Spaniards to come to his aid. If the proposed league and the consequent advance of 300,000*l*. was not at once to be obtained, would they not lend his master 150,000*l*. in his present straits, and defer the remainder till after the signature of the league? If even that was not to be had, he would content himself with 100,000*l*., half to be paid at the end of the month, and half three or four weeks later. He would give his personal security for its repayment in November. The Spaniards replied that they had no orders to lend the money, but added a general assurance of their master's goodwill, which can hardly have conveyed much satisfaction to Strafford.[2] Almost at the

---

[1] Rossingham's *Newsletter*, July 27, *S. P. Dom.* ccclxi. 32.

[2] Velada, Malvezzi, and Cardenas to Philip IV., $\frac{\text{July 23}}{\text{Aug. 7}}$, *Brussels MSS. Sec. Esp.* cclxxxv. fol. 47.

same time, Cottington was making application to the French Agent for a loan of 400,000*l.* It is hardly necessary to add that the request did not meet with a favourable reply.[1]

The Queen, too, had her share of disappointment; the reply to the request which had been made in her name, in the height of the tumults in May, arrived from Rome. The answer was plain enough. If Charles would become a Catholic, he should have both men and money. Six or eight thousand soldiers, who would serve the King to their last breath, would be sent in vessels which would arrive under the pretext of fetching alum. Unless he became a Catholic it was impossible to do anything for him.[2]

The complete failure to obtain money increased the difficulty of keeping order among the soldiers. So far had the distrust of the English army gone that it was seriously proposed to levy two regiments of Danish horse, and to bring them into England to keep order amongst the mutineers; and this project was only abandoned through the absolute impossibility of finding the money for the levy.[3]

If Danish soldiers were not to be had, at least the English officers might be empowered to execute martial law. "You may now hang with more authority," wrote Northumberland in forwarding these instructions to Conway; "but, to make all sure, a pardon must come at last." The whole expenditure on the forces, he added, till the end of October, would be 300,000*l.*, 'towards which we have not in cash nor in view above 20,000*l.* at the most. If some

---

[1] Montreuil's Despatch, $\frac{\text{July 30}}{\text{Aug. 9}}$, *Bibl. Nat.* Fr. 15,995, fol. 104.

[2] Barberini to Rossetti, June $\frac{29}{35}$. Rossetti to Barberini, $\frac{\text{July 31}}{\text{Aug. 10}}$, *R. O. Transcripts.*

[3] Giustinian's Despatch, $\frac{\text{July 24}}{\text{Aug. 3}}$, *Ven. Transcripts.* That this was so

speedy way be not found to get the rest presently, I do not think that I shall pass the Trent this year.'[1]

1640. July 25. Communion rails pulled down.

In the Eastern counties the unruliness of the soldiers assumed a new form. At Bocking the clergyman was so ill-advised as to attempt to propitiate the men by the gift of a barrel of beer and fifty shillings. They took his money and his beer, got drunk, and rushed into the church. There they pulled up the Communion rails, brought them out and made a bonfire with them in the street. In various other places in Essex, churches were invaded and the Communion rails pulled down. At Penfield, near Braintree, and at Icklington in Cambridgeshire, the minister was chased out of the parish.[2]

July 28. The Yorkshire petition.

At the back of this ill news came a great petition from the gentlemen of Yorkshire. Not only did they complain of the violence of the soldiery quartered amongst them, but they proceeded to say that the billeting of these men in their houses was a breach of the Petition of Right.

July 30. It is presented to the King.

The petition was presented to the King at Oatlands on the 30th. Strafford would have had it rejected as an act of mutiny in the face of approaching invasion.[3] His daring spirit never quailed, but he could no longer inspire his fellow-councillors with his

---

is shown by the instructions given on Aug. 6 by Christian IV. to his ambassadors Ulfield and Krabbe. They were to propose to Charles the cession of the Orkneys to Denmark, either for money or for hired soldiers, as Christian had heard from General King of Charles's wish to have soldiers from Denmark. When the ambassadors arrived it was too late, and they said nothing of the Orkneys, and Charles was equally silent about the soldiers. This information has been kindly communicated to me by Dr. Fredericia from the Copenhagen archives. See his *Danmarks ydre politiske Historie, 1635-1645,* p. 258.

[1] Northumberland to Conway, July 25, *S. P. Dom.* ccclxi. 16.

[2] Maynard to the Council, July 27. Warwick to Vane, July 27, *Ibid.* ccclxi. 23, 24.   [3] *Rushw.* iii. 1,214.

own audacity. To them the case, as well it might, seemed altogether desperate. Peace, they thought, must now be bought at any price. Roe, the opponent of the debasement of the coinage, was to carry the news to the City that negotiations were to be opened, and to ask once more for a loan, which it was fondly hoped would be readily granted, as the money was needed to pay off the soldiers and not for purposes of war. Roe went to Guildhall as he was bidden, but he went in vain. He was told that grants of money were matters for Parliaments, and not for the citizens of London. As for themselves they were quite unable to find the money, the Londonderry plantation having 'consumed their stocks.'[1]

If it was unlikely that the Londoners would place confidence in the honeyed words of the King now that he was in such desperate straits, it was still less likely that, after the experience of the pacification of Berwick, the Scots would reopen a negotiation which took no account of their present demands, and which, even if it gave them all for which they asked, might be subsequently explained away by the interpretation which it might please Charles to place upon his words. They had long ago made up their minds that a lasting peace could only be attained after an invasion of England, and that it would be necessary to come to an understanding not with the King alone, but with an English Parliament. Every piece of intelligence which reached them from the South must have convinced them that they had no longer, as in 1639, to fear a national resistance. The circumstances of the dissolution of the late Parliament had put an end to

---

[1] Rossingham's *Newsletter*, Aug. 4, *S. P. Dom.* ccclxiii. 33. Montreuil's Despatch. Aug. $\frac{8}{10}$, *Bibl. Nat.* Fr. 15,995, fol. 107. Giustinian's Despatch, Aug. $\frac{7}{17}$, *Ven. Transcripts.*

that. Personages of note and eminence had entered into communication with their commissioners, and had given them assurances, which they had no reason to doubt, that Parliament, if it met, would take up their cause, and would refuse to grant a sixpence to the King unless he consented to put an end to the war.[1] If nothing had passed since, the knowledge of the emptiness of the Exchequer, of the growing resistance to the various attempts which had been made to wring money from Englishmen, and of the mutinous temper in which the troops were marching northwards, must have convinced the Covenanting leaders that the time had now arrived in which they might strike hard without fear of consequences.

There can be little doubt, however, that secret communications had passed between the Scots and the English leaders. Before Loudoun had left London he had been in communication with Lord Savile, the son of Strafford's old rival, who had inherited the personal antipathies of his father, and whose hatred of Strafford placed him by the side of men of higher aims than his own. To him, as the recognised organ of the English malcontents, Johnston of Warriston addressed a letter on June 23, just at the moment when Leslie's army was first gathering at Leith. After expressing the not unnatural desire of the Scottish leaders for a definite understanding with the English nobility, it asked for an extension of the National Covenant in some form to England, in order that the Scots might distinguish friends from foes, and for a special engagement from some principal persons that they would join the invading army at its entrance

---

[1] The communications through Frost, noticed by Burnet (*Hist. of Own Times*, i. 27) seem to relate to the period before the Parliament.

CHAP. IX.
1640.
July 8.
Answer of the Peers.

into Northumberland, or would send money for its support. This letter passed through Loudoun's hands, and the answer was forwarded by Savile some days after the Scottish nobleman had set out on his return. It was signed by Bedford, Essex, Brooke, Warwick, Scrope, Mandeville, and himself. It contained a distinct refusal to commit a treasonable act, and an assurance that the English who had stood by their side in the last Parliament would stand by their side still in a legal and honourable way. Their enemies were one, their interest was one, their end was one, 'a free Parliament,' to try all offenders, and to settle religion and liberty. This letter failed to give satisfaction in Scotland. Nor was its deficiency likely to be supplied by an accompanying letter, full of the most unqualified offers of aid from Savile himself. The Scots pressed for an open declaration and engagement in their favour. In the end of July or the beginning of August, Savile sent them what they wanted. He forged the signatures of the Peers with such skill that, when the document was afterwards submitted to their inspection, they were unable to point out a single turn of the pen by which the forgery might have been detected.[1]

Aug.
Savile's forged engagement.

[1] I have probably surprised many of my readers by the facility with which I have accepted Oldmixon's letters (*Hist. of Engl.* 141) as genuine. Oldmixon's character for truthfulness stands so very low that historians have been quite satisfied to treat the letters as a forgery. The internal evidence of their authenticity is, however, very strong. The letters of Johnston, of the Peers, and of Savile are written in so distinct a style, and that style so evidently appropriate to the character and position of the writers, as to require in a forger a very high art indeed—art which there is nothing to lead us to suppose that Oldmixon possessed. The allusions to passing events cannot all be tested, but there is none which I have succeeded in testing which is incorrect. The prediction that the troops would be on the Borders on July 10 indeed anticipated reality by ten days; but this is just the mistake that Johnston was likely

Encouraged by these communications, Leslie had in July taken up his post in Choicelee Wood, about

CHAP. IX.
1640.
July.

to make, and which a skilful forger would avoid. On the other hand, the strongest evidence in favour of the letters is derived from the argument by which Disraeli satisfied himself of their supposititious character. He asks how Oldmixon came to place the seven names at the end of the Peers' letter when he assures us that those names were cut out from the original? My answer to this is that the letter which Oldmixon produces is not what he says it was. The story of cutting out the names is borrowed by him from Nalson (ii. 428). Now there can be no doubt what the paper described in Nalson really was. It was a declaration and engagement on the faith of which the Scots said they had invaded England, and which they said the English Lords had broken. The letter in Oldmixon contains no engagement which was not fulfilled. There can be no doubt, therefore, that the forged paper was a different one from that which he has printed, and that it contained a promise of actual assistance. Nalson's evidence is of the highest authority as being an extract from the *Memoirs* of the Earl of Manchester, who, as Lord Mandeville, was one of those whose signature was forged. On the hypothesis that the letters were Oldmixon's forgery, we have to face the enormous difficulty that, after producing letters so wonderfully deceptive as the others were, he did not take the precaution of forging one from the Peers which would bear the slightest resemblance to the description which he himself had given of it. On my hypothesis everything is easily explained. Oldmixon met with these letters either in the original or in copy. Being either careless or dishonest, or both, he was not content to give them simply for what they were, but must needs give them out for the lost engagement for which Charles had sought in vain. The dates, too, as we have them, support this view. The Peers' letter is said to have been sent off from Yorkshire on July 8, about ten days after Loudoun left London. Manchester in his *Memoirs* says that the engagement was sent after Loudoun had been released, and had been some few weeks in Scotland. I would add that Henry Darley, the reputed bearer, was in York on July 28, signing the Yorkshire Petition, and it would be likely enough that Savile was encouraged to the forgery by the temper of the signers of that petition. If so, Darley's journey would be, as I have suggested, in the end of July or the beginning of August. Further, Henry Darley was arrested by a warrant from Strafford, dated Sept. 20, and confined in York Castle till he was liberated by the Long Parliament (*Lords' Journals*, iv. 100. *Hist. MSS. Com. Rep.* iv. 30). The only piece of internal evidence against these letters is the reference to Lord Warriston, when he was not till later a Lord of Session. He was, however, a Scotch Laird, and a Scotch Laird might easily pass into a Lord in an English letter, his official title being that of Baron. My attention has been called by Lieut.-Col. Alexander Fergusson to the fact that John Napier, the inventor of logarithms,

four miles from Dunse.¹ He, too, had difficulty in obtaining money and provisions for his army, and for some weeks he was obliged to content himself with keeping a small force upon the Borders till supplies came in sufficient quantities to enable him to gather his whole army for the projected invasion. Nor were political divisions wanting to add to his distraction. The huge Committee of Estates was but a cumbrous substitute for government; and, as the prospect of a reconciliation with Charles melted into the distant future, the Covenanters can hardly be blamed for looking around for some temporary form of executive which would give unity of control to their action. Naturally the name of Argyle was uppermost in their thoughts, and plans were discussed, in some of which it was proposed to constitute him dictator of the whole country, whilst in others he was to rule with unlimited sway to the north of the Forth, whilst two other noblemen were to receive in charge the southern counties.

To such a scheme Montrose declared himself bitterly hostile. He was still under the delusion that it was possible to establish an orderly constitutional and Presbyterian government, with Charles at its head. Whether this notion were wise or foolish, it was shared, at least in theory, by a large majority of

whose position was exactly that of Johnston, calls himself on the title-page the Baro de Murchistoun, and he also tells me that he is informed on high authority that in charters of such estates it was customary even to use the word Dominus of the owner. Oldmixon calls Johnston Sir Archibald Johnston, Lord of Warriston, which is clearly an anticipation of his subsequent title. It may, therefore, be argued that the Lord Warriston in the letter is the result of Oldmixon's ignorance. Yet after all, Johnston was Lord of Warriston, not because he was a judge, but because he was proprietor of the estate. For Savile's acknowledgment of the forgery, see p. 437.

¹ Outside the wood is a spot marked as Camp Moor on the Ordnance Map.

his countrymen, and when he entered into a bond with eighteen other noblemen and gentlemen to protest against 'the particular and direct practising of a few,' and to defend the Covenant within the bounds of loyalty to Charles, he only said plainly what few of his countrymen would care openly to deny. This Bond of Cumbernauld, as it was called, took but a sentimental view of the position of affairs. But Scotland is a land in which sentiment is peculiarly strong, as long as it does not require the positive neglect of the hard facts of daily life. Amongst the signers of the Bond were such undoubted Covenanters as the Earl Marischal, who had been joined with Montrose in his attacks upon Aberdeen, the Earl of Mar, to whose keeping Stirling Castle had been safely trusted by the national Government, and Lord Almond, who was at that time second in command of the army destined for the invasion of England. The Bond itself was kept secret, but the feelings which prompted its signature were well known. In the face of this opposition it was impossible to persist in establishing a new Government, which would have shocked the conscience of the nation. It was arranged that half the Committee of Estates should remain at Edinburgh, whilst the other half should accompany the army to the field. It would be time enough to settle what the future constitution of Scotland was to be when the objects of the invasion had been attained. In the policy of the invasion itself both parties were agreed.[1]

The small numbers of the forces on the Borders, combined with the rumours of want of money, deceived the English commanders. Up to August 10 Conyers and Erneley from Berwick, and Conway from

<small>The English commanders do not expect an invasion.</small>

[1] Napier, *Memoirs of Montrose*, i. 262. *Memorials of Montrose*, i. 183, 254.

CHAP. IX.
1640.
Aug.

Newcastle, reported constantly that no invasion was to be expected, or that at most a mere foraging raid was intended.[1] At Court the truth was better understood. The Scottish nobility and clergy who had taken refuge there had friends in Scotland who took care to keep them properly informed of passing events.[2] But the knowledge of the danger did not make it any the easier to resist it. There was the old vacillation in Charles's mind. One day, orders were given to disband the regiments which had been told off to serve under Hamilton, because it was understood that the men would break out into mutiny rather than set foot on board ship. Another day orders were given to bring them back to their colours. The preparations for coinage of base money were suspended without being absolutely countermanded. A fresh attempt to obtain a loan from the City companies separately having broken down, the French and Dutch merchants residing in London were asked, with equal want of success, for a small loan of 20,000l.[3]

Vacillation at Court.

Strafford deserted.

Amidst all this welter of confusion Strafford felt the ground slipping away beneath his feet. To what purpose had he placed himself in the forefront of the battle, had bullied aldermen, and cried out for the enforcement of ship money and coat and conduct money, if none of the things which he recommended were really done? Except in himself 'thorough' was nowhere to be found. A bewildered king, a com-

---

[1] Conway to Northumberland, July 28. Conyers to Windebank, July 29. Conyers to Conway, Aug. 4. Erneley to Windebank, Aug. 5, *S. P. Dom.* ccccli. 58, cccclxi. 40, cccclxiii. 31, 39.

[2] Vane to Conway, Aug. 3, *Clar. St. P.* ii. 101.

[3] Northumberland to Conway, Aug. 11, *S. P. Dom.* cccclxiii. 71. Joachimi to the States General, Aug. $\frac{11}{21}$, *Add. MSS.* 17,677 Q. fol. 225.

mander-in-chief who had no heart for the war, officials who shrunk from the responsibility of illegal action —these were the instruments which he found to his hand at the time when, as he firmly believed, the whole future well-being of his country was at stake. Whatever was to be done he must do it alone in spite of Charles, if it could not be done otherwise. On one part of the world alone could he look with satisfaction. The Irish army was not mutinous and disorderly like the English peasants. The infantry was already at Carrickfergus. The cavalry had not yet gathered to its rendezvous, but it was ready to rise on a word from him. In the first week of August he had purposed to cross the Irish Sea.[1] Once in Ireland he would be free from the trammels of courtiers and the weakness of a man whom he had seen too closely to respect him as he had respected him from a distance. At least, that master had had no hesitation in giving him full power over his Irish force. With dangers gathering thickly around him in England the old idea of using that trusted soldiery to compel obedience elsewhere than in Scotland took formal shape in the patent by which the command was entrusted to Strafford. He was to be 'Captain-General over the army in Ireland, and of such in England as the King by his sign manual shall add thereunto, to resist all invasions and seditious attempts in England, Ireland, and Wales, and to be led into Scotland, there to invade, kill, and slay.' These troops he might conduct into 'any of the King's dominions with power to suppress rebellions or commotions within any of the three kingdoms or Wales.'[2]

The patent was indeed but a copy, with unimport-

[1] Wandesford to Ormond, Aug. 25, *Carte MSS.* i. 240.
[2] Abstract of Strafford's Patent, Aug. 3, *Carte MSS.* i. 220.

ant alterations, of the patent which had been granted to Northumberland.[1] But it can hardly be doubted that if need had arisen Strafford would have been ready to take advantage of its widest terms. Yet, what were soldiers without money? Once more, on the 8th, Strafford pressed the Spanish Ambassadors for an instant loan. His demand for 300,000*l.* had sunk to 100,000*l.* a fortnight before. Now he declared that he would be well content with 50,000*l.* If the Cardinal Infant would lend that, he should have the whole of the Irish Customs as his security. He would be allowed to levy 6,000 Irishmen for the Spanish service, and to hire twenty English ships to reinforce the Spanish fleet in the coming spring. The Ambassadors recommended the Cardinal Infant to comply with the request.[2] But events were hurrying on rapidly in England, and it might be too late before the answer came.

Into Strafford's inner soul during these distracting months it is impossible to penetrate. Save by fierce expressions of contempt, he never betrayed his chagrin. His hard destiny had yet to be fulfilled. He had built the edifice of his hopes on the shifting sand. He had misconceived the conditions of political life in the England of his day, and facts were already taking upon him their terrible revenge.

Not yet had the iron entered into his soul as it was to enter in the coming weeks. On August 10 Conway at last convinced himself that an invasion in force was imminent. Conway was a brave and tried soldier, but he was not the man to uphold a sinking State. Strafford, in his place, would have seized

---

[1] Strafford's Patent, Aug. 3, *Carte MSS.* i. 397.
[2] Velada, Malvezzi, and Cardenas to the Cardinal Infant, Aug. $\frac{8}{18}$, *Brussels MSS. Sec. Esp.* cclxxxv. fol. 149.

upon an authority which was not lawfully his, and, by threats and encouragements, would long ago have fortified Newcastle. Conway had remonstrated that the place was in danger, and when he was told that he could have no money for the fortifications, had quietly acquiesced in his helplessness. He now wrote a doleful letter to Northumberland. Newcastle, he said, was utterly indefensible. At the utmost it might be guarded for a day or two. He had written to Astley to send him men from Selby, but men without money would ruin the country worse than the Scots. He had also written to Sir Edward Osborne, Strafford's Vice-President of the Council of the North, to put the Yorkshire trained bands in readiness, and to inform him how the country and the gentry stood affected. With his scanty numbers it was impossible for him to do anything against a whole army.[1]

CHAP. IX.
1640.
Aug. 10.

Astley could do little to help. By the 11th 12,800 men had arrived at Selby, about half the number with which the Scots were preparing to cross the Tweed, and of these 3,000 were entirely unarmed. All depended on the supply of money. The week before there had been a mutiny for want of pay, and a soldier had been hanged by martial law. Osborne's reply was equally discouraging. The Yorkshire trained bands were completely disorganised. Arms which had been lost in the last campaign had never been replaced. Four colonelcies were vacant, and it was impossible to find men in the county fit to fill them 'who stood rightly affected as to his Majesty's service.' If the men were called out, the gentry would refuse to lead them out of their own county. "I am persuaded," wrote the Vice-President, "if Hannibal were at our gates some had

Aug. 11.
State of the forces in the North.

Aug. 14.
Feeling in Yorkshire.

[1] Conway to Northumberland, Aug. 10, *Clar. St. P.* ii. 102.

rather open them than keep him out. . . . I think the Scots had better advance a good way into Northumberland without resistance than we send this army to encounter them without pay; for then, without all question, they will prove more ravenous upon the country than the Scots, who, for their own ends and to gain a party here, I believe will give the country all the fair quarter that may be, which our men neither can nor will do."[1]

An invasion welcomed by a large part of his subjects, and regarded with indifference by the rest, such was the pass to which Charles had been brought by eleven years of wilful government. At Whitehall everything was in confusion. The attacks upon the Communion rails had spread from Essex to Hertfordshire. Laity and clergy were of one mind in protesting against the oath enjoined by the new canons. Everywhere there was lukewarmness and ill-will.[2] Northumberland vowed that if he was to take the command he would not go without money.[3] Now that it was too late, pressing orders were sent to Conway to fortify Newcastle by the forced labour of the townsmen.[4]

The coming of the Scots was preceded by two manifestoes—one in the shape of a broadside for popular distribution, the other as a small pamphlet for more leisurely perusal. The Scots protested that the matter must at last be brought to an issue. They could not afford to continue in arms during interminable negotiations. They were therefore coming

[1] Astley to Conway, Aug. 11, 13, *S. P. Dom.* cccclxiii. 73, 93. Osborne to Conway, Aug. 14, *Clar. St. P.* ii. 105.
[2] Salisbury to Windebank, Aug. 13. G. Beare to W. Beare, Aug. 13, *S. P. Dom.* cccclxiii. 90. 98.
[3] Montreuil's Despatch, Aug. $\frac{13}{23}$, *Bibl. Nat.* Fr. 15,995, fol. 109.
[4] Windebank to Conway, Aug. 14, *S. P. Dom.* cccclxiii. 99.

to England to obtain redress of grievances from the King. But, with all respectful language towards Charles, they made it clear that it was not from him but from a Parliament that they expected redress. The last Parliament had refused to assist him to make war on Scotland. The next one would bring to justice Laud and Strafford, the instigators of the evil policy which had been pursued, and would relegate the Scottish Councillors who had been guilty of a like fault to a trial in their own country by the laws of Scotland. The invading army would do no man any wrong, would shed no blood unless it were attacked, and would pay ready money for all the supplies which it consumed.[1]

CHAP. IX.
1640.
Aug. 14.

Charles's policy of using English forces against Scotland was recoiling on his own head. Both nations were alike sick of his misgovernment. The personal union of the Crowns would prove but a feeble link in comparison with the union of the peoples. The Scots had appealed from the English King to the English Parliament.

Appeal to Parliament.

Copies of the Scottish manifesto were circulated in London on the 12th.[2] Charles was never wanting in personal bravery. At a council held on the 16th, he announced his intention of going in person to York, to place himself at the head of his disordered army. He would listen to no objections. In vain Hamilton suggested that an army ill-affected and ill-paid might not be the better for the King's presence. In vain Holland asked whether the King would have any money when he arrived. In vain, too, Strafford, refusing to believe in the reality of the risk, and

Aug. 12.
The manifesto in London.
Aug. 16.
The King announces that he will go to York.

---

[1] Information from the Scottish nation, *Treaty of Ripon*, 70. The intentions of the army, *Spalding*, i. 321.

[2] Montreuil's Despatch, Aug. $\frac{12}{22}$. *Bibl. Nat. Fr.* 15,995, fol. 109.

thinking that a Scottish invasion would sting England into loyalty, declared that he was not satisfied that Newcastle was in danger, and that if the Scots came in 'it would not be the worse for his Majesty's service.' Charles rightly felt that the post of honour was in the North. Only by appearing in person could he prove the untruth of the statement in the Scottish manifesto that what had been done had been done by evil counsellors rather than by himself.[1]

Aug. 17. Answer to the Yorkshire Petition.

The next few days were spent in preparation. On the 17th a sharp answer was returned to the Yorkshire Petition,[2] criticising its inaccuracies, and explaining that the Petition of Right was never intended to do more than to enact that soldiers billeted should pay for the provisions they consumed.[3] This loose interpretation of the duties which he owed to his subjects did not prevent Charles from holding his subjects to the very letter of the law towards himself.

Aug. 19. The trained bands called out.
Aug. 20. Tenants in knight-service summoned.

On the 19th he issued orders to the Lords Lieutenants of the midland and northern counties to call out the trained bands for immediate service. On the 20th, he directed that all persons holding by knight-service should follow him to the field, as their tenures bound them to do, though he added that he was ready to accept fines in lieu of service.[4] The now familiar order to the sheriffs to pay-in the arrears of ship money was once more issued. To prevent further ill-feeling during the King's absence on the ground of the etcetera oath, Laud was directed to suspend its administration till October.[5]

[1] Minutes of Council, Aug. 16, *Hardw. St. P.* ii. 147.
[2] P. 399.
[3] Privy Council to the Council of York, Aug. 17, *S. P. Dom.* cccclxiv. 17.
[4] The King to the Lords Lieutenants of certain counties, Aug. 19, *S. P. Dom.* Proclamation, Aug. 20, *Rymer,* xx. 433.
[5] *Hardw. St. P.* ii. 151.

For the army thus hurriedly ordered to be got together it was now necessary to find a commander. Northumberland had always been hopeless of any good result, and his health had now broken down under the strain.[1] There was but one man capable of occupying the post. With the title of Lieutenant-General, Strafford was to be placed at the head of the English army. It was finally arranged that Hamilton's mutinous men should be disbanded.[2] The Irish army was to be left to shift for itself. The ruin in the North was to come under the hand of Strafford.

CHAP. IX.
1640. Aug. 20.
Strafford to command the English army.

Not that Strafford was in any way despondent. He utterly refused to believe that Newcastle was indefensible, or that the trained bands of the North would not rally to the King when once he was amongst them.[3]

On the morning of the 20th the King set out from London. That night the Scottish army, some 25,000 strong, crossed the Tweed at Coldstream. Montrose was the first to plunge into the river to lead the way.[4] Leaving the garrison of Berwick on their flank, the Scots pushed steadily on. They issued a proclamation assuring the men of Northumberland that they would not take a chicken or a pot of ale without paying for it. They brought with them cattle and sheep for their immediate necessities. Spectators who watched the blue-bonneted host as it passed, wondered at its discipline, and stared at the Highlanders with their bows and arrows. Strafford, when all military force appeared to be melting away, had

The King sets out. The Scots cross the Tweed.

---
[1] It has often been suspected that this illness was a feint to escape the responsibility of commanding, but the letters amongst the State Papers leave no doubt of its reality. See especially Garrard to Conway, Oct. 6, *S. P. Dom.*
[2] Windebank's Notes, Aug. 29, *S. P. Dom.* ccclxiv. 45.
[3] Strafford to Conway, Aug. 18, *Ibid.* ccclxiv. 27.
[4] *Baillie*, i. 256.

encouraged himself with the hope that an invasion would open the eyes of his countrymen in the North to the reality of their danger. In Northumberland, at least, no such result was visible. "They," wrote Conway of the Scots, "deal very subtily. They hurt no man in any kind, they pay for what they take, so that the country doth give them all the assistance it can. Many of the country gentlemen do come to them, entertain and feast them."[1] The calculated courtesy of the Scots was not without its exceptions. Estates of recusants, with the lands of the Bishop or the Chapter of Durham, were regarded as lawful prey, to which no mercy was to be shown.

In London, after the King had left, everything was in confusion. "We are here, and in every place," wrote Sir Nicholas Byron, "in such distraction as if the day of judgment were hourly expected."[2] Charles's system of government had not been such as to gather round him men capable of taking the initiative in moments of peril. The Council was at its wits' end. The City, once more applied to, persisted in its refusal of a loan.[3] At last an expedient was thought of which offered some relief for the immediate necessity. It was known that the East India Company had just received a large consignment of pepper. On the 22nd Cottington appeared before the Company, and offered to buy the whole at a price above that at which it was immediately saleable. The Company refused to deal with the King, but they agreed to accept the substantial securities of private persons for the payment of the money by instalments within a year. The general result was that by the end of the month

---

[1] Conyers to Conway, Aug. 21. Conway to Vane, Aug. 22, 26, *S. P. Dom.* ccclxiv. 60, 61, 84.

[2] Byron to Conway, Aug. 21, *S. P. Dom.* ccclxiv. 63.

[3] Windebank's Notes of Business, Aug. 22, *S. P. Dom.* ccclxiv. 45.

Cottington saw his way to the receipt of 50,000*l*., advanced upon interest at the rate of 16 per cent., about double the rate at which money was usually attainable.[1]

<small>CHAP. IX.
1640.
Aug. 22.</small>

It might well be doubted whether even this provision would arrive in time. When the King reached York on the 23rd, his first thought was to urge upon the Council his need of money. "Certainly," he wrote on the 27th, "if ye send us none or little, the rebels will beat us without striking a stroke."[2] Amidst the universal discouragement, Strafford's voice was alone raised in calm assurance. The actual invasion of the Scots, he said, was more to the King's advantage 'than should have been had we been the aggressors.' The English army, too, would be at Newcastle before the Scots, 'and so secure the place.'[3]

<small>Aug. 23.
The King at York.

Aug. 24.
Strafford's confidence.</small>

If Strafford was over-sanguine, his hopes were not entirely without foundation. The county of Durham offered to turn out its trained bands, and to send 2,000 men to defend the fords of the Tyne. On the 24th the King collected round him the lords and gentry of Yorkshire, and adjured them to form a second line of defence on the Tees. In the presence of their Sovereign the gentlemen of Yorkshire laid aside their grievances for a time, and offered to follow where he should lead, within the county, on the receipt of a fortnight's pay. "I must tell you," wrote Vane, "had not his Majesty been in person, I do not conceive it had been possible to have induced this county to have risen by any other means, so great was the distemper when his Majesty arrived here; and by

<small>The Durham and Yorkshire trained bands.</small>

---

[1] *E. I. C. Court Minutes*, Aug. 22, 26. Warrant, March? 1641, *S. P. Dom.*

[2] The King to Windebank, Aug. 23, 27, *Clar. St. P.* ii. 91, 92.

[3] Strafford to Cottington, Aug. 24, *S. P. Dom.* ccclxiv. 86.

CHAP. IX.
1640.
Aug. 24.

this you see that the person of a king is always worth 20,000 men at a pinch." Encouraged by the example of Yorkshire, Charles ordered that the nine counties lying nearest to the southern border of that county should be summoned to send their trained bands to the common defence.[1] In the meanwhile, the Council was not idle in London. So great did the danger appear, that they appointed Cottington Constable of the Tower, to prepare that fortress to stand a siege. Arundel was appointed Captain-General of all his Majesty's forces to the south of the Trent, and was directed to put into execution the Commission of Array, calling out a levy of all able-bodied men to the defence of the country.[2]

Time wanting to the King.

It was all too late. Time would in any case have been needed to weld these heterogeneous elements into a disciplined army, and time was not even allowed to unite the forces which Charles already had at his disposal. The Scots were hastening their march, in spite of the heavy rains which had soaked the roads and impeded their progress. Over the King's army there was no commander present, except himself. Strafford had been delayed by necessary preparations in London, and had been overtaken at Huntington by an attack of his old disease. In spite of failing health

Aug. 27. Strafford's appeal to Yorkshire.

he pushed on to the scene of duty. On the 27th he was at the King's side at York, adjuring the Yorkshire gentry to give up their demand of a fortnight's pay. They were bound by their allegiance, he said, to follow his Majesty to resist invasion at their own costs; ' bound,' he repeated, ' by the common law of England,

[1] Yorkshire Petition, Aug. 24, *Rushw.* iii. 1231. Vane to Windebank, Aug. 25, *S. P. Dom.* ccclxiv. 95.

[2] Windebank's Notes, Aug. 25, 26, *S. P. Dom.* ccclxiv. 94. Order for the Commission of Array, Aug. 26, *Rushw.* iii. 1,233.

by the law of nature, and by the law of reason.' They were no better than beasts if they now hung back.¹

Worn out by fatigue and disease, Strafford had made his last effort for a time. He would gladly have hurried to the front, but his bodily weakness chained him to York. Racked with pain, he sent off an impatient letter to Conway, bidding him to defend the passage of the Tyne at any cost.²

When Strafford's letter reached Conway, it found him in no mood to undertake anything heroic. Having been on the spot for some months, he had taken

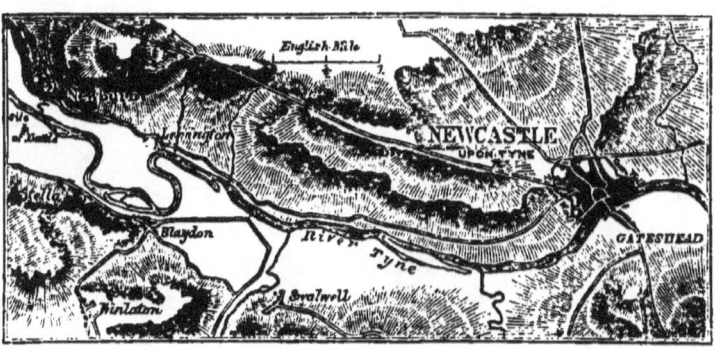

a truer measure of the military position. Astley had hurried up to Newcastle, and for some days the inhabitants had been labouring hard at the necessary fortifications. But there was no chance that the work would be completed before the Scots arrived. To meet the Scots in the field he was totally unprepared. It was true that by this time the two armies were about equal in numbers. But even if the composition of the two forces had been equal, the Royal army was too scattered to make resistance. Twelve thousand foot and five hundred horse were with the King at York. Ten thousand foot and two thousand

¹ Strafford's Speech, Aug. 27, *Rushw.* ii. 1,235.
² Strafford to Conway, Aug. 27, *Clar. St. P.* ii. 107.

horse were with Conway and Astley at Newcastle. If the Scots succeeded in crossing the Tyne not only would the English army be cut in two but, as Gateshead was still unfortified, Conway's troops at Newcastle would be entirely at the mercy of the enemy.[1]

Strafford's advice was the best possible under circumstances which admitted of none that was good. He recommended Conway to lead out the bulk of his force to stop the passage of the Tyne.[2] The suggestion reached Conway too late. Like most weak men, that officer was attempting to gain two incompatible objects at the same time. He divided his army into two parts. About two-thirds he left to garrison Newcastle, though he was perfectly aware that the town could not be defended on the south. With the other third, about 3,000 foot, and 1,500 horse,[3] he marched out on the evening of the 27th to hold the ford at Newburn, about four miles above Newcastle.

The Tyne at Newcastle is a tidal river, only passable at low water. Low tide on the 28th was between three and four in the afternoon, and as the Scots had not reached the spot on the preceding evening, Conway had some time to make his preparations. Not much that was effectual could be done. The river winds among flat meadows which lie between steep banks rising up at the distance of about half a mile from one another. Any force placed to defend the ford would, therefore, be commanded by the northern height, which at this place slopes down to the water's edge. Yet simply, it would seem, to

---

[1] Conway to Vane, Aug. 26, *S. P. Dom.* cccclxv. 3.

[2] Strafford to Conway, Aug. 27, *Ibid.* cccclxv. 10. In the *Clar. St. P.* ii. 108, the force of the advice is lost by the number of the foot which Strafford wished to see Conway take with him being misprinted as 800 instead of 8,000.

[3] The numbers are variously given.

avoid the charge of cowardice, Conway prepared to defend with inadequate means, an indefensible position.¹ He threw up two small works, one close to the river, the other a little in the rear. In each of these he placed 400 men and four guns, whilst he drew up his horse at a small distance to the eastward, to be ready to charge the Scots after they reached the shore in confusion. His headquarters were at Stella, on the top of the southern height, where the remainder of his men were kept in reserve.

CHAP IX.
1640.
Aug. 28.

When the Scots arrived they occupied themselves with planting cannon in a commanding position. The English were the first to fire, but they could do but little damage from the low ground. For three hours their guns were unanswered. Then, when the tide was running low, the Scottish ordnance began to play upon the enemy. The English bulwarks gave Conway's soldiers but little defence against the plunging shot. The raw troops, who had never before seen a gun fired in anger, began to murmur against their officers. Why, they asked, had they been kept there night and day? Why had not men come from Newcastle to relieve them? At last a shot struck to the ground some of the defenders of the nearest work. The rest threw down their arms and fled.² The men in the

The Scots cross the ford.

---

¹ I do not think it is presumptuous in one without military knowledge to speak strongly on this point. In the summer of 1880 I visited the spot, and the impossibility of resistance appeared to me to be evident even to the most unpractised eye.

² Dr. Burton (*Hist. of Scotl.* vii. 109) quotes Conway as saying in his Narrative that 'the soldiers were unacquainted with the cannon,' and interprets this as meaning that 'they were not aware of their existence till they opened fire.' Conway's words, as given in the *Clar. St. P.*, are: 'the soldiers were *new*, unacquainted with the cannon,' meaning that they had never been under fire before. Conway's discretion in posting his men in such a place cannot be saved on the plea that he did not know that the Scots had cannon. The reports of the spies in the *State Papers* prove the contrary.

other work soon followed their example. By this time the Scots had begun to cross the river. Their horse charged the English cavalry, and drove it off the level ground. Astley did his best to rally his men at the top of the hill; the Scots followed them there, and charged once more, with Leslie in person at their head. The English horse broke and fled, leaving some of their officers as prisoners in the hands of the enemy. They did not draw rein till they reached Durham. The infantry fell back on Newcastle.[1]

To remain at Newcastle was to be caught in a trap. Early in the morning of the 29th, therefore, Conway and Astley marched out with all their force, leaving the town to its fate. Before many hours had passed, Sir William Douglas presented himself at the gate with the usual promises of good treatment. His countrymen, he said, had come to petition for their religion, their laws, and their liberties; but they had brought with them a sword to defend themselves against all who might attempt to hinder them from reaching the King. They were ready to pay for all that they consumed. The next morning Newcastle was occupied in force by the Scots. They seized the King's Custom House, and took for their own use the stores which had been abandoned by the retreating army.[2]

On the night of the 30th, Conway, having rejoined his fugitive horse, arrived with his whole force at Darlington. Strafford, who was there to receive them, wrote cheerfully to the King.[3] To his bosom friend, Sir George Radcliffe, he poured forth a wail of despair. "Pity me," he wrote from Northallerton, to

---

[1] *Rushw.* iii. 1236. *Balfour*, ii. 384. *Baillie*, i. 256. Conway's Narrative, *Clar. St. P.* ii. 108. Vane to Windebank, Aug. 29, *S. P. Dom.* ccclxv. 38. Dymock to Windebank, Sept. 10, *S. P. Dom.*

[2] Narrative of the Scots' entry, Aug. 29, *S. P. Dom.* ccclxv. 50, i.

[3] Strafford to the King, Aug. 30, *S. P. Dom.* ccclxv. 49.

which place he had gone, to put himself at the head of Conway's men, "for never came any man to so lost a business. The army altogether necessitous and unprovided of all necessaries. That part which I bring now with me from Durham, the worst I ever saw. Our horse all cowardly; the country from Berwick to York in the power of the Scots; an universal affright in all; a general disaffection to the King's service, none sensible of his dishonour. In one word, here alone to fight with all these evils, without any one to help. God of his goodness deliver me out of this the greatest evil of my life."[1]

CHAP. IX.
1640.
Aug. 30.

Strafford spoke truly. Not the scaffold and the raging crowd, thirsting for his blood, were the worst of evils. In the inexplicable and utter failure of hopes conceived with a lofty purpose, lies the tragedy of life to him who cannot humbly bend beneath the stroke, and ask, in all seriousness of purpose, whether the work which had for long years seemed to him so lofty and heroic were, indeed, other than a fabric of his own self-will.

Strafford soon took heart again. But for the temper of the soldiers, the mere military position was even better than it had been before the rout at Newburn. There was no longer a danger of an interruption of the communication between the two divisions of the army. The Scots, indeed, had pushed on to Durham, and occupied the line of the Tees. From Durham there had been a sudden flight of the cathedral clergy, the Scottish Dean, Dr. Balcanqual, who knew himself to be specially obnoxious to the invaders, as the author of the Large Declaration, being foremost in the hasty exodus, so that far into the next century the Durham boys were in the habit of greet-

[1] Strafford to Radcliffe, Sept. 1, Whitaker's *Life of Radcliffe*, 203.

ing a breathless fugitive with scornful cries of "Run away Dr. Boconcky."[1] But the flight of a few dignitaries of the Church could not affect the military position. The King was concentrating his forces at York, and whether he advanced to Conway, or summoned him to his assistance, the united armies would be about equal in number to that of the invaders.

Unhappily for Charles it was very far from being a question of numbers alone. The army was without heart or discipline. The nation was equally without heart or discipline. There was a widespread conviction that the cause of the invaders was the cause of the invaded as well. "I must tell you," wrote Vane to Windebank, "it is strange to see how Leslie steals the hearts of the people in these northern parts. You shall do well to think of timely remedies to be applied, lest the disease grow incurable, for I apprehend you are not much better in the South." A postscript added the alarming news that Leslie had already quitted Newcastle, and was pushing farther on in pursuit.[2]

Already the Committee to which the government had been entrusted during the King's absence, was at its wits' end. Information was brought that Essex, Warwick, Bedford and his son Russell, Saye, Brooke, Pym, and Hampden, were in close conference in London. Such a gathering boded no good to the tranquillity of the Government. Yet the Committee did not dare to attack them openly, to make them smart for it, as Strafford had said of these very men in his speech after the dissolution. Neither could they resolve to let them alone. They weakly sent

---

[1] My friend, Professor Hales, pointed out to me this anecdote in Surtees' *History of Durham*.

[2] Vane to Windebank, Aug. 30, *Hardw. St. P.* ii. 164.

Arundel to Bedford to recommend him 'as of himself' to go back to his duties as Lord Lieutenant of his own county, and they suggested to Essex, through one of his friends, that it would be well for him to offer his services to the King. The Queen, too, agreed to write him a civil letter to the same effect. Anything more that his Majesty might suggest, they were ready to do.[1]

CHAP. IX.
1640.

Not by such means as this was Charles's authority to be made good. The Peers and Commoners who met in London, were but taking the step which they had always intended to take. In the letter forwarded by Savile in July, they had engaged to support the Scottish advance by a demand for a Parliament. That demand they now put into shape. On the 28th, the day of the rout at Newburn, a petition was signed, which was probably only a copy with slight alterations of the Remonstrance, to avoid the presentation of which the Short Parliament had been dissolved. It ran over the grievances of the military charges, of the rapine caused by disorderly soldiers, of the innovations in religion, of the increase of Popery and the employment of Recusants in military commands, of the dangerous employment of Irish and foreign forces,[2] of the urging of ship money, of the growth of monopolies, and the intermissions of Parliament. They then turned to the remedies. They asked that a Parliament might be summoned in which the authors and counsellors of their grievances might be brought to trial, and that negotiation might be opened for a peace with the Scots, in order that both kingdoms might be united 'against the common enemy of their reformed religion.'

The Opposition meeting.

Aug. 28. Petition of the Peers.

[1] Windebank to the King, Aug. 31, *Clar. St. P.* ii. 94.
[2] Probably alluding to the Danish contingent, which was talked of then and later. See p. 398.

The addition of the demand for the punishment of his advisers was all that the King had gained by his rejection of the terms of the Short Parliament. The petition as it stands was doubtless the handiwork of Pym; but Pym's signature was not affixed to it. By customary usage the Peers were regarded as the born counsellors of the King, and it was in that character that twelve Peers now approached the throne. To the names of six of the signatories of the letter to the Scots—Bedford, Essex, Brooke, Warwick, Saye, and Mandeville—were added those of Exeter, Hertford, Rutland, Mulgrave, Howard of Escrick, and Bolingbroke.[1] Behind these names was England itself.

Before the petition was made known, Charles had sent to his Council in London for its advice as to the steps to be taken if the Scots should disregard his shattered army and march upon London.[2] Already, before the request arrived, the Council had come to the conclusion that it was itself too weak for the burden thrust upon it. An army there must be in the South to second the efforts of the King. But where were officers to command it or money to pay it? The idea suggested itself that, as the Peers had supported Charles against the Commons in the last Parliament, they might still be found on his side. It was asked whether some of the noblemen might not be won over if they were called to share in the deliberations of the Council.

The next day, when Charles's missive arrived, the notion developed itself further. The idea that it was possible to raise money any longer by preroga-

---

[1] Petition of the Peers, Aug. 28, *S. P. Dom.* ccclxv. 16. The copy in Rushworth, which, as Ranke has pointed out, is incorrectly printed, contains the names of Bristol and Paget in the place of those of Exeter and Rutland.

[2] Vane to Windebank, Sept. 1, *S. P. Dom.*

tive was only mentioned to be rejected. Manchester suggested that not merely a few peers but all should be summoned. They were the born counsellors of the King. In the reign of Edward III., such an assembly, the Great Council of the Lords, had assisted the King with large sums of money without any Parliament at all. Shrewder members of the Council urged that it would be as easy to summon Parliament at once as it would be to summon the Peers, and that the former alternative would be far more useful. But it was something to put off the evil day for a season, and a formal recommendation was forwarded to Charles to summon the Peers to meet in London as soon as possible.¹ So out of heart were the Councillors now, that they were already taking measures for strengthening the fortifications of Portsmouth as a last place of refuge for the King.²

Charles did not as yet share in the terrors of his Council. He still believed it to be possible to rally the kingdom round him. "Tell the Earl Marshal and all the Council," he wrote to Windebank, "that we here preach the doctrine of serving the King, every one upon his charge, for the defence of the realm, which I assure you is taken as canonical here in Yorkshire; and I see no reason why you of my Council should not make it be so understood there."³ His confidence was not entirely without foundation. The Yorkshire trained bands were moving at last. One regiment marched into York on the evening of the 3rd, and the greater part of the remainder was expected on the following day. Vane was once more in good spirits. "We shall have a gallant army," he

---
¹ Memorial of the Council, Sept. 2, *Hardw. St. P.* ii. 168. Observations of the Council, Sept. 3, *S. P. Dom.*
² Windebank's Notes, Sept. 2, *Ibid.*
³ The King's Notes, Sept. 2, *Clar. St. P.* ii. 96.

wrote. "God send us hearts to fight. We shall have horse and foot sufficient." It was for Juxon and Cottington to provide them in good time with money and provisions.[1]

It was the last thing that Juxon and Cottington were capable of doing. The truth of his weakness was to be brought home to Charles through the emptiness of his Exchequer. In the meanwhile he had to bend his ear to voices to which he was unaccustomed. On the 4th, after the occupation of Durham, the Scots sent in a supplication, couched in the usual humble terms, asking that their grievances might be redressed with the advice of an English Parliament.[2] Almost at the same time, Mandeville and Howard arrived from London with the petition of the twelve Peers.

Whilst the King's Council was debating on the answer to be given to demands which, coming from such opposite quarters, seemed to be concerted together, Windebank's messenger arrived with the news that the Council in London recommended the summoning of the Peers. It was at once received as the only possible solution of the difficulty. Very likely Charles only regarded it as a means of gaining time. Lanark, Hamilton's brother, who was now Secretary for Scotland, was ordered to announce to the Scots that the King had summoned the Peers to meet at York on September 24. But if they would express their demands more particularly, he would, by the advice of the Lords, give a fitting answer, and, in the meantime, he expected the Scots to advance no farther.[3] The twelve Peers were

[1] Vane to Windebank, Sept. 3, *Clar. St. P.* ii. 98.
[2] Petition of the Scots, Sept. 4, *Rushw.* iii. 1,255.
[3] Lanark's Reply, Sept. 5, *Ibid.* 1,256.

expected to be contented with a similar reference to a meeting of the Great Council.

It was not likely that they would be well pleased with so long a delay. In all outward form the petition was addressed to the King by twelve Peers, and by them alone. Care was now taken that copies should be distributed in London. One of these fell into Manchester's hands, and Manchester carried it to the Council.

There can be little doubt that the publication of the petition was the work of Pym. The force which popular support had given to the Scottish Covenanters had not been lost upon him. Earlier Parliaments had been wrecked because they had confined themselves to Parliamentary procedure. The echo of their debates had hardly reached the popular ear. Resolutions confined to the journals of the Houses could be torn out by the King. Documents prepared by committees could be seized and burnt. What was needed now was to bring the House of Commons into living connection with the wave of feeling which tossed outside its walls. In the Short Parliament Pym had stood forth as the leader of the Commons. He was now to stand forth as the popular agitator as well.

Two of the Peers, Hertford and Bedford, went boldly before the Council, and asked the Councillors to join with them in signing the petition. The Councillors naturally refused to do anything of the kind. It was very strange, said Arundel, that they should 'desire the Scots to join in the reformation of religion.' The two lords were asked whether they knew of any Covenant like that of Scotland in England. They asserted that they knew of none. They declared that the Council of Peers could grant no money. Nothing but a Parliament could give

CHAP. IX.

1640. Sept. 6.

Copies of the Petition spread abroad.

Popular support sought.

Sept. 7. Hertford and Bedford before the Council.

CHAP. IX.
1640.

Sept. 9.
The King's
feelings.

Sept. 11.
Demands
of the Scots
discussed.

The Scots
demand a
contribution.

satisfaction. As for the petition, it was not theirs alone. It was supported by 'many other noblemen and most of the gentry.'[1]

Far away in the North, the King hardly yet felt the force of the tide which was running against him. His chief pre-occupation was the difficulty of finding money. "I see," he wrote to his ministers on their refusal to meddle further with the debasement of the coinage, "ye are all so frightened ye can resolve on nothing."[2] It was evident now that money was only to be had by the goodwill of his subjects. But at York it seemed not altogether impossible that the subjects would now see their true interests. On the 11th, the Council was summoned to consider the answer to be given to the Scottish demands, which had at last arrived, and which formulated, more clearly than before, the expectation of the invaders, that all the Acts of the last session would be accepted and the persons named as incendiaries be delivered for trial.[3] The message, galling as it was to the King, was accompanied by news which raised his hopes. The money which the Scots had brought with them was already exhausted. The assurance that they would pay their way had held good till they had gained their object. They now informed the magistrates of the two counties of Northumberland and Durham, together with the magistrates of Newcastle, that it was for them to support the invading army, at the cost of 850*l*. a day. Tenants of the Bishop and Chapter were forced to pay rents by anticipation to the Scottish commanders.[4] Deserted

---

[1] Windebank's Notes, Sept. 7, *Treaty of Ripon*, 79. Windebank to the King, Sept. 7, *Clar. St. P.* ii. 110.
[2] The King's Notes, Sept. 9, *Clar. St. P.* ii. 112.
[3] The Scots to Lanark, Sept. 8, *Rushw.* iii. 1,258.
[4] Petition of Tenants, *Rushw.* iii. 1,272.

houses were freely plundered, but those who remained at home and paid the contribution, suffered nothing.¹

CHAP. IX.
1640.

Such news was worth much to the King's cause in Yorkshire. Strafford's expectation that Englishmen would rally round the King when they once understood what a Scottish invasion was, seemed destined to be realised. On the 10th the King had held a review of the army. In the eyes of Vane it was all that could be desired. "Braver bodies of men and better clad," he wrote, "have I not seen anywhere, for the foot. For the horse, they are such as no man that sees them, by their outward appearance, but will judge them able to stand and encounter with any whatsoever." What was better still, the Yorkshire trained bands did not now stand alone. The counties of Nottingham and Derby were ready to send their men as soon as they were bidden, and some of their horse had already come in. Leicestershire was equally prepared. Stafford and Lincoln still held back, but hopes were entertained that they would not be wanting. It was evident that the men of central England were unwilling to become tributary to a Scottish army.²

Sept. 10.
The review at York.

Encouraged by these demonstrations of returning loyalty, Charles sent a short answer to the Scots, referring them to the Council of Peers for their answer, and demanding the immediate delivery of the prisoners taken at Newburn.³

Answer to the Scots.

Charles, however, was not out of his difficulty. His army cost him 40,000*l*. a month, and he himself acknowledged that he would be undone unless he had

Want of money.

¹ Vane to Windebank, Sept. 16, *Hardw. St. P.* ii. 180.
² Vane to Windebank, Sept. 10, *S. P. Dom.* Sept. 11. *Hardw. St. P.* ii. 172. Newport to Nicholas, Sept. 11, *S. P. Dom.*
³ Lanark to the Scots, Sept. 11, *Balfour*, ii. 402.

two months' pay secured.¹ There was still uncertainty whether the Yorkshire gentlemen would take the pay of their trained bands on themselves. They drew up a petition demanding a Parliament. Strafford called them together again, obtained the rejection of the petition, and a direct offer to support their trained bands till the meeting of the Great Council. Strafford took them at once to the King. Charles received them most affably, and told them that in future he would require no more from them than 6,000 men instead of 12,000, that he would excuse them from the obligation of scutage, and that the heirs of those who might be killed in his cause should be freed from the claims of the Court of Wards.

So far had Strafford succeeded. Charles was not slow in acknowledging his obligation. On the day on which the offer of the Yorkshiremen was made he held a special chapter of the Order of the Garter, and invested the Lord Lieutenant with the blue riband.²

What were Strafford's hopes and fears at this conjuncture we shall never know. Probably he hoped to deal with the Peers and even with the Parliament, which he must have foreseen to be inevitable, as he had dealt with the gentlemen of York. The Scottish invasion would drive them to rally round the throne, Charles would come forward with graceful concessions, and the old harmony of the Elizabethan government would be restored.³

¹ The King's Notes, Sept. 11, *Clar. St. P.* ii. 114.
² Vane to Windebank, Sept. 13, 14, *Hardw. St. P.* ii. 176, 177. Rushworth's statement (iii. 1,265) that the Yorkshiremen insisted on retaining their demands for the summoning of Parliament is refuted by this evidence.
³ There is a noteworthy echo of the hopefulness which at this time prevailed at York in a letter from Pocklington to Lambe, Sept. 14, *S. P. Dom.*

But for the strength of Puritanism it is possible that he would not have calculated amiss. Of the living force of religious zeal he had no understanding. It had little place amongst his neighbours in the North.

CHAP. IX.
1640.
Sept. 13.

In the South, where the danger was less pressing, there was none of that revival of loyalty which had so unexpectedly arisen. In London especially, the progress of the Scots was regarded as a national triumph. When the news of Conway's rout arrived it was received with every demonstration of joy.[1] Placards were set up calling on the apprentices to rise for the reformation of religion, 'which, in plain English,' as Windebank explained, 'is the defacing of churches.' The Lord Mayor and Aldermen, however, had no intention of allowing a repetition of the riots of the preceding spring, and the attempt was promptly suppressed.[2] The Scots hastened to relieve the citizens from any fear that their material interests would be affected, by assuring them that the all-important coal trade should remain open as before.[3] The Council soon heard with alarm that a petition, not very dissimilar from that of the twelve Peers, was circulating in the City, and had already received numerous signatures. They at once ordered the Lord Mayor and Aldermen to put a stop to the scandal. But their efforts were entirely fruitless, and they found that the clergy had a petition of their own in preparation as well. They could think of nothing better than to recommend the King to imprison the bearers of both petitions as soon as they arrived at York. Charles was already growing impatient of the weakness of his

Feeling in London.

The London petition.

Petition of the clergy.

Sept. 18.

[1] Giustinian's Despatch, Sept. $\frac{4}{14}$, *Ven. Transcripts.*
[2] Windebank to the King, Sept. 7, *Clar. St. P.* ii. 113.
[3] The Scots to the Lord Mayor, Sept. 8, *Rushw.* iii. 1,259.

Ministers. "I could wish," he wrote on the margin of Windebank's despatch, "ye would show as much stoutness there as ye council me to here."¹

These tidings from the South were overwhelmingly convincing of the necessity of summoning Parliament. Yet Charles hesitated long. "Notwithstanding the Lords of the Council's advice for a Parliament," wrote Vane on the 18th, "I do not find in his Majesty yet any certain resolution for the same."²

There was one man, however, by his side who was now ready to persuade him that resistance was hopeless. Hamilton had no wish to be given up to his countrymen to be prosecuted as an incendiary. He begged the King to allow him to leave the country. He had urged Strafford and Laud, he said, to do the same thing, 'but the earl was too great-hearted to fear, and he doubted the other was too bold to fly.' One way, indeed, remained more dishonourable than flight, and that was one to which Hamilton had lowered himself in the preceding year. He might betake himself to Charles's opponents, might speak their words and accept their principles, in order that he might betray their counsels to the King. This was the service which Hamilton proffered, and which Charles accepted with gladness.³

Whatever might be the result of Hamilton's intrigue, his despondency could not fail to make an impression on Charles. It could make no real difference in the position that a party of Scotch horse which had come plundering into Yorkshire was captured or slain almost to a man.⁴ The news from

¹ The King's Notes, Sept. 20, *Clar. St. P.* ii. 117.
² Vane to Windebank, Sept. 18, *Hardw. St. P.* ii. 181.
³ *Clarendon*, i. 218. Mr. Disraeli's suggestion that this story is but a repetition of an earlier one seems to me unsatisfactory.
⁴ Vane to Windebank, Sept. 20, *Hardw. St. P.* ii. 183.

Scotland was most depressing. Dumbarton had surrendered on August 29. On September 15 Ettrick's garrison, wasted by scurvy caused by the failing of fresh water, gave up the Castle of Edinburgh. Feeble and tottering, the brave defenders of the fortress stepped forth with drums beating and colours flying. Their resolute bravery was no commendation in the eyes of the populace of Edinburgh. But for a guard of soldiers, which had been providently assigned to them, they would have been torn in pieces long before they reached Leith.[1] A few days later Nithsdale's fortified mansion of Caerlaverock was taken by the Covenanters. The National Government was supreme from north to south.[2]

The news of the loss of Edinburgh Castle was known to the King on the 22nd. On that day the London petition was presented to him. It bore the signatures of four aldermen and of ten thousand citizens. The Councillors in London were bidden to abandon the thought of imprisoning either the organisers of this petition, or Burgess, by whom the petition of the clergy had been conveyed to York.[3]

It was impossible longer to resist the universal cry for a Parliament. Even if Charles had remained deaf to the wishes of his subjects, his financial distress would have been decisive. The pepper-money would support his army for a few weeks longer, and then the catastrophe would surely come. He would be as powerless to hold his forces together in Yorkshire as he had been powerless to hold them together in Northumberland the year before.

[1] *Balfour*, ii. 403. Drummond to Hog, Oct. 3, *S. P. Dom.*
[2] *Baillie*, i. 258. A story of the massacre of the garrison was circulated in England, but was soon contradicted.
[3] Vane to Windebank, Sept. 22, *Hardw. St. P.* ii. 184.

1640.
Sept. 24.
The King's speech to the Great Council.

On the 24th the Great Council met in the hall of the Deanery at York. The King's speech gave clear evidence of the distraction of his mind. He had called the Peers together, he said, that by their advice he might proceed to the chastisement of the rebels. Then, lowering his tone, he announced the issue of writs for a Parliament to meet on November 3, and asked for counsel, not on the best mode of chastising the rebels, but on the answer to be given to their petition, and on the means of keeping the army together till the meeting of Parliament. "For so long as the Scotch army remains in England," he said in conclusion, "I think no man will counsel me to disband mine, for that would be an unspeakable loss to all this part of the kingdom by subjecting them to the greedy appetite of the rebels, besides the unspeakable dishonour that would thereby fall upon this nation."

Traquair's narrative.

In the afternoon the Peers met again. Traquair, by the King's command, repeated the narrative which had moved the Council in the preceding winter to declare the Scottish demands to be inadmissible. Evidently Charles had not yet abandoned the hope that the Peers would support him in the position which he had taken up. Such was not the view of the situation which they took. At Bristol's motion they resolved to name sixteen of their own number as Commissioners to negotiate with the invaders. Every one of the seven who had signed the letter forwarded by Savile, reappeared amongst the number, and the remainder were favourable to a good understanding with the Scots.

Commissioners to treat.

Bristol's leadership.

Whatever their private opinions might be, the Lords had clearly accepted the leadership of Bristol. His old loyalty was a sufficient guarantee that he would be no favourer of revolution, whilst he was known to be entirely hostile to the new system of government. No other Peer could compete with him in capacity for the conduct of the negotiation.[1]

CHAP. IX.
1640.

The next day the Peers took the King's financial difficulties into consideration. It was acknowledged that at least 200,000*l*. were needed. Strafford urged the necessity of supplying the money at once. If that army were to be dissolved the country would be lost in two days. He was not for fighting now. If they remained on the defensive they would wear out the Scots. The question of overpowering the Scots was not the foremost one with the other Peers. Now that a Parliament was to meet, said Bristol, the City would be ready to lend. It was ultimately resolved to send a deputation to London to collect a loan of 200,000*l*. on the security of the Peers.[2]

Sept. 25.
The Peers engage their security for the City loan.

It remained to be considered on what terms the negotiations should be opened. The King proposed that the Pacification of Berwick, that vague and inconclusive arrangement which had been subjected to so many interpretations, should be taken as the basis of the understanding. Was it not, asked the King, dishonourable to go further than the Pacification? If he had had his way he would have secured the support of the Lords in refusing the Acts of the late Parliament. He would not acknowledge that he must look upon the Scots as capable of dictating terms. Bristol took the more sensible view. "If his Majesty were in case," he said, "it were best to bring

Sept. 26.
Terms of negotiation.

[1] Vane to Windebank, Sept. 24, *Hardw. St. P.* ii. 186. *Rushw.* iii. 1,275.

[2] Sir J. Borough's notes of these and the subsequent meetings of the Great Council are printed in *Hardw. St. P.* ii. 208, from *Harl. MSS.* 456. The printed copy cannot always be relied on; Mandeville's speech, for instance, is attributed to Savile at p. 209.

436   THE SCOTTISH INVASION.

CHAP. IX.
1640.

Sept. 29. Instructions to the Commissioners.

Oct. 2. Meeting at Ripon.

Scottish demands.

them on their knees: but now, considering their strength, Newcastle and the two provinces taken, we must now speak of the business as to men that have gotten these advantages."[1] Charles was not to be moved. In the instructions finally given, he declared his intention of keeping the Scottish castles in his own hands. As to such acts as were derogatory to his crown and dignity, he had instructed Traquair, Morton, and Lanark to inform the Scots of his pleasure.[2]

There could be little doubt what that information would be. The point, however, would not be raised for some little time. The Commissioners of the two nations met at Ripon on October 2. It was evident, from the first, that the Scots were aware of the strength of their position.

Loudoun, who took the lead on their side, said plainly, that his countrymen would not be content without taking into consideration events which had happened since the Pacification; and he also took objection to the presence of six persons who had been named as assistants to the English lords, especially as one of the number was the obnoxious Traquair, pointed out as one of the incendiaries at whose trial and punishment they aimed.[3]

The Scots seem to have been surprised at the tenacity with which Bristol, without contradiction from his fellow-Commissioners, fought them inch by inch. They had entered England under the belief that they had received from seven of the Commissioners present a positive offer of armed assistance, and they could not understand how those very men

[1] *Hardw. St. P.* ii. 225.
[2] *Rushw.* iii. 1,283.
[3] Borough's *Treaty of Ripon* (Camd. Soc.), 1–17. Commissioners to the King, Oct. 2, *Rushw.* iii. 1,289.

should be found supporting the arguments against their claims. That evening, Loudoun and Johnston applied anxiously to Mandeville for an explanation, charging him and the other six Peers with a breach of their signed engagement. To this unlooked-for accusation Mandeville answered that he knew nothing about the matter. Loudoun and Johnston replied that the whole negotiation had passed through Savile's hands, and that he would be certain to bear witness to the truth. The next day, accordingly, Savile was sent for and interrogated. Prevarication in such company was useless, and he boldly acknowledged the forgery. He had acted as he had, he said, from motives of patriotism, and the only thing to be done, now that his falsehood was discovered, was to take advantage of its results for the common good.

Chap. IX.
1640. Oct. 3. Meeting between Loudoun, Johnston, and Mandeville.

Savile's confession of forgery.

Savile's treachery was easily condoned. It was not likely that he would ever be trusted again by those whom he had tricked; but if, as is probable, he had been the medium through whose hands genuine as well as forged writings had passed, it is easy to understand the mixed motives of those who concurred in passing over so odious a treachery. Naturally, too, the English Lords were anxious to obtain from the Scots the incriminating paper. The Scots refused to give it up, but they cut out the supposititious signatures and burnt them in Mandeville's presence.[1]

Savile's treachery condoned.

[1] *Nalson,* ii. 427. The story is extracted from Mandeville's own *Memoirs.* Dr. Burton comments on it, that 'the doubts that any such affair ever occurred are strengthened by the absence of any reference to it in Mr. Bruce's *Ripon Papers.*' Surely he could not have been serious in supposing it likely that the official note-taker of the Conference would be invited to be present at this interview! The passage in question is to be found in a fragment now known as *Add. MSS.* 15,567, which is thus identified as a portion of the long-lost *Memoirs* of the Earl of Manchester. Its importance will be seen when the narrative reaches Strafford's arrest.

CHAP. IX.
1640.
Oct. 5.
Progress of the negotiation.

In the open discussions which followed, the question of the assistants was settled by the compromise that they might give advice without showing themselves at the public conferences. Then came a debate on the terms on which a cessation of arms was to be granted. The Scots declared that nothing short of 40,000*l*. a month would satisfy them during their occupation of the northern counties, and that this payment must last until the conclusion of peace. The English Commissioners referred the demand to the King.

Sept. 29.
State of London.

Before Charles gave his answer he was in possession of better news from London than he had been accustomed to receive. In the last days of September the exasperation of the citizens had been daily growing. At the election of the new Lord Mayor, they shouted out that they would have none who had opposed the petition to the King, and set aside the aldermen who stood highest on the list, and who, according to the usual custom, would have been elected without further difficulty. The greater part of the votes were divided between Geere, who had given his support to the petition, and Soames, who had been sent to prison for his resistance to the loan. Riots, too, broke out in two of the city churches where Dr. Duck, the Bishop's Chancellor, had irritated the people by calling upon the churchwardens to take the usual oath to present offenders against the ecclesiastical law. In one of them the summons was received with shouts of No oath! No oath! from the crowded assembly. An apparitor, who unwisely spoke of the disturbers as a company of Puritan dogs, was hustled and beaten, and was finally carried off to prison by the sheriff who had been summoned to restore order. The Chancellor was glad enough to escape in haste, leaving his hat behind him.¹

All this was changed for a time by the arrival of the Peers from York. On October 2 an informal meeting was held, in which a number of the richer citizens appeared in the midst of the Common Councillors. As Bristol had anticipated, the declaration of a Parliament carried all before it. The Lord Mayor was invited to write to the City Companies to ask them to lend 200,000*l.* on the security of the Peers.²

The news of the success of the application to the City reached York on the 6th,³ the day on which the Great Council met to take into consideration the Scottish demands. The King had no certain advice to give. He hesitated between the risk of exasperating the Scots, and the indignity of buying off the vengeance of rebels. Strafford had no such hesitation. "This demand," he said, "hath opened our eyes. Nothing of religion moves in this business." "The Londoners' example," he added, "hath much turned my opinion." Once more he was beginning to think that the Scottish exorbitance would give the King the support that he needed. He was for taking the defensive, and leaving the Scots to do their worst. Some, indeed—Lord Herbert of Cherbury, amongst them—were equally prepared to proceed to extremities. But the general feeling of the Peers inclined the other way, and on the following day the King proposed that the negotiation should be removed to York, apparently with the intention of bringing his personal influence to bear upon the Scottish Commissioners.⁴

CHAP. IX.
1640.

Oct. 2. The City agrees to a loan.

Oct. 6. Debate in the Great Council on the Scottish demand.

Oct. 7. The negotiation to be removed to York.

¹ Rossingham's *Newsletter*, Oct. 7, *Add. MSS.* 11,045, fol. 122. Windebank to the King, Sept. 30, *Clar. St. P.* ii. 125.
² The Peers' deputation to the King, Oct. 3, *S. P. Dom.*
³ Vane to Windebank, Oct. 6, *Hardw. St. P.* ii. 193.
⁴ *Hardw. St. P.* ii. 241.

The answer of the Scots to the Royal command was a blank refusal to obey it. They had not forgotten how some of their number had been detained in London when employed on a similar negotiation. They would not, they said, trust themselves in the midst of an army of which Strafford was the commander. They were empowered to name him 'as a chief incendiary.' In the Irish Parliament he had had no better name for them than traitors and rebels, and he was now doing his utmost to bring the negotiation to an end.[1]

Doubtless the Scots had received tidings from their friends at York of the speech delivered by Strafford two days before. They could not know of a proposal fiercer still which he was that very day penning, to be submitted to Radcliffe. His thoughts in these days of trouble must often have passed over the Irish Channel to that army which, but for the want of money, he would have brought over the sea to join in the attack upon the invaders. He knew, too, that there were in the North of Ireland 40,000 able-bodied Scotsmen, and that if Argyle chose, as had been threatened, to go amongst them he would find an army ready to his hands. In desperation he clutched at the notion of rousing the Irish House of Commons, which had met again at Dublin on the 1st, against these invaders upon Irish soil. If the Irish Parliament were to declare for the banishment of these men the Irish army would be strong enough, armed though the Scotchmen were, to carry its behest into execution.[2]

Wisely indeed did Radcliffe give his word against this terrible project. It would have filled the North of Ireland with carnage, with the sole result of rous-

[1] The Scotch Commissioners' answer, Oct. 8, *Rushw.* iii. 1,292.
[2] Whitaker's *Life of Radcliffe*, 206.

ing the indignation of England against the perpetrators of such a crime. The habit of driving straight at his object, undeterred by the miseries which would be wrought in attaining it, had been growing upon Strafford. To crush the Scots was the one object for which he now lived. On the 6th he had proposed to deliver up the populations of Northumberland and Durham to the tender mercies of the invaders. On the 8th he proposed to give over the Province of Ulster to blood and flame. It was not for nothing that the Scots had named him as the chief incendiary.

Strafford was not to have his way. The refusal of the Scots to come to York was meekly accepted. The negotiation was renewed at Ripon with the sole object of obtaining a modification of their demands. At last they agreed to accept a continuance for two months of the 850*l.* a day, or about 25,000*l.* a month, which they were drawing from the two counties, on condition that the first month's payment should be secured to them by the bonds of the leading gentry of the counties, given on assurance that the King would recommend their case to Parliament; and that the second month's payment should be provided for in a way to be hereafter settled—a stipulation which plainly pointed to a Parliamentary engagement.

On these terms, a cessation of arms was granted. The two northern counties were to remain in the possession of the invaders till the conclusion of the treaty. As soon as this arrangement was made, Henderson blandly informed the English Commissioners that they had the best of the bargain, as it was 'more blessed to give than to receive.' As the day for the meeting of Parliament was now approaching, it was arranged that further negotiations should be carried on in London, and on the 26th the Commissioners of the two countries met for the last time at Ripon.[1]

The resolution to yield to the Scottish demands in their modified form, had probably been influenced by unsatisfactory news from London. The election of the Lord Mayor, indeed, had ended in a compromise. Neither Acton, who was supported by the King's Council, nor Soames, the candidate of the popular party, had been chosen. The choice of the electors had fallen upon Alderman Wright, the second on the list. But Charles cared far less about the London Mayoralty than he did about the London loan, and it must have been a real shock to his mind when he learned that the City Companies would only lend him a quarter of the sum for which he had asked. He would have to wait for the rest till Parliament met.[2]

Unless, too, the Parliament could supply him with authority as well as money, the most disastrous consequences might be expected. In London at least the order which he had painfully laboured to establish, was entirely set at nought. On the 22nd the mob dashed into the High Commission Court, as it was preparing to sentence a Separatist, tore down the benches, seized upon the books, and threw the furniture out of window. Laud, at least, maintained his courage to the last. He called on the Court of Star Chamber to punish the offenders if they did not wish to be called in question by the populace for their sentence on Prynne, Burton, and Bastwick. But the Court of Star Chamber was no longer responsive to

[1] *Treaty of Ripon*, 27.
[2] Windebank to the King, Oct. 14, *Clar. St. P.* ii. 129.

his call. It was thought more prudent to indict some of the rioters before the Lord Mayor and some Aldermen sitting on a Commission of Oyer and Terminer. The grand jury could not agree to find a true bill against the prisoners, and the proceedings came to nothing. The result of this leniency was a fresh riot on the following Sunday. St. Paul's was invaded by the rabble, and a large quantity of papers, found in an office, were torn in pieces, in the belief that they were the records of the High Commission.[1]

On the 28th the Great Council was gathered together for the last time, to advise on the acceptance or rejection of the compact made at Ripon. Even Strafford did not venture to recommend the latter course now, and the King's assent was therefore given to the arrangement. But he distinctly declared that the payment was a voluntary act on the part of the gentry. He would enforce no man to pay the Scots.

The Great Council then broke up. It had not met in vain. It had done the utmost that was possible under the circumstances. It had obtained breathing time for the nation at the least expense which the hopelessness of immediate resistance would admit of. By selecting Bristol as its leader, it had declared equally against the extreme party which would have dragged an unwilling nation into staking its honour and safety upon the chances of a war to be waged by a beaten and undisciplined army, and against an equally extreme party which had looked with favour upon a hostile invasion. More than this, it had saved Charles from himself—from that hopeless vacillation

[1] Rossingham's *Newsletter*, Oct. 27, Nov. 3, *Add. MSS.* 11,045, fol. 128, 130.

which delivered him over as a prey to rash violence on one day, and to unreal submission on the next.

What chance was there that the influence of Bristol would be maintained in the coming Parliament? It was not likely that a House of Commons elected in such a time of suspicion and excitement, would be content with any measures which would be easily accepted by the King. It was not likely that the King, accustomed as he was to the exercise of arbitrary power, would accept meekly the restrictions which even moderate men sought to place upon him. Times were coming when such men as Bristol might well despair of the ship of State. He was not likely to secure the mastery over the coming Parliament. Nor was it at all likely that he would secure the mastery over the King. The feelings with which Charles looked forward to meeting the assembly which he had been compelled to call into existence, are doubtless admirably expressed in the opening pages of that little book which, if it be indeed a forgery, was the work of one possessed of no ordinary skill in the delineation of human character, and which was, in all probability, written by no other hand than that of Charles himself.

"I cared not," so runs the passage, "to lessen myself in some things of my wonted prerogative, since I knew I could be no loser if I might gain but a recompense in my subjects' affections. I intended not only to oblige my friends, but mine enemies also, exceeding even the desires of those that were factiously discontented, if they did but pretend to any modest and sober sense. The odium and offences which some men's rigour in Church and State had contracted upon my government, I resolved to have expiated by such laws and regulations for the future as might not only rectify what was amiss in practice, but supply what was defective in the Constitution. I resolved to reform what I should, by free and full advice in Parliament, be convinced of to be amiss, and to grant whatever my reason and conscience told me was fit to be desired."[1]

Between Charles's conception of his place in the English nation and the sad reality, there was, indeed, a great gulf.

[1] *Eikon Basilike*, ch. 1.

INDEX.

ABE

ABELL, Alderman, bargains on behalf of the Vintners, 76
Aberdeen, nature of its Royalism, 159; Montrose's first visit to, 161; his second visit to, 223; Aboyne at, 237; Montrose's third visit to, 242; the Earl Marischal and Monro at, 386.
Aboyne, Viscount (James Gordon), escapes from Montrose, 205; proposes to rouse the North, 216; taken by the Earl Mareschal, 223; his reception by Hamilton, *ibid.*; his proceedings at Aberdeen, 236; sends to Hamilton for help, 237; defeated by Montrose, 241; is chased through the streets of Edinburgh, 247
Adkins, Alderman, imprisoned for refusing to lend money to the King, 346
Aerssens, Francois van, arrives to explain the conduct of Tromp in the Downs, 297
Airlie, Earl of (James Ogilvy), burning of his house, 388
Aldermen committed to prison, 345; set at liberty, 351
Anabaptists, attempts to suppress, 288
Antrim, Earl of (Randal Macdonnell), proposes to raise a force for the West of Scotland, 153; failure of his project, 207
Archer, John, tortured and executed, 358
Argyle, Earl of (Archibald Campbell), his authority in the Highlands, 160-175; his character, 176; declares in favour of the Glasgow Assembly, 177; refuses to come to Berwick, 248; his policy in the Scottish Parliament, 256; directed to defend the Western Highlands, 367; argues that Parliament may meet in defiance of the King's demands, 369; his rule in the Highlands, 386; his raid upon Athol, 387; burns the House of

ARU

Airlie, 388; returns to the West, 389; talk of making him dictator, 404
Armstrong, Archie, discharged from his post as the King's jester, 132
Army, the English, preparations for the raising of, 191; its want of enthusiasm, 211; Verney's criticism of, 215; reinforcements ordered for, 219; good spirits of, 224; want of discipline in, 226; numbers of, 227; despondency of, 231; discomforts of, 232: preparation for collecting it again, 303; condition of the cavalry of, 371; dissatisfaction of the men pressed for, 377; Catholic officers distrusted by, 379; want of discipline of, 380; mutinous conduct of, 394; collects at Selby, 409; distribution of, 417; review of, 429
— the Irish, Strafford's proposal to levy, 305; alleged intention of employing it in England, 336; its rendezvous at Carrickfergus, 407
— the Scottish, expected to occupy the border, 210; occupies Kelso, 229; forces Holland to retreat, 230; encamps on Dunse Law, 233; Baillie's description of, 234; prepares to invade England, 400; encamps at Choicelee Wood, 403; crosses the Tweed, 413; its conduct in Northumberland, 414
Arundel, Countess of, her conversation with Con, 23
— Earl of (Thomas Howard), sent to strengthen the border fortresses, 149; appointed to command the first army against the Scots, 192; is the only peer who wishes to act vigorously against the Scots, 212; his proceedings at Dunse, 225; appointed captain-general to the south of the Trent, 416

448   INDEX.

ASS

Assembly of the Church of Scotland, the, appealed to by the Covenanters, 146; is summoned to meet at Glasgow, 165; divine right claimed for, 167; electoral machinery of, 167; its representative character, 169; meets at Glasgow, 171; is dissolved by Hamilton, 175; continues to sit, and abolishes episcopacy, 177; appointed to meet at Edinburgh, 241; bishops summoned to, 246; its proceedings at Edinburgh, 252.

Astley, Sir Jacob, sent to prepare for war in the North, 189; his discouraging report, 385; gathers troops at Selby, 409; goes to Newcastle, 417; tries to rally the troops after the rout of Newburn, 420

Athol, Earl of (John Murray), seized by Argyle, 387

Aylesbury, houses burnt by mutineers at, 349

BAILLIE, ROBERT, his opinion on the riots at Edinburgh, 117; describes the army on Dunse Law, 232; attacks Laud's system, 357

Balcanqual, Walter, Dean of Rochester, writes *The Large Declaration*, 198; made Dean of Durham, 199; flies from Durham, 421

Balmerino, Lord (John Elphinston), revises the Covenant, 126; argues that Parliament may meet in defiance of the King's commands, 369

Baner, General, his successes in Germany, 259

Bankes, Sir John, his argument in the ship-money case, 62

Bastwick, John, his early life and *Flagellum Pontificis*, 4; his *Apologeticus* and *Litany*, 5; his trial in the Star Chamber, 6; execution of the sentence on, 9; his imprisonment, 11

Bedford, Earl of (William Russell), takes the lead in draining the Great Level, 86; votes against interfering with the Commons, 321; recommended to go home, 423

Bellasys, Henry, attacks the military charges, 327; is imprisoned, 344; set at liberty, 351

Bellièvre, M. de, negotiates with Charles on behalf of Tromp, 266; wishes to support the Scots, 300; is recalled, 301

Berkeley, Justice, his opinion in the ship-money case, 66

CAE

Bernhard of Weimar, his victories on the Upper Rhine, 187; death of, 263

Berwick, Charles arrives at, 224; signature of the treaty of, 241; Conyers commands the garrison of, 291

Bishops, Laud's opinion on the authority of, 8
— the Scottish, excite the jealousy of the nobles, 97; their part in the organisation of the Church, 102; their share in the preparation of the new Prayer Book, 103; are attacked as the authors of the change, 120; protest against their remaining in the Council, 122; accused before the Edinburgh Presbytery, 170; are attacked by Hamilton, 173; their declinator read, 174; secretly protest against the legality of the Assembly of Edinburgh, 251; abolished by the Assembly, 252; Charles refuses to rescind the Acts against, 255; abolished by Parliament, 257

Bocking, destruction of Communion rails at, 399

Boteler, Lord (John Boteler), his change of religion, 17

Breisach captured by Bernhard of Weimar, 187

Brereton, Sir William, his account of his travels in Scotland, 100

Brickmakers, Corporation of the, 72

Bridge of Dee, Montrose's victory at, 242

Bristol, Earl of (John Digby), advises the King not to advance to Berwick, 219; asserts that the lords wish for a Parliament, 236; urges Strafford to recommend another Parliament, 353; gives an account of Strafford's conversation, 354; assumes the leadership of the Great Council, 434

Brooke, Lord (Robert Greville), refuses to follow the King to the war, 192; refuses the military oath, 212; votes against interfering with the Commons, 321

Buckinghamshire, slow payment of ship money in, 358

Bullion, seizure of, 392

Burgess, Cornelius, carries the Ministers' petition to the King, 433

Burton, Henry, his sermons, *For God and the King*, 4; his trial in the Star Chamber, 6; execution of the sentence on, 9; his triumphal progress and imprisonment, 11

CAERLAVEROCK holds out for the King, 201; surrenders, 433

INDEX. 449

CÆS

Cæsar, Sir Charles, buys the Mastership of the Rolls, 206
Canons, the new English, passed by Convocation, 360
— the Scottish, proposed by the King, 101; submitted to Laud and Juxon, 103; issue of, 104; are revoked by the King, 164
Cardenas, Alonso de, is suspended from intercourse with the Court, 183; refuses the loan of Spanish troops to Charles, 193; applies for gunpowder, 264; negotiates with Charles for aid to Oquendo, 265; negotiates with Newport, 268
Cardinal Infant, the (Ferdinand of Spain), sanctions negotiation with Gerbier, 182; refuses to send Spanish troops to England, 193
Carlisle, garrisoned, 191
— Earl of (James Hay), votes against his conscience, 324
— Lady, her relations with Strafford, 293
Carrickfergus, the Irish army at, 407
Catholics, the, Laud urges the persecution of, 14; Charles's feeling towards, 15; their converts, 17; proclamation against, 22; improved position of, 23; their contribution to the Scottish war, 228; burning of the books of, 352; proposal to get money for, 377; appointed as officers in the army, 394
Chambers, Richard, brings an action against the Lord Mayor, 69, 372; postponement of the case of, 381
Charles I., his position after eight years of unparliamentary government, 1; orders the publication of Laud's speech, 9; his feeling towards the Catholics, and his friendliness towards Con, 15; hesitates to suppress Con's proselytism, 19; issues a proclamation against the Catholics, 22;- his opinion of Laud's character, 23; his conduct in Williams's trial, 34; undertakes to finish the draining of the fens, 90; causes of his failure, 91; his love of art, 92; his policy in Scotland, 97; purposes an alteration of the worship of the Church of Scotland, 99; writes to the Scottish bishops about a new Prayer-book, 101; receives the news of the riots in St. Giles', 112; cannot acknowledge his mistake, 114; orders the enforcement of the use of the Scottish Prayer-book, 115; persists in demanding obedience, 117; directs the removal of the Council and the Session

CHA

from Edinburgh, 118; refuses to give an immediate answer to the petition about the Prayer-book, 121; seeks the advice of Traquair, 122; issues a proclamation in defence of the Prayer-book, 123; asserts that he has not consulted Englishmen on his Scottish policy, 133; finds it difficult to resist the Scots, 136; resolves to gain time with the Scots, 137; demands the surrender of the Covenant, 138; sends Hamilton a declaration, 141; orders Hamilton to obtain the surrender of the Covenant, 142; prepares for war, 144; permits Hamilton to return, 145; declares that he will only press the Prayer-book in a legal way, 146; feels despondent, 149; informs the English Privy Council of the state of Scottish affairs, 150; his treatment of Montrose, 157; authorises the meeting of an Assembly and Parliament in Scotland, and orders the circulation of a new confession of faith, 162; offers to limit episcopacy, and directs that a new covenant shall be signed, 165; Charles declares that he is preparing for war, 171; drifts into war, 179; his foreign relations, 180; wishes to support the Elector Palatine, 181; carries on secret negotiations with Spain, 182; allows Mary de Medicis to land, 185; prepares for war with Scotland, 189; asks for Spanish troops, 193; orders the publication of Laud's *Conference with Fisher*, 197; states his reasons for going to war with Scotland, 198; rides into York, 205; issues a proclamation favouring the tenants of Scots in rebellion, 209; advances to Durham, 213; sends Aboyne to the Firth of Forth, 216; issues a second proclamation to the Scots, 217; allows Hamilton to negotiate, 218; orders reinforcements, 219; orders Hamilton to return if necessary, 220; arrives at Berwick, 224; his proclamation described as a Satanic temptation, 225; financial distress of, 227; sends for Hamilton, 231; finds that the nobility do not wish to fight, 232; sees Leslie's army on Dunse Law, 233; opens negotiations with the Scots, 237; takes part in the discussions, 238; is unable to keep his army together much longer, 239; negotiates for Scottish soldiers for the Palatinate,

VOL. I.   G G

CHA

243; disputes the interpretation put by the Scots on his engagements, 244; summons bishops to the Assembly, 246; believes himself to have been misrepresented by the Scots, 247; complains that the pacification of Berwick has not been observed, 248; his altercation with Rothes, 249; returns to Whitehall, 250; directs the Scottish bishops to protest against the legality of the Assembly, 251; wishes to introduce ministers into the Scottish Parliament, 254; refuses to rescind the Scottish Acts establishing Episcopacy, 255; orders the prorogation of the Scottish Parliament, 258; his relations with the Continent, 259; seeks the help of Spain, 260; objects to the Dutch claim to the right of search, 261; orders Pennington to protect the Spanish fleet, 262; hopes to gain advantage from the position of the Spanish fleet in the Downs, 264; negotiates secretly with Spain, 265; makes offers to France, 267; sends his nephew to Alsace, 268; renews his negotiations with Spain, and is angry at the battle in the Downs, 273; and at his nephew's imprisonment, 273; makes Wentworth his counsellor, 275-278; sends back the Scottish Commissioners, 280; agrees to summon Parliament, 282; obtains a loan from the Council, 283; appoints Vane secretary, 294; liberates Valentine and Strode, 295; assures Rossetti of his protection, 296; offers the Princess Elizabeth to Prince William of Orange, 297; proposes a marriage alliance with the King of Spain, 298; receives the letter written by the Covenanters to the King of France, 301; hears the Scottish Commissioners, 301; expects to influence Parliament by the intercepted letter of the Covenanters, 306; sends the letter to the King of France, 307; opens the short Parliament, *ibid*; appeals from the Commons to the Lords, 319; expresses his confidence in Strafford, 322; puts pressure on the Lords, 324; consults his Council on the best mode of dealing with the Commons, 325; announces a dissolution, 330; dissolves the Short Parliament, 331; measures taken by him in preparation for a new war with Scotland, 344;

CHU

opens a negotiation with Spain, 346; hesitates to support Strafford, 348; proposals to prorogue the Scottish Parliament, 352; visits Strafford in his illness, 356; persists in the war with Scotland, 357; orders the prorogation of Convocation, 359; commits Goodman to prison, 366; orders the further prorogation of the Scottish Parliament, 367; thinks of compelling the City to furnish soldiers, and of negotiating with the Scots, 373; sends Loudoun to renew negotiations in Scotland, 390; orders the debasement of the coinage, 392; offers to make peace with the Scots, 396; countermands the debasement of the coinage, 397; hesitates in face of the expected Scottish invasion, 407; resolves to go to York, 411; answers the Yorkshire Petition, 412; sets off from London, 413; writes from York of his need of money, 415; orders trained bands to be sent north, 416; consults the Council on the steps to be taken if the Scots march southwards, 424; expects that all men will serve in defence of the realm, 425; resolves to summon the Great Council, 426; hopes that his subjects will support him, 428; reviews his army, 429; cannot make up his mind to summon Parliament, 432; announces to the Great Council that he has summoned Parliament, 434; authorises negotiation with the Scots, 435; proposes the removal of the negotiation from Ripon to York, 439; accepts the terms agreed to at Ripon, 443; his expectations from the Long Parliament, 444

Charles Lewis, Elector Palatine, is defeated by the Imperialists, 181; invites Bernhard to assist him, 260; goes to France, 268; is imprisoned, 274

Chevreuse, the Duchess of, arrives in England, 184; advises the Queen to visit Berwick, 240; proposes a marriage alliance between the Royal Families of England and Spain, 298

Chillingworth, William, his early life, 42; comparison of his opinions with those of Laud, 43; his intercourse with Falkland, 44; his *Religion of Protestants*, 46

Choicelee Wood, Leslie's army at, 403

Church of England, the, failure of Charles's attempt to restore harmony to, 1

INDEX 451

CIT

City. *See* London, City of
Clarendon, Earl of (Edward Hyde), criticisms on his *History of the Great Rebellion*, 326, 328
Coal-shippers, the regulation of the trade of, 73
Coat-and-conduct money, speeches against, 325; slow returns of, 357; pressure to collect, 391
Coinage, the, proposed debasement of, 392, 396
Coke, Sir John, threatened with dismissal, 292; dismissed, 294; gives information on a misstatement of the Queen's, 296
Colchester, ecclesiastical court at, 286
Colvill, William, intended to go to France, 299; sets out for, 301
Commissioners of the opponents of the Scottish Prayer-book chosen, 120; protests of, against the bishops sitting in the Council, 122; appoint a Committee known as the Tables, 125
— of the Scottish Parliament arrive in London, 301; plead before the King, 302; are imprisoned, 307; are set at liberty, with the exception of Loudoun, 352
Commissions of Array, issue of, 382
Committee of Eight, the, consults on Scottish affairs, 279; Traquair's narrative before, 281; consulted on the proposed war with Scotland, 333
Commons, the House of, grievances discussed in, 309; determines to take grievances before supply, 320; wishes to get rid of arbitrary taxation, 325; debates the King's demand for twelve subsidies, 326
Communion, the, indictment of a minister for refusing to administer to the congregation in their seats, 288
— Table, the, Laud's view on the position of, 8; declaration of the new canons on, 361; destruction of the rails of, 399, 410
Con, George, arrives as Papal Agent at the Queen's court, 15; his language about Laud, 16; his influence with the Queen, 16; attempts to make proselytes, 17; urges the Queen to support his proselytism, 19; his contest with Laud, 21; his opinion of Newcastle's character, 24; returns to Rome, and dies, 295
Contribution, the general, demanded for the Scottish war, 206; small results of, 227; analysis of, 228

COU

Convention of Estates meets at Edinburgh, 366
Convocation, subsidies voted by, 319; continues sitting after the dissolution of Parliament, 359; grants subsidies, 360; passes canons, 360; the right to sit after the dissolution questioned, 365; dissolution of, 366
Conway, Viscount (Edward Conway), appointed to command the Horse against the Scots, 291; mutiny of his troops, 371; wishes to execute a murderer by martial law, 383; urges the necessity of fortifying Newcastle, 384; is ordered to exercise martial law, 398; believes that an invasion is imminent, 408; declares Newcastle to be indefensible, 409; his position at Newcastle, 417; occupies the ford at Newburn, 418; is defeated, 419; arrives at Darlington, 420
Conyers, Sir John, appointed to command the garrison of Berwick, 291
Corporation, the new, 81
Corunna, sailing of a Spanish fleet from, 263
Cottington, Lord (Francis Cottington), takes Williams's part, 34; presses the Lord Mayor and Aldermen for a loan, 240; becomes a member of the Committee of Eight, 279; his speech in the Committee of Eight, 336; sent to ask the City for a loan, 396; attempts to obtain a loan from France, 398; raises money for the Crown on pepper, 414; appointed Constable of the Tower, 416
Council, the Great, its summons recommended, 425; resolution of the King to call, 426; meets, 434; gives security for a loan, 435; last meeting of, 443
— the Privy, is informed of the state of affairs in Scotland, 149; committee on Scottish affairs appointed from, 150; does not expect to get money enough for the army, 227; presses the Lord Mayor for a loan, 237; agrees to the calling of a Parliament, 282; offers a loan to the King, 283; proposes to burn a heretic, 289; its opinion asked on the projected dissolution of the Short Parliament, 330; amount raised by loan from, 353; attempts to enforce payment of ship-money and coat-and-conduct money, 357; recommends the summoning of the Great Council, 425; Hertford and Bedford before, 427

G G 2

452 INDEX.

COU

Council, the Scottish, explains the difficulty of enforcing the use of the Prayer Book, 115; finds the opposition too strong, 116; ordered to remove from Edinburgh, 118; hesitates to support the King, 146
Covenant, the King's, ordered to be substituted for the National Covenant, 165; protestation against, 166; few signatures obtained to, 167
— the Scottish National, its substance, 126; its signature in Edinburgh, 130; is circulated in Scotland, 133; signatures exacted to, 134; its surrender demanded by the King, 141; Wentworth's opinion of, 154; proposal to oppose it with another confession of faith, 162
Covenanters, the, terms demanded by them, 141; refuse to surrender the Covenant, 143; engage to disperse, 145; appeal from the King to the Assembly and Parliament, 146; are encouraged by Hamilton, 147; engage not to choose an Assembly before Hamilton's return, 164; protest against the King's proclamation, 166; accuse the Bishops before the Presbytery of Edinburgh, 170; appeal to the English people, 196; write to Essex, 213; negotiate with Hamilton, 220; invited to Berwick, 248; communicate with the King of France, 299; intercepted letter of, 301, 306; question the right of the King to prorogue Parliament, 367
Coventry, Lord (Thomas Coventry), lends money to the King, 283; dies, 291
Craven, Lord (William Craven), taken prisoner by the Imperialists, 181
Crawley, Justice, his judgment in the ship-money case, 66
Crew, John, imprisoned, 344
Croke, Justice, his judgment on the ship-money case, 67
Cromwell, Oliver, his proceedings in connection with the draining of the fens, 89; nickname of 'Lord of the Fens' applied to, 90
Crosby, Sir Patrick, attacks Wentworth, 275; is sentenced in the Star Chamber, 276
Cumberland, Earl of (Henry Clifford), commands at Carlisle, 191
Cumbernauld, the bond of, 405

D ALKEITH, gunpowder stored at, 141; taken by the Covenanters, 201

EDI

Dalzell, Lord (Robert Dalzell), created Earl of Carnwath, 258
Danish troops, proposal to introduce into England, 398
Davenant, John, Bishop of Salisbury, his remark on the position of the Communion table, 8
Denbigh, Earl of (William Fielding), Con's contempt for, 18
Dickson, David, is ready to persuade those who hesitate to sign the Covenant, 130; accompanies Montrose to Aberdeen, 161; Moderator of the Assembly of Edinburgh, 252
Divino right of kings, the, view of the canons on, 262
Dorset, Earl of (Edward Sackville), his duel referred to by Bastwick, 7; threatens the Vintners, 76; charges Hamilton with treason, 207; makes excuses for lawyers who had drunk confusion to the archbishop, 352
Drummond, of Hawthornden, William, approves of the King's proclamation, 166
Dumbarton secured for the King, 145; seizure by the Covenanters of the castle of, 201; again captured by the Covenanters, 433
Dunfermline, Earl of (Charles Seton), sent to open negotiations with the king, 235; visits Charles at Berwick, 249; arrives in London on a mission from the Scottish Parliament, 279; his overtures to Bellièvre, 300
Dunglas, Leslie's camp at, 224
Dunse, Arundel's proceedings at, 225
Dunse Law, occupied by the Scots, 233
Durham, city of, occupied by the Scots, 421
—, county of, trained bands of, 415

E AST INDIA COMPANY, the, its bargain for the sale of pepper to the King, 414
Edinburgh, riot at the reading of the new Prayer Book at, 109; second riot at, 116; third riot at, 118; signature of the Covenant at, 130; negotiation for the surrender of the castle of, 145; purchase by Hamilton of the castle of, 170; seizure by the Covenanters of the castle of, 200; Ruthven in command of the castle of, 246; riot at, 247; opening of the Assembly at, 252; opening of the Parliament at, 253; bad condition of

EGL

the castle of, 303; siege of the castle of, 324, 367; surrender of the castle of, 433

Eglinton, Lord (Alexander Montgomery), directed to watch the west coast of Scotland, 366

Eikon Basilike, quotation from, 444

Elector Palatine. *See* Charles Lewis.

Elizabeth, Electress Palatine, and titular Queen of Bohemia, hopes for assistance from Scottish soldiers, 243
— the Princess, marriage with Prince William of Orange proposed for her, 297

Elphinstone, Sir William, attacked by the mob at Edinburgh, 247

English Army, the. *See* Army, the English

Esmond, Robert, alleged manslaughter of, by Wentworth, 275

Essex, destruction of communion rails in, 399
— Earl of (Robert Devereux), appointed second in command in the first war against the Scots, 192; receives a letter from the Covenanters, 213; votes against interfering with the Commons, 321

Estates of the realm, new definition of the, 318

Etcetera oath, the, enjoined, 364; suspended, 412

Ettrick, Lord (Patrick Ruthven), his position in Edinburgh Castle, 303; fires upon the town, 324; continues to hold out, 389; surrenders, 433

Eure, Lieutenant, murder of, 394

Excise, proposed, 281

FABRONI denies that the Queen Mother is coming to England, 185

Falkland, Viscount (Henry Cary), his death, 39
—, Viscount (Lucius Cary), his early life, 38; his character, 40

Fens, the drainage of, 83

Finances, the, flourishing condition of, 70; distress of, 227

Finch of Fordwich, Lord (John Finch), reads the Covenanters' letter to Parliament, 308; obtains an adjournment of the House of Lords, 311; his speech to the Short Parliament, 319; approves of the prolongation of Convocation, 359

Finch, Sir John, Chief Justice of the Common Pleas, his conduct at Prynne's trial, 6; his judgment in the ship-money case, 67; appointed Lord

HAM

Keeper, 292; created Lord Finch, 308. *See* Finch of Fordwich, Lord

Forest Courts, the, 71

Forthar, burning of the Earl of Airlie's house at, 388

France, navy of, 188; proposed loan from, 377; attempt to obtain a loan from, 398

Frederick Henry, Prince of Orange, proposes a marriage between his son and the Princess Mary, 297

GAGE, Colonel, suggests that Spanish troops may be used in England, 193

Garway, Henry, Lord Mayor, threatened for refusing to lend money to the King, 345; attempts to distrain for ship-money, 372

Geere, Alderman, committed to prison, 346

Genoese loan, a, proposed, 377

Gerbier, Balthazar, carries on a secret negotiation at Brussels, 182

Glanville, John, attacks ship-money, 327

Glasgow, the Assembly meets at, 171

Goodman, Godfrey, Bishop of Gloucester, retains his bishopric after conversion to the Roman Catholic Church, 365; is committed to prison, 366

Gordon, Lord, accompanies Huntly to Edinburgh, 204

Gordon, Sir Lewis, imprisoned by the Covenanters, 303

Great Council, the. *See* Council, the Great

Great Level, the, drainage of, 86

Grey Friars' Church, signature of the Covenant at, 130

Grimston, Harbottle, early life and character of, 309; placed in the chair of the Committee on Grievances, 317

Gun, Colonel, alleged treachery of, 242 *note*

HACKNEY coaches, licences for, 82

Hales, John, of Eton, his character and opinions, 49; his conversation with Laud, 52; becomes a Canon of Windsor, 53

Hall, Joseph, Bishop of Exeter, his *Episcopacy by Divine Right*, 318; forced to beg pardon for insulting Saye, 319

Hamburg, Congress at, 180

Hamilton, the Marchioness of, failure of Mrs. Porter to convert, 18

Hamilton, the Marquis of (James Hamilton), makes money by the Vintners, 76; obtains a patent for

HAM

licensing hackney coaches, 82; his character, 138; is sent as commissioner to Scotland, 140; threatens Rothes, 141; arrives at Edinburgh, 143; suggests that an explanation may be added to the Covenant, 144; proposes to advise the calling of an Assembly and Parliament, 145; secretly encourages the Covenanters, 147; returns to England, 148; his second mission to Scotland, 162; attempts to divide the Covenanters, 163; returns again to England, and comes back to Scotland with fresh overtures, 164; advises that the Assembly be allowed to proceed to business, 169; purchases Edinburgh Castle, 170; presides in the Assembly of Glasgow, 171; his account of the Assembly, 172; his displeasure with the Bishops, 173; advocates war, 174; dissolves the Assembly, 175; reports on his mission before the English Council, 179; charged by Dorset with treason, 207; sent to the Firth of Forth, 209; writes from Yarmouth complaining of his troops, 210; occupies Inchkeith and Inchcolm, 214; despairs of success, 215; proposes concessions to the Scots, 217; negotiates with the Covenanters, 220; his opinion on the chances of the war, 221; sends two regiments to Berwick, 222; his reception of Aboyne, 223; ordered to come to Berwick, 232; arrives at Berwick, 236; advises Charles to abolish episcopacy, 237; is abused by the mob at Edinburgh, 246; resigns the Commissionership, 248; is authorised to talk freely with the Covenanters, 248; becomes a member of the Committee of Eight, 279; supports a proposal to call a Parliament in England, 281; advises Charles to send Loudoun to Scotland, 390; objects to Charles's journey to York, 411; proposes to betray the Scots, 432

Hamilton, William, created Earl of Lanark, 258

Hampden, John, his ship-money case, 58; Wentworth's opinion of his treatment, 153; speaks in the Short Parliament, 326

Hatfield Chase, drainage of, 83

Hay, Sir John, made Lord Provost of Edinburgh, 116; is unable to quiet

HIG

the mob, 119; suggests that the opponents of the Prayer-book shall choose Commissioners, 120

Health Office, proposal to erect a, 86

Henderson, Alexander, draws up a petition against the Scottish Prayer-book, 113; appears before the Council, 115; takes part in drawing up the Covenant, 126; is ready to persuade those who hesitate to sign the Covenant,130; accompanies Montrose to Aberdeen, 161; is the probable author of the protestation against the King's Covenant, 166; is chosen Moderator of the Assembly of Glasgow,172; his speech in the Assembly, 174; puts the question whether the Assembly can judge the Bishops, 175

Henrietta Maria, Queen, is urged by Con to make proselytes, 16; her contest with Laud, 19; treats the proclamation against the Catholics with contempt, 22; receives money from the Londonderry fines, 81; Richelieu's overtures to, 184; begs that her mother may be allowed to land in England, 185; urges the Catholics to contribute to the Scottish war, 228; proposes a contribution by the ladies, 229; talks of visiting the army, 240; gains over Charles to the French, 267; supports Leicester and afterwards Vane for the Secretaryship, 294; is afraid lest Parliament will attack the Catholics, 295; begs the King to protect Rossetti and to keep the Catholic Lords in Parliament, 296; her high estimation of Strafford, 322; assailed for her part in politics, 350; her overtures to Rome, 351; protects the Catholics, 377; is refused a loan by Rome, 398

Herbert of Cherbury, Lord (Edward Herbert), proposes to resist the Scots, 439

Hertford, Earl of (William Seymour), votes against interference with the Commons, 321

Hertfordshire, resistance to coat-and-conduct money in, 358

Heylyn, Peter, publishes *A Coal from the Altar*, 36; his account of a conversation with Hales, 53

High Commission, Court of, its sentence on Bastwick, 5; Act Book of, 286; riot in, 442

Highlanders, use of bows and arrows by, 230; their fear of the cannon, 242

INDEX. 455

HOL

Holborne, Robert, his argument in the ship-money case, 61; argues for the Earl of Bedford in the case of the fens, 91
Holland, Earl of (Henry Rich), holds forest courts, 71; appointed to command the Horse in the first Scottish war, 192; votes unwillingly by the King's orders, 324; objects to Charles's journey to York, 411
Hope, Sir Thomas, said to have instigated the riot at St. Giles', 111; supports the petitioners against the Prayer-book, 121; his conversation with Rothes, 3c2
Hopton, Sir Arthur, conveys to the Spanish Government Charles's proposals about the fight in the Downs, 298
Hotham, Sir John, attacks the military charges, 328; is imprisoned, 344; is sot at liberty, 351
Hull, a military magazine to be created at, 170
Huntly, Marquis of (George Gordon), his influence in the Highlands, 160; proposed by Hamilton as Lieutenant of the North, 174; appointed Lieutenant of the North, and dismisses his troops, 202; his interview with Montrose, 203; is carried to Edinburgh, 204; refuses to sign the Covenant, 205; retires to England, 386
Hutchinson John, his character, 28
Hutton, Justice. his judgment in the case of ship-money, 67; employed to mediate in a dispute about Hatfield Chase, 85
Hyde, Edward, opposes Hampden in the Short Parliament, 326

INCHCOLM, occupied by Hamilton, 214
Inchkeith, occupied by Hamilton, 214
Inverury, Huntly at, 202; plundered by Montrose, 203
Ireland, Wentworth's government of, 150

JARS, the Chevalier de, released from captivity, 184
Joachimi, Albert, protests against the protection given to Spanish soldiers, 261
Johnston of Warriston, Archibald, left at Edinburgh on behalf of the opponents of the Prayer-book, 118; reads a protest at Stirling, 124; proposes the renewal of the Covenant, 126; is

LAU

chosen clerk of the Assembly of Glasgow, 172; argues that Parliament may meet in defiance of the King's commands, 369; writes to Lord Savile, 401
Junto, the, *see* Committee of Eight
Juxon, William, Bishop of London (Lord Treasurer), revises the Scottish canons, 103; offers to find 200,000*l* for the Scottish war, 144; finds he cannot raise the money, 150; becomes a member of the Committee of Eight, 279

KEBLE, John, his opinion on the churches in Scotland, 101
Kelso, a Scottish army at, 229; Holland's march to, 230
Kent, behaviour of the soldiers pressed in, 349
Kilvert, Richard, brings charges against Bishop Williams, 33; presses the Vintners for money, 77
Kimbolton, Lord, *see* Mandeville, Viscount
Knight-service, tenants by, ordered to follow the King to the field, 412
Knott, Edward, his *Charity mistaken*, 44

LAMBETH, attack of rioters upon, 349
Lanark, Earl of (William Hamilton), announces to the Scots that the King has summoned the Great Council, 426
Large Declaration, the, its publication, 198
Latitudinarianism, influence of, 52
Laud, William, Archbishop of Canterbury, his efforts to promote unity in the Church, 2; attempts to suppress unlicensed publications, 3; his speech at the trial of Prynne, Burton, and Bastwick, 7; his opinion on the ceremonies, and on the royal authority, 8; publication of his speech, 9; his dissatisfaction with Prynne's speech in the pillory, 11; libels on, 12; urges measures against the Catholics, 14; Con's talk about his conversion, 16; urges the King to stop Con's proselytism, 19; his contest with the Queen, 20; is too easily frightened by the Puritans, 32; employed by Williams as mediator, 34; his conversations with Hales, 52; increases the tithes paid to the City clergy, 81; his opinion on the churches in Scotland, 99; revises the Scottish Canons and Prayer-book, 103; insists

LEI

upon the use of the Scottish Prayer-book, 112; saves Archie Armstrong from a flogging, 133; regrets the Queen Mother's visit, 186; his *Conference with Fisher* published, 197; his opinion of the Pacification of Berwick, 250; urges the King to support Wentworth, 277; becomes a member of the Committee of Eight, 279; supports the proposal to summon Parliament, 281; thinks the Church is conformable, 286; refers Trendall's case to the Council, 289; Northumberland's ill opinion of, 294; proposes the adjournment of the House of Lords during the sittings of Convocation, 311; his speech in the Committee of Eight, 336; libellous placards against, 348; does not expect the prolongation of Convocation, 359; suspends Bishop Goodman, 366

Leicester, Earl of (Robert Sydney), a candidate for the Secretaryship, 292

Leith, fortifications of, 214

Lennox, Duke of (James Stuart), favours Williams, 35; forged speech attributed to, 170

Leslie, Alexander, his early life, 195; appointed to the command of the Scottish army, 196; enters Aberdeen, 203; is expected to appear on the Border, 210; encamps at Douglas, 224; marches to the Borders, 231; encamps on Dunse Law, 233; respect shown to him, 234; proposes to provide soldiers for the Elector Palatine, 243; prepares to invade England, 391; encamps at Choicelee Wood, 403

Lewis XIII., King of France, refuses to allow his mother to return to France, 186; birth of his son, 187; disavows having communicated with the Covenanters, 307

Lilburn, John, charged with importing unlicensed books, 30; his trial and sentence in the Star Chamber, 31

Limerick, Wentworth at, 151

Lincolnshire, drainage of fens in, 86

Lindsay, Bishop of Edinburgh, tries to quiet the rioters at St. Giles', 109; escapes with difficulty, 110

Lindsey, Earl of (Robert Bertie), ordered to take men to Berwick, 191

Linlithgow, the King's proclamation at, 121

Loftus of Ely, Viscount (Adam Loftus), his dispute with Wentworth, 276; prosecution of, 278

London, the city of, growth of buildings

MAN

in, 78; prohibition of new buildings in, 79; reduction of the fine on, 80; tithes payable to the clergy of, 81; proposal to extend the municipal boundaries of, *ib.*; importance of, 93; its institutions, 94; asked for a loan for the Scottish war, 206; another loan demanded of, 229; pressure put on, 239; a loan again demanded from, 307; threats used by Strafford to the citizens of, 345; attempt to extract ship-money from, 372; objects to furnish men for the Scottish war, 373; refuses to lend to the King, 396; rejects Roe's request for a loan for the King, 400; petitions for a Parliament, 431; loan guaranteed by the Peers from, 435; election of a Lord Mayor of, 438-442; loan by, 442

Londonderry, case of, in the Star Chamber, 80

Lord's Day, the, attacks on the Puritan conception of, 2

Lords, the House of, refuses to adjourn during the meetings of Convocation, 311; questions Mainwaring's appointment to a bishopric, 317; Charles's appeal to, 320; supports the King, 321; maintains its position by a decreased majority, 323

— of the Articles, the, reconstruction of, 253

Lorne, Lord (Archibald Campbell), his feeling about the new Prayer-book, 111. *See* Argyle, Earl of

Loudoun, Earl of (John Campbell), revises the Covenant, 126; visits Charles at Berwick, 249; arrives in London on a mission from the Scottish Parliament, 279; his overtures to Bellievre, 300; imprisoned by the King, 301; examined, 309; sent back to negotiate in Scotland, 390; enters into communication with Savile, 401

Lycidas, the, its publication, 25; its attack on the Laudian system, 26

Lyttelton, Sir Edward, his argument in the ship-money case, 60

MAINWARING, Roger, Bishop of St. David's, his appointment to a bishopric questioned, 317

Maltsters and brewers, regulation of the trade of, 75

Malvezzi, the Marquis Virgilio, arrives as Spanish ambassador to England, 346; Milton's reference to, 346, *note* 2

Manchester, Earl of (Henry Montague),

INDEX. 457

MAN

lends money to the King, 283; urges the citizens to lend money, 307; suggests the summoning of the Great Council, 425
Mandeville, Viscount (Edward Montague), appealed to by the Scots, 437
Mar, Earl of (John Erskine), treats with Hamilton for the surrender of Edinburgh Castle, 145; holds Stirling Castle for the Covenanters, 201
Marischal, Earl (William Keith), drives the royalists out of Aberdeen, 223; accompanies Monro to Aberdeen. 386; signs the Bond of Cumbernauld, 405
Martial law, question of the right to exercise, 383; Conway ordered to exercise, 398
Mary de Medicis, her stay at Brussels, 184; proposes to visit England, 185; arrives in London, 186; her apartments threatened, 349
—, the Princess, marriage with Prince William of Orange proposed for her, 297
Mastership of the Rolls, sold to Sir Charles Cæsar, 206
Maxwell, John (Bishop of Ross), said to wish to be Treasurer, 111
Melander, negotiation for the purchase of his troops, 181
Meppen seized by the Imperialists, 181
Michell, David, insulted for refusing to sign the Covenant, 135
Michelson, Margaret, declares that the Covenant came from heaven, 167
Middleton, John, storms the Bridge of Dee, 242
Military charges, the, objections taken to, 325, 327, 328
— oath refused by Saye and Brooke, 212
Milton, John, his *Lycidas*, 25; his attack on the Laudian system, 26; his reference to Malvezzi, 346, *note 2*
Mint, the, debasement of the coinage at, 392
Monopolies, corporate, 71
Monro, Colonel, his regiment kept on foot, 248; sent to the North of Scotland, 385
Monsigot, his mission to England, 185
Monson, Sir John, appears against Williams, 35
Montague, Richard, becomes Bishop of Norwich, 287; his account of his diocese, 288
—, Walter, urges the Queen to secure proselytes, 16; is employed as agent for the Catholic contribution, 208
Montreuil, M. de, his evidence on the

NEW

King's intention to employ the Irish army in England, 337
Montrose, Earl of (James Graham), his early years, 157; takes part with the Covenanters, 158; his first entry into Aberdeen, 161; appears at Turriff, 201; his second entry into Aberdeen, 202; his interview with Huntly, 203; carries Huntly to Edinburgh, 204; allows Aboyne to escape, 205; refuses to plunder Aberdeen, 223; defeats Aboyne at the Bridge of Dee, 241; enters Aberdeen the third time, 242; visits Charles at Berwick, 248; his Parliamentary policy, 255; signs the letter of the Covenanters to the king of France, 302; urges that Parliament should be prorogued in obedience to the King's commands, 369; his ideas compared with those of Strafford, 370; attempts to protect the House of Airlie, 388; cause of the weakness of his policy, 390; his hostility to Argyle's dictatorship, 404; signs the Bond of Cumbernauld, 405; crosses the Tweed at the head of the army, 413
Morocco, the King of, surrenders English captives, 56
Mountnorris, Lord (Francis Annesley), attacks Wentworth, 275
Murford, Nicholas, invents a new mode of making salt, 75

NAPIER, Lord (Archibald Napier) his opinion on the political employment of the clergy, 98
Neile, Archbishop, objects to foreign Protestant worship in Hatfield Chase, 85; is consulted on the proceedings in the case of Wightman and Legate, 289; advises the burning of Trendall, 290
Newburn, Conway posts himself opposite, 418; victory of the Scots at, 419
Newcastle, necessity of fortifying, 384; fortifications not completed at, 418; occupied by the Scots, 420
—, Earl of (William Cavendish) character of, 24; lends money to the King, 283
Newport, Earl of (Mountjoy Blount), his anger at his wife's conversion, 19; bargains with Cardenas and Oquendo, 264, 268; declares that he had voted against the King by mistake, 324
—, Lady, tries to prevent her father

NOR

from changing his religion, 17; changes her own religion, 18
Northumberland, Scottish invasion of, 414
Northumberland, Earl of (Algernon Percy), is appointed Lord Admiral, 137; approves of Tromp's proceedings, 261; is puzzled by contradictory orders, 266; becomes a member of the Committee of Eight, 279; appointed General of the army, 291; his ill opinion of Laud, 294; sees no advantage in an offensive war, 355; despondency of, 353, 384; predicts failure, 394; orders Conway to exercise martial law, 398

OGILVY, Lord (James Ogilvy), created Earl of Airlie, 258
—, Lord (James Ogilvy), left to keep the House of Airlie, 388
Olivares, Count of, Duke of San Lucar, suspects Charles's sincerity, 182; refuses an alliance with Charles, 298
Oñate, the Count of, wishes to build a large chapel, 20
Oquendo, Antonie de, is defeated in the Straits of Dover, 263; takes refuge in the Downs, 264; is promised assistance by Newport, 269; is defeated in the Downs, 272
Orange, Prince of, see Frederick Henry
Ormond, Earl of (James Butler), supports Wentworth in Ireland, 151
Osbaldiston, Lambert, writes an attack on Laud, 197; escapes punishment, 198
Osborne, Sir Edward, gives a discouraging account of the state of Yorkshire, 409

PALATINATE, proposal to send Scottish soldiers to, 243
Pargeter, William, refuses to pay coat-and conduct money, 381; his case postponed, 382
Parliament, the English, proposal to summon, 281. *See* Parliament, the Short
—, the Irish, proposal to summon, 283; votes money to the King, 304; objects to the mode in which subsidies are levied, 374
—, the Scottish, is summoned to meet in Edinburgh, 165; day of its meeting fixed, 241; constitutional changes in, 253; formation of parties in, 255; demands further concessions from Charles, 258; prorogation of, 280; the King orders its further prorogation, 367; passes the Bills before it,

PYM

370; appoints a Committee of Estates, 371
Parliament, the Short, expectation that it will be overawed by military force, 284; elections to, 306; opening of, 307; threatened with a dissolution, 325; is dissolved, 331; character of its work, 331
Peers, petition of, for a Parliament, 423
Pennington, John, sent to the Firth of Forth, 200; approves of Tromp's proceedings, 261; keeps the peace in the Downs, 264; receives unintelligible instructions, 269; is present at the Battle of the Downs, 272
Pepper, money raised on the sale of, 414
Perth, Articles of, their enforcement, 99
Petition of Rights, the alleged infringement of, 399
— of the City of London, 431; presented to the King, 433
— of the Peers, 423
Pfalzburg, the Princess of, carries on a negotiation with Gerbier, 182
Physicians, the College of, report on overcrowding in London, 80
Porter, Endymion, is sent with a message to Cardenas, 270
—, Mrs., converts her father on his death-bed, 17; fails to convert Lady Hamilton, 18
Post-office, establishment of a, 82
Potter, Dr., replies to Knott's *Charity Mistaken*, 44
Prayer-book, the new Scottish, its preparation ordered, 101; is drawn up, 105; attempt to read it at St. Giles's, 109; its use suspended in Edinburgh, 112; Henderson's petition against, 114; difficulty in enforcing the use of, 115; supplication against, 120; Charles's defence of, 123; absolutely revoked by the King, 164
Pregion, John, a witness in Williams's case, 34
Press, the unlicensed, 3; Star Chamber decree against, 14
Prynne, William, his *Divine Tragedy*, 3; his *News from Ipswich*, 4; his trial in the Star Chamber, 6; execution of the sentence on, 9; his triumphal progress and imprisonment, 11; Wentworth's opinion of his treatment, 152
Pym, John, speaks on grievances in the Short Parliament, 311; his opinion on Parliamentary privilege, 312; his

INDEX. 459

view of the ecclesiastical grievances, 313; complains of the civil grievances, 315; proposes a remedy, 317; induces the Commons not to vote supply before their grievances are redressed, 323; resolves to move that the King be requested to come to terms with the Scots, 330; is probably the author of the petition to the Peers, 424; appeals to the people, 427

RABY, Strafford offends Vane by taking a title from, 294
Radcliffe, Sir George, rejects Strafford's advice to turn the Scots out of Ulster, 440
Rainsborough, Captain, commands an expedition to Sallee, 56
Rainton, Alderman, committed to prison, 345
Rheinfelden, battle of, 187
Richelieu, Cardinal, acquires the services of Melander's army, 182; wishes to be on friendly terms with the Queen, 184; supposed to stir up troubles in Scotland, 188, 260; wins over the officers of Bernhard's army, 267; supports Tromp, 271; refuses to help the Scots, 300; is satisfied that he has kept clear of the Scots, 307
Ripon, negotiation with the Scots at, 436; conclusion of an agreement at, 441
Roe, Sir Thomas, sent to the Congress at Hamburg, 180; his account of the desolation of Germany, 259; opposes the debasement of the coinage, 393; asks the City for a loan, 400
Rossetti, Count, arrives as Papal Agent, 295; application for money and men made to, 351; threat to murder, 359
Rothes, Earl of (John Leslie), objects to the introduction of the English Prayer-book into Scotland, 121; appeals to the gentry for support, 124; revises the Covenant, 126; his interview with Hamilton, 141; visits Charles at Berwick, 248; his altercation with Charles, 249; his conversation with Hope, 302; argues that Parliament may meet in defiance of the King's commands, 369
Rudyerd, Sir Benjamin, his speech in the Short Parliament, 310
Rupert, Prince, taken prisoner by the Imperialists, 181
Ruthven, Patrick, General, made Governor of Edinburgh Castle, 246; created Lord Ettrick, 258. *See* Ettrick, Lord

ST. GILES', riot at, 109
St. John, Oliver, his argument on ship-money, 58; is employed in the case of the fens, 90; his satisfaction at the dissolution of the Short Parliament, 332
Sallee, expedition to, 56
Salt-works, the. 74
Sabbath, the, Puritan conception of, 3
Savile, Sir William, asks that ship-money may be abolished, 327
—, Viscount (Thomas Savile), receives a letter from Johnston of Warriston, 401; forged invitation sent to the Scots by, 402; confesses his forgery, 437
Saye and Sele, Lord (William Fiennes), opposes the legality of ship-money, 58; objects to follow the King to the war, 192; refuses the military oath, 212; is insulted by Hall, 319; votes against interfering with the Commons, 321
Scotland, rivalry of the nobles and bishops of, 97; condition of the Church of, 98; intention of Charles to alter the worship of, 99; Brereton's account of, 100; new Prayer-book proposed for, 101; ecclesiastical organisation of, 102; character of the bishops of, 103; preparation of canons and a Prayer-book for, *ibid.*; dislike of the new Prayer-book in, 107; resistance to the Prayer-book in, 109; proceedings of the Privy Council of, 111; growth of the opposition to the Prayer-book in, 113; National Covenant of, 126; its religion, 134; Wentworth's plea for the treatment of. 154; training of its soldiers in Germany, 194; favourable terms offered by Charles to the tenants of, 209; resistance to Hamilton of, 214; its coercion resolved on, 281; its relations with France, 299; overtures made to Bellievre, on behalf of, 300; recommencement of war in, 324
Scottish Army, the. *See* Army, the Scottish
— manifestoes, 410
Selby, collection of troops at, 409
Separatists, failure of the Church Courts to suppress, 288; burial of one of their number, 289

Session, Scottish Court of, ordered to remove from Edinburgh, 118
Seymour, Sir Francis, attacks the ecclesiastical grievances, 311
Shields, salt-works at, 74
Ship-money meets an actual need, 55; attacked as illegal, 56; Hampden's case of, 58; collection of the arrears of, 69; reduced levy of, 190; paid in slowly, 206; again demanded, 281; attacked by Glanville, 327; enforced payment of, 345; slow return of, 357; difficulty of collecting in London, 372
Soames, Alderman, committed to prison, 345
Soap-makers, Corporation of the, 73
Southampton, Earl of (Thomas Wriothesley), votes against interfering with the Commons, 321
Southesk, Earl of, imprisoned by the Covenanters, 303
Southwark, riotous assemblages at, 348, 358
Spain, Charles's secret negotiations with, 182, 346; attempt to obtain a loan from, 397
Spanish troops, proposed employment of, in England, 193; sent to Flanders in English ships, 261
Spottiswoode, John, Archbishop, is made Chancellor of Scotland, 97; has St. Giles' cleared of rioters, 110; advises the suspension of the old and new Prayer-book, 112; recommends concession, 132
Star Chamber, the, trial of Prynne, Burton, and Bastwick in, 6; decree against unlicensed books in, 14; trial of Lilburn in, 31; case of Williams in, 33; second case of Williams in, 197
Starchmakers, the, 75
Stirling, proclamation read at, 123; castle of, held for the Covenanters, 201
Strafford, Earl of (Thomas Wentworth). *See* Wentworth, Viscount, appointed Lieutenant-General of the army against Scotland, 291; supports Leicester for the Secretaryship, 292; his relations with Lady Carlisle, 293; urges the retention of Coke as Secretary in preference to Vane's appointment, 294; application of the Queen to, 296; is considered a Puritan by Rossetti, 297; crosses to Dublin, 303; obtains subsidies from the Irish Parliament, 304; proposes to levy an Irish army, 305; returns to England, and advises Charles to appeal from the Commons to the Lords, 320; his conduct compared with that of Wellington, 321; favour shown him by the King and Queen, 322; recommends the King to conciliate Parliament, 325; supports a dissolution, 332; his conversation with Conway on the justice of the King's cause, 333; his speeches on war with Scotland in the Committee of Eight, 334; suggests the bringing in of the Irish army, 336; his intention of doing so discussed, 337; his constitutional views, 341; threatens the Lord Mayor and Aldermen, 345; negotiates an alliance with Spain, 346; asks the Spanish Ambassadors for money, 347; his plans abandoned by the King, 348; charged with failure by the courtiers, 351; serious illness of, 353; his conversation with Bristol, 354; his opponents at Court, 355; his convalescence, 356; asks for strong measures, 383; finds fault with the City merchants, 392; advocates the use of a debased coinage, 393; attempts to obtain a loan from Spain, 397; treats the Yorkshire petition as an act of mutiny, 399; his patent empowering him to command the Irish Army, 407; presses the Spanish Ambassadors for a loan, 408; disbelieves in any danger from the Scots, 411; appointed to command the English Army, 413; expresses confidence, 415; appeals to the Yorkshire men, 416; his illness, 417; his advice to Conway, 418; complains of the state of the Army, 420; receives the Order of the Garter, 430; hopes that the Great Council will resist the Scots, 439; proposes to drive the Scots out of Ulster, 440
Straits of Dover, battle in the, 263
Strathbogie pillaged by Monro, 386
Strode, William, set free from prison, 295
Suffolk, Earl of (Theophilus Howard), sent to prepare for the Spanish troops, 271
Supplication, the general, against the Scottish Prayer-book, 120
Sutherland, Earl of (John Sutherland), signs the Covenant, 130
Sydserf, Thomas, Bishop of Galloway,

INDEX. 461

TAB

attacked by the Edinburgh mob, 119; suggests that the opponents of the Prayer-book shall choose Commissioners, 120

TABLES, the appointment of, 125; are not dissolved immediately after the pacification of Berwick, 248
Taylor, John, carries on an unauthorised negotiation at Vienna, 183
Torture, judicial, last employment of, 359
Traquair, Earl of (John Stuart), his political position, 111; laments the position of affairs in Scotland, 120; suggests that the English Prayerbook may be introduced, 121; objects to the organisation of the Commissioners, 121; begs that the King may be propitiated, 122; his advice to Charles, *ibid.*; regrets the position of affairs after the signature of the Covenant, 131; stores gunpowder at Dalkeith, 141; fails to keep Dalkeith, 201; arrest of, 207; attacked by the mob at Edinburgh, 247; appointed Lord High Commissioner, 248; his instructions, 249; his management of the Assembly, 252; selects the Lords of the Articles, 253; ordered to prorogue Parliament, 280; his narrative before the Committee of Eight, 281; his report before the Council, 282; is sent back to Edinburgh, 284; brings to Charles the letter proposed to be sent by the Covenanters to the King of France, 301; refuses to return to Scotland, 352; his narrative to the Great Council, 434; refusal of the Scots to admit him to the negotiation at Ripon, 436
Trendall, John, proposal to burn, 289; his subsequent history, 290
Trevor, Baron, and his judgment in the ship-money case, 67
Tromp, Admiral, takes Spanish troops from English vessels, 261; defeats the Spaniards in the Straits of Dover, 263; blockades the Spaniards in the Downs, 264; defeats the Spaniards in the Downs, 272
Turriff, Montrose appears at, 201; the Trot of, 222

VALENTINE, Benjamin, set free from prison, 295

WEN

Vane, Sir Henry, becomes a member of the Committee of Eight, 280; appointed Secretary, 294; supports a breach with the Short Parliament, 325; declares that no less than twelve subsidies will be accepted, 328; proposes a defensive war, 334; discussion on the value of his paper of notes, 335-337; sent to ask the City for a loan, 396
— Sir Henry (the younger), Joint-Treasurer of the Navy, 291
Velada, the Marquis of, sent to England as Spanish ambassador, 298; arrives in England, 346
Vermuyden, Cornelius, drains Hatfield Chase, 83; drains the great level, 86
Verney, Sir Edmund, his opinion of the war with Scotland, 213; criticises the English army, 216; gives a despondent account of the position of affairs at Berwick, 231
Vintners, the, are compelled to pay an imposition, 76

WANDESFORD, Sir Christopher, Lord Deputy of Ireland, his grief at Strafford's illness, 356; gives way to the Irish Parliament, 375
Wedderburn, James, Bishop of Dumblane, his suggestions on the Scottish Prayer-book, 105
Wemyss, the Earl of (John Wemyss), helps Bishop Lindsay to escape, 110
Wentworth, Viscount (Thomas Wentworth), mediates in a dispute about Hatfield Chase, 85; his progress in the West of Ireland, 150; criticises the treatment of Prynne and Hampden, 152; his opinion of the Earl of Antrim, 153; gives advice on the treatment of Scotland, 154; offers money for the Scottish war, 191; cross-examines Antrim, 207; his opinion on the Scottish war, 208; his case against Crosby and Mountnorris, 275; his conduct to Lord Chancellor Loftus, 276; arrives in England and becomes the King's adviser, 278; his ascendency in the Committee of Eight, 279; advises the calling of a Parliament, 281; heads the subscription to the Councillor's loan, 283; created Earl of Strafford, 291. *See* Strafford, Earl of

WES

Westminster, proposal to extend the municipal boundaries of, 81
Weston, Baron, his judgment in the ship-money case, 66
William John, Bishop of Lincoln, Star Chamber prosecution of, 33; second prosecution of, 34; publishes *The Holy Table, Name and Thing*, 36; his sentence, 37; fresh prosecution of, 197
Winchester, Marquis of (John Paulet), offers money for the war with Scotland, 192
Windebank, Sir Francis, complains of the difficulty of getting money for the army, 227; advises the King to extort money from the City, 240; negotiates with Cardenas, 265; becomes a member of the Committee of Eight, 279; speaks like a zealous Catholic, 295; employed to negotiate with

YOR

Rossetti, 351; his view on the mutinies, 385
Windebank, Francis, gains the confidence of his soldiers, 395
Wither, George, his verses, 32
Wren, Matthew, Bishop of Norwich, his views on the unity of the Church, 2; revises the Scottish Prayer-book, 103; becomes Bishop of Ely, 287

YARMOUTH, salt-works at, 75; Hamilton's expedition at, 210
York, James, Duke of, his future appointment as Lord Admiral arranged, 137
Yorkshire, petition from, 399; unreadiness to resist the Scots in, 409; offers to support the King, 415; Strafford's appeal to, 416; petition for a Parliament from, 430

END OF THE FIRST VOLUME.

LONDON : PRINTED BY
SPOTTISWOODE AND CO., NEW-STREET SQUARE
AND PARLIAMENT STREET

www.ingramcontent.com/pod-product-compliance
Lightning Source LLC
Chambersburg PA
CBHW051847300426
44117CB00006B/298